A HISTORY OF
BRITAIN

A HISTORY OF
BRITAIN

AT THE EDGE OF THE WORLD?
3000BC–AD1603

SIMON SCHAMA

talk miramax books

NEW YORK

Frontispiece: 'The Ditchley Portrait' of Elizabeth I,
by Marcus Gheeraerts the Younger, *c.* 1592

Library of Congress Cataloging-in-Publication Data

Schama, Simon.
A history of britain : at the edge of the world? : 3000 BC–AD 1603 / Simon Schama.
p.   cm.
Includes bibliographical references and index.
ISBN 0-7868-6675-6
1. Great Britain—History—To 1485.
2. Great Britain—History—Tudors, 1485–1603. I. Title.

DA130 .S44   2000
941—dc21   00-061442

Picture credits appear on page 415.

First Edition

10 9 8 7 6 5 4 3 2 1

CONTENTS

For
Michael Sissons –
true Brit

The cradle rocks above an abyss, and common sense tells us that our
existence is but a brief crack of light between two eternities of darkness…
Nature expects a full grown man to accept the two black voids, fore and aft,
as stolidly as he accepts the extraordinary visions in between. Imagination,
the supreme delight of the immortal and the immature, should be limited.
In order to enjoy life we should not enjoy it too much.
I rebel against this state of affairs.

VLADIMIR NABOKOV, *Speak, Memory*

I shall cheerfully bear the reproach of having descended below the dignity
of history if I can succeed in placing before the English of the nineteenth century
a true picture of the life of their ancestors.

THOMAS BABINGTON MACAULAY, *The History of England*

Those conquered kings pass furiously away;
gods die in flesh and spirit and live in print
each library a misquoted tyrant's home.

ROBERT LOWELL, 'End of a Year' from *History*

ACKNOWLEDGEMENTS

I doubt whether the BBC wants to think of itself as a repatriation service, but the fact is that *A History of Britain* has been a homecoming to the country I've not lived in for twenty years and a subject I've not taught for ten. Returning expatriates, vision clouded either by sentimentality or by hypercriticism, may not be the most dispassionate narrators of their nation's history. When Janice Hadlow (then of BBC2) first asked me to think about tackling a television history of Britain, my immediate response was that my distance from the debates of specialists obviously disqualified me from the job. But Janice urged me to think of that distance not as a liability but a potential strength, something that would make me earn my understanding through reacquaintance and give me some connection with viewers and readers who themselves would be anything but experts (although regular encounters with taxi-drivers who turn out to know *everything* about the battle of Hastings and the Black Death have made me wonder about that assumption). By betting that the excitement of rediscovery would outweigh the perils of unfamilarity, Janice, with Alan Yentob and Michael Jackson – who together conceived the project – were making a huge gamble. As far as we are concerned it has been the gamble of a lifetime.

In the end, it was impossible not to respond positively to Alan and Janice's passionate belief that a history of Britain was the kind of thing that television was made to do: to inject fresh energy and drama into well-known stories and bring less well-known ones before the biggest possible public; to restore and reanimate history as a shared public enthusiasm, something not remote from our contemporary lives but fully a part of it, especially at a moment when the whole issue of national allegiance and identity is once again a serious question rather than an easy assumption.

Though there is one name on the cover of this book, *A History of Britain* has been, from beginning to end, a collective work, inconceivable without the courageous talents and inexhaustible energies of my friends and colleagues at the BBC. Martin Davidson has been, throughout, an extraordinary partner in this work: sharp-focused, imaginative and (when the going seemed rough) able to bring calm, clear thinking to a project and to a narrator not famous for his mastery of those qualities. I have been incredibly lucky to have worked with a team of producers willing to share my own often idiosyncratic vision and from whom I have learned more than can ever properly be repaid within the conventions of these acknowledgements: Clare Beavan, Ian Bremner, Martina Hall, Liz Hartford, Tim Kirby, Janet Lee and Paul Tilzey. Mike Ibeji, together with Ian Bremner, put in an astonishing amount of hard work to help fill in the monumental gaps in my knowledge of medieval history and point me towards the scholarship and issues with which I needed to engage. I'm also deeply grateful to a tireless and intrepid band of research assistants on both textual and visual sources without whom the enterprise would have been hopelessly handicapped: Melisa Akdogan, Alex Briscoe, Amy Eisner, Karen Green, Patrick Keefe, Joanne King, Ben Ledden and Chloë Schama. As cameraman for the majority of programmes in the series Luke Cardiff has been, literally, a visionary. And at BBC2 I've been sustained throughout by the committed support of Paul Hamann and Jane Root. Making sure that a television presenter–writer is kept from going completely off the rails has to be one of the most demanding jobs in the world and I can only thank Sara Fletcher, Claire Sharp and Theresa Lydon of the History Unit of BBC2 for their loyalty, efficiency and thoughtfulness both on location and off.

At Columbia University I'm deeply grateful to Provost Jonathan Cole for giving me the extended leave needed to tackle this apparently interminable work and to my colleague David Armitage for all kinds of scholarly help and inspiration. John Brewer, Stella Tillyard, Amanda Foreman, Eliot Friedman, Mindy Engel Friedman, Jonathan Gili, Tanya Luhrmann, Jill Slotover and Terry Justo have all been good friends to the intrinsically hubris-laden nature of this enterprise and to its author.

This book is, though, far more than a 'tie-in' to the television series, and treats the subject matter and issues of our history at greater length and in much closer detail than a mere transcript of our scripts would allow. Stuart Proffitt read the manuscript with his usual eagle eye and pointed out, as ever, ways small and big in which it might be improved. Margaret Willes made many helpful suggestions on early drafts. Professor Andrew Pettegree and Dr John Hudson were kind enough scrutinize the text for glaring errors but any that remain are mine alone. At BBC Worldwide I'm fortunate to have had in Martha Caute a generous, patient and discriminating editor, and I'm also grateful to Sheila Ableman, Sally Potter and Chris Weller for their sustained belief in the importance of tackling the subject on the scale it undoubtedly deserves. At Talk Miramax, Tina Brown and Jonathan Burnham have been committed to bringing *A History of Britain* to the widest possible public in the United States. From the minute she heard about it, Tina has been a fanatic enthusiast for the whole project, well beyond the call of our friendship.

Over the years of its writing and production, a project of this scale has taken more than the wear and tear usually inflicted on the family of the arch-culprit and I'm grateful as always to Ginny, Chloë, Gabriel and Gus for the daily doses of love and domestic happiness that have immunized me from exhaustion. At Peters, Fraser & Dunlop, Vanessa Kearns has always been ready to help smooth my and my family's extended stays in Britain and much else besides.

A History of Britain has been, throughout, an amazing act of faith by a small group of people – Alan Yentob, Janice Hadlow, Martin Davidson, my television agent Rosemary Scoular – all of whose unswerving belief in the project and in its author has been the most touching (and unnerving) event in this writer's long career as an historian. But one of my fellow-travellers – Michael Sissons – deserves the lion's share of thanks, not just for giving me the courage to tackle this project and see it through to realization, but for helping me fulfil my life as a writer over thirty years of shared adventure. He has ever been the pilot in the storm.

PREFACE

History clings tight but it also kicks loose. Disruption, as much as persistence, is its proper subject. So although the great theme of British history seen from the twentieth century is endurance, its counter-point, seen from the twenty-first, must be alteration.

Both hanging on and letting go made themselves felt in the two public ceremonies – a drizzly coronation and a frost-nipped funeral – which spoke most powerfully to my post-war generation about what it meant to be British. Admittedly, in June 1953 a bracing sense of change was not the most obviously dominant mood. Two years before, in the Festival of Britain (a self-consciously centennial commemoration of the Victorian Great Exhibition of 1851), there had been a strenuous official attempt to persuade us eight-year-olds, in our grey flannel shorts and saggy knee-socks, that we should now think of ourselves as 'New Elizabethans'. The heraldic symbol of the coming technological Valhalla was the Skylon – Brancusi out of Isambard Kingdom Brunel – a slender steel cylinder, tapering to points at both ends like an industrial bobbin and suspended by cables so light that it seemed to float a few feet over the South Bank promenade with no visible means of support. But in the spring of 1953 bewitching visions of a sleekly engineered scientific future did, indeed, weigh nothing beside the vast machinery of reverence being cranked up for the coronation of Elizabeth II. To be sure, fitful efforts had been made to advertise the event as a moment of rejuvenating change. But no one was really fooled. For all the communiqués about 'an association of free nations', the Commonwealth over which the young queen presided was, transparently, the brave face put on the loss of empire. The parade of pith-helmeted and bush-hatted troops from the 'loyal dominions' along with more exotic detachments from what were still, in 1953, known as 'British possessions' dutifully trotted along the Mall in their allotted order – a post-imperial durbar in all but name. And when the queen set off on her post-coronation world tour, primary school children like us followed her progress by sticking little flags in all the many regions of the globe still (no matter what their ostensible status in the modern world) reassuringly tinted the dusty rose-red of the old empire. In William McElwee's *The Story of England*, published in 1954, it was still possible to look forward to 'the peaceful evolution of backward races throughout the empire' made 'possible under British leadership'. And the faces behind the net curtains in Omdurman Gardens and Mafeking Close were still those of the colonizers, not the colonized.

There was one gawky contemporary cuckoo growing apace in the nest of tradition, and that, of course, was television. But although the broadcast of the ceremony in Westminster Abbey, seen by 27 million viewers within Britain and as many as a quarter of the world's population in all, was an epochal moment in the history of mass communications, it very nearly didn't happen. For months the queen herself and all her principal advisers let it be known that while they were prepared to have the processions to and from the abbey televised (as had also been the case with her wedding in 1947), the ceremony of the crowning itself was to be preserved in its sacrosanct mystery from the common electronic gaze. Eventually – swayed, it has been suggested, by the intervention of Richard Dimbleby – she relented. But to re-run that television coverage is to see just how completely the latent cheekiness of the medium was subdued by the enfolding stateliness of the coronation rituals. The cameras were put in their place and made to stand up straight where they were told and to pay attention when they were bidden. Anything as intimate as a close-up of the queen herself, needless to say, was strictly prohibited, so that many of the most memorable shots of the ceremony are the remote views from the galleries high above the nave, peering down at the grandeur. And whatever the credits might have read, the real producers of the event were the Duke of Edinburgh, in his capacity as Chairman of the Coronation Executive Committee; the Archbishop of Canterbury, Geoffrey Fisher, who was intent on maximizing the mystical and sacrificial aspects of the rite; the Grand Chamberlain, the Marquess of Cholmondeley; and, most important of all, the Earl Marshal, the Duke of Norfolk, who was required to rule on matters as critical as whether rabbit-fur was an acceptable substitute for ermine on the trim of aristocratic robes. (It was.) Over the black-and-white pictures (which themselves have the quality of official state photographs) poured, with honeyed smoothness, the deferentially modulated tones of the commentators-royal: the ripely hushed baritone of Richard Dimbleby for the abbey solemnities and the excitable, lilting tenor of Wynford Vaughan Thomas for the street procession. For that matter, the twenty-seven-year-old at the centre of all this seemed herself to have been crystallized, as if in some ceremonial alembic, into the role of monarch, the open, often broadly smiling face of the young woman settling into the impassive mask of royalty. Millions of the loyal, gathered in front rooms, peering at the 9-inch screens that had been magnified with strap-on image enhancers, watched the heavily crowned, massively mantled figure, the train flowing endlessly behind her, as she swayed down the nave of Westminster Abbey to the roar of the choir and the oceanic swell of the organ, the ancient Saxon-Frankish shout 'May the queen live forever' echoing off the columns.

Out in the streets and in the country, novelty was certainly not uppermost in the national mind-set. Analogies between the two Elizabethan reigns were endlessly drummed home. The Earl Marshal was, after all, a Howard Duke of Norfolk, just as there had been a Howard Norfolk Earl Marshal for the coronation of the first Elizabeth. *The Souvenir Book for Essex Children* emphasized the parallels between the reign of the first Elizabeth: 'a time when the English people faced a crisis, namely the great struggle with Spain. Now in 1953 Queen Elizabeth the Second has come to the throne at an equally critical time. Two great wars have been fought when the nation has stood and suffered.' But, it promised, 'if we are loyal and steadfast, history will tell that the reign of our Queen Elizabeth will be worthy to rank with that other Good Queen Bess'.

With all this fixation on the unbroken continuity of British history, it seemed only natural (or, at the very least, fated) that it should be Winston Churchill who should be in office as prime minister, presiding over the accession and enthronement of the new monarch. For in Churchill's person the classical distinction between history as deed and history as report had become moot. Looking back over his entire career, had there ever been a time when Churchill had not both written about, and acted on, British history? Two weeks before the coronation, at a lunch for Commonwealth parliamentarians, Churchill told an American schoolboy (who, for better or worse, would go on to be a presidential speechwriter): 'Study history, history, history. In history, lie all the secrets of statecraft.' Certainly, in his own mind the writing and doing were so entangled that it was virtually impossible to say which was cause and which effect. Even at the hour of supreme crisis in 1940, it might be argued, the difference that Churchill made to the destiny of the nation was as much a matter of words as deeds: his instinctive (and perfectly justified) belief that to bet on the future it was indispensable to reconnect the country with its passion for its past. Although he was in his late seventies at the time of the coronation, Churchill seemed virtually imperishable, clearly enjoying reminding the queen at a great banquet held beneath the medieval hammerbeam roof of Westminster Hall that he had faithfully served her great-great-grandmother (Victoria), her great-grandfather (Edward VII), her grandfather (George V), her father (George VI) and now her. And the tutelary partnership between this young queen and the indomitable patriarch seemed to both press and public a perfect emblem of the happy marriage between old and new that was supposed to typify the coming epoch of the new Elizabethans.

But three weeks after the coronation, on 23 June, having (one assumes) entertained the Italian prime minister at a dinner with a speech about the Roman conquest of Britain, Churchill collapsed in a chair, the victim of a massive stroke. Its effects carefully disguised from public view, he continued in office and, in fact, made an astonishing recovery. But, as he put it, 'the zest was diminished'. Like the particular kind of Britain he cherished, he was mortal after all, and when he died twelve years later, in the freezing winter of 1965, the obsequies took place in a culture hot for novelty. Churchill, after all, could hardly be expected to have survived a time-loop so complete that the whiskers and the military epaulettes and frogging he had last seen in the imperial army of Queen Victoria had returned as the whimsical costume of rock bands. The 12th Earl of Home had been replaced in Downing Street by a Labour prime minister, Harold Wilson, who hymned the 'white heat of the scientific revolution', and the burial place of the first Saxon kings, Winchester Cathedral (for reasons still mysterious to me), had become a pop song sung by Frank Sinatra. But England stopped swinging ('like a pendulum do') long enough to grieve. Indeed, on 30 January 1965, the day of the funeral, Big Ben's pendulum was stopped altogether for the duration of the obsequies. And in the unmeasured time it took to carry Churchill's coffin, cut from ancient Blenheim oaks and carried on a grey gun-carriage to St Paul's, where, in a break from protocol, the queen waited before the altar to pay her respects, then out again past the enormous crowds braving the bitter chill on the streets, down to Tower Pier and aboard the launch *Havengore*, past the docks where the cranes of the Port of London were made to dip in salute, and on to the train at Waterloo, carrying the body westward past a man standing on his flat roof, dressed in his RAF uniform and saluting, towards Bladon churchyard, a mile or so from Blenheim where he was born; in that time the cutting-edge glamour of the new Britain was utterly engulfed by the immense epic of the national past. Out from its lair ambled the old beast history, prowling the streets and monuments and daring any King's Road smart alec to make jokes at its expense.

Which included me and my mates. For between the coronation and Churchill's funeral, we had become, we supposed, serious readers of history, meaning, *inter alia*, Fernand Braudel, A.J.P. Taylor, E.P. Thompson, Marc Bloch, J.H. Plumb, Asa Briggs, Denis Mack Smith and Christopher Hill (who came to our school and spoke, with a brave, charismatic stammer, of Milton and Muggletonians), but which, very definitely, did not mean Churchill or his loyal echo and eulogist Arthur Bryant. Bryant's rustic rhapsody on late eighteenth-century Merrie England, about to face the crisis of the French revolutionary wars in *Years of Endurance 1793–1802* (published, not coincidentally, in 1942), was precisely the kind of thing that drew from us hoots of knowing derision.

> Within the candle-lit windows of the wayside cottage and the farmhouse on the hill Old John Bull would sit dozing with his pot beside the kitchen fire, the dog and cat asleep at his feet, the good wife at her wheel, the pretty maid his daughter coming in with her pail, the tinder box on the shelf, the onions and flitches hanging from the ceiling…In the tavern down in the village old England still lived on where over their pipes and bowls gathered round the bare rude table, the local worthies with russet, weather-beaten faces cracked their jokes and trolled their song.

But Bryant's drowsy sentimentality, we also thought in more high-minded moments, was really less of a joke than a menace. It was a kind of literary opium, calculated to lull asleep a public that we wanted jolted awake to the bleaker and more contentious realities of past and present. Our radical rewrite of Bryant's idyll would have read:

> In front of the tavern down in the village, Old England lived on in the gibbet from which swung the decomposing remains of the local rick-burners and poachers who had been so presumptuous as to attack, in their several and unlaw-ful ways, the propertied despotism of the complacent squirerarchy.

Something along those lines, anyway. And in place of the great procession of tableaux from which Churchill constructed his chronicle of Britishness – Runnymede, Tilbury, Trafalgar – we wanted to substitute pages from the life of the people – the armed peas-ants at Blackheath in 1381, the Levellers at Putney, the Chartists at Kennington in 1848.

All the same, back home for the funeral and moved partly by furtive piety and partly by a curiosity as to what it had been in Churchill's *A History of the English-Speaking Peoples*, which my father had given me many years before, that first kindled my passion for history, I dusted off the red volumes. Passages read at random duly made me squirm with embarrassment, but just as many startled me with bursts of irresistibly gorgeous rhetoric and unimpeachable common sense. The only possible, unanticipated, response, was mixed feelings. On the one hand, the unblushing Churchillian epic of progress, much of it inherited from Macaulay – a bullishly insular, romantically princely, axiomatically Protestant, Whiggishly parliamentary, *English-*speaking Britain, cast as the nursemaid of democracy, the hope of the West, the guardian of the moral genius of the common law and the perennial hold-out against fanatical tyrannies – couldn't possibly be sustained as the definitive 'meaning of British history'. But then again, neither could it be airily dismissed as a deluded anthology of patriotic fairy-tales. It had been when my father explained to me that the ghostly letters 'PJ', dimly outlined in white paint on the railway-cutting wall in the seaside town of my childhood, meant 'Perish Judah' and warmed to his speech, explaining that Churchill had been what stood between the Mosleyite slogan and its realization, that I properly understood that for his generation the belief in the island fortress of freedom had been less a hollow platitude than a necessary article of faith. Buried within the fabulous mythology, could there be, I let myself wonder, if only for an instant, a gritty little nugget of truth?

Thirty-five years on, both authorized versions of the British past – the Churchillian and the socialist – have fallen steeply out of favour. Labour history, initiated at the same time as the Labour Party and largely written by its Fabian founders, has withered on the shrivelled vine of that older Marxist politics, and a centrist political establishment, eager to forget the 'Red Flag' along with the rest of the regrettably obscurantist relics of the class war, seems unlikely to put the history of organized labour at the centre of its curriculum for future citizens. Gone, too, is the empire over whose demise Churchill swore he would not preside. The colonized, promised by Westminster that the British legacy would be parliamentary democracy and the rule of law, took the promise at face value and decided to move to the source to enjoy those blessings, which was not exactly what the proconsuls had meant. Omdurman Gardens all over the country are now populated by precisely the people whose subjugation the street names commemorate, and for them, the imperial triumphalism of the saga of what Churchill repeatedly called 'the island race' is understandably at best incomprehensible and at worst egregiously offensive.

Not for everyone, of course. The massive audience for radio readings from *This Sceptred Isle*, largely based on unreconstructed readings from Churchill's history, testifies to the continuing capacity of his text to feed the popular hunger for heroic narrative. As part of the thriving yesteryear industry, this seems perfectly acceptable to the masters of the *Zeitgeist*, a heritage entertainment for senior citizens, like country-house tours and costume dramas, a gently narcotic dose of nostalgia, harmless enough if not consumed while driving or operating heavy machinery.

But this is not at all what Churchill meant when he offered that American schoolboy his advice or, for that matter, put pen to paper, still less what his intellectual ancestor Macaulay wanted from his own compelling, dazzlingly crafted narratives. For both of them, it was a living instruction or it was nothing: not a spare-time luxury but a requirement of informed citizenship. Both would have been horrified to see British history and British modernity treated as if they were mutually exclusive rather than mutually dependent.

And yet they are partly to blame for the predicament of poor old Clio, History's muse, subjected either to embalming or eviction and dragged out of the attic like a dotty aunt in eccentric dress, smelling a bit of mothballs, given an occasional airing for a special occasion and then hastily returned to her quarters, where she shares space with mildewy Gladstone bags and antimacassars. For it was the Whig historians who were so determined to insist on the insularity of British history and who took as a truism that the meaning of British history was synonymous with its separateness. In this steadfast belief they were not, in fact, invariably wrong. There are moments – significant moments, like the late Elizabethan sixteenth century or the Hanoverian mid-eighteenth century – when British (or anyway English) history is, indeed, an unmistakable peculiarity. The conviction that it was the work of history to sift from the unruly mass of past data material that seemed to signpost the way towards the 'British difference', towards the realization of a nation state called Great Britain or the United Kingdom, was what gave its narratives the virtues of tremendous clarity and coherence.

But now that the United Kingdom itself has become not a truism but a question – along with many other institutions that the Churchillian historians once assumed to be perpetual – that clarity looks like over-confidence, and the history that assumed the inevitability and permanence of the British difference suddenly seems misleading. Those teleological signposts were pointing, after all, the wrong way. Is it better not to read this sort of history, better not to read any sort of British history if it is going to perpetuate illusions of isolationism in an increasingly globalized world?

But to collude in the minimization of British history on the grounds of its imagined 'irrelevance' to our rebranded national future, or from a suspicion that it does no more than recycle patriotic pieties unsuited to the global marketplace, would be an act of appallingly self-inflicted, collective memory-loss. The damage done would vindicate Cicero's warning that cultures without history doom themselves to remain trapped in the most illusory tense of all, the present, akin to small children who know neither whence they have come nor whither they go. And it would be a *gratuitously* willed amnesia, too, for the histories that presupposed a single, unchanging national personality embedded within the different periods of the past are not, in fact, the only British histories imaginable.

Imagine instead a British history in which alteration, mutation and flux, rather than continuity and bedrock solidity, are the norm; a history that does not lead inexorably to a consummation in the unitary state of Great Britain but that sees that period – only, after all, three centuries old, barely as long as Roman Britannia – as just one epoch among many in the evolution of these island nations. This would be a history in which national identity – not just in Britain, or in England, but in Scotland, Ireland and Wales – was not a fixed but a decidedly shifting and fluid quality; a history in which the allegiance that mattered might, from generation to generation, from place to place, be a matter of clan or class, town or manor, language or dialect, church or club, guild or family, rather than of flag and dynasty. It would be a history in which the ragged frontiers of regions might count for a lot more than the fixed borders of countries; in which north–south divisions within Scotland and Wales could be as profound as those between either of them and their English neighbour. It would be an elastic history of nationhood, with England or Scotland sometimes closer in spirit and interest to France and even to Rome than to each other; but at other times genuinely and wholeheartedly (for good or ill) bound together within the British union. But it would also be a history which does not try to abandon the necessary impurity of Britishness for some cleaner, tidier, smaller concept of nationality, but instead embraces that historical impurity as a strength. The unity presupposed by a 'united kingdom' may be no more coherent, in the end, than the unity of a 'united states', and no less worth defending, for precisely its generous heterogeneity. Finally this history might be a history respectful of contingency, mistrustful of inevitability, indifferent to any predetermined route or destination; a history refusing to take for granted (as the victors' texts always want) that the way things turned out was the way they were always meant to be; a history that can see, but for a happenstance – Harold not falling out with his brother; Anne Boleyn giving birth to a healthy son; Oliver Cromwell not dying when he did – an altogether different outcome. How likely, after all, was it, for a clairvoyant of the 1750s to prophesy that, by the century's close, Britain would end up, not with colonies that spoke, for the most part, English, but with colonies that spoke, for the most part, Bengali and Urdu?

There is a risk, of course, of lost moorings in these kinds of British histories, of the familiarity of the bulldog breed, island race story going astray amid countless competing alternatives, a risk of the consoling simplicity of the old story being traded in for the bewildering confusion of the new. But Clio, properly respected, is the least straightforward of the muses. Her beauty lies in the complexity, not the simplicity, of her truth. Which is why her votaries, attentive to the sometimes difficult and winding path they must follow, are sworn to tell stories in order to make the journey easier. For in the end, history, especially British history with its succession of thrilling illuminations, should be, as all her most accomplished narrators have promised, not just instruction but pleasure.

CHAPTER

1

Writing his *Britannia* in the glory days of Elizabeth I, William Camden, the anti-quary and historian, saw no reason to be coy. His country was, as everyone knew, 'the most famous island without comparison of the whole world'. And what made it especially enviable, he also knew, was its weather. Britain was, he rejoiced, 'seated as well for aires as soile in a right fruitfull and mild place. The aire so kinde and temperate that not only the Summers be not excessive hot by reason of continual gentle winds that abate their heat…but the winters are also passing mild.' It was this sweet fertility, Camden thought, that had made Britain so irresistible to the ancients. In 'Happie Britaine', according to the Roman writer known as the panegyrist of Constantine (whom the Elizabethans believed had been born there), 'the forests were without savage beasts and the ground voyd of noisome serpents. Contrariwise an infinite multitude there is of tame cattle with udders strutting full of milke.' Thus blessed, the historian Tacitus conferred on Britain the best compliment that could occur to any Roman: that it was *pretium victoriae* (worth the conquest). For not only did it grow everything, except (alas) the olive and the vine, it was also, literally, a gold mine. Silver was abundant there too, as were pearls, although he had heard they were grey like the overcast rain-heavy skies and that the natives only bothered to collect them when they were cast upon the shore.

Remoteness, then, did not mean outlandishness. If Tacitus, or, for that matter, Camden had been able to travel back in time as well as space to the most distant of all the British isles, the place they knew as the Orcades (which we call Orkney), and get there before the palaces of Mycenae and the pyramids of Egypt were built, before Stonehenge went up on the Wiltshire plain, they would have seen something that would have confirmed their most benign expectations: a seaside village.

From the Orcadians of 5000 years ago you expect, perhaps, ritual monuments: great columns and circles of standing stones. What you don't expect is domesticity. Instinctively, we imagine Neolithic Britons huddled in primitive dwellings gouged

AT THE EDGE
OF THE WORLD?

The Ring of Brodgar on Orkney.

out of the face of a rocky cliff. The hamlet of Skara Brae, miraculously preserved beneath a seal of dunes and grass until a great tempest around 1850 blew away the concealment of millennia, is anything but the habitat of savages clinging to a dangerous shore. Its original settlers probably migrated across the Pentland Firth from Caithness on the Scottish mainland. The sea and the air were a little warmer than they are now, and once they had established themselves a few hundred feet away from the water's edge in sandstone houses (the slaty stone easily hacked away with antler picks), they could harvest red bream, corkfin wrasse and the mussels and oysters that were abundant in the shallows. On land that is now thought unfit for any kind of food crops, the Skara Brae villagers managed to grow barley and even wheat. Cattle provided meat and milk; dogs were kept for hunting and for company. During the Neolithic centuries there would have been at least a dozen little houses here, half-dug into the ground for comfort and safety – a thriving, bustling little community of fifty or sixty souls, with both public places and privately walled-off houses, connected by narrow, stone-lined lanes and alleys. It was, by any definition, a true village.

Its one-room dwellings were proper homes: 320 square feet of floor space, divided up into all the social activities we associate with domestic life. In the middle, clearly marked by the stones, was a great hearth, for cooking and warmth. At one end of the room was a water-filled tank to keep live bait, perhaps limpets, and against the walls were sleeping areas, the beds made snugly welcoming with layers of straw and feathers and covered, rather luxuriously, with blankets of hide and fur. The channels running from the inside to the outside of the dwellings have even suggested to archaeologists that the prehistoric Orcadians may actually have had their own loos.

But the Skara Brae houses were not just shelters. They housed culture. They had, it turns out, what we like to call 'style', for the dramatic visual centres of their living rooms were dominated by large stone dressers. On their shelves they displayed carved stone balls, decorated with circles and spirals, grooved clay pots and jars, with scalloped rims and zigzag patterns, or, perhaps, bone bead necklaces and costume pins. To gaze at these objects, surviving from so distant a time, is to be confronted with the great paradox of all history: that it is at all times a dialogue between the alien and the familiar. The past, especially a past as remote as prehistoric Orkney, might indeed be a foreign country, but somehow, uncannily, we feel we have been there before. So although conscientious historians must resist the temptation to imagine themselves back into the company of Neolithic Orcadians, it is hard to walk between the houses, built, with ecological economy, on the mounds of their own organic rubbish – shellfish remains and compost – and not feel in the midst of a thriving little world – well-fed, well-housed and, by the standards of the time, well-off.

Given the rudimentary nature of the available tools, which were fashioned from sharpened animal bones or the grey sandstone of Orkney, it would have taken countless man-hours to make not just these domestic dwellings but also the great ritual circles of stones like those erected at Brodgar, where the population of the villages gathered to mark the passage of the seasons and to give thanks to their gods for the harvest or for being spared from disaster. So we can be sure that places like Skara Brae were not just isolated settlements of fishers and farmers. Its people belonged to some larger society, and one that was sophisticated enough to mobilize the army of toilers and craftsmen needed to make these monuments and stand them on end.

Because nothing seemed more important than to give their dead a fitting resting-place, Neolithic architects and their masons kept their most phenomenal achievement for their collective tombs, palaces of the defunct, which are as majestic and darkly beautiful as anything you might find in Minoan Crete or pre-Roman Etruria. These are, as it were, our British pyramids, and in keeping with our taste for understatement, they reserve all their impact for the interior. Outside, from the air, the mausoleum at Maes Howe is no more than an unassuming mound, a swelling on the landscape.

When a new body needed interment, the stone plug sealing the tomb entrance would have been pulled away by a detail from the village. The body was then carried or dragged through the opening in the earth. The builders made the 30-foot passageway narrow and so low that the bearers of the body would have had to stoop sharply, perhaps in an attitude of respect, as they made their awkward way down a stone corridor, lit only once a year by the wan rays of the winter solstice and smelling dankly of the underworld, a death-canal constriction, before they were able to stand erect at last in a lofty chamber, tapering upwards towards an indeterminate vault, black like the northern sky. Some of the tombs were elaborately decorated with swirling circular patterns like waves or the breeze-pushed clouds. Before the Vikings robbed these tombs in the ninth century, they would have been loaded with jewels and ornaments, laid down to garland the dead on their passage to the beyond, and sometimes with the cadavers of dogs and eagles. In some tombs, like those at Midhowe, on the nearby island of Rousay, the dead were laid on stone shelves in neat cubicles, their knees drawn foetally up to their chests as if waiting to be reborn; in other places, like Maes Howe, those rating special treatment were buried in side-tombs opening on to the main chamber, while the hoi polloi of the Orcadians would have been dumped into a common ossuary, packed with the bones of countless predecessors, a crowded waiting room to the Neolithic afterworld.

Life at Skara Brae must have continued in much the same way for centuries. New houses were built on the midden dumps of their predecessors, and the little

Left: The Neolithic sandstone houses of the village at Skara Brae. The living rooms were dominated by large stone dressers (top) on which the prized objects such as pots and bonebead necklaces (above) were displayed.

colony gradually rose above sea-level. But around 2500BC the island climate seems to have got colder and wetter. The red bream disappeared, and so did the stable environment the Orcadians had enjoyed for countless generations. Fields were abandoned, and the farmers and fishers migrated, leaving their stone buildings and tombs to be covered by layers of peat, drifting sand and, finally, grass. Until the Vikings – with an extraordinary nose for loot – burrowed or hacked their way in, the great burial chambers lay undisturbed and carpeted with bones.

Over the centuries that followed a protracted struggle took place for good land, not just in Scotland but all over Britain. Forests were cleared at such a rate that around 1000BC Iron Age Britain was not, as was once romantically imagined, an unbroken forest kingdom stretching from Cornwall to Inverness but rather a patchwork of open fields, worked with rudimentary ploughs to harvest beans and grains, dotted here and there with woodland copses giving cover for game, especially wild pigs, and intensively worked to stoke forges and supply timber for the building of the circular huts and houses in which most of the population lived. It was, in fact, a countryside already beginning to resemble, in outline, the landscape you can see from your aeroplane seat three millennia later.

There was, however, one big difference. In the centuries before the Roman invasions, when the pressure of population on available land was at its most intense, farmers were in increasing need of reliable protection. They got it from the great hill-forts that dominated Iron Age Britain, like those visible (especially from the air) in terraced contours at Danebury in Hampshire and Maiden Castle in Dorset. Lofty seats of power for the clan chiefs, they were defended by concentric rings of dug earthworks, timber palisades and ramparts, or, if there were ample supplies of easily quarried stone nearby, by bristling walls, several feet thick, or, as in the brochs of Scotland and Wales, by great windowless towers, many feet high, which still survive in remote places like Mousa in Shetland or Gurness in Orkney.

Behind those daunting walls and terraced stockades, however, the world was not in panicky retreat. The Iron Age Britain into which the Romans eventually crashed was a dynamic, expanding society. Protected by the hillforts, arable and pastoral farms established themselves beyond the walls. Inside, the military character of many of the sites was fading, as they became instead true embryonic towns, some of them undefended, and most with recognizable street patterns, places of ceremony and worship and rich with forges and workshops. From these workshops came the spectacular metalwork with which the elite decorated their bodies – armlets, pins and brooches, carved mirrors and, not least, the heavy gear without which no self-respecting British warrior would step into his war-chariot: sword hilts and horned helmets figured with curling patterns like unfurling ferns or the astonishing stylized bronze horses, endearingly melancholy in expression like so many Eeyores resigned to a bad day in battle.

These tribal cultures were not just warring, but trading with each other. It used to be thought that these finely wrought works of art had been brought by a great Celtic migration, travelling from central and northern Europe around 500BC and awakening the sleepily primitive natives of the islands to a higher state of culture. But we now know that this sophisticated culture of warriors, druid-priests and artists developed spontaneously within Britain itself, importing – and also exporting – within trade zones that divided the island longitudinally: western Scotland and Wales south all the way to Brittany; southeastern England with northern Gaul and the Low Countries. So this was, in all important ways, an indigenous British culture, which had evolved in contact with, rather than having been conquered or settled by, continental Europe. Iron Age Britain, after all, had grown up on sites that had been occupied for thousands of years. Although the stone henges and burial barrows that marked its landscape had been built at least a millennium before, it seems likely that ritual practices still took place on these ancient sites.

But was it a civilization? The Roman historians of the invasions, from Caesar himself to Tacitus, didn't think so, not least because 'civilized' meant, by definition, dwelling in cities. Although the Romans called the undefended town centres of the British tribes *oppida* (towns), by Latin standards they were still primitive timber settlements, with wattle and daub huts, a far cry from even the simpler stone-built cities of the Mediterranean world. And they wrote off as hideous savages the barbarian warriors who appeared before them in battle, covered in bright blue body paint, waving their long, slashing swords, blowing war-trumpets and yelling unintelligible war-cries, in much the same way as the soldiers of the Victorian empire would describe their 'primitive' enemies in Africa and India.

But suppose they had seen the extraordinary artefacts produced by the Picts, who left behind astonishing carved stones with symbolic hieroglyphs of birds, oxen and fish, and frieze-like reliefs of long-robed, bearded and coiffed warriors, which looked for all the world as if they had been directly transplanted from Assyria rather than being created in the valley of the Tay. Suppose they had come across sculptures like the haunting stone head, found on Anglesey, with its archaic, secretive smile, the deep-set eyes half-closed as if in some mysterious devotional trance, the nose flattened, the cheeks broad, the whole face so spellbindingly reminiscent of the ancient Mediterranean busts they might have encountered in the Greek islands or Etruria. Would they have conceded that this was, in fact, a work of art? Probably not, especially when they noticed that the top of the head had been scooped away like a boiled egg to make room for some votive offering. For this might have confirmed the gruesome stories heard from some of the more cultivated barbarians encountered in the Roman world (for there were many) of cults of decapitated heads – not to mention ritual sacrifices and drownings – which were said to be a special feature of British religion. Some of the natives even appeared to believe that, unless swiftly buried and preferably in a deep well, the heads would continue to reproach those who had parted them from their trunks.

So why should the Romans have wanted to have gone to Britain, to the edge of the world, to an island of talking heads? For despite Tacitus' fantasy of a British El Dorado, a commander as canny as Julius Caesar is unlikely to have been persuaded that the island was indeed 'worth the conquest' had not hard-headed political considerations within Rome itself pushed him in the direction of a British adventure. In the middle of the first century BC he was restlessly sharing power with two other triumvirs, Pompey and Crassus, and a brisk triumph would unquestionably establish him as the senior partner. And he would not be going to Britain as an ignorant outsider. In all likelihood, it was delegates from British tribes themselves who offered Caesar a perfect opportunity to pose as peace-maker, arbitrator, overlord. Nothing could be further from the truth than to imagine a confederation of united British tribes massing shoulder-to-shoulder at the cliffs to resist the Latin invader. Two of those tribal kingdoms – the Catuvellauni in what is now Hertfordshire and the Trinovantes in Essex – were seen by many of the others in the south, east and west as threateningly expansionist and aggressive, and calling in the Romans as allies must have seemed a way to stop them. (When, three-quarters of a millennium later, the British came to establish their own new Roman empire, it was through very similar overtures to the indigenous population that they would secure their own foothold in India.) It was, after all, Commius, the king of the Atrebates, who came with Caesar on the original expedition and who must have supplied over-optimistic intelligence about its prospects. The enterprise of Britain would not, then, be a journey into the unknown, the legions bringing light to the heart of barbarian darkness. It was because Britain was a *known* quantity – its famously mild winters, its cornucopia of food supplies, its obliging native allies – and because Caesar probably thought of the campaign as a limited exercise, a show of superiority rather than a wholesale colonization, that it must have seemed so temptingly feasible. Sitting in sunlit Rome at the height of his powers, a little giddy with invincibility, Caesar must have imagined a nice little sideshow, a triumph on the cheap. Faced with the glittering armour of the legions and the eagle standards, the barbarians would simply line up to surrender. They would understand that history always fought on the side of Rome.

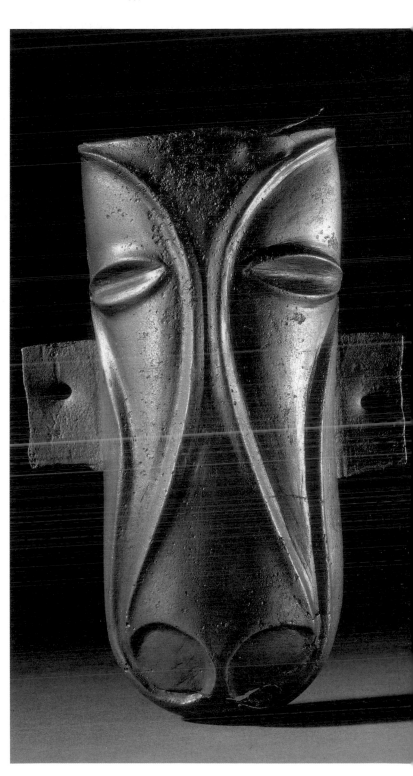

Above: The 'Hendy Head', found a few years ago on a farm on Anglesey. Made of local sandstone, it was probably carved in the pre-Roman Iron Age.
Right: A small bronze horse mask, found in Iron Age earthworks at Stanwick in North Yorkshire; first century AD.

But, as it turned out, geography did not. Two years in succession, in 55BC and 54BC, Caesar's painstaking logistics were turned into a bad joke by the one element that was supposed to have been dependably friendly, the weather. On the first campaign, with a force of 12,000 infantry and 2000 cavalry on the water, fierce gales blew the ships carrying the horses and their troopers back to Gaul before the rest of the fleet had even made a landing. And on both occasions stormy high tides and violent winds smashed the boats that had managed to make it to the Kentish beaches. Where Caesar had imagined the disciplined Roman troops ploughing their way through the British warriors in open combat, what he actually had to deal with, once his troops moved inland, was an enemy that melted away, spookily, into the woods, reappearing only to launch deadly hit-and-run raids. Although the Romans crossed the Thames at Brentford on the second campaign, Cassivelaunus, the king of the Catuvellauni, remained elusively undefeated, and, deprived twice in a row of reinforcements or winter supplies, Caesar had no option but to come to a political, face-saving settlement with the king, extracting promises (not worth very much) that Cassivelaunus would leave the Roman allies among the British in peace. Cicero, whose brother was serving with Caesar's army, put a brave face on the failure by writing off the botched expeditions as not worth the trouble. Gold and silver had not materialized, nor was there 'any booty apart from captives, and I fancy you won't be expecting them to be highly qualified in literature or music'.

Memories of the British fiasco must have rankled, however. By the time the Romans returned, ninety years later in AD43, the mood in Rome had become more aggressively imperialist. In the great Latin verse epic of empire-building, the *Aeneid,* Virgil has Jupiter proclaim: 'I have set upon the Romans bounds neither of time nor space.' Even so, the irritation of a Britain eluding Roman grasp would not itself have been enough to persuade the successors of Julius and Augustus of the need for an all-out campaign of conquest had not Roman credibility as a reliable supporter and protector of its allies been on the line. For if Caesar had abandoned Britain, the Britons had not abandoned Rome. In the decades before the invasion of 43, trade between Roman Gaul had never been more active; bulky goods going south, fancy goods going north. Rome itself was full of disaffected sons and rivals of the dominant British kings, in particular Cunobelinus (whom Shakespeare called Cymbeline), who had put together a formidable power base in the southeast. His death in AD41 and the predictable squabbling among heirs were almost certainly the occasion for his many enemies among the British tribes – the Iceni of East Anglia, the Regnenses in what would be Sussex – to present the disarray as a now-or-never moment for a new Roman campaign.

Perhaps because there had already been so many false starts – Tiberius procrastinating; Caligula never getting beyond the harbour front – Claudius, the club-foot stammerer, on the face of it the most unlikely conqueror of all, was determined to get it right. If it were to be done at all, Claudius must have reckoned, it had to be done in such massive force that there was no chance whatsoever of repeating the embarrassments of Julius. He was not so secure on his throne as to be able to afford even a mixed result, and because the politics of the British tribes were so notoriously unstable and their attitude to hostages indifferent, there could be no thought of a limited holding campaign. This time it had to be serious. So Claudius's invasion force was immense, some 40,000 troops, the kind of army that could barely be conceived of, much less directly encountered, in Iron Age Britain. Even this armada, however, got off to a comical false start, for although it was commanded by some of the most rock-solid veterans of the empire, the rank-and-file troops took one look at the fleet at Boulogne and refused point-blank to embark – until, that is, a personal letter arrived from the emperor himself. This duly came, although it probably didn't help that the letter was delivered by Claudius's personal manservant, an ex-slave known as Narcissus!

Claudius succeeded where Julius Caesar failed, through a brilliantly synchronized campaign of concentrated military ruthlessness and shrewd political pragmatism. His commanders, such as Aulus Plautius, understood the developing society of the Britons well enough to know that by seizing the largely undefended *oppida* they would strike at the heart of the British aristocracy – its places of status, prestige and worship. But in place of those Iron Age centres of conspicuous consumption and display, the Romans could, of course, offer to those sensible kinglings who reached for the olive branch rather than the battle javelin something of a completely different order of magnificence. Faced with the choice, Togidubnus, king of the Regnenses, who had already tasted enough of the Roman good life to know just how good it could be, signed on with alacrity as an ally. After the conquest, he was duly rewarded with wealth and status. He became Tiberius Claudius Cogidumnus, styled himself *legatus Augustus* and built a spectacular palace at Fishbourne near Chichester, which was decorated with brilliantly coloured mosaic floors, the kind of house imaginable, until now, only amid the olive groves of Latium, not the pear orchards of the South Downs.

Togidubnus was not the only important tribal chief to take a pragmatic view of what was in the best interests of himself and his people. All the way through the island the Romans found support from local chiefs, who assumed that their alliance would strengthen rather than weaken their local authority. The fourth-century Roman historian Eutropius wrote that the king of Orkney submitted to Claudius at the time

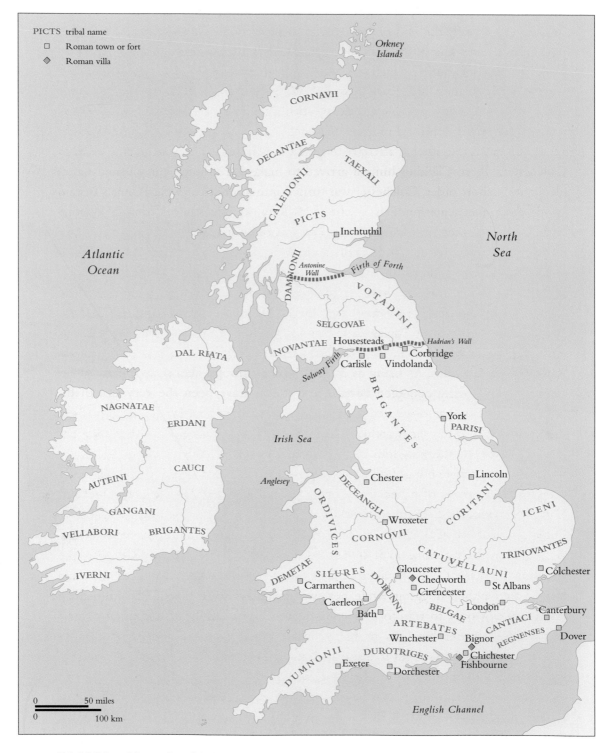

PICTS tribal name
□ Roman town or fort
◆ Roman villa

*Orkney
Islands*

CORNAVII

DECANTAE

TAEXALI

CALEDONII

*Atlantic
Ocean*

PICTS

□ Inchtuthil

*North
Sea*

DAMNONII

*Antonine
Wall*   *Firth of Forth*

VOTADINI

SELGOVAE

NOVANTAE   Housesteads   *Hadrian's Wall*
                  □ □   □   □ Corbridge
                  Carlisle Vindolanda
      Solway Firth

BRIGANTES

NAGNATAE

ERDANI

Irish Sea

□ York
PARISI

AUTEINI

CAUCI

Anglesey

DECEANGLI

□ Chester

□ Lincoln

CORITANI

ICENI

GANGANI

BRIGANTES

ORDIVICES

CORNOVII

□ Wroxeter

VELLABORI

IVERNI

DEMETAE

SILURES

□ Carmarthen

DOBUNNI

CATUVELLAUNI

TRINOVANTES

Gloucester
◆ Chedworth   □ St Albans   □ Colchester
□ Cirencester

□ Caerleon

BELGAE   □ London   □ Canterbury

Bath □

ARTEBATES

CANTIACI

Winchester □   Bignor ◆   REGNENSES   □ Dover

DUMNONII

DUROTRIGES

◆ Chichester
Fishbourne

□ Exeter

□ Dorchester

English Channel

0   50 miles
0   100 km

Tribal Britain and the coming of the Romans.

of the invasion of AD43, but until shards from Roman amphorae of a type that became obsolete by the end of the century were found at Gurness, this seemed far-fetched. Now we know that in the Iron Age broch, turned royal palace, as much as in the hillforts of southern England, there were shrewd local rulers who knew very well which side their bread was buttered. With the individual kings of the British tribes atomized, it was possible for the Roman army to pick them off one by one as they rolled their machine through the island. One of the sons of Cunobelinus was beaten in battle; the other, Caratacus, retreated north. Behind him he left the town of Colchester, where Claudius himself arrived to make a triumphal entry seated on an elephant. In short order, Colchester was turned into a model of what Roman Britain would look like: a metropolitan centre, with long, straight streets, formidable stone walls, packed markets, imposing temples and grandiose statuary. It may not have been Britain's first town, but it was certainly its first city, and a place where it was possible to be *both* Roman and British.

For a while it must have seemed almost too easy. The fugitive son of Cunobelinus, Caratacus, was handed over by the obliging Queen Cartimandua of the Brigantes in the north of England and paraded in chains in Rome. He behaved with such dignity, however, that, in a famous scene of imperial magnanimity, he was pardoned by Claudius. As many as 50,000 Roman troops, almost an eighth of the entire imperial army, occupied Britain, and it may have been the very size of the military garrison that prompted some of its junior commanders to overplay their hand, especially once the watchful Claudius had been succeeded by the indolent Nero in AD54. In the kingdom of the Iceni the careful conventions by which the local aristocracy were bought off and co-opted into the Roman alliance were brutally discarded for a show of naked force. Trying to pre-empt trouble when her husband King Prasutagus died, Boudicca had already offered to share her realm with Nero. Instead, in a show of suicidal arrogance and brutality, the local administrator had it declared a slave province as if it had resisted rather than collaborated with the Romans. To make the point about exactly who owned whom, Boudicca was then treated to a public flogging while her two daughters were raped. The immediate result was not only to transform a willing, even eager, family of collaborators into implacable enemies but also to bring about exactly what the more intelligent Romans all along had sought to avoid: an immense coalition of the disaffected sweeping through an entire region of the country.

With the cream of the Roman troops tied down suppressing an insurgency in remote north Wales, in AD60 Boudicca's army marched towards the place that most symbolized the new world the Britons had almost inadvertently allowed to happen:

Colchester. It helped that it was lightly garrisoned. After a firestorm march through eastern England, during which Roman settlements were burned one by one, it was the city's turn. The colonists retreated to the one place where they must have felt they would be safe – the great temple precinct that had been built by Claudius – but Boudicca's army proceeded to demolish the place, knocking the emperor's head off its bust and throwing it into the river Alde. (The ritual drowning of bodies or of severed heads in wells or rivers was a traditional practice of the British tribes, and Boudicca's army may have been making the point that their culture was still very much alive.) With thousands of terrified Romans huddled in the inner sanctum, the precocious imperial city was set alight. Cowering behind their walled-in sanctum, the colonists must have smelled the advancing smoke and scorch before they, too, were incinerated in the remains. A bowl of carbonized dates, a relic from the firestorm, tells you all you need to know about Boudicca's revenge.

Her victory couldn't last. Elated by the destruction of Colchester, Boudicca's army snowballed in size, and this, paradoxically, may have been its undoing. Once it had to face a disciplined army – Roman troops rushed back from Anglesey – the uncontrollable horde that the British force had become became a victim of its own unwieldiness. Women and children who had gathered in wagons at the rear of the battlefield obstructed the manoeuvrability of the war-chariots and foot soldiers once the Roman legionaries had managed to carve a way through. The congested melée turned into a gory, chaotic slaughter, and Boudicca took her own life rather than fall into the hands of the Romans.

Lessons had been learned the hard way, at least by some. If we believe the history left by his son-in-law Tacitus, Julius Agricola, the general in charge of the pacification of Scotland and Wales, tried to avoid the causes of rebellion by 'putting his own house in order' and making every effort to govern with integrity and justice. Agricola also wanted to draw the boundary line of Britannia at the Clyde and Forth, leaving the logistically difficult Highlands to the tribes known as the Caledonians. But, as usual, it was impossible even for a prudent general to sit on his hands while barbarians attacked Roman forts with impunity. In 79 an enormous pan-European pitched battle took place on the slopes of an unidentified Highland mountain, certainly north of the Tay, which Tacitus calls Mons Graupius, where 30,000 of the Caledonians and their northern allies engaged with the Roman legions and their Dutch (Batavian) and Belgian (Tungrian) auxiliaries. The result was a slaughter of 10,000 of the natives and 360 Romans. The most remarkable pages in Tacitus's history are not the battle scenes, with their predictable gore, but the speeches he puts into the mouths of the opposing commanders, especially the Caledonian general Calgacus, who delivers the first of the great back-to-the-wall, anti-imperialist speeches on Scotland's soil, a ringing appeal for his native country's freedom:

> here at the world's end, on its last inch of liberty, we have lived unmolested to this day, defended by our remoteness and obscurity…But there are no other tribes to come; nothing but sea and cliffs and these more deadly Romans whose arrogance you cannot escape by obedience and self-restraint. Robbers of the world, now that the earth falls into their all-devastating hands, they probe even the sea; if their enemy have wealth they have greed…[neither] East nor West has glutted them…To plunder, butcher, steal, these things they misname empire: they make a desolation and they call it peace.

We have no evidence, of course, that Calgacus ever said any such things. The impassioned appeal for freedom comes straight from Roman republican, rather than Celtic tribal, rhetoric of which we can know nothing. Yet this kind of burning sentiment would echo down the generations. Like the identity of 'Britannia' itself, the idea of a free Caledonia was, from the first, a Roman invention.

'*Perdomita Britannia et statim omissa*' (Britain was subjugated and straight away let slip) was Tacitus's damning verdict on Roman policy after all his father-in-law's Herculean efforts in the north. Tacitus was an armchair warrior, unburdened by the practical responsibilities of governing an overstretched empire that, at the turn of the second century, extended from rebellious Judea to insubordinate southern Scotland. But there was one emperor, Spanish by birth, the most thoughtful of them all, who had grown wise on years of campaigning on behalf of his predecessor, Trajan, and his impossibly far-flung empire and who well understood the virtues of containment. And he was destined, in Britain, at any rate, to be remembered by a wall.

Hadrian's Wall is too often imagined rather like a frontier fort in Indian country, with the US cavalry peering nervously through the palisades and straining to hear the war-drums, a structure sweating paranoia from every stone. But it wasn't like that at all. The wall, all 73 miles of it, 7–10 feet thick and 15–20 feet high, running from the Tyne to the Solway Firth, was begun around AD122, shortly after Hadrian's imperial tour of inspection in Britain. The logic of its engineering and its breathtaking ambitiousness bear all the hallmarks of Hadrian's personal touch. There is no doubt that it was initially a response to the endemic insubordination of those whom the Romans sometimes referred to, rather loftily, as the 'Brittunculi' – the wretched little Brits – and, especially in the first fifty years of its life, it was certainly above all a military base, with troops stationed along the 'milecastles' and turrets, which appeared every 500 yards) along its line. Hadrian, who came to inspect its progress in 122, clearly thought of it as marking the limit of the regions of Britannia that could plausibly be made into a governable Roman province. The Brigantes, amid whose territory the wall was built, had originally been a compliant ally under their Queen Cartimandua, but she had been challenged by her husband, Venutius, who attempted a full-scale revolt, and by the end of the first century the Northumbrian countryside was not thought of as a region particularly hospitable to Roman colonization.

By the time Hadrian died in 138 the wall had done its work of containment well enough for his successor, Antoninus Pius, to push the frontier north, deep into Scotland, to a turf wall built from the Clyde to the Firth of Forth, confining the hostile Picts (literally the 'painted ones' or *picti*) to what Tacitus had called the northern 'island' of Caledonia. Now that they were no longer on the first line of defence, forts such as Housesteads and Corbridge developed into something more like upcountry hill stations and centres of bustling business than anything resembling a Roman Checkpoint Charlie. The wall was rarely thought of as a *cordon sanitaire*, something that would hermetically seal off Roman Britain from the rest of the island to the north. The idea was less to prevent movement than to control and observe it. If there was a killing to be made it would be measured less in bodies than in *denarii*, the takings from the customs tolls imposed on goods travelling from one side of the wall to the other. That way, traders and suppliers who were making money from the presence of the military would also be paying for the country's defence, a kind of protection that the Romans would have been horrified to have considered as a racket. Rather than thinking of Hadrian's Wall as a fence, it might be more accurately seen as a spine around which Roman control of the north of Britannia toughened and stabilized.

If we can now imagine a place like Vindolanda fort, about halfway along the length of the wall, as not such a bad posting, it is because our sense of what life was like for the soldiers at the wall forts and for the population who lived around them has been transformed by one of the most astonishing finds of recent Roman archaeology. For twenty-five years, archaeologists have been cutting slices of the soil, from 23 feet deep, broad enough to see, when inspected sideways on, in a kind of cross-section of the ancient past, whether the dirt retains any of the paper-thin, postcard-size, wooden tablets on which the men and women of Vindolanda recorded the comings and goings of their daily life. Written in ink, fragments have survived rather in the way one might imagine (though this is increasingly unlikely in the age of e-mail) the little bits of receipts, credit card payment stubs, junk mail and circulars that we casually toss aside. They have opened a window on to what the world of the Roman fort was really like.

Hadrian's Wall from the air.

Suppose you were a trader in fish sauce, that ubiquitous and smelly table condiment of the Roman Empire, without which, it seems, no soldier could face a day's duty, and you were making a delivery to Vindolanda. The first thing that would strike you was how very few soldiers actually seemed to be around. When a tally was taken in May AD89 no fewer than 456 out of the fort's nominal strength of 756 were either absent or sick. Then you might notice that the soldiers who were there didn't look especially Roman, but were rather tall, lanky types with fair hair and pink cheeks, which makes sense since most of them were in fact Dutch (Batavian) or Belgian (Tungrian) auxiliaries. There also seemed to be a lot of people around doing strictly non-military jobs: building workers, cobblers, vets and armourers. You would also see enviable luxuries: a hospital for the sick, communal latrines, a heated bath-house and enormous granaries. If you were asked to stay for a meal, you would probably accept, because you knew they ate well: oysters and roe-deer venison, goat's meat and pig's trotters, garlic, olives and radishes. And you would be reminded that it was a global empire you were serving by the presence of exotic pepper in your diet. There would, of course, be the usual grousing about the shortage of beer and gossip about which lads got which jobs and what exactly they had to do to get them; when they would next get a chance to go on a boar-hunt; how long their stint was before they could get out of the army and get their citizenship as a reward; the laziness or the excellence of their slaves; and juicy tittle-tattle about the station commander, Flavius Cerealis, and his wife Sulpicia Lepidina and her social world.

On the third day before the Ides of September, sister, for the day of the celebration of my birthday I warmly invite you to make sure that you come to us, as your arrival will make the day more enjoyable for me if you are present. Give my greetings to your Cerealis. My Aelius and my little son send him theirs. I shall expect you sister. Farewell, sister, my dearest soul as I hope to prosper and hail.

Although at the beginning of the four centuries of Roman rule distinctions between Latins and Britons were brutally sharp, sometimes drawn in blood, by the late second and third centuries, Britannia – especially in lowland England from the Weald to the Lincolnshire Wolds in the east, and from Devon to Carlisle in the west – had settled down into a hybrid, polyglot, rather easy-going province, not the nightmare of perpetual insurrection it must have seemed at the height of Boudicca's revolt.

Of course, not everyone among the native population of Britannia enjoyed the fruits of Roman rule equally. For the vast majority of country-dwellers, who continued to speak their Celtic tongues, it was just a case of one kind of landowner

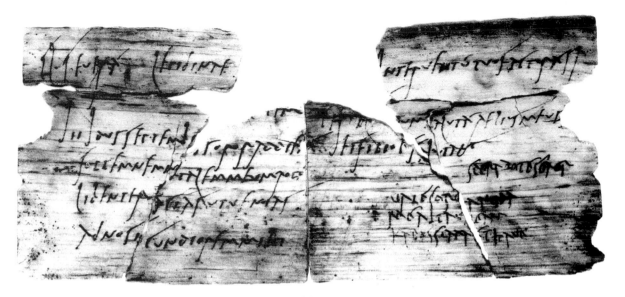

Part of a letter from Claudia Severa, wife of the commander of a neighbouring fort, to Sulpicia Lepidina at Vindolanda.

replacing another. The warriors of the British tribes, who had enjoyed high status for their performance of military services for the chief, were probably the most traumatized of all, shoved aside by the professional army of the Romans and faced with a choice of joining the unfamiliar world of urban society or of staying on the land as masterless peasant cultivators. In the top tier of society, however, a remarkable hybridization took place, just as everywhere else in the Roman Empire at its height, with the distinctions between natives and newcomers increasingly blurred. It is not exceptional to find a tombstone erected at Carlisle by a Roman from Palmyra, Syria, to his wife Regina, a British ex-slave. And beneath the veneer of official Roman religion, all kinds of native British-Celtic cults survived. In a first-century grave at Corbridge a beheaded skeleton was buried along with a batch of bodies who were buried with their boots, the better perhaps to march into the afterlife.

The most deservedly famous of all these hybrid icons is the cheerful face that greeted poolside devotees (along with a group of carved bathing beauties) as they entered the colonnaded porch of the temple of Sulis Minerva at Bath. In keeping with a place that may have been built to its state of classical opulence and grandeur by that unapologetic celebrant of Romano-British good feeling Togidubnus (a.k.a. Tiberius Claudius Cogidumnus of the palace of Fishbourne), whose territories now stretched all the way into the west country, there are allusions in the relief sculptures to the imperial magnificence of Claudius and Vespasian. But Togidubnus was a true cultural cross-breed, and it would have been just like him to have concocted a signature deity for the baths that was part-Roman (with suggestions of the Gorgon's head) and part Celtic, perhaps Sol, old Sunshine himself, who warmed the cockles of the Romans, if not in the Mendip air, then certainly in the steaming waters of Aquae Sulis.

Bath was the quintessential Romano-British place, at the same time mod-con and mysterious cult. On either side of it were a pair of Iron Age forts, Little Solsbury and Bathhampton, and given the native British reverence for the waters, Togidubnus was almost certainly taking advantage of his new position to build on the kind of site that, in the older culture, it would have been sacrilegious to turn into a spa. In its prime, Bath was a huge extravaganza of buildings constructed over a spring, which gushed a third of a million gallons of piping hot, bright orange (from the mercuric oxide) water, 104°F (40°C), up into the bathing pools every day. To soak at Bath was to give both your body and your soul a good cleaning, ablution and devotion. Much of the bathing – as well as the gossip, flirtation and deal-making that was bound to go on in the steamy drip of the spa – took place in the austere grandeur of the Great Bath (with second thoughts on something injudicious said or done perhaps occur-ring in the subsequent cold dip that was meant to close the pores). But the real heart of the place was the sacred spring, where the water gathered in a ferny grotto. A specially cut window allowed devotees of the presiding deity, the *genius* of the place, Sulis Minerva herself, to look over the spring towards an altar erected in her honour, and it also let bathers throw a little something in the waters to attract her attention.

From the trove of objects taken from the drain during excavations of 1878, it is apparent that the more one wanted a favour, the more lavish the offering – a bag of gems, a pair of earrings. What was wanted, it appears from the stones, was some-times a blessing, sometimes a curse on faithless lovers – 'By this Tacita is cursed and declared putrefied like rotting blood' – and especially on the casual petty-thieves for whom Bath must have been a goldmine: 'Whether pagan, Christian, whosoever; whether man or woman, boy or girl, slave or free, has stolen from me, Ammianus, this morning six silver pieces, from my purse, you Lady Goddess are to extract them from him.'

Bath was not the only place where Romano-Britons could wallow in the well-being of the province. From the great trading centre of Londinium, through settle-ments like Gloucester, which had begun as a retirement colony for Roman soldiers, to Colchester, which had risen, phoenix-like, from its burned ruins to become a majestically imposing city, the island was dotted with towns of between 15,000 and 20,000 citizens. It was the beginning of authentic urban life in Britain. And although in the country the vast majority of the peasantry still spoke Celtic tongues, by the third century AD the descendants of the old British warrior nobility grew up

Top: The Great Bath, built towards the end of the first century AD and later extended, in Roman Bath.
Above: Romano-British head from the pediment of the Temple of Sulis Minerva, Bath.

speaking and writing Latin, even though they must have been conscious of being part of a native elite. Once educated, they could join the government of the towns as *curiales* (councillors) and live in town houses with engineered water supplies, which would be connected to their houses if they could afford it. Nothing remotely like this degree of hydraulic and sanitary convenience would be available again in Britain until the nineteenth century. The tables of the governing class were stocked from markets, to which farmers, who could now raise crops for a cash market, brought fresh produce, and their houses were full of goods made in Britain, such as Dorset black earthenware, the best competition for the imported Samian redware that flooded the Roman Empire. There were animal games in the theatre, dull council meetings in handsome stone assembly rooms and ostentatious suburban villas, seldom more than half a day's ride from town, with walls painted with faux architectural details to make them seem even grander.

It is quite wrong to think of the third or even the early fourth century AD as the twilight zone of Roman Britain. Whatever the problems of metropolitan Rome, with usurper succeeding usurper with dizzying speed and obligatory bloodshed, the sun was still shining on Britannia. Some of the most stunning creations of Romano-British art were created in this period, like the splendid villa at Bignor in Sussex, or the showy hotel at Dover, known as the 'Painted House', its rooms now buried several feet below the surface of the street. To anyone arriving in the province from Gaul and lucky enough to be lodged in this place, there would have been no thought at all that this was the architecture of 'decline'.

At some point, however, Dover's significance for Britannia changed from being a port of entry to being a defensive stronghold, and the welcome mat gave way to the keep-out sign, in the shape of massive walls, which at one point cut right through what would once have been the Grand Hotel's lobby.

This sea-change from expansive optimism to fretful caution did not happen overnight. Roman Britain died very slowly, with neither a bang nor a whimper, but with rather a long-drawn-out sigh. And not for any lament for the imagined lost liberties of Celtic Britain, but rather for Mother Rome herself. If we ask what was wrong with Roman Britain, the answer is: not much, not, at any rate, in the third and fourth centuries. The trouble was not here but there. Ironically, as the taproots of Roman-British culture ran more deeply and more strongly, the metropolitan centre of the empire began to subside into anarchy, with multiplying emperors, conspiracies, murders and usurpations. The very core of Roman rule, legitimacy, itself became problematic. When a new currency was issued from Rome, it met with resentment and resistance in Britain. It was precisely because Britannia seemed to be one of the strongest, rather than one of the weakest, of the provinces, that when military strong men raised the standard of revolt in York or London, they did so not in the name of national independence but as reformers who were more Roman than the Romans – the saviours of the empire who would descend from the chilly north to save the languid eternal city from itself.

The most extraordinary of these men was Carausius, who started his career as a pilot-helmsman in the muddy waters of the Belgian coast and rose through the ranks as a captain commissioned to sweep the North Sea of pirates. Rather than render to Caesar what was Caesar's, Carausius proceeded to use his prizes to build a formidable power base, going all the way in 286 and having himself declared emperor. A succession of British historians, not least the great eighteenth-century writer Edward Gibbon, romanticized Carausius as an authentic early British king, an Alfred before his time, a mariner-hero. But Carausius was really an adventurer, who used Britain as an operational base to advance his imperial ambitions. Styling himself Marcus Aurelius Carausius, after the most philosophical of emperors, he dressed up his military exploits with cultural self-promotion, minting coins that referred to the onset of a new golden age, and himself as the 'Renovator of Rome'. Carausius's publicity machine may have been so good that it tempted his own second-in-command, Allectus, to believe that he could easily take it over. So in 293 he murdered Carausius and promptly minted his own coins before going down in defeat to a Roman army of repression. But the general at whose feet defeated London kneeled and who was hailed as 'Restorer of the Light' was Constantius, the deputy of the Emperor Maximian and father of Constantine.

Compared to the disasters unfolding on the empire's eastern frontiers, where the barbarian armies were slicing deep into its territories, Britain must have seemed, at least superficially, an impregnable rock. The defensive line of Hadrian's Wall was supplemented now by a chain of nine 'Saxon Shore' forts, begun by Carausius and strung strategically along the eastern and southern coasts, from Brancaster in Norfolk to Portchester in Hampshire. But manpower had, in fact, been seriously drained by returning many of the troops to the continental empire, where they were desperately needed. And this attrition did not go unnoticed by Rome's enemies, for in 367 something unprecedented happened: a co-ordinated onslaught by three separate sets of raiders. From across the North Sea came Anglo-Saxons, who penetrated the Saxon Shore forts and killed their commanders. Other fortresses, traditionally assumed to be solid, were pierced by warriors who came from lands that had never fallen under Roman rule: Picts from central and northern Scotland and the Gaelic Dal Riata (usually, and much more confusingly, referred to as the 'Scoti') from Ireland. Villas

Mosaic from the late Roman villa at Bignor, near Chichester in Sussex, fourth century AD.

were sacked and burned, and towns were terrifyingly cut off from any kind of relief or reinforcement. The chronicler Ammianus wrote of London being surrounded by gangs of looters, who pushed crowds of captured men and cattle along the roads.

It was not all over with Britannia. Two years after the shock of the barbarian raids, a semblance of Roman law and order had been restored and the garrisons strengthened. But the end of the fourth century undeniably saw a crisis. Ironically, some of the country's helplessness in the face of outside attack was due to its being too well-adjusted to Roman government. The continuity of town life that lay at the heart of the system presupposed adequate defence. But that had been left to professional troops and foreign and native auxiliaries, who could no longer be relied on (whatever the promises from Rome) to stay put when needed. Bereft of that protection, the most Romanized regions of the province could not suddenly conceive of an improvised self-defence, much less do something about it. It was on the less urbanized fringes of Britannia – in Wales, Devon and Cornwall, and in the far north for example, where the old British sub-Roman warrior class had been less integrated into Roman government – that it was possible to mount some resistance, usually led by local autocrats and helped by rugged topography. One of them actually reoccupied the deserted fort of Birdoswald on Hadrian's Wall as his military headquarters.

Military peril engendered economic crisis. In the heartland of Roman Britain generations of farmers had prospered by producing for the town markets. With those markets now imperilled by barbarian raids, the vital connection between town and country snapped, leaving many of the villagers to resort to cattle- and sheep-droving. Those who stayed had no reason to be particularly loyal to the Romano-British. As long as they were left alone, why should they care who lorded it over Britain? For the unfree country people, the changes that were so traumatic for their rulers were just a matter of exchanging one lot of masters for another. So when, in 410, the Emperor Honorius responded to requests for help from Britain by writing to the leading citizens of Britannia that from now on they would have to defend themselves from their own resources, Romano-patriotic resistance was hardly on the cards.

In any event, Honorius had little choice. Alaric the Goth had sacked Rome and he had moved his capital, temporarily, to Ravenna from where he wrote his farewell to Britain. From now on, the empire would be run from Constantinople, and Britain, which had not been a top priority for Italy, was now no priority at all for the new Rome East. Thoughtful historians are constitutionally allergic to critical dates, preferring instead to de-dramatize 'turning points' into long-term developments. But 410 was, in fact, one of the genuinely fateful moments in British history. Alaric the Goth had sacked Rome, and the last two legions departed. It was not like Hong Kong in

1997, with flags flying, pipers piping and the governor in his chariot driving seven times around the courtyard pledging to return. Doubtless, many among the Romano-British hoped and even assumed that, some day, they would see the eagles back. Others – town councillors, magistrates, tax-collectors, potters, poets, musicians and, not least, the new Christian priests – who were facing the murky, uncertain future, told themselves that it was bound to happen, that they could not expect to look to Mother Rome forever, that the empire was half-infested with barbarians anyway, that they could hire themselves some barbarians to deal with other barbarians, and that, somehow, they would manage to see the crisis through. But in the meantime, just to be prudent, they would bury their treasure in a hoard – coins, gems, medals – and when the worst was over they would pull it up again and into the light of civilization.

The best the Romano-British could do was to opt for what seemed the least evil. At first, the warriors from the north German coast – southern Denmark, Jutland and Lower Saxony – sailing upriver in their 'wave-horses' seemed a boon, not a curse. Some sort of force was needed to stop the Picts in the north and the Dal Riata in the west from exploiting the yawning vacuum of power left by the exit of the legions, and an enterprising local despot like Vortigern saw in the Saxons his very own private army – muscle that would be his to command – and a way to make himself supreme in his corner of southeast England. What was more, he must have reckoned that the Saxons – just a few hundred of them – could be had on the cheap. What did they know or care about ruling? So Vortigern offered them a patch of land on the isle of Thanet, and after they had duly dealt with the marauding Picts, pushing them back north, he saw no reason to go on paying them.

This was one of the more spectacular misjudgements in British history. Around 440 the Saxon warriors expressed their displeasure at being double-crossed by going on a rampage, the likes of which made the raids of 367 look like a picnic. In 446 the distraught Britons, acutely aware of what Vortigern had unleashed on southern and eastern England, made a last frantic appeal to Rome. It was recorded in his *De Excidio Britanniae* (The Ruin of Britain) by the monk Gildas, who was living in Wales in the mid-sixth century:

> To Aetius, thrice consul, the groans of the Britons…The barbarians push us to the sea; the sea pushes us back on the barbarians. Between these two kinds of death, we are either drowned or slaughtered.

Gildas saw the disasters of the fifth and sixth centuries – famine, petty tyranny and the ravaging of 'a pack of cubs [which] burst forth from the lair of the barbarian lioness' – as a punishment ordained by God for the violation of his commandments by the stiff-necked and haughty Romano-British and even by Christians, who 'should have been an example to the whole people [but who] lay about, most of them, in drunken stupor'. But in making the events of British history sound as much as possible like the plagues of Old Testament scripture and in the interest of poetic colour – 'fragments of corpses covered with a purple crust of congealed blood looked as if they had been mixed up in some dreadful wine-press' – Gildas exaggerated the scale and the speed of the destruction. The 'multitudes' of the barbarian warriors were, in fact, scattered bands, who settled (when they settled at all) rather thinly in the south and east of the country. They were tough and threatening to be sure, and were a tiny minority in a population still, in the sixth century, overwhelmingly Romano-British. And the disproportion in numbers made possible famous moments of resistance, such as the improvised action at St Albans (Verulamium), where Saint Germannus prevailed by deploying the mightiest weapon of all, war-cries of 'Hallelujah', or the battle in north Britain, perhaps in southern Scotland, described in the Welsh epic *The Gododdin* written by the bard Aneirin, where the three British kings, Cynri, Cynon and Cynrhain, and their 300 warriors, 'wearing golden torques' and seated on 300 fiery stallions, took on the Saxons. The most famous of all these episodes of resistance was the battle of Mount Badon, probably fought in 516, and for some time thought to be somewhere around the hills overlooking Bath. Much later, in the eighth century, the monk-historian Nennius imagined the victor of Mount Badon to have been none other than Arthur, the last of the Christian-Roman warriors to hold out against the hordes of darkness, but the holy aura of Camelot and a king given his vocation by a Celtic wise man are a poetic fantasy that lights up the sparsely chronicled emptiness of these uncertain, and perhaps unknowable, times. The hero of Mount Badon is much more likely to have been the kind of man described by Gildas as a Roman aristocrat, perhaps an ex-officer, Ambrosius Aurelianus, whose second name still has a ring of gold to it.

For all the epic glamour of these tales, the fifth and sixth centuries were not, in fact, a time when the hosts of light and darkness fought over the prostrate body of the island. A tidy compartmentalization of British history, with the wholesale destruction of Roman Britain immediately followed by its violent reincarnation as Anglo-Saxon England, bears no relation to the experience of the vast majority of the inhabitants of Britain. The governing institutions of the Roman province did, indeed, fall away, but much of the social practices and culture and even the language of the old Britain persisted long after the arrival of the first few bands of Saxon mercenaries and freebooters. For many generations Romano-Britons and North Sea warriors must have lived alongside each other, as neighbours rather than implacable foes. Since the Saxons, Jutes and Angles were themselves looking for already-worked land with *in situ* peasantry (for they had no intention of stooping to farming themselves) and since the only interest the unfree country people had was in calculating which kind of overlord offered the more secure protection, there was an easy fit between the new and the old.

The make-do changes that were forced on the island came about as much in response to its economic isolation from the old world of the continental empire as to the threats from Saxons. There was certainly contraction. Some towns, like Exeter (Isca Dumnoniorum) were abandoned altogether; others shrank. Roads, bath-houses, marketplaces and theatres fell into disrepair. And at some point between 490 and 550 the bread ovens at Wroxeter (Viriconium) in Worcestershire were fired up for the last time. But what happened at Wroxeter is a good instance of what must have been happening in many towns in this time of transition: an adaptation rather than an obliteration. When the bath-house no longer functioned, its tiles were used for paving. When the roof of its basilica threatened to fall in, the citizens took down the building themselves and within the shell constructed a new timber-winged building in the Roman style, still commodious, whether used for private or public purposes.

Eventually, however, the adaptations became ever more makeshift and the fabric of Roman life increasingly threadbare, until it did, indeed, fall apart altogether. Those who remained most deeply attached to the idea of Roman Britain evidently felt, by the middle and late sixth century, that they were unlikely to be able to sustain it any longer in the classic heartland of Britain – the south and east, where Jutes (in Kent), Angles (in East Anglia) and Saxons (in the south) were arriving and settling in disruptively greater numbers. They migrated to the north and west, or sometimes, in search of a remnant of the old trading and market economy of the empire, some of the British took ship for the Roman province of Gaul and Armorica (Brittany).

Certainly by the seventh century, Britannia was truly a thing of the past and four cultures shared the islands of Britain. There was a vestigial 'Britain' hanging on in the west, southwest and Wales; these people were no longer Romano-British but spoke and wrote in Celtic. The Dal Riata Gaels, who lived in Ireland, the Hebrides and western Scotland, were part of this tradition. North of the abandoned walls and forts the loosely confederated Pictish kingdoms, for the most part still pagan and speaking a language that remains uncertain, were firmly established in Scotland. And 'England' – the pagan realm of the Anglo-Saxons and Jutes – was planted in the east, all the way from Jutish Kent to the Saxon kingdom of Bernicia in Northumbria, with its stronghold at Bamburgh on the Northumbrian coast.

Like many invaders, the Saxon chiefs and kings had a hankering to possess what had gone before them – the old Roman ideal of the *regnum Britanniae*, the kingdom of the Britons – and they often built settlements on the ruined remains of old Roman-British towns, not least, of course, London, but in no other respect did they remotely resemble that culture. Their political power rested on the spoils of war and on the unwritten custom of the clan. The blood feud and the inhumation of bodies were standard practice among them. This does not mean, however, that the early Anglo-Saxon kingdoms were places of subhuman brutality and ignorance, perpetrated by thugs in helmets. War was not a sport; it was a system. Its plunder was the glue of loyalty, binding noble warriors and their men to the king. It was the land, held in return for military service, that fed their bellies; it was the honour that fed their pride; and it was the jewels that pandered to their vanity. It was everything.

Although the great Anglo-Saxon poem *Beowulf,* written at some point between the seventh and the tenth centuries, is an epic fantasy of a monster-slaying hero, its vision of *ceorls* (free warriors) feasting in the great timbered hall of their 'ring-giver' lord could not have been far from the truth. The 'breast mail', helmet and golden standard presented to Beowulf are exactly reminiscent of the body-jewellery and armour taken from the Sutton Hoo ship burial. And if the spectacular quality of the Sutton Hoo artefacts is anything to go by, it is no wonder that warriors would be willing to devote their lives to a lord who could deliver such glittering prizes. One such lord was Raedwald of East Anglia, who died around 625 and who is the best candidate to be identified with the king who was laid out in the 85-foot-long Sutton Hoo ship, along with his splendid, rather Roman-looking armour – helmet, mailcoat, sword, shield and spears. The ship was then dragged from the river Deben in Suffolk, up an embankment and sunk into a custom-dug trench. In the middle a huge coffin contained the king and his treasure, and when the proper obsequies had been done, the boat was settled in its grave and earth mounded over it so that it stood out on the horizon, a wave-horse riding to the afterlife. The origin of the pieces discovered in the ship and in separate burial mounds made clear the astonishingly global reach of the Anglo-Saxon raiders and traders: silver from Byzantium, gold coins from Gaul, Romano-British enamels, yellow silk from Syria and a North African bowl with carvings of a camel and a lion. But the most spectacular item of all may well be a great gold buckle, alive with writhing serpentine creatures over its massively wrought surface.

Was the Sutton Hoo warrior's resting-place to be pagan Valhalla or the Christian paradise? Among the treasure was a pair of spoons, one with 'Saul' engraved on its shaft, the other with the Christian 'Paul'. And although it seems that Raedwald himself had been dissuaded by his wife from making the leap to Christianity, it was not long before many of his contemporaries among the five kingdoms of Anglo-Saxon England did. The history of the conversions between the sixth and the eighth centuries is another of those crucial turning points in the history of the British isles, but it is not just an episode in the history of religion. Just as much as the exit of the legions marks the isolation of Britain from Rome, the age of the conversions marks its return. And, paradoxically, the process began in a country that had never been touched by Roman rule in the first place: the land the Romans called Hibernia, which was populated by the Gaelic tribes of the Dal Riata.

It is important to remember that the most famous of the early missionaries to Ireland, St Patrick, was, in fact, a Romano-British aristocrat, a *patricius* or patrician, as he called himself. His father was a pillar of the ruling class – a town councillor and landed gentleman, with servile peasants at his beck and call – and like so many of his class trying to cling to the Roman way, he was deacon in the Christian Church. So there was nothing remotely Irish about the teenager who was kidnapped and sold into slavery, probably from a home somewhere in southwestern England, by Dal Riata raiders some time in the early fifth century. By his own account, until this disaster Patrick had been idle and callow, but during his six long years of servitude as herdsman in the 'forest of Foclut' (by tradition believed to be Slemish in County Antrim) he had time to consider and repent of his former life: 'My faith grew and my spirit stirred and…I would say up to a hundred prayers a day. I would wake to pray before dawn in all weather: snow, frost or rain and I felt no harm as I now realize the Spirit was within me.'

After he had escaped, probably to Brittany, had taken instruction and been ordained, Patrick spent years in the places where Christianity had sunk the deepest roots – Gaul, and in particular the cathedral city of Auxerre. So to the image of Patrick the Romano-Brit we must now add Patrick the European Christian. He was then visited by prophetic dreams. The first told him to return home to Britain. The second, once he was in Britain, was a vision in which a man came from Ireland bearing a letter from the people of Foclut imploring him, the 'holy boy, to come and walk among us'. So some time around 460 Patrick became the Paul of the Dal Riadic western isles, a wanderer, putting his life at risk and doing, in fact, what no other Christian evangelist had ever dared to do by going beyond the limits of the old Roman Empire, to Ultima Thule, 'the ends of the earth', to preach the gospel to the heathens. It was not an easy mission. In Ireland he seemed to the local kings to be an enemy, a spy from Rome; to the fathers of the Roman Church he was wasting his time on incorrigible heathens. But despite hostility and spells of captivity, Patrick took the good fight to the foe, targeting traditional pagan sites and festivals at which to do his preaching.

This may, in fact, have been a less confrontational tactic than it first seems, since it was common (if controversial) for missionaries to 'lead' the pagans to Christ by grafting the ancient animist cults of water and woods on to Christian purposes. The Dal Riata kings, after all, still liked to boast of their descent from pagan gods, so it made sense to co-opt sacred springs as sites of baptism, venerated, spirit-inhabited groves of trees as temples of the living cross, and traditional hillforts and burial mounds as places of preaching. And there were other ways in which Patrick and his successors used the circumstances of Celtic Ireland to further their mission. The rigid organization of the Roman Church, with its disciplined hierarchies of bishops and its stress on a single centre of authority, might have been a hard sell to take to the passionately parochial 150 kings of Ireland. Patrick was determined to establish his own independence from the Roman-dominated British Church, with its insistence on obedience to territorially organized bishops. He understood that the monastic ideal of retreat, which he had learned in Gaul, perfectly matched the needs of local royal clans and that it could be presented to them as a family matter.

Columcille, the 'holy dove' (Columba, in the more familiar Latin form of his name), had an even better grip on the convergence between secular and spiritual purposes because he (like his biographer St Adomnan) came from the exceptionally powerful Antrim clan of the Ui Neill. The clans were, after all, first and foremost tribal communities, presided over by the father figure of the *ri tuach*, and Columcille would certainly have understood that for the king, the founding and endowment of a monastery could be thought of as the kind of gift that, like the donation of land or horses to a loyal warrior, established obligation; it was a gesture from which the donor was sure to get something in return – cattle, wealth or good fortune in battle, and perhaps not least a literate class, who might give written form to his commands. This was probably what the king, Conall mac Congaill, had in mind when, in 563, he granted Columcille land on the small fertile island of Iona, off the coast of Mull. The island rapidly became the headquarters of Columcille's missions, both west to the Irish Dal Riata and east through the Hebridean isles and Argyll. Throughout these lands and islands the local kings would supply the land for the monks, peasants who could supply them with barley and honey, the labour to build their cells and work in the forge and sons for an abbot and monks and daughters for nuns. It was as if they were building a holy *cashel* – feathers in their caps, grace for their soul. So monasteries like Aran off the gull-swept Irish coast, with their stone walls, circular beehive cells and encircling stone *cashel* walls, almost look like strongholds: encampments for God.

And this coming together of the kingly and the sacred realms must have seemed consummated when, around 574, Columcille actually ordained one of the Dal Riata kings, Aedan mac Gabhrain, as a Christian priest.

At some point in the early seventh century one of the Bernician kings, Oswald, asked Iona to send a mission to preach in his kingdom, and St Aidan's arrival in the northeast shortly after is properly seen as the beginning of a momentous epoch: the gathering-in of all the peoples of Britain within the Christian flock.

The chronicler of that extraordinary work was the Jarrow monk, Bede. To all schoolboys of my generation he was always the 'Venerable Bede', and that venerability, smelling a bit of the hairshirt and the cloister, not to mention that daunting title of his *Historia ecclesiastica gentis Anglorum* (*Ecclesiastical History of England*), was enough to suggest that Bede might not be a page-turner. In fact, however, Bede is the first consummate English story-teller; an artful retailer of wonders, a writer of brilliantly imaginative prose, capable of conjuring up the fire-light and roasting meat of the timbered halls of the Saxon kings or the death throes of a great war-horse. Although he spent virtually his entire life in the Northumbrian monastery of Jarrow, where he had been deposited by his parents when he was seven years old, Bede's was one of the least cloistered minds of early medieval England. He was a clear-eyed observer of the earthiness of the Anglo-Saxon world, of its bloody feuds, its unpredictable, sometimes infantile, dynastic quarrels, as well as its credulous enchantment by magic. It was his acute understanding of the foibles of sinners as well as the virtues of saints and his lack of illusions about the difficulty of keeping the converted to the straight and narrow that makes him so persuasive a narrator.

Bede had been a child in 664 when the Synod of Whitby had debated the issue of the precise dating of Easter (named as a baptized version of the pagan festival of Eostre). To us, the quarrel might seem petty, but for the respective partisans of the Celtic Irish and the Roman Churches it was crucial. For if they could not agree on the date of the Lord's Passion, what else could they be expected to have in common? And despite the strong presence of the Irish, it was the Roman party that won the day, and Bede grew up in a monastery dominated by Romanism. So it is no surprise that Pope Gregory the Great gets a lion's share of credit for the conversion of the Anglo-Saxons, for it was Gregory who dispatched Augustine to evangelize the Jutish kingdom of Kent in 597. The pope had identified Aethelbert, the king of Kent, as a strong conversion prospect since he had married a Frankish Christian princess, Bertha, and allowed her to keep a chapel in the city of Canterbury, together with a bishop imported from France. Bede's story is the opposite of a lightning conversion. Originally the king kept the missionary isolated from his subjects on the isle of

Iron helmet from the Sutton Hoo ship burial. The nose and mouth are made of gilt bronze and the eyebrows are cast bronze inlaid with silver wire. Dated from before AD 665.

Thanet. It was only when Augustine and Queen Bertha, praying together, began to attract a following that Aethelbert himself was won over. And it was as a result of their daughter, Aethelburga, marrying Edwin, the king of Northumbria, that he, too, became a convert. Throughout his history Bede sees, without any starry-eyed sentimentality, what kind of incentives could overcome the deep mistrust and anxiety of the pagan kings when they were asked to desert their traditional gods. In a world full of fighting the prospect of the Lord of Hosts fighting on their side was, at least, worth pondering. And then there was sheer curiosity. Edwin of Northumbria, for example, summoned a meeting of wise men to advise him on the adoption or rejection of the new Church and improbably begins with the high priest of the old religion admitting that his cult has no 'virtue or advantage'. He is followed by a Saxon noble, who makes the single most touching speech in Bede's entire history, which is all the more credible for being an argument for conversion based on nothing more than a gambler's fretful hunch.

> Such seemeth to me, my lord, the present life of men here on earth…as if a sparrow should come to the house and very swiftly flit through…which entereth in at one window and straightaway passeth out through another while you sit at dinner with your captains and servants in wintertime; the parlour being then made warm with the fire kindled in the midst thereof, but all places being troubled with raging tempests of winter rain and snow. Right for the time it be within the house it feeleth no smart of the winter storm but after a very short space of fair weather it soon passeth again from winter to winter and escapeth your sight. So the life of man here appeareth for a little season, but what followeth or what hath gone before that surely we know not. Wherefore if this new learning hath brought us any better surety, methinks it is worthy to be followed.

It is typical of Bede to put this clinching speech, so startling in its pragmatism, in the mouth of a nobleman. For the Church in Anglo-Saxon England (just as in Ireland and Pictish Scotland) was a natural extension of the aristocracy and was dominated by men and women of high birth. The twin monasteries of Jarrow and Monkwearmouth had been founded in the seventh century by Benedict Biscop, an ex-warrior-lord, a *thegn*, at the Northumbrian court, who had become a monk after travelling through Frankish Christian Europe. Grandeur mattered to these lordly abbots, conscious as they were of being the next generation of purified Romans. St Wilfrid, the aristocratic bishop of York, deliberately used part of Hadrian's Wall to build at Hexham a basilica worthy of Roman authority. And their monasteries and churches were decorated with aggressive magnificence (in contrast to the simplicity and austerity of the Irish church). Biscop had brought back from his travels in Italy teams of stonemasons, glaziers and jewellers and shot-silk hangings embroidered with the scriptures and lives of the saints. He also imported a singing master from Rome to teach the monks the chant as sung at St Peter's. And when one of these princes of the Church travelled he was followed by an imposing retinue, as many as eighty monks, just as if he had been a great lord. Attacked on a beach in Sussex, St Wilfrid's men swore, in the Anglo-Saxon style, to fight, 'death with honor or life with victory'.

The monasteries needed manpower for their most exacting work – copying the sacred texts and histories of the early Church – and places like Jarrow and Lindisfarne were production-lines of books that would ensure the survival of Latin and Christian literature, and they needed an industrial approach to carry it off. It took over 2000 parchment folios to copy the works of Gregory the Great; 500 calf-skins to make a single bible. And although Lindisfarne, founded by the Iona monk St Aidan, was originally a simpler place than Jarrow, it, too, had a jewellery shop that could work on the binding and cases made for its own glorious bible, decorated by the monk Eadfrith. Eadfrith is, arguably, the first English master artist to whom we can put a name. Along with the many unknown brethren who worked with him on the Lindisfarne bible (inscribing, for example, over 10,000 little red dots around a single folio capital), he brought to sacred art the ancient British feeling for the coiling, curling, spiralling line, first visible in Neolithic jewellery. Remarkably, the same beaked, serpentine creatures that twist over the Sutton Hoo buckle reappear on the densely beautiful 'carpet pages' of the Lindisfarne Gospel, a startling testimony to the fusion between pagan and Christian motifs with which the greatest Anglo-Saxon art is saturated.

The Lindisfarne Gospels were almost certainly intended for the shrine of the abbey's most charismatic holy man, St Cuthbert, whose life was recorded in a separate work by Bede. It is a biography that exemplified the need of the Anglo-Saxon Church, not just for scholars and figures of authority such as St Wilfrid, but for men who seemed to personify the beatific simplicity of the earliest Christian hermits. Cuthbert came from the same high-status family as St Wilfrid and Benedict Biscop, but although he dutifully obeyed the Roman line that had been laid down after the Synod of Whitby, his own training had been more in keeping with the Irish tradition of ascetic simplicity, and he spent a great deal of time striding about the Cheviots, tending both human and woolly flocks and visiting the sick and poor. He became a prior at Lindisfarne when he was thirty years old, and his reputation for mysterious saintliness had already provoked comment among the monks of the Northumbrian coast. There was, to begin with, his habit of stealing away and, some said, standing knee-deep in freezing seawater and chanting the psalms – the kind of habit in which innocence and ostentatiousness seemed suspiciously mixed. When he was visiting Coldingham abbey he was surreptitiously followed by a brother who did, indeed, find Cuthbert up to his shins in the rockpools, singing away while the moon shone down. All scepticism melted at daybreak, however, when the saint was seen kneeling on the sand while two sea otters emerged from the water and rubbed their furry bodies on his feet to make them warm and dry.

Even Lindisfarne was too gregarious for Cuthbert's meditations, however, so when he was forty he retreated still farther, out to the island of Farne, where he was left alone to grow barley and commune with the puffins. When, in 684, the Northumbrian king, Egfrith, wanted to persuade Cuthbert to return to the mainland as bishop, it was the king who had to make the journey over the choppy waves to Farne in a predictably futile attempt at persuasion. It was, in any case, too late. Cuthbert died in 687. The monks came to fetch his body from Farne and when they reached Lindisfarne, the boat was met by a huge assembly of the pious chanting psalms. Eleven years later, when the brethren of Lindisfarne decided to raise a shrine in his honour and disinterred him from the chapel of St Peter, they found to their amazement that his body showed no signs of decomposition.

It was because St Cuthbert was so passionately venerated that, in 793, before the men called 'the wolfcoats' and 'the berserks' could do his remains any harm, that the Lindisfarne monks, knowing that precious shrines were a favourite target of the Viking sea-raiders, took his body from Lindisfarne and spent seven years wandering with it, looking for some safer place of refuge. For in that year, *The Anglo-Saxon Chronicle* reports:

> dire potents appeared over Northumbria...immense whirlwinds and flashes of lightning and fiery dragons were seen flying through the air. A great famine followed and a little after that, on the 8th of June, the ravages of heathen men miserably destroyed God's church at Lindisfarne.

If you look hard enough, it is possible to find some good in any culture (except, perhaps, some candidates from the twentieth century), and in recent years, for the best possible motives, historians of the Vikings have been at pains to dispel the mythology that theirs was a sail-and-slash-burn-rape-and-pillage culture. It is known now that it was pressure of population on poor Scandinavian land that got them into their boats in Norway and Denmark and that they came bearing amber, fur and walrus ivory (as well as a bad attitude), and that their sagas were full of epic heroics. It is certainly true

An ornamental carpet page from the Lindisfarne Gospels,
made at Lindisfarne about 698.

that when the Vikings (in the tenth century, for example) settled down as colonizers (and even as farmers) the dynamism of their trade and the beauty of their artefacts perhaps offset their ferocious belligerence. Cities such as Dublin and York thrived under their overlordship, enough for the latter to have recently invented a 'Jorvik' theme park, devoted to projecting a warmer, cuddlier image of the Vikings.

But with the best will in the world, the idea of the early Vikings as speedy Baltic commercial travellers, singing their sagas as they rowed to a new market opening, doesn't ring quite true. Towards the end of the eighth century the reeve Beaduheard in Dorchester went to meet what he innocently supposed was a fleet of peacefully inclined Norse trading ships. He directed them to the loyal royal estate and was thanked for his helpfulness by an axe in the face. The Vikings were certainly partial to one kind of inventory – people (including women), whom they sold as slaves. A thousand such slaves were taken from Armagh in one raid alone in 869. A burial dated to 879 contained a Viking warrior with his sword, two ritually murdered slave girls and the bones of hundreds of men, women and children – his very own body count to take with him to Valhalla.

So it seems likely that the inhabitants of ninth-century Britain would have had some difficulty in finding the Norsemen ethnographically fascinating, being too busy defending themselves against dismemberment or being dragged off into captivity. Just because so many of the tales of their early impact on Anglo-Saxon life are alarmingly violent, and because they come from Anglo-Saxon, Church sources, does not necessarily mean they were untrue. Gaelic sources tell much the same story. At Strangford Lough, the ancient abbey closely associated with St Patrick's earliest preaching in Ireland, was completely destroyed. In 795 another of the iconic sites of the Christianization of Britain – Iona – was sacked, and in 806 sixty-eight of its monks were killed. Houses, then, which were vulnerable to attack from rivers, loughs or coastal estuaries had very good cause to take the Viking threat seriously. A small cathedral at Bradwell-on-Sea in Essex, founded in the seventh century by a far-ranging mission from Northumbria, had been built on the foundations of a Roman fortification, and the monks must have been grateful for the solid masonry defences while they waited nervously for Viking raids, which they knew, sooner or later, would strike fast and fierce.

On the positive side, however, there was one thing that the Vikings did manage to do – albeit inadvertently – and that was to create the need for a consolidated kingdom of England and of Alba, too, which eventually became known as Scotland. This was not what they had in mind when their longships sailed swiftly and lethally upstream. What they had in mind, principally, was loot. The Vikings came from a

Scandinavian society that was itself a near-anarchy of warrior lords, making gestures of allegiance to their kings in Denmark and Norway, but for the most part being permitted to operate as freebooters, taking as much land, plunder and captives as they wished. Better the marauder away than the marauder at home. The idea, before the Vikings began to settle themselves in occupied areas of eastern and northern England, was to inflict enough violence on a kingdom for its ruler to buy them off, preferably in hard silver. The principle was crude, but the delivery of the violence was efficient, and it hit the Saxon kingdoms at a time when they were themselves divided both between and within each other. The marriage alliances between the Saxon states had proved, under pressure, to be no guarantee of military solidarity, especially when Viking damage might be thought of as a calamity for somebody other than yourself. In fact, some of the Saxon rulers repeated the mistakes of the Romano-British four centuries before, by actually welcoming the invaders as a useful auxiliary.

Before he died in 735 Bede had worried a great deal about whether the Christian tree of belief had been planted deeply enough to survive the threats he saw coming from both pagan resurgence in the shape of the Norsemen and the new militant religion of Islam, which had thrust deep into the heart of Christian Spain and France. But even Bede's pessimism couldn't begin to imagine the scale of devastation that the Vikings would inflict on Northumbria, not only on Lindisfarne, but on his own monastery at Jarrow, and at Monkwearmouth and Iona, the capture of York and, most painful of all, the burning of the great libraries of the monasteries. When he heard of the annihilation at Lindisfarne, Alcuin of York, the court scholar to Charlemagne, the great Frankish Holy Roman Emperor, wrote: 'Behold the church of St Cuthbert, spattered with the blood of the priests of God.'

By smashing the power of most of the Saxon kingdoms, the Vikings accomplished what, left to themselves, the warring kings, earls and thegns in England and the mutually hostile realms of Dal Riata and Pictland in the north could never have managed: some semblance of alliance against a common foe. After two decades of attacks in the north, the Pictish king Constantine I, consciously taking his name from the first Roman-Christian emperor, defeated the Dal Riata and united the kingdoms in 811. Likewise, it took the threat of common, irreversible catastrophe for the rulers of what remained of non-Viking England to bury their differences and submit to the overlordship of a single king, a king of all England. To attract this kind of unprecedented allegiance, such a figure would have to be exceptional, and Alfred, of course, fitted the bill. The Tudors thought him inspiring enough to award him, alone of all their predecessors, the honorific appellation of 'Great' in direct analogy with Charlemagne, Charles the Great. And for all the mythology about Alfred, it can't be said that they were wrong. The Anglo-Saxons called him *Engele hirde, engele dirling* (England's shepherd, England's darling).

When he was born – in Wantage in 849 – the youngest son of King Aethelwulf and the grandson of King Egbert of Wessex, that realm, through the usual combination of war and marriage, had replaced the midland kingdom of Mercia as the dominant Saxon kingdom. The Vikings were still largely thought of as periodic inconveniences, mounting raids, stealing as much as they could from shrines or busy Saxon market towns like Hamwic (the ancestor of modern Southampton), extorting money and then mercifully departing to enjoy the proceeds. But of late their fleets had been getting bigger – thirty, thirty-five ships at a time – and their stays were becoming ominously more protracted. In the 850s they began to stay through the entire winter in Thanet and Sheppey in Essex. In 850 a fleet, which *The Anglo-Saxon Chronicle* put as high as 350 ships, captured Canterbury and London and sent the Mercian king, Berhrtwulf, packing. Nor could silver be relied on any longer to keep them at arm's length. In 864 the ealdormen (noblemen) of Kent had duly coughed up but the Vikings had decided to put the area to the sword anyway, just for the hell of it. The following year, 865–6, was the year in which the great Christian kingdom of Northumbria was destroyed at the hands of the biggest Viking fleet Britain had yet seen, with York falling in 867. By 876 the Northumbrian lands were being shared out among their principal chiefs. In 869 it was the turn of the king of East Anglia, Edmund, who, sick of making the usual payments, turned to resistance and suffered decapitation and impalement. It was now obvious to Aethelred, the king of Wessex, and to his only surviving brother, Alfred, that they, too, could not avoid confronting the Vikings for very much longer.

Much of what we know about Alfred comes from the biography written by the Welsh monk Asser, invited to the king's court and doubtless eager to sing his praises. Allowing for idealization, though, the portrait somehow has the ring of truth, even the child already hungry for learning. Asser's most famous tale of the boy-wonder describes Alfred's mother offering to give a decorated book of Anglo-Saxon poetry to whichever child could learn the contents. Needless to say, Alfred not only committed the poems to memory but recited them out loud to his mother, half bookworm, half show-off.

But these were not bookish times. In 868, with the Vikings wintering in Mercian Nottingham, Alfred was married, in an obvious tactical alliance, to Eahlswith, whose mother was a member of the Mercian royal family. By 870 the Danes were in Reading, a direct challenge to the kingdom of Wessex. In 871 the two brothers, Aethelred and Alfred, fought a series of battles culminating in the victory of

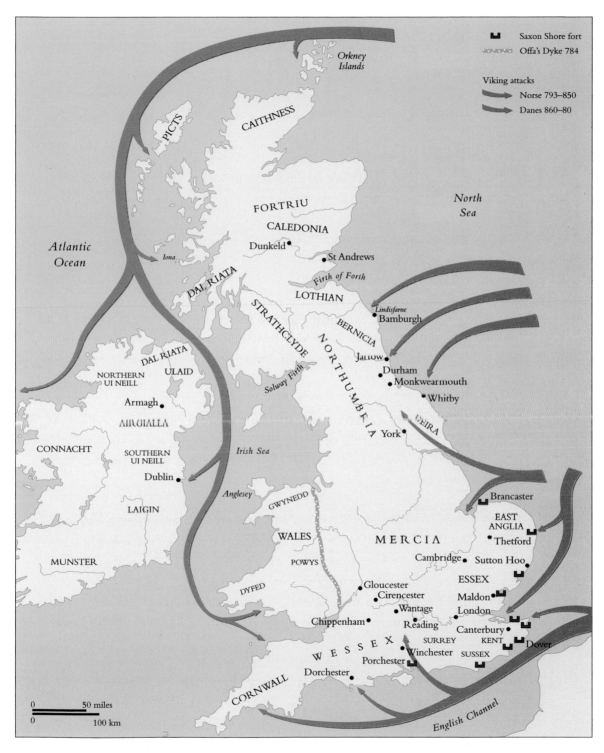

Anglo-Saxon kingdoms and the coming of the Vikings.

Ashdown. But before he could enjoy the success, Aethelred died, leaving Alfred the kingdom. The news that a second, enormous Viking army had come to Reading was not reassuring. With the collapse of Wessex apparently imminent, the entirety of Anglo-Saxon England seemed about to go the way of Roman Britain.

But then a series of small miracles intervened. The one failing in the otherwise impressive Viking killing machine was its tendency to congratulate itself on victory by splitting itself into pieces; not so much divide and conquer as conquer and divide. Presumably confident it could never be withstood, the great pagan Viking armies of 865 and 871 went their separate ways. In 874 some of the senior class of 865 returned to Norway, the rest settling down in Northumbria for the long term. The junior class of 871, led by a *jarl* (chieftain) called Guthrum, moved to Cambridge, from where it calculated it would make Wessex, to the south and west, its very own milch-cow. When Guthrum moved on Gloucester, this seemed about to happen.

For the moment, Alfred had no choice but to temporize, making treaties and exchanging hostages with Guthrum in an attempt to get the Vikings out of Wessex and into Mercia. For a while, the tactic seemed to work, even though Alfred must have been pessimistic about holding a pagan like Guthrum to any kind of sworn oath. Sure enough, on Twelfth Night, January 878, in the dead of winter and knowing that Christians like Alfred were distracted with celebrating the Epiphany, the Vikings launched a surprise attack on the royal Wessex town of Chippenham. The plan must have included the capture of the king and it very nearly succeeded. Virtually defence-less, Alfred was forced to take flight.

What happened next is the heart of Alfred's legend. A fugitive in the bullrush-choked swamps of Athelney, he began to turn the tide against the enemy, using the inaccessible bogs as a defensive stronghold. Asser describes the prototype of the guerrilla fighter, leading 'a life of great distress amidst the woody and marshy places of Somerset [with] nothing to live on except what could be foraged from raids', reduced to begging hospitality from peasants, including the swineherd's wife, who gave him such a bad time for burning her cakes. The stories, both then and later, have the tone of scripture (or at least apocrypha): a proud king reduced to abject destitution and stoical humility (especially when dressed down by an indignant woman); but then, when flattened by misfortune, blessed with the inspiration to take hold of his and his country's destiny. In one of the many later stories surrounding the wandering king on the run, no less a person than St Cuthbert (who else?) appears and asks to share his meal. The king obliges. The stranger vanishes only to appear in full saintly get-up, promising eventual success and urging Alfred, like Gideon, to trust in God and blow blasts on his battle horn to summon his friends.

By the spring of 878 Alfred had managed to piece together an improvised alliance of resistance, and at King Egbert's stone, on the borders of Wiltshire and Somerset, he took command of an army that, two days later, fought and defeated Guthrum's Vikings at Edington. It was a victory so complete that Alfred was able to pursue them all the way back to Chippenham and besiege them for two weeks before the Viking chief capitulated. And this was no ordinary surrender. Guthrum was sufficiently impressed by the power of Alfred's battle-god that he decided forthwith to enrol in the ranks of the Christian soldiers along with thirty of his warriors. Accepting baptism at the church of Aller in Somerset, Alfred stood godfather to Guthrum, raising him from the font. The hitherto fiercely pagan Viking lords were now clad not in armour but, head to foot, in the soft white cloth of converts; their baptismal garments removed on Alfred's royal estate at Wedmore as the solemn ceremonies were completed. So the victory over Guthrum was both martial and spiritual. Alfred had made a believer of him and received him into the community of the English Church, so it was now possible to make a sacred, binding treaty (so the king must have hoped anyway) in which Guthrum agreed to be content with his mastery of East Anglia and desist from attacking Wessex, Mercia or the territories of Essex and Kent, also ruled from Wessex proper. And this seems to be more or less what happened. Guthrum withdrew to Hadleigh in Sussex where perhaps he spent a bucolic retirement pottering about in un-Viking like harmlessness.

Alfred was much too intelligent to be carried away by a premature sense of triumph. A single *jarl* and his army had been defeated, not the whole of the Viking power in England. By the end of the ninth century it was more than ever clear that the Norsemen were in the island for the long haul, no longer as raiders and pirates but as colonists. Alfred's best hope was containment, for a *modus vivendi* with a Christianized and, therefore, relatively peaceable Viking realm. And although it was not quite the epic of historiographical legend, Edington did make the Viking kings pause in their sweep across the island and bought Alfred fourteen years of priceless respite, a period in which he constructed a formidable chain of thirty defensive forts called *burhs*, permanently manned garrisons, strategically based on the accumulated military wisdom of generations of ancestors: Iron Age hillforts, Roman roads, and Saxon dykes and ditches. His part-time army of the *fyrd*, raised from the thegns who owed service to his senior lords, was now equipped with horses, and put on rotational shifts of duty, so that whenever and wherever the Vikings appeared, they would always have a serious opposing force to contend with. When the Vikings did return in the early 890s, as Alfred had anticipated, they no longer had the operational freedom they had enjoyed in their marauding heyday in the middle of the ninth century. Alfred's campaign forced the Vikings to settle for much less than half of the country, and a border running through East Anglia, eastern Mercia and Northumbria hardened into a frontier between Danish and Saxon England.

It was, at best, a stand-off. But when in 886 Alfred entered London (which he had refounded on its old Roman site, rather than the Mercian-Saxon *Lundenwic* sited near present-day Aldwych and the Strand), something of a deep significance happened. He was, as Asser wrote, acclaimed as the sovereign lord of 'all the English people not under subjection to the Danes'. And it was at this time that he began to be called 'King of the Anglo-Saxons'. Some coins of the period actually go further and style him *rex Anglorum* (king of the English), the title with which his grandson Aethelstan would be crowned in 927. So there can be no question that during Alfred's lifetime the idea of a united English kingdom had become conceivable and even desirable. The exquisite 'Alfred Jewel', which was found not far from Athelney, bears an extraordinary enamelled face, perhaps like the similar Fuller brooch, its staring eyes symbolizing Sight or Wisdom, a wholly apt quality to celebrate an omniscient prince. The 'Alfred Jewel' is inscribed on its side with the legend *Aelfred mec heht gewyrcan* (Alfred caused me to be made). The same perhaps could be said of his reinvention of an English monarchy.

In truth, the Anglo-Saxon kingdom of England was still as much a work in progress as was the mac Aailpin kingdom in Scotland under Kenneth I. But by the time he died in 899, Alfred certainly had transformed the office of kingship itself. What had been a warrior chieftaincy, the giver of rings (and Alfred was still celebrated as the greatest ring-giver of all) was now also an institution of classical and biblical pretensions. The king who was the translator of the psalms could never have been far from thinking himself as a new David or Solomon. Like David, he would be the right arm of the Church of God – and a sword found at Abingdon suggests just how seriously he took this role. Like Solomon, Alfred assumed that the authority of the king should rest on something other than the arbitration of force, namely justice. So he was the first of the kings to set about combining the different law codes and the penalties for their infraction into a single, coherent whole and having them written and translated so that his subjects (or at least the half of them that were free, for it must always be kept in mind that Saxon England was a slave society) could have access to royal justice as a matter of course. To be sure, the justice that Alfred offered was kept well within the bounds of realism. Aware of the hopelessness of attempting to outlaw the blood vendetta, Alfred merely insisted that the king should regulate it, giving a grace period, for example, to the attacked party to come to terms before he was set upon. Pained by the memory of the Viking burning of monastic libraries, Alfred also

The Alfred Jewel.

saw the king as an educator. In his translation of Boethius's *De consolatione philosophiae* (*The Consolation of Philosophy*) Wisdom gets the best lines, but Alfred's commitment to instruction was also of a practical kind. Establishing schools, not just for his family and the court but for all his nobility, was a statement of intent that henceforth those who presumed to govern in the name of the king should do so as literate, educated men, rather than the bearers of swords and the takers of purses.

It was an extraordinary thing that Alfred's most fervent conviction was that the condition of exercising power was the possession of knowledge. Of how many other rulers of British realms could that truly be said?

The Saxon kings had come a long way from the ferocious pagan axemen of the *adventum* to the makers of libraries! Of course, this vision of a peaceful, studious Anglo-Saxon Wessex was more of a noble ideal than an imminent reality. More than half the country was securely in the grip of the Vikings, and although in the tenth century the sovereignty of the Wessex-based kings of England would extend to the border of the Tweed, it was on condition that the Viking zone of control, the 'Danelaw' as it came to be known, would enjoy its own considerable autonomy. By the end of the tenth century a second coming of aggressive Viking raids would once again attempt to reach deep into the territory of Anglo-Saxon England, and early in the eleventh century a Danish king, Cnut, would reign over the whole country south of Hadrian's Wall. But he would reign largely as the beneficiary of the Anglo-Saxon government established by Alfred and his successors.

Although the dynasty of the house of Wessex was battered and bloodied through all these years of tribulation, and was often on the point of being wiped out altogether, the ideal of English kingship that had crystallized under Alfred persisted. And it is one of the most profound ironies of early British history that it was, at heart, a Roman ideal of rule, which was implanted in the breasts of the Saxon cultures usually thought of as having buried the classical tradition. This was equally true north of the Tweed, where the kings of Alba (as they called the old Pictland after 900) named their sons alternately with Gaelic and Latin names — so that a Prince Oengus would be brother to a Prince Constantine. Alfred had, in many ways, been the most Roman of Saxons. When he was just a child, in 853, his father, Aethelwulf, had sent him on a special mission to Rome where Pope Leo IV had dressed the little fellow in the imperial purple of a Roman consul and set around his waist the sword-belt of a Romano-Christian warrior. In 854–5 he had spent another whole year in Rome with his father, collecting the kind of memories, even of the Palatine hill in ruins, that an Anglo-Saxon would hardly forget. Learning Latin in his adult life and translating Pope Gregory's *Pastoral Care* finally set the seal on this ardent Christian Romanism.

And during the pontificate of Pope Marinus II, Alfred inaugurated the tradition by which every year, in return for freeing the English quarter of the city from taxes, the alms of the king and people of England would be sent to Rome, a tradition that ended only with the reformation of Henry VIII.

Of course, the Rome to which Alfred was evidently devoted was not the pagan empire from which Claudius and Hadrian had sent their legions into the island, inventing Britannia. It was, rather, the new Roman Christian empire. If Alfred had had a model in mind for his own exalted concept of kingship it surely would have been Charlemagne, and Alfred's policy of bringing learned clerics to court seems to have been in direct emulation of the Frankish Emperor. All the same, when his great-grandson, Edgar, was crowned, twice over, in 973 with solemnities designed by Dunstan, the Archbishop of Canterbury (who must have known something about antiquity), the rituals that remain at the heart of English coronation to this day – the anointing, the investment with orb and sceptre, the cries of acclamation, 'Long live the king, may the king live forever' – owed as much to the Roman as to the Frankish tradition. And where did those two coronations take place? In the two places in England that most profoundly embodied the fusion of Rome and ancient Britain: Bath and Chester.

For whatever else he understood about this, Edgar was bright enough to know that, if he were to survive, the one thing a king of England could not afford was insularity.

Historians like a quiet life, and usually they get it. For the most part, history moves at a deliberate pace, working its changes subtly and incrementally. Nations and their institutions harden into shape or crumble away like sediment carried by the flow of a sluggish river. English history in particular seems the work of a temperate community, seldom shaken by convulsions. But there are moments when history is unsubtle; when change arrives in a violent rush, decisive, bloody, traumatic; as a truck-load of trouble, wiping out everything that gives a culture its bearings – custom, language, law, loyalty.

1066 was one of those moments. Lately, a campaign has been waged to minimize the significance of the battle of Hastings, beginning with elaborate exercises in name-correction. And the battle did indeed happen, not at Hastings itself, but many miles inland at a place the Saxons called 'senlach' and the Normans corrupted into 'sang-lac', the lake of blood. But nomenclature is surely beside the point. The point is whether what happened in south-east Wessex in the autumn of 1066 was a faint tremor, barely disturbing the routine of a settled society or, as most historians have assumed, the opening of a massive fault-line in the continuity of our history: the end of something and the beginning of something else. Was it, in fact, an annihilation?

It is certainly true that, for the majority of the population of Anglo-Saxon England (let alone the rest of Britain), 1066 was mostly a matter of exchanging lords. The slaves at the bottom of Anglo-Saxon society who could be bought and sold could hardly have cared less what language their masters spoke. Peasant villeins (unfree tenants or serfs) ploughed their fields, fed swill to their pigs, prayed to avoid poverty and pestilence and watched the seasons roll round. But it's always possible, of course, by looking at events from the point of view of the apolitical, to see even the greatest enormities as marginal to the imperturbable rhythms of social routine. And it's a truism that every spring, the grass came up green again. But this year there were bones under the buttercups and the entire governing class of Anglo-Saxon England,

CONQUEST

The battle of Hastings from the Bayeux Tapestry.

some 4000 or 5000 thegns, had been made to vanish and authority, wealth, men and beasts had been given to foreigners. You could survive and still be English. You could even speak the language. But politically you were now a member of the underclass, the inferior race. You were a peon. You lived in England, but it was no longer your country. And that change, by any standards, was a trauma.

A change of overlord was nothing new in England. Exactly a half-century before the battle of Hastings, in 1016, the country abruptly became, in effect, the southern-most province of a great Baltic–Danish maritime empire, ruled by its Christian king, Cnut. This had not been an inevitable change, but neither was it altogether a surprise. At the end of the tenth and the beginning of the eleventh century all the old night-mares had come back to haunt the Anglo-Saxon kingdom. Viking raids had resumed with a vengeance in the 990s, but unlike the earlier expeditions, which had been free-booting affairs, carried out by opportunistic *jarls* in search of a killing, they were now more like the colonial arm of official Danish policy. Shut out of continental Europe by the military power of the Ottonian monarchy, the Danes had reverted to their ambition of breaking out from the *de facto* frontiers of the Danelaw in eastern England, destroying the power of the Saxon realms of Wessex and Mercia and sub-jecting the entire country between the river Tweed and the Welsh borders to their rule. The battle of Maldon in 991, on the Essex shore, lamented in a great Anglo-Saxon epic poem, at which the ealdorman of Essex, Byrhtnoth, was killed and defeated by the Viking prince, Olaf Tryggvason, has the resonance of a national rather than just a regional disaster. It came at a time when the authority of the reigning king of Wessex, Edgar's youngest son, Aethelred, had already suffered so badly from the Viking offensive that he could not be sure of the allegiance of many of his leading ealdormen and thegns. The conversion of his name 'Aethelred' (good counsel) into a nickname 'Unraed' (bad counsel) was a painful joke, and although recorded only after the Conquest might well have been contemporary – an ominous sign of the loss of deference. After the battle of Maldon the Vikings began to exact heavy tribute from Saxon lands, which, without guaranteed protection (or the threat of retribution) from Aethelred, the Saxons often chose to pay, thereby subsidising the long-term presence of further Viking fleets. The elaborate chain of power and allegiance that Alfred and his successors had put together seemed to be coming unstrung.

But not completely and not yet. Although the Danish king, Sweyn I, a pious convert to Christianity, made no secret of his ambition to become king of England, it took twenty years of grim campaigning before it came within reach. First, he had to defeat his principal Viking rival, Tryggvason, who became king of Norway in 995; then he had to persuade the majority of English ealdormen to assent to his kingship.

By 1013 this had indeed taken place. But within a few years, fathers gave way to sons: Sweyn I died unpredictably in 1014, leaving the kingdom to his son, Cnut. Aethelred followed in 1016, survived by his son, Edmund Ironside. In October 1016 Ironside suffered a disastrous defeat at Ashingdon in Essex at the hands of Cnut and was forced, despite his more direct claim to the throne, to make a treaty. The house of Wessex was to keep its own realm, full of estates, churches and abbeys, but the Danes were to have everything else. Then, later that same year, in November 1016, without any warning, Edmund followed his father to the grave, and the last piece of England dropped sweetly into Cnut's lap. Two years later he inherited Denmark from his brother.

Did England now become as thoroughly Danish as it would be Norman fifty years later? Much of the country, from York through East Anglia – and beyond England in the Norse earldom of Orkney and the Viking port city of Dublin – could already be said to have been colonized, in the sense that their economic and cultural life was redirected northeast and east towards the trading empire of Scandinavia. The countless towns with name-endings in -by and -thorp bear the marks of their Viking origin to this day. But in Wessex and Mercia it was much less clear who was colonizing whom. Cnut began his reign in the usual way with a wedding and a slaughter. In 1002 Aethelred had had no compunction about ordering a general massacre of Danes, the better to pre-empt a fifth column. Now it was Cnut's turn to wipe out his major competitor, Edmund Ironside's brother Eadric, as well as those Saxon magnates whom he suspected of disloyalty, in particular the earls of Mercia and East Anglia, whose earldoms were given to the Viking nobles, Eric and Thorkell the Tall, who had delivered the throne of England to him. That was the way things were done in the Mafia-like world of eleventh-century Europe: a nice clean slate, with no athelings (nobles of royal descent) left to cause problems later on. Finally, Cnut lost no time in taking Aethelred's widow, Emma, as his own wife even though she was old enough to be his mother.

But the marriage of Emma and Cnut was designed less for carnal joy than political convenience. It was another aspect of what was, in effect, a hostile take-over, rather than a complete effacement. For although he made his Danish friends into powerful earls, Cnut was shrewd enough to run England the English way. He would have been foolish to think of doing anything else since he had inherited the most intensively administered, best organized government in early medieval Europe (and, by the time Cnut had finished with it, the most heavily taxed as well). Late Anglo-Saxon England was politically volatile but institutionally stable. Beyond the mayhem at court and the bloodshed of the battlefield, churches were being built, cases were

Top: Viking spearheads and axes found near London Bridge.
Above: King Cnut and Queen Emma present an altar cross to New Minster, 1031.

being heard in court, merchandise was being produced and marketed and a strong and copious coinage was being minted. And from the few fragmentary survivals we can see that this was also a culture of great sophistication and versatility. The stunning ivories, dazzlingly coloured psalters, intensely emotional Passion scenes, vividly animated birds and beasts, coming from the great ecclesiastical powerhouses of Winchester and Canterbury, are the equal of the best work to be found anywhere in Christian Europe.

In the nineteenth century medieval historians saw in Anglo-Saxon government the foundation of institutions they themselves recognized and celebrated, and while there was a good deal of retrospective sentimentalization about an imagined Saxon 'golden age', they were not completely wrong. South of the Humber, England was divided into the shires that persisted to 1974, each one with a court to administer royal justice and governed by the powerful ealdormen who governed in the king's name. And the shires were themselves subdivided into smaller jurisdictions, called hundreds, with their own courts, which all freemen were supposed to attend and which were held monthly, presumably to hear local disputes and misdemeanours. A famous law from Aethelred's time even mentions a 'jury' of twelve thegns, deputed to seek out and bring malefactors to trial, an institution usually thought of as the invention of the twelfth century. In the hide – the land deemed adequate to support a free family, but usually about 120 acres – the government had the basic statistical unit, always rounded up, through which it could assess the liability of shires, hundreds and burghs for taxes and the military draft. At the local level the reeve was responsible for law, taxes, the upkeep of roads and the provision of men for the *fyrd* (the part-time soldiery, mostly thegns and their beholden tenants, obliged to do military service). With this governmental machinery at their disposal, it was no wonder that the Anglo-Saxon kings felt empowered to legislate. And when they made laws eliminating cattle-rustling and sent them, signed and sealed, to their senior magnates, the ealdormen, and then on through the sheriff, they expected those writs to be faithfully obeyed.

There was, then, no reason for Cnut to upset the heavily laden apple-cart that was early eleventh-century England. He kept its bishops in place, and Wulfstan, Archbishop of York, who had been responsible for much of Aethelred's moralizing legislation, continued undisturbed in his authority. It was Wulfstan who must have been responsible for Cnut's decision to issue a code of laws (thus aligning himself with Alfred and Edgar), with all kinds of headmasterly homilies reminding clergy and laity of their proper duties: reminders about abstinence from meat in Lent; instructions on what part of a dead earl's property the king might lawfully claim; how a cottager's wife might defend herself when stolen property, put there without her knowledge, was discovered in her house. Cnut even began the practice of addressing public letters to his subjects, an early exercise in royal damage limitation, offering a kind of contract to the stubbornly disaffected: 'I will shut down my raiding parties if you submit peacefully to my rule.'

In so far as Cnut was a successful Danish colonialist, bringing England twenty years of respite from what had been constant warfare, it was because he was prepared to govern the country the Saxon way and from England, rather than as an absentee emperor based in Scandinavia. Add to that his mistrust of the few Viking nobles, like Thorkell the Tall, whom he had promoted to earldoms, and his dependence on shrewd, well-informed English advisers becomes all the more obvious. Such men had to know about hides and taxes; loyalty and conspiracy; when to cosset the Church and when to fleece it; these men could smell treasure or treason miles away, however deeply it was buried. To be reliable, such men also needed to be unconnected with the old royal house of Wessex. And if these new men did their work well, and loyally, Cnut made them noble and rich, powers in the land.

No one laboured more conscientiously or was more lavishly rewarded than Earl Godwine. He had risen far, fast. The son of a South Saxon thegn, Wulfnoth, he had excelled as a freelance pirate raider along the south coast of England in the years when authority was slipping from Aethelred's grasp. So Godwine appreciated early on the Danish connection between violence, riches and government. On his way up he took care that he married a Danish aristocratic wife, Gytha, and gave his children Viking names, like Sweyn and Harold. He was, in his own person, a symbol of England's adaptation to the reality of Viking power. And in short order he made himself indispensable as a source of intelligence and enforcement, permitting the king to present himself as Cnut the wise, Cnut the just, Cnut the magnanimous, while his enemies were expeditiously seen off. So, by 1018 Godwine the ex-pirate made it all the way to becoming Earl Godwine, and he was given great estates and the patronage of grand abbeys in the choice region of the old kingdom, Wessex. Since kings in those days were still prodigal wanderers, moving from estate to estate, sponging off the local magnates, the earl and the king saw a great deal of each other. It was a relationship of perfect, mutual parasitism. And it was too good to last.

In 1035, by most standards a capable ruler, Cnut died at Shaftesbury before he had reached the age of forty. His two sons, Harthacnut and Harold, the offspring of different mothers, were both in a position to claim the throne and both did, since there was no assumption, either in Danish or Saxon conventions, of the automatic succession of the eldest. Queen Emma, now widow to two kings of England, had thrown her support behind Harthacnut. But a war had broken out between the Danish and Norwegian realms of Cnut's empire, and Harthacnut decided to fight his battles in Scandinavia. So the earls of Mercia and Northumbria, members of the *witan*, the national council consisting of the great secular and spiritual magnates of the country, nominated his half-brother, Harold 'Harefoot', the son of Cnut's former wife Aelgifu, and, needless to say, just as soon as he realized its inevitability, Godwine came round to the idea of Harold as king.

But there was, in fact, a third possibility for the succession: an English possibility. For the dynasty of Wessex had not been entirely wiped out in the Danish years. Two children of Aethelred and Emma, Alfred and Edward, survived and were living across the English Channel in the duchy of Normandy, where they had been sent for their own protection during the grimmest period of the Danish onslaught on Saxon England. Desperate for help against the Danes, Aethelred had earlier made an alliance with Duke Richard of Normandy. At the time it made a great deal of sense. His wife, Emma, was a daughter of the Norman dukes, and the warrior state, stretching across a great crescent of territory in what is now northwestern France, was a dependent vassal state of the kingdom of France only on paper. In reality, it was very much its equal or senior. Many generations before, the Normans, whose dynastic founder had been known as Ralf, or Rollo the Viking, had done things the Norse way: using hit-and-sail violence to extract plunder; using the plunder to finance a further sailing; and amassing enough power to extort political privileges and implant themselves in the body of their victim-host, in their case, late Carolingian France. But it would be misleading to think of the connection the house of Wessex made with the Dukes of Normandy as another case of 'our Vikings against their Vikings'. For by the late tenth and early eleventh century, the dukes had long since made the amphibious evolution to creatures of the land, trading in their longboats for war-horses taken from Spain and bred in stud-farms in Normandy itself. The old Norse halls had given way to motte-and-bailey castles: strongholds set atop earthwork mounds, surrounded by palisades and deep-dug ditches. And the defensive strength of those early castles meant that while the dukes were early feudal territorialists, commanding power through their client-magnates, they were constantly in the saddle, fighting off rebellions and defections and keeping shaky coalitions together by bribing prospective allies with the bait of the confiscated lands of their enemies. Politically chaotic, ducal Normandy hummed with piety. Like the house of Wessex, the dukes were patrons of new monasteries, and it was in the eleventh century that handsome Romanesque stone churches began to appear, as well as the first spectacular stone castles like the one at Falaise where, in 1027, an illegitimate son was born to Duke Robert and a tanner's daughter called Herlève. With all this disorderly energy flowing through Normandy, it could only be a matter of time before the duchy was thought of as the coming power in northern Christian Europe.

Growing up in that world, it was not surprising that the Wessex princes, Alfred and Edward, imagined that some day, with Norman help, they would be restored to the throne they believed had been usurped by the Danes. And when Cnut died in 1035 they even imagined that their mother Emma might look with favour on their claim. She herself seemed to have encouraged the initiative. In 1036, although they must have known the enterprise was fraught with risk, Alfred and Edward arrived in England, by different routes, to sound out their mother on their prospects. Edward sailed to Southampton but having dipped his toe in the waters of English politics judiciously withdrew it and sailed back to Normandy. Alfred paid the price for his optimism. At first, all seemed to go well. He was met by the Earl Godwine, who must have seemed the soul of cordiality, entertaining his guest at his hall in Guildford and even going through the motions of becoming Alfred's vassal, his 'sworn man', by returning to the allegiance of the house of Wessex. The prince relaxed — fatally. For Godwine handed him over to Harold Harefoot's men, who proceeded to butcher Alfred's entourage, tear out the young man's eyes and mutilate his body. What was left of him was dragged off mercilessly to Ely, where he died of his terrible wounds.

Harold Harefoot lived only another four years to enjoy his triumph. His half-brother, Harthacnut, returning from Scandinavia in 1040 to succeed to his father's legacy, delivered his own obituary on Harefoot's reign by exhuming his body from the royal tomb at Winchester and having it thrown in the Thames. Anxious to exculpate himself from any responsibility in the murder of Prince Alfred, Godwine delivered an eighty-man warship to the new king and submitted himself for a trial in which, as expected, he was acquitted. In 1041, pressing this reconciliation with the Saxon nobility further, Harthacnut invited Alfred's brother, Edward, to return to England. Harthacnut was not making these overtures out of any sentimental good-will, however. He knew he needed the support of the great Saxon earls if he was to repel his Viking rival, the Norwegian king, Magnus I, who certainly thought he had as good a claim to the throne as the Dane. In the end, it was an agreement between the two Scandinavian kings, by which the kingdom of England would pass to whichever survived the death of the other, that bought Harthacnut time. From the beginning, then, Edward was something of a pawn in the grand strategies of the Viking powers. And if he made the crossing from Normandy in all innocence, he must still have been at least queasy about the decision, given the fate of his brother. But a year later Edward's prospects seemed suddenly to have brightened when

The seal of Earl Godwine.

Harthacnut unexpectedly died, 'falling to the ground with terrible convulsions' while drinking the health of one of his retainers at the wedding feast, a Viking exit if ever there was one.

It took no time at all for Earl Godwine to propose to the rest of the *witan* that Edward now become king. There were still two Scandinavian contenders – Harthacnut's Danish kinsman, Swein Estrithson, and Magnus I, the king of Norway – but Edward had the enormous advantage of being in the right place at the right time and, through Godwine's persuasion, also having the support of the earls of Mercia and Northumbria. Godwine's calculation was that with a weak Saxon on the throne rather than a strong Viking, he would be in a much better position to be the *de facto* governor of the realm. So Edward, later known as the Confessor, was crowned at Winchester on Easter Day 1043 according to the rites invented for Edgar by Abbot Dunstan. He was thirty-seven years old and unmarried. And despite the usual acclamations and each of the nobles doing homage, Edward might still have felt a chill of anxiety, not least because his own mother (who seemed to have enjoyed her reign as Cnut's queen rather more than her reign as Aethelred's) was shamelessly campaigning to have Magnus, king of Norway, put on the throne of England and her son set aside!

Like Cnut, Edward had little choice but to take things very much as he found them. To keep the king of Norway at arm's length he needed the support of the earls of Mercia and Northumbria, and no matter how much his stomach may have churned at the memory of the fate of his brother Alfred every time he looked at the Earl of Wessex, he could not afford to do without Godwine's help. After all, Godwine owned almost as much land – and with it the loyalty of client thegns and their foot soldiers – as the king. His son, Harold, had been elevated to the earldom of East Anglia, vastly expanding the territorial base of Godwine's power. Whichever way Edward looked at it, the old monster was the undisputed leader of the *witan* and the controller of patronage in Church and state. And there was nothing the king could do about it; not yet, anyway. So when Godwine made him an offer he couldn't refuse – his daughter Edith in marriage – she duly became queen. No children were born to the couple, however, and later it was thought that Edward had taken a vow of chastity or that he had some sort of insuperable distaste for the sex act. It was just as possible that by keeping his distance from Edith, Edward was deliberately thwarting Godwine's ambition to insert his own family into the royal line of succession by creating a grandchild who would be heir to the throne of England. In any event, Edward was not yet the ascetic miracle-worker and healer of the sick he became in later legend. Early in his reign Edward was much like any other red-blooded member of the house of Wessex: hunting, drinking and raging with the best of them.

The model for Edward's leadership could as easily have been Norman as Anglo-Saxon, however. After all, Normandy, his mother's birthplace, had been more of a home to him than anywhere else, and he spoke Norman French and looked to Duke Robert of Normandy as a protector and guardian. In addition, the dukes of Normandy had supported his and his brother's cause (even if inadequately) against the Danish kings while his mother Emma (the Gertrude in this saga) had decided to sleep with them. When Edward thought of himself as a patron of the Church, it was the Norman style of sponsoring reforming orders that he had in mind. And many, if not most, of his small personal following, such as his nephew Ralph the Timid, were either Norman, French or Breton.

Although he was twenty years his senior, Edward would have seen little William the Bastard growing up at the ducal court, somehow blessed with whatever it took to survive. When William was just seven or eight years old and much was still made of his illegitimacy, his father, Duke Robert, decided to express his appreciation for the Lord's support in vanquishing his domestic enemies by going on pilgrimage to the Holy Land. He died in 1035 on the homeward journey, leaving his little bastard no better than a lamb thrown to the wolves. The wolves lost no time, killing William's steward in his bedchamber, probably in front of the boy's eyes. A witness to all this turmoil, which was so much like his own misadventures, Edward might have been impressed by the way in which the boy survived. He had last seen him when he was thirteen years old, but from England, where the king's authority seemed so frustratingly circumscribed, Edward may well have looked enviously at the progress of the young duke as he overcame conspiracy and adversity and eventually triumphed (with the help of the French king) over a formidable confederation of rebel nobles. Somehow William had managed to put together the aggressively centralizing state that eluded all the Anglo-Saxon kings.

Taking a leaf from the book of the audacious, risk-taking duke of Normandy, around 1050 Edward began to build up his own party of supporters, some of them with cross-Channel connections. Most crucially, the bishopric of London had been given to Robert, a monk from the immensely important abbey at Jumièges, who in 1051 became Archbishop of Canterbury. The king also found land in Lincolnshire, East Anglia and the West Country for his French and Norman allies. The most important was his nephew, Earl Ralf, the son of his murdered brother Alfred, who had come to England with him in 1042. In Herefordshire they created a little Normandy, complete with the first castles in England and retinues of Norman knights. None of this was done as part of a strategic conspiracy to pave the way for a Norman succession. Edward's immediate concern was rather to defend the western borders of Mercia and

Wessex against the expansionism of the Welsh princes of Gwynedd and Powys. But if, in so doing, he managed to build a power base that would free him from dependence on the Godwines, so much the better.

By 1051 he must have thought he was strong enough to make a move and was spoiling for a trial of strength with the earl and his family. Edward's Norman brother-in-law, Eustace of Boulogne, travelled to England, arriving at Dover with a retinue of knights. A fight broke out over the worthiness or unworthiness of their lodgings, and it ended with one of the knights being wounded and his assailant being stabbed to death by the Normans. By the time the fracas was over the body count reached twenty. Furious at the affront to his kinsmen, Edward demanded that the whole city of Dover be punitively 'harried' – the legal term for being sacked and pillaged. The royal servant assigned to do the job was Godwine, within whose territory the outrage had occurred. But Godwine was no idiot. He knew that he had been neatly trapped into a lose-lose dilemma. His choice was either inflicting pain on his own dependents, thereby alienating his power base, or being accused of disobedience by the king. He chose the latter. At Gloucester, where he had been summoned to give an account of his refusal to do the king's bidding, Godwine found himself confronted by a small army consisting of the royal troops strengthened by reinforcements from Earl Siward of Northumbria. Godwine was prepared to clear himself in a ritual ceremony of oath-swearing, but Edward was no longer interested in these arcane rites. Refusing Godwine a safe-conduct, the king went so far as to call out the *fyrd*. Godwine was removed from his earldom and offices along with his sons. He was also obliged to surrender his property and estates to the king and given just five days to clear out of the kingdom. The Godwines left in two parties. The earl himself, together with his sons Sweyn and Gyrd, sailed to Flanders, where a third son, Tostig, had married the daughter of the count, while his other sons Harold and Leofwine exited though the West Country to Ireland. Edith, the queen and their sister, was left virtually hostage to Edward's triumph and, more or less repudiated by the king, was shut up in a convent.

It was the high point of Edward's reign, still only eight years old. He must have thought himself worthy of his Norman education and a master of the political game. He seemed free of his Godwine custodians and, perhaps, almost revenged on his brother's murderers.

But how far did he go to press his advantage? Norman chronicles of the Conquest insist that what happened next was the cornerstone of William's claim to the throne. For it was at this point that Edward made Robert of Jumièges Archbishop of Canterbury, and sent him to Rome to have the promotion confirmed by the pope.

Ruins of the abbey church of Jumièges in Normandy.

En route, according to those same sources, Robert was instructed to make a detour to Rouen, where he was said to have informed William that Edward intended to make him his heir. The Norman chronicles are, of course, retrospective propaganda, and if succession was assumed through proximity of kinship, William's claim was implausibly remote – no better than second cousin of Edward, once removed! But closeness of family ties was certainly not the only criterion determining the succession in the absence of immediate heirs. And the childless Edward – who did not wish to see the throne revert to the Viking dynasties from which he had wrested it, still less to the Godwines – might at least have toyed with the idea, in the brief euphoria of his victory in 1051–2. But if he was making so radical, even subversive a move just to spite his rivals, Edward must have known that he was creating terrible mischief for the future. For in the Anglo-Saxon tradition, the succession was not in the gift of kings unless they had the consent of their high council, the *witan*.

Whether or not he was brooding on a Norman succession, Edward had barely begun to enjoy his ascendancy when it went sour on him. By being reputed to favour 'foreigners' he had alienated the critical support of the earls of Mercia and Northumbria, who began to make discreet noises to the Godwines about a return. (In fact, virtually the entire crisis of Anglo-Saxon England was to turn on the difficult relationship between the north and south of the country.) Godwine, of course, needed only the slightest prompting to launch a comeback. With the help of his son's Flemish in-laws, he mustered a formidable fleet, united with the separate fleet commanded by Harold and Leofwine, at the Isle of Wight, and ravaged the island to make the point that King Edward was no protector. With recruits drawn from his old Wessex domains (who might well have appreciated his earlier refusal to sack Dover), Godwine sailed all the way to London, past London Bridge – a good sign that the citizens were on his side – anchoring at Southwark on 14 September 1052. The royal fleet sent to meet him refused to fight. Edward's coup had rebounded on him as a disastrous humiliation.

Godwine was restored to his earldom and, together with his family, declared innocent of all the crimes of which he had stood accused. The Normans and French who 'had lately come into the kingdom' were expelled, and the property of the Norman archbishops of Canterbury and Dorchester and the baronial enclaves on the Welsh borders were confiscated and divided among old Godwine, his son Harold and Queen Edith. 'Good Law', meaning law that was something other than the arbitrary will of the king, was promised to the people.

Who now ruled England? King Edward, mortified by his climb-down, had authority but little power. The Godwines had power but dubious authority. Duke

William of Normandy might have already had irresponsible but beguiling promises whispered in his ear, but the debacle of the Normans in England must have made his chances seem extremely remote. The earls of Mercia and Northumbria must have supposed the king a broken reed, but they had no intention of grovelling to the Godwines. Further off still, the new king of Norway, Harald Hardrada, variously known as 'the thunderbolt of the North' and the 'greatest warrior under Heaven', certainly thought of himself as having a strong claim and aimed at restoring the Anglo-Scandinavian empire of Cnut. Still further off, in remote Hungary, lived yet another, not entirely improbable, contender for the throne: the grandson of Aethelred, the son of Edmund Ironside, Edward's nephew, known as 'the Atheling'. Every so often, emissaries would arrive on the grassy Danubian plains from remote England enquiring whether he wouldn't, after all, care to return to 'his' kingdom. In 1056, with his two small boys, he did just that – and died a long way from Lake Balaton, in the hall of some Saxon thegn, the very next year.

The Godwines emerged from the crisis of 1051–2 stronger than ever. King Edward, on the other hand, must have been bitterly aware of the limitations of his power. Unable to exercise his will as secular commander, he increasingly concentrated on the realm spiritual. This did not mean any kind of retreat from the world. Although his hagiographers paint a portrait of the confessor-king spending days in prayer and fasting, poring over sacred literature and devoting himself to acts of healing and charity, Edward was also taking advantage of the movement that placed abbeys and monasteries under direct royal (rather than aristocratic) patronage. When he planned to build a great Benedictine house on Thorney island, upstream from London, and name it West Minster after St Peter – in complement to the East Minster of St Paul – there was little doubt that it would be as much a centre of royal power as of piety. And it would, of course, be built as a Norman Romanesque basilica, with columns enclosing arched aisles very much in the manner of the great abbeys at Jumièges and Fécamp. For that matter, if you pray hard enough, of course, God will take care of your enemies, or so Edward might have thought when his old antagonist Godwine suddenly expired in 1053, barely a year after his triumph in the contest of their wills. The story told by the Norman chroniclers was that, at a feast, the king had confronted Godwine with the murder of his brother Alfred, and the old earl had choked on a morsel of bread, caught in his throat as he attempted to defend himself. More probably it was a stroke, as the Abingdon manuscript of *The Anglo-Saxon Chronicle* tells that while Godwine was at dinner with the king at Winchester, 'he suddenly sank down against the footstool, deprived of speech' and that he remained helpless and mute for some days before dying.

Politically, however, the king had little cause to rejoice. The godfather of the clan gone, the Godwineson band of brothers now controlled England virtually unchallenged. Not all of them had survived unscathed. Sweyn, the eldest, seems to have been a dissolute psychopath, whose career makes *King Lear*'s Edmund look positively monkish by comparison. Having had to run for his life after abducting and raping the abbess of Leominster, he compromised his comeback by murdering his own cousin while he had been under safe-conduct. Although he had been pardoned by the king, Sweyn went on a pilgrimage to Jerusalem and died on the way back. His death meant that the core territory of the Godwine empire, the earldom of Wessex, now passed to the next oldest, Harold. During the mid-1050s and early 1060s history turned dramatically the Godwinesons' way. In 1055 the earl of Northumbria died, allowing the next brother, Tostig, to succeed him. An abortive rising in East Anglia dropped another earldom into the hands of Gyrd, and when there were no more earldoms to go round, a new one in the strategically crucial territory from Buckinghamshire to Kent was created for Leofwine. But it was as the commander of an army sent to crush a revolt in north Wales – a country believed geographically impossible to pacify – that Harold's reputation for Caesar-like force was made. In 1063 the prince of Gwynedd and Powys, Gruffydd ap Llewellyn, whose territories had expanded east of Hereford, was rash enough to form an insurrectionary alliance with the earl of Mercia. Together with a second army commanded by Tostig and encouraging the *huscarls* (armed retainers) to fight, unarmoured, partisan-style in the hills, the Godwine armies waged a ferocious war of attrition against the Welsh. Villages and farms were devastated, leaving, as Gerald of Wales would put it in the twelfth century, 'not one that pisseth against a wall'. The response of Harold's counter-insurgency campaign, when his soldiers were decapitated by the Welsh, was the summary execution of civilians. When Gruffydd's own men had had enough, they sliced off his head and sent it to Harold as a token of capitulation.

Harold now presided over an empire of patronage and military power. He was at the height of his powers: tall and charismatically good-looking, he was as politically shrewd as his father but with the gangsterish rough surface buffed up into aristocratic polish. Evidently an efficient administrator and someone who understood the machinery of Anglo-Saxon government, Harold was also, when the need arose, a formidable general, adapting his tactics to the very different terrains of the wet, low country of East Anglia or the mountains of Snowdonia. Those campaigns, ostensibly fought for King Edward, also suggest that Harold, well before he was king, was intensely concerned with hacking out some sort of territorial cohesion for the kingdom of England, and especially with pre-empting alliances between disgruntled earls

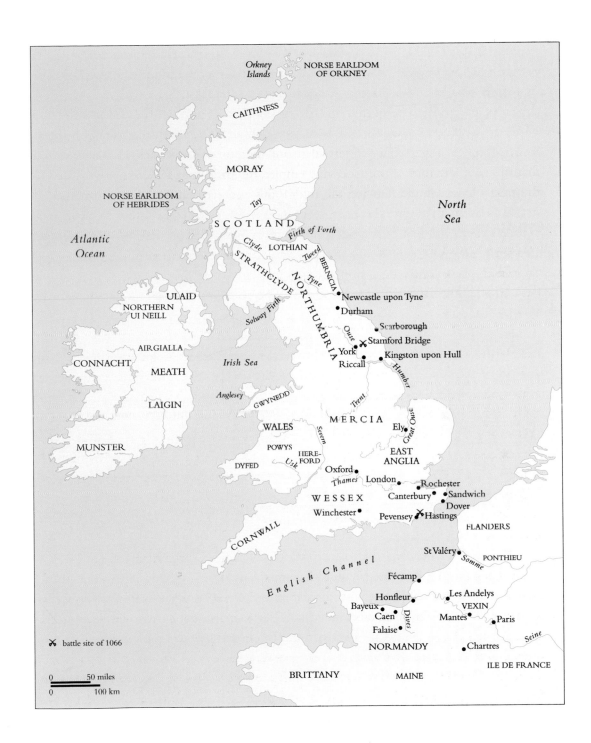

The British Isles and Normandy *c.* 1065–6.

and the wide range of potential allies available for trouble within the British isles: Welsh princes, Scots kings, Norse kings of Dublin, Norse earls of Orkney and Caithness. There could be no question of any kind of unitary kingdom just yet – the earldoms would stay – but by keeping them in the family, Harold was trying to ensure that they would not act like independent powers.

In the aftermath of his victory in Wales in 1063, Harold Godwineson seemed to have everything: land, riches, a dynamic band of brothers. He had married his vanquished enemy Gruffydd's widow Ealdgyth. Now he was Edward's indispensable man, keeping enemies from his borders. Was it possible for him, now, to dream royal dreams? Was it possible for him *not* to? It would have meant a change in dynasty in England, but with Edward unlikely to bear children, this would happen anyway. And if Harold looked north of the border to the history of King Macbeth of Scotland he might have found as much encouragement as discouragement for his ambitions. For there was a curious parallelism about the fate of the two kingdoms. The mac Ailpin dynasty of kings of Alba (called Scotland by the mid-tenth century) had made itself dominant in the same way as the kings of Wessex – by becoming the paramount force to hold off the Vikings. By the early eleventh century the kingdom of Strathclyde in the southwest of Scotland was virtually absorbed into its power, and the Scottish kings, like their English counterparts, had developed a rite of solemn inauguration at the Abbey of Scone, and through Church patronage they had developed the same Solomonic sense of themselves as the descendants of Alfred and Edgar. Like the Wessex kings, too, they had to contend with regions of unconquerable Viking settlement, Norwegian rather than Danish, and concentrated on the earldom of Orkney, which had made a crucial crossing over the Pentland Firth to Caithness. Like Edward the Confessor, the last of the mac Ailpin kings, Malcolm II, was childless. His successor, Duncan, claimed the throne in 1034 through the female line, but his grip was always shaky and contested. As if to compensate for his insecurity, Duncan thrashed around looking for military victories – first against the Northumbrian English at Durham, then in the north against the Earl of Orkney – and failed. When he attempted to force his will on the northern *mormaer* of Moray (*mormaer* was the name given to a local magnate who possessed what was, in effect, a private army), Duncan was killed in battle.

The *mormaer* of Moray was Macbeth, and he came to the throne in 1040 not by murder but through the decision of the battlefield. He also lasted a lot longer than the panicky, guilt-ridden usurper of Shakespeare's play – seventeen years, in fact – holding on to power with the help of an alliance with Thorfinn, the earl of Orkney. In the end, in 1057, Macbeth was defeated and killed in battle by Duncan's son,

Malcolm III Canmore. But if Harold was looking to learn lessons from the true history of Macbeth, the prospect of a seventeen-year reign, a prudent alliance with helpful northern allies and periodic trials by arms might not have seemed such a cautionary tale. And if Harold was making judicious cross-border comparisons he would have been heartened by the fact that Duncan, unlike Edward the Confessor, had two surviving sons to take up his cause.

All the signs must have seemed auspicious. But then, in 1064, Harold's ambitions seem to have been blown off course. The precise point of Harold's fateful journey, which ended up in William's court, remains tantalizingly uncertain. The Bayeux Tapestry, the incomparable work of Norman propaganda history, commissioned for William's half-brother Bishop Odo, makes the voyage the beginning of its story, apparently in keeping with the official claim of Norman historians that Harold had been sent by Edward on a mission to confirm the king's promise to award the succession to Duke William. But in all probability, by 1066, the year of his death, Edward had, with good or ill grace, abandoned whatever dreams he might have had during his brief ascendancy fifteen years before of a Norman succession. Almost all of the other contenders – Viking, Atheling or Godwine – were more plausible than William. And why should Harold have gone out of his way (literally) to expedite an arrangement so obviously contrary to his own interests? Even the tapestry, created in all likelihood by *English* women embroiderers, is enigmatic, even non-committal about the reasons for Harold's sea journey. Its opening images of the earl are conspicuously heroic – the dashingly moustachioed rider, hawk at the wrist, feasting in his beautiful Saxon abbey church at Bosham near Chichester; the salt-of-the-earth noble, bare-legged in the water, helping his men pole the ship away from its mooring, then taking the helm as it sails into the Channel.

What happened thereafter, though, is less disputed and is faithfully recorded in the tapestry. Whether or not his boat was forced to make an unplanned landing by a storm at sea, Harold was captured by Guy of Ponthieu, on whose territory he had arrived, and handed over to Guy's liege lord, Duke William. For Guy, taking wrecks and hostages was akin to a cottage industry, but he had fallen foul of the duke before for over-abusing his power, and once William was informed of Harold's presence little time was lost before he was taken to the duke. The embroiderers now make it plain that Harold and his followers found themselves in an alien world. The Saxons sport their characteristic moustaches and, despite their predicament, carry themselves with a certain sense of bravura. The Normans ride enormous horses (which in actuality were a lot smaller than modern mounts) and shave the *backs* of their heads. For a while the duke and the earl seem to act like comrades in arms, William taking Harold

with him on campaign in Brittany, offering his daughter to Harold in marriage and
making a Norman match for Harold's sister. But comrades were not equals. In the
embroidery, William makes Harold one of his knights and bestows armour on him. This
would have required an act of feudal homage, the Saxon placing his hands inside those
of the Norman duke and agreeing to put his life and loyalty at William's command.

It seems possible that, subsequently, Harold did swear some sort of oath to Duke
William. Oaths were taken with deadly seriousness in medieval Europe, so exactly
what form the oath took would matter immensely in the coming conflict. The
sources closest to the Godwine view maintained that Harold had sworn merely to be
William's man in Normandy, with no bearing on anything connected to the English
succession. The Norman chronicles, on the other hand, insist that Harold had taken a
solemn vow to defend and advance William's right to the throne of England and even
to create garrisons for the duke in advance of his taking lawful possession of the
realm! And since the essence of the Norman case against Harold would be that he
had perjured himself, the most imaginative of their propagandists, such as the twelfth-
century writer Wace, had him swearing unwittingly on a chest full of holy relics that
the duke had covered with a cloth. 'When Harold placed his hand upon it, the hand
trembled and the flesh quivered but he swore and promised...to deliver up England
to the duke.' Once again the embroiderers become wonderfully devious at this critical moment of their story, for by lining up the boat taking Harold back to England
immediately after the scene of oath-taking, they give the unmistakable impression
that the vow was the price of his freedom: that it had been extracted under duress.

Just how Harold saw his position on his return from the disastrous stay in
Normandy will always remain obscure. Whatever his motives for the voyage, it seems
inconceivable that, with Edward ailing, there was not *some* intention of talking over
the glaringly critical issue of the succession with William. The most likely scenario is
that Harold intended to try and reconcile the duke to his succession and perhaps even
assumed that the exchange of brides would seal their alliance. But at some point (as
not infrequently happens in the indirect course of informal negotiation), misunder-
standings hardened, and Harold, not at all a free agent, found himself in the position
of talking not about his own succession but the duke's!

Once returned, though, there was absolutely nothing in his conduct to suggest
that he now thought of himself as William's deputy in England. What we do know is
that the decision he took in the winter of 1065 on the fate of the earldom of
Northumbria was so shockingly at odds with the entire tradition of Godwine clan
solidarity that it makes sense only in terms of Harold planning a bid for the throne
of England himself. What he did was to sell his brother Tostig down the river.

Harold on horseback, with a hawk on his wrist, leaves
for the coast; from the Bayeux Tapestry.

In eleventh-century Europe, of course, brothers were perfectly capable of behaving like Edgar and Edmund in Shakespeare's *King Lear* if a throne was at stake. Harold merely evicted Tostig from the earldom of Northumbria where he had been installed a decade earlier. But since he turned his brother into an implacable enemy he might just as well have killed him outright. And this was more than a domestic row. The war between the Godwine brothers, so little noticed in so many of the textbook histories, was as bloodily fateful as anything in the epics or sagas. In the end, the enmity of Tostig would cost Harold his throne and his life. The family feud killed off Anglo-Saxon England.

Of course, Harold knew he was taking a huge risk in alienating his brother, but in 1065 he may have felt he had no choice. A serious rebellion had broken out in the north (always a field of opportunity for Scottish kings and Viking earls), a rising largely provoked by Tostig's own misplaced zeal in insisting on abolishing the laws of Cnut that permitted the blood feud. It didn't help that Tostig was also busy creating his own personal army and that he robbed religious houses and bled the country for taxes to pay for it. Nor was he much of a protector to Northumbria. The earl, who had been off on pilgrimage to Rome and on the Welsh campaign in 1063, seemed to have no military answer to the cross-border raids mounted by Malcolm III from Scotland. Worse than being a bully was being an impotent bully. In the inevitable uprising all 200 of Tostig's guards were hunted down and killed, and Tostig himself was declared outlaw. The rebel thegns then invited Morcar, the young brother of the earl of Mercia, to be their new earl. Harold was sent by King Edward to negotiate an end to the revolt rather than to crush it by force. Once it was clear that the thegns wouldn't countenance Tostig's return, Harold must have calculated that, with Edward old and ailing, it would be suicidally imprudent to alienate the leading nobles, especially if he was going to have to face an invasion threat from Norway.

Tostig, who for some time had been suspicious about where his brother's loyalties lay, was furious to learn that Harold had agreed to his removal and replacement by Morcar. He went into exile, consumed with rage, bent on revenging himself on Harold, who had committed what he called the 'unnatural act' of betraying a brother. In Flanders, a guest of his father-in-law, the count, Tostig must have remembered his father's brief spell in limbo, the careful creation of a fleet of retribution and the triumphal return to power, and must have supposed that he would follow in old Godwine's steps.

It was not to work out quite as Tostig planned. But nothing in the year ahead, 1066, was to work out quite as planned. The end of 1065, according to *The Anglo-Saxon Chronicle,* was marked by a ferocious tempest, which destroyed churches, houses and halls and uprooted great ancient trees, sending them flying through the air. At such a time men were prone to visions and forebodings, especially if, like Edward the Confessor, they were plainly coming to the end of their days.

Around the deathbed of the last of the sons of Aethelred the Ill-Advised, at his newly completed palace at West Minster (if the Bayeux Tapestry is to be believed) were gathered those who mattered: Queen Edith, Harold's sister, restored, somewhat, to favour, wiping away a tear with her veil; Stigand, Archbishop of Canterbury; and, not least, Harold himself. The king stretches out his hand and touches Harold's fingers, signifying some gesture of delegation. But for what – as regent, *subregulus* or as king? If he were really designating Harold successor, Edward would have set aside the claim of his own great-nephew Edgar the Atheling. Whatever he did would be trouble. According to the later author of the *Vita Aewardi*, before he died, Edward managed to rouse himself to make an utterance. But instead of speaking his mind on the succession, the Confessor unburdened himself of a dream or, rather, a nightmare. Two monks whom he had known in an earlier life had come to his deathbed, warning that the sins of the English had been so grievous that God had given the realm to evil spirits for a year and a day. The king asked the monks if penance and sincere contrition would commute the sentence and was told that this would not happen until a growing tree, felled halfway down the length of its trunk, came together of its own accord and grew green with leaf. This was interesting but unhelpful in resolving the succession problem. So when the *witan* behaved predictably and offered Harold the throne, he accepted, and the funeral of one king on the Feast of Epiphany 1066 was followed, later the same day, by the coronation of another, Harold II. The new king, hoping for the best, issued coinage bearing the word PAX ('peace') on its face. But in April 1066, the hairy star, Halley's comet, was seen in the spring sky (not, as the Tapestry melodramatically has it, on the night of Harold's coronation!) and no one supposed this could be anything but an ill omen.

England had a new king before most of its people were aware that the old king had died. Although the historian John of Worcester, writing in the next century, praised Harold for repealing unjust laws and legislating just ones, virtually the entire helter-skelter nine months of his reign were overwhelmed by a sense of crisis. Harold's first act was to make sure that the northern earls, to whom he had sacrificed his brother, would now live up to their end of the bargain and behave loyally. To bind them closer he took the sister of the Earl of Mercia as a new wife. And for a while the strategy seemed to have paid off. With the north secure, Harold could concentrate his defences in the south, and it was there that Tostig made an appearance in the spring, with ships acquired in Flanders. But the coast was so well defended that he

Top: Halley's comet seen above Westminster in April 1066, with ominous longboats in the border below; from the Bayeux Tapestry.
Above: Silver penny with the head of Harold on one side and PAX (peace) on the reverse.

got no further than the Isle of Wight. Repelled in southern England, Tostig sailed up the east coast to his old duchy of Northumbria. But instead of being greeted by 'welcome home' signs, he was smartly seen off by the troops of Harold's new loyalists, Earl Morcar and Earl Edwin. Faced with desertions, Tostig carried on, going north to seek refuge with the Scots king Malcolm III. With his brother out of the way, Harold concentrated on dealing with his main headache: the Duke of Normandy.

A Norman historian, William of Jumièges, describes how William heard the news of Harold's coronation at Westminster while hunting in his ducal forest at Quévilly near Rouen:

> going forth to the chase with many pages and esquires…when the Duke…learned all the truth, how that Edward was dead and Harold made king he became as a man enraged and left the craft of the woods. Oft he tied his mantle and oft he untied it again; and spoke to no man, neither dared any man speak to him. Then he crossed the Seine in his boat and came to his hall and entered therein: and sat down at the end of a bench, shifting his place from time to time, covering his head with a mantle and resting his head against a pillar.

Whatever the truth of this wonderfully vivid account, it's certain that William took the affront personally. The Earl of Wessex was his sworn vassal, had put his hands in his. And in all likelihood, William, who had been building a formidable bloc of territories, had jumped the gun by letting it be known that before too long England would be added to them. Now his claim looked like an empty boast.

His first action was to send an indignant protest to Harold at the outrageous violation of his oath. A later English source has Harold replying that he had been chosen king by the *witan* (as must certainly have been the case) and that he could never have promised anything that he was patently unauthorized to alienate. The Bayeux Tapestry shows that work was immediately under way to build an invasion fleet, but the legal and political preparation was as important to William as the military planning since, once the rage abated, he must have known that an attempted invasion of England would be a huge gamble. Consulting his feudal magnates did not produce the unanimous enthusiasm he was looking for. To many of them, the risks far outweighed the incentives. When William then stood on his ducal authority and attempted to levy a feudal host, he was told that the obligations of his vassals went as far as the water's edge.

What changed their mind? In a word, the Church. William's second strategy had been to get to Westminster by way of Rome and to turn the cause of England into an internationally authorized crusade. Deeply influenced by his friend Lanfranc of Bec, Abbot of Caen (and later Archbishop of Canterbury), William had already positioned Normandy as the friend and ally of the papacy in its struggle against the domination of lay rulers. The hottest issue of the eleventh century was whether secular rulers should be able to appoint and invest bishops or whether this right belonged to the successors of St Peter in Rome. Bishops were not, after all, just senior clergy. They had immense power, wealth and influence in their sees, and the struggle over their appointment was as much a matter of politics as theology. By siding with Rome, William felt sure he could depend on a friendly reception when he sent Lanfranc to seek papal blessing for a campaign against Harold. Lanfranc was known to consider the English as little better than barbarians or quasi-pagans, and he would have had no hesitation in (mis)representing the Godwine supremacy in England as a classic example of the thuggish bullying of the Church by over-powerful magnates. Lanfranc could produce a roll call of infamy. The Godwines had despoiled the Church; they had kicked out the lawful Archbishop of Canterbury, Robert of Jumièges, appointed by King Edward, and replaced him by the Bishop of Winchester, Stigand, who had been excommunicated by five popes and who was in such bad odour that even Harold thought it prudent to be crowned instead by the Archbishop of York.

The record of Godwineson diplomacy in Rome had, in any case, not been encouraging. In 1061 Harold had sent Tostig to try to persuade the ardently pro-Norman Pope Nicholas II that the English Church was not the sink of corruption it was commonly thought to be in Rome. The mission would have been an outright disaster had not Tostig's train been set upon by a Tuscan bandit–nobleman on his way back, giving him the unforeseen opportunity to upbraid the pope on law and order. The memory of this, however, might not have predisposed his successor Alexander II to look kindly on the Anglo-Saxons. In any event, the pope gave William his formal blessing, invested the duke with the papal banner and ring and even allowed him to wear one of the holy relics on which it was said Harold had committed perjury.

It is quite impossible to understand the events of 1066 without comprehending the immense significance of the religious and Roman dimension. Between them, William and Lanfranc had managed to convert a personal and dynastic feud into a holy war, and once this was known, many of the nobles who had fought shy of the original proposal flocked to William's sanctified banner. There were not just Normans, but also Bretons and Flemings. The matter of England had now become the cause of Christian Europe, and nothing good could come of this for its new king.

This was all the more ironic since it appears that during the first months of his reign Harold was acutely solicitous towards the Church and took steps to restore unlawfully taken land and property. But he was too late. Blissfully ignorant of what had happened in Rome, he busied himself with the practical needs of defence. And here he proved one of the most phenomenal military organizers in British history. As the crack troops of his army he could call on an elite of 3000 or so *huscarls*, professional soldiers trained to wield a two-handed axe that, if swung with enough momentum, could slice through a horse and rider at a single blow. The *huscarls* fought on foot, although many of them might come to the battle on horse, and they were protected by hide-covered wooden shields, both circular and kite-shaped, by conical helmets with nasal protectors and trousered chain-mail hauberks, which were a prized possession. The mass of the English army, though, was made up by the *fyrd*, the part-time troops supplied on demand by Harold's 4000 thegns and, in any event, obliged to serve for forty days every year. This would give Harold at least 10,000 to 13,000 soldiers, in addition to the *huscarls*. The core of the army could be stationed on the south coast, close to the fleet, which Harold had rapidly requisitioned from the Kent and Sussex ports. This was, after all, Godwine country, where every abbey, village and harbour was known intimately. So if William was going to come he would have to launch himself at the king's strongest defences.

Whether he understood this or not, the duke was not taking any chances. At the mouth of the river Dives in northern France he had put together an immense expeditionary force, the biggest since the Emperor Claudius's army of invasion. There may have been as many as 6000 horses, three for each knight: the *destrier*, the great war-horse charger, and two smaller animals, one to carry the knight's squire and a third to carry his weapons. The fleet numbered 400 ships, packed tight with men and mounts, and smaller supply boats with the army's initial provisions, although they intended to live off the land in England just as soon as they could. By 10 August this vast armada was ready. Two huge fighting forces, bent on each other's annihilation, faced each other across the Channel.

And then – nothing. William waited for the southerly wind that never came. Harold waited for William, who never came. Neither of them could really afford the delay. William's horses (which were, literally, in clover) had just about exhausted the local supply of hay, and his men had eaten their way through the harvest. But Harold's position was even more serious, for by the first week in September he had kept the *fyrd* and the little navy in battle position for longer than their stipulated forty-day tour of duty. Doubtless he had been impressing on them the imminence of the danger from Normandy. But nothing irks a mass of soldiers more than indeterminate waiting, and the longer they waited, the more grumbling there must have been from men who were eager to be back home, getting in their own harvests and rejoining their wives and children. Eventually this pressure became irresistible, and on 8 September Harold demobilized the *fyrd* and his flotilla of boats. A week or so later the king left Bosham and returned to London, where, according to one chronicle, he began to suffer from a mysterious and obstinate pain in the leg; not an auspicious omen for a king who fought on foot. Perhaps his cramps were trying to send a message, for on 12 September, just before Harold left the south coast, William's armada had finally put out to sea. Only a sudden gale, pushing the fleet east, to the mouth of the Somme, prevented it from making the Channel crossing.

A week later, on 19 September, Harold got bad news from a different and completely unexpected quarter. His estranged brother Tostig, together with the king of Norway, Harald Hardrada, the 'thunderbolt from the north', and as many as 10,000 men had landed in Northumbria and had already burned Scarborough, Cleveland and Holderness to the ground.

Harold must have supposed that he had seen off Tostig in the spring, but during the summer, while Harold was putting his defences in place, rumours had circulated that Tostig was wandering around Europe looking for allies, even going to Normandy to talk to Duke William. Not many of the stories were credible, but one of them was only too true: that Tostig had made contact with the alarming Hardrada in Norway. The Norwegian interest in, and claim on, the throne of England went back at least to the reign of Cnut. Hardrada's predecessor, King Magnus, had been a great force to contend with in the North Sea world, which then extended from Northumbria, through eastern Scotland to the Norse earldom of Orkney. One of Harold's more effective military campaigns on behalf of King Edward in the 1050s had been to prevent Magnus from invading East Anglia. Hardrada claimed that Magnus and Cnut's son, Harthacnut, had signed an agreement delivering England to whichever of them survived the other, a promise reneged on by the Saxon kings. And no matter how flimsy the Norwegian claim might be, it could hardly be more lightweight than William's or Harold's, who had no kin relationship to his predecessors at all. Hardrada also arrived with a fearsome reputation as a warrior of superhuman strength: exceptionally tall – 6 feet 4 inches; a veteran of countless wars, from Scandinavia to Russia and Byzantium; lauded by the bards (including himself) as a hero for the ages; and capable of acts of legendary cruelty. Shortening a siege by tying burning wood chips to the tails of little birds, which flew to their nests in the eaves of houses, thereby setting the town alight was pretty much Hardrada style. So it was a great coup for Tostig to have enlisted his support, no doubt by persuading the Norwegian king that Harold's distraction with Normandy offered the perfect opportunity for a surprise attack. In return, he would have his earldom back and perhaps, in the new reign, be his chief man, playing Godwine to Hardrada's Cnut. They are likely to have met in Orkney, where the two young earls joined the army. When Tostig saw the vast fleet anchored in the Flow, his bitter little heart must have skipped a beat at the thought of the damage that was about to be inflicted on his brother. Their war-machine would be invincible and unstoppable, a legend to be sung by the bards.

The first of the three great battles of 1066 would have done nothing to alter that view. It took place on 20 September at Fulford, just outside York, between a swamp and the river Ouse. To get to York – the prosperous Viking city of Jorvik – where Hardrada planned to winter, his boats had sailed far upriver along the Humber and then the Ouse, anchoring at the village of Riccall. Barring the way to York at Fulford were the forces raised by Edwin and Morcar. They were still teenagers, and their troops were untested, but they managed to do surprisingly well against the wedge of the Norsemen, even advancing from their position until Hardrada personally led a ferocious counter-attack that broke the English line. Their dead lay so thick in the marshes that, as the Norse bard Snorri Sturlasson gloated: 'the war-keen Norsemen/could cross on the corpses.'

York/Jorvik was now an open city, and Hardrada was shrewd enough to try and rally its population by refraining from sacking the town. The Northumbrians responded by agreeing to join the army on its march south. Hostages were delivered to ensure that promise was kept, but by the terms of the capitulation a further 500 hostages were to be taken from the shire, and the village of Stamford Bridge, 8 miles east of York, was chosen as the place where they would be surrendered on 26 September. It must have seemed a perfectly routine business. Hardrada took Tostig along to enjoy the moment, leaving a third of his troops behind at Riccall. But when they got to Stamford Bridge what they saw was not a bunch of shambling, forlorn hostages but a huge army. Snorri Sturlasson wrote that: 'when their weapons glittered, it looked like a sheet of ice.' Hardrada and Tostig duly froze. The Norwegian asked the Saxon what it meant. Tostig replied it meant trouble. It meant Harold.

The English king had done the impossible. Hearing of Hardrada's landing on 19 September he had left London the next day, mobilizing his *huscarls* and the disbanded *fyrd* en route. Gathering strength, the army moved at an astounding lick, covering a 190 miles in five days, a speed conceivable only if at least some of the thegns and weapons were carried on horseback. But many of the *fyrd* must have jogged brutally north up the Roman road, javelins, axes and all. By 24 September they had reached York, which, Jorvik or not, quietly opened its gates to them. On the morning of the 25th they were ready to surprise Tostig and Hardrada.

Surprised they certainly were – to the point at which Tostig is thought to have suggested a tactical withdrawal to the safety of the ships at Riccall to regain their full troop strength and armour. Typically, Hardrada rebuffed the advice as chicken-hearted and the mêlée got under way. There are no reliable eye-witness accounts, either for Stamford Bridge or Fulford, but both Norse and Anglo-Saxon traditions describe the Norsemen fiercely defending the bridge itself, their shield-wall pushed back by the onslaught of the English axes and swords, until the span was held by a single unarmoured 'berserker', who was finally removed only when an English soldier floated beneath the timbers of the bridge in a swill-tub and stabbed the Viking from below through gaps in the planking. Once the bridge was cleared, the battle raged on on the other side. Eventually the Viking soldiers summoned from the ships made a belated appearance, but they were too late to affect the outcome. The Norse warriors were so depleted that the English had broken their line. At the end, the surviving warriors gathered around their chiefs, with Hardrada swinging his axe beneath his standard of the Land-Waster, before dying of an arrow in the throat. Tostig is said to have picked up the raven flag before he too was cut down in his turn.

The carnage was so complete that the Viking remnant ran for their boats, harried as they fled. The young Orkney earls and Hardrada's sons were spared on condition they departed England and vowed never to return. From the hundreds of boats that had sailed from Norway under the midnight sun, just twenty-four were needed to carry the survivors back home. A year later Hardrada was buried in the Church of St Mary in Niadro in northern Norway. With him was buried the Anglo-Scandinavian state begun in the reign of Alfred. Lying beneath the Land-Waster Harold found his dead brother, and he took what was left of him to be interred in York Minster.

But Harold had time neither to grieve nor to exult. For on 26 September, a day after the battle of Stamford Bridge, the wind suddenly veered at the port of St-Valéry, at the mouth of the Somme, where William's fleet had been frustratingly holed up. Priests were firmly of the view that it had been the exhibition of the relics of St Valéry that had worked the miracle. On the 27th William was at sea once more, his fleet sailing due north, as he stood at the helm of the *Mora*, the ship provided by his wife Matilda. The Bayeux Tapestry shows him wearing an expression of unforgiving command. The next day he needed it, as first light revealed the *Mora* sailing alone in the swelling sea, not a sail in sight. While his crew and men panicked, William ate breakfast. His ship had, in fact, merely outrun the others, which were weighed down with horses and weapons. Two ships had apparently foundered. 'Not much of a soothsayer,' was his response to news that the official clairvoyant of the expedition had been lost along with one of the boats. 'Couldn't foretell his own end.'

The first sight of England would have been the towering cliffs of Beachy Head, but it would have taken little reconnoitring to find a safe beaching at Pevensey, below an apparently stern Roman fort that, on further investigation, turned out to be an undefended shell. Had the *fyrd* still been in the positions of three weeks earlier, or had Harold's defending fleet not been holed up at the Isle of Wight expecting William to sail in that direction, it would have been a different story. But now the Normans were able to unload one of the three prefabricated timber castles they had brought with them and construct it on a mound of earth within the fort, as if in declaration that they were heirs to the Romans.

Without any organized army to oppose them, the Norman army moved through the Sussex countryside at will, grabbing whatever food they needed but proceeding with the nervous wariness of men in an alien landscape. William himself was anxious about being bottled up amid the boggy watercourses and hills of the area and being thwarted in an effort to move out of their beach-head to the London road. For the time being the Normans took food from the helpless natives as and when they needed it and burned whatever couldn't be seized. One of the most harrowing scenes from the Bayeux Tapestry (a work full of mutilated bodies) is the picture of a mother and child setting out as fugitives from the burning remains of a building, perhaps their house. It's the very first image in European art that makes space for the ruin of victims. The Bayeux embroiderers were not, of course, pacifists, but they did go out of their way to see the Conquest as something involving more than the strategics of the powerful. Both in the borders and the main picture space, the embroidery is full of the life of the common people: porters and archers, cooks and spear-carriers; Bishop Odo presiding at a ritual feast almost like Christ at the Last Supper, but also two soldiers whacking each other with shovels.

By the time the Norman army had settled in around Hastings, Harold was back in London after another brutal, high-speed march. Having beaten back the threat of the Norsemen and his own brother, it must have seemed inconceivable that he was going to have to do it all over again within a week or two. The damage inflicted on the victorious army at Stamford Bridge made it unthinkable to use the surviving part of the *fyrd*, however high their morale. It would have been equally inconceivable, on the other hand, *not* to use the *huscarls,* who were indispensable in any force strong enough to have a chance of resisting the Normans. Who would be their commander, though, was a serious question. A tradition has Harold's brother, Gyrd, asking the king if he, and not his older brother, might lead the defending troops. This was, in fact, a sensible request. Should the battle be won, all well and good; should it be lost, Harold would still be available for a second line of defence, and it would by no means be a

simple matter for William to proceed unopposed to London. Harold, though, may
have felt that, when all was said and done, the king had, without question, to be present in person to rally his troops against the invader. To dodge the confrontation with
William was to concede, somehow, that there was something illegitimate about his
authority. Messages reiterating the charge of perjury that had arrived from the duke
in the week before the battle had obviously stung Harold – as had been intended. The
quarrel was now something akin to a matter of knightly honour, and Harold
evidently felt he had, throughout, behaved entirely honourably.

Even more important was the issue of when he should engage William's army.
The most reasonable strategy would have been to wait until his army could be reinforced by the *huscarls* from Northumbria who had survived Fulford and until he
could add to the strength of the *fyrd* from the shires beyond his immediate home base.
Potentially, Harold could call on perhaps 30,000 or 40,000 more *fyrdsmen*, numbers
that would, in the end, have made William's position completely untenable. But
Harold believed that all these arguments were outweighed by the imperative need to
keep William bottled up amid the woods and waters of south Sussex and to prevent
him, at all costs, from breaking out and having the freedom to roam at will in the
southeast. He may even have thought that the duke might be expecting reinforcements from Normandy and that his best chance of facing him with relatively even
forces was to do it at once. And then, perhaps, Harold may have been a little too
elated with his success at Stamford Bridge, believing, fatally, in his own invulnerability.

He must also have believed that the logistics of the likely battle favoured the
defending force. All the Saxon army had to do was to stand its ground and prevent
William from breaking through to the London road. Once his own army was in
Sussex, food and hay would be much harder to come by for the Normans. Winter
was not far ahead, and what had happened to Julius Caesar would happen to William.
Deprived of freedom of manoeuvre and food, the invasion would lose its momentum, and the invaders would head back to the beaches.

First, though, the decisive blow had to be struck. On 12 October, without waiting to see if the northern earls would join him, Harold left London with his two
brothers, Gyrd and Leofwine (whom he foolishly insisted join him in a display of
dynastic solidarity), and 2000 or 3000 *huscarls*. A fresh batch of the *fyrd* was to be
mobilized through the thegns and was to assemble by an old grey apple tree, the 'hoar
tree', which stood at the crossing of the tracks leading out of Hastings and towards
London. There, by the blasted tree, Harold would plant his banner of the Fighting
Man; there, on the ridge of Senlach, ready or not, the English would make a stand
against William of Normandy.

Top: The Roman fort at Pevensey, in Sussex, where the Norman invaders landed.
Above: Saxons *huscarls* defending the ridge of Senlach; from the Bayeux Tapestry.

It was the morning of Saturday, 14 October 1066, Julian Calendar, the feast-day of St Calixtus, the slave-born convict pope. If you had been Saxon *huscarl*, you would be standing on the brow of the hill (it was a great deal steeper than it is now), looking down at the opposition some hundreds of yards away. You're exhausted from the gruelling march the king forced on you – 58 miles in three days! Perhaps he wanted to surprise the Normans as he had surprised Hardrada. But they had been quite unsurprised. Either side of you, in a long line, the shield-wall is strung out, perhaps a thousand paces, flank-to-flank, battle-axes and javelins whetted. They had better be sharp. Behind you are the men of the *fyrd*. They have seen some action, and they keep their swords and helmets at home for just such an occasion as this. In the centre you can see the king with his brothers standing at their banners: the Wyvern, the Golden Dragon of Wessex, and the king's own standard of the Fighting Man. You believe in this king. He has courage and good sense. You saw him destroy Hardrada, and you know he will be steadfast. Down below, you can hear the Norman horses. You have never faced a charge of knights before. But then, they have to ride uphill. Perhaps that's why you think you hear them chanting psalms.

If you were a Norman foot soldier you would be praying that the gentlemen on horses know what they're doing. All around you is the scraping of metal: the sharpening of swords; the mounting of horses. You peer up to the brow of the hill and see a thin, glittering line. You cross yourself and toy with the linked rings of your coat of mail. Can they dull the blow of an axe? You've never faced axes in battle before. You turn about and watch the archers check the tautness of their bowstrings. Other foot soldiers are shuffling into place behind the archers. No one seems to care very much where they stand. You take your spear and sword. Behind you are the *gonfalons* (the pennants of the knights): Bretons to the left, Flemish to the right. You feel better that you are in the centre, with the duke and his brothers. And better still when you see the banner of the Holy Father, reminding you that God is fighting with you and that the duke is going into battle with the pope's ring.

It would be nice if the most poetic accounts of battles happened to be true and if this one had actually begun the way the chronicler Wace described it, with the minstrel Taillefer arrayed for combat, riding out from the Norman ranks and singing the *Chanson de Roland,* throwing his sword high in the air, catching it by the hilt and then charging full-tilt at the English line, killing three before being struck down in a hail of spears. But the reality was probably more prosaically deliberate: a slow advance of archers as they got within range and unloosed their arrows, then the foot soldiers breaking into a run, and finally the knights, charging to the sound of Norman trumpets and battle cries of *Dex aie*, 'God is our help'. Before they were on the English line, they could hear the rhythmic drumming on the shields and the shouts of *Goddemite*, 'God Almighty', and then just the murderous smashing and crashing of horses and the thrusting of weapons, the thud of arrows and swords on leather-covered shields and men hitting the ground and screams of the wounded: a grinding labour in progress.

For about an hour William sent his triple-formation troops – archers, infantry, cavalry – uphill. Some of the horses made it all the way to the shield-wall, where they crashed against it like a reef. But most of the Norman horsemen, especially in the early stages of the battle, were not especially eager to make contact with the English axes. So they rode close enough to the English line to be able to unloose their javelins, which they hoped would pierce the shields, but then wheeled about under a protective shower of arrows and retired downhill to await another charge. Nothing much was going to come of this, and by midday nor had it. The Saxon shield-wall hadn't budged an inch. And there was a limit, perhaps, as to how many charges the Norman cavalry could make. It was, in fact, exactly this gathering sense of elation in the English ranks that the cavalry attacks were faltering that led to a crisis. The left flank of William's army, the Bretons, recoiled in such disarray, with horses stumbling back over infantry, that a part of the *fyrd* were unable to resist the temptation to turn the moment into a rout. They broke ranks and followed the Bretons down the hill. At this critical moment in the early going, the English army might indeed have won the whole day if a concerted attack, led by the king, had been made. But Harold was conservative in his tactics, knowing that neither the Flemish right nor the Norman centre had broken and remaining convinced that the essential requirement for his army was to maintain its strength and let the enemy simply exhaust itself, against the shield-wall. Failing to take the lead in a concerted advance, Harold momentarily lost control of crucial sections of his army. As they ran down the hill, William, who had been rumoured to be dead and who had, indeed, had horses cut from under him, threw back his helmet to show he was very much alive, regrouped the ranks of the Norman centre and wheeled around to encircle the pursuing Saxons, cutting them off from their own line. They retreated to a little hillock, fighting as best they could without heavy armour, but were cut down, one by one.

The battle was a long way from being over. It would be six hours before it was decided – one of the longest battles in all medieval history – but the rally of the Norman knights was surely a turning point. It demonstrated the difference in flexibility in the two armies: William adapting the different elements of his forces to shifting circumstances; Harold locked into his stolid defence, soaking up punishment until the enemy was so weakened that it could be pushed over. Towards the middle of the

A mother and child leave their burning house; from the Bayeux Tapestry.

afternoon, however, it seems to have been the English, not the Norman, army that was being ground down by attrition. William deliberately sent what Norman historians insist were 'feigned' retreats by his knights. Feigned or not they had the effect of shortening the English frontline where *huscarls* had fallen. Very gradually the more lightly armed and protected *fyrd* had to take their place, and those behind them became more exposed to Norman arrows shot high in the air and falling behind the front rank. Thinned out or not, the Saxon line remained glued to its hill until quite late in the day. At some stage, though, weak points were sufficiently exposed for some of the Norman cavalry to get up on the western brow of the hill, from which point it charged the depleted Saxon line directly. Right in the thick of it was Harold, probably with his brother Gyrd, and when the king was struck in the eye with the arrow (for the tapestry leaves no room for ambiguity) the wound was fatal, not just to the king but to his army, especially since both of his brothers died in the fighting as well, Leofwine probably much earlier, Gyrd at the end. Around them were the bodies of countless *huscarls*, who fought to the bitter end as light faded from the field.

Once the banners had fallen, what was left of the English line disintegrated. For the surviving members of the *fyrd* it was time to save their necks, find their families or just to get out of harm's way. The fighting was not quite over with, though. A company of Norman knights, who were pursuing stragglers at full gallop, charged into the wooded gully of the *'Malfosse'*, were ambushed and their horses chopped down. Many knights were killed, and Eustace of Boulogne, their leader, was hit so hard that 'blood ran from his nose and mouth' so that he had to be carried from the field.

Harold's mutilated body was identified by his mistress, Edith Swan-Neck, who was walking through the heaps of dead. She recognized the dead king 'by marks on the body, known only to her'. William had the body buried on the beach, beneath a stone slab, as if permanently confronting the inevitability of his doom. Harold's mother, Gytha, offered gold to the duke to reclaim her son's body but was contemptuously rebuffed. At the exact point where Harold had planted his standard, William determined to make good his oath to God that, should he be given a victory, he would build an abbey of thanksgiving. But before he could indulge himself in these grandiose gestures, he had to make sure that he had won, not just a single battle, but the war for England. He had lost at least a quarter of his army in the carnage at Senlac ridge, and not long after the rest were stricken by a violent epidemic of dysentery. And if William had supposed the remnant of the English nobility would come flocking to him at Hastings, offering submission and allegiance, he was going to be badly disappointed.

With the Godwine family destroyed, the key players were Stigand, Archbishop of Canterbury, and Aeldred, Archbishop of York, together with the two northern earls, Edwin and Morcar, whose levies, had they been on the field at Senlac, might well have changed the outcome of the battle. Keeping them back meant, at least, that they had something to bargain with, or so they must have supposed. Their first instinct was to proclaim Edgar the Atheling, the very last of the old Wessex line – Edmund Ironside's grandson and Edward the Confessor's great-nephew – as king. But he was still only a boy, a pawn in the hands of the English rearguard.

So as soon as his troops recovered their stomachs, William needed to give a practical demonstration of what was to be gained from submission and what would be lost by resistance. The usual swath of fire and plunder was cut through the countryside of southeast England and, not surprisingly, it did the trick. One by one, the great centres of Anglo-Saxon England crumbled – Canterbury, Winchester (where Harold's sister Edith, Edward the Confessor's widow, handed him the keys to the city and to the abbey, the necropolis of the Saxon kings). Suddenly, Edwin and Morcar had second thoughts about making the boy Edgar king and departed for their earldoms in the hope of preserving them. Their assumption was that the Norman Conquest would be very much like the Danish: a foreign figurehead would simply co-opt the great men and the governing institutions of Anglo-Saxon England. But there was never the remotest chance that William would actually govern through some sort of political and social fusion of the old and the new, of Saxon and Norman. The elementary condition on which he had been able to mobilize his great army in Normandy in the first place had been that the victors should possess the spoils. And now that the colonization of England required a continuing, heavy presence of men in arms, he fully intended to live up to his bargain and deliver the properties, lands and estates of the English nobles, to his own vassals.

William knew that no conquest worth its name would be secure without the occupation of London, but instead of tackling the city directly he sent his army around it in a green-belt excursion, perhaps with the aim of starving it into surrender if need be. By the time he crossed the Thames at Wallingford, however, Archbishops Stigand and Aeldred, and Edgar the Atheling were ready to kneel in submission. The last of the Saxon line was now William's hostage, and there was no one left from the old *witan* who could possibly lead any kind of concerted resistance. On Christmas Day 1066, Westminster Abbey saw its third royal ceremony within a year: the coronation of King William I. There was an effort to make this a hybrid of Saxon and Norman rites. Read in English by Aeldred of York and in French by Geoffrey, Bishop of Coutances, the rite of Dunstan, which had been created for King Edgar's coronation at Bath in 973, was enacted but with the addition of a rite used for the kings of France – the anointing with the sacred oil, the chrism. Perhaps this, finally, made William the Bastard a legitimate king.

It was almost a year since Edward the Confessor had made his deathbed prophecy, and perhaps some of those who had been in attendance in Westminster thought that the many thousands of English dead were atonement enough and that the tree of England might now repair itself and grow green again. But the demons had not quite departed. On his coronation day William had prudently posted knights outside the abbey to deal with anyone who was not demonstrating unconfined joy at the great event. When the guards heard the shouts of acclaim from within, the *vivats*, they concluded that some sort of assault was under way, for which the standard response was to set fire to every building in sight. The historian Orderic Vitalis wrote:

> as the fire spread rapidly through the houses the people who had been rejoicing in the church were thrown into confusion, and a crowd of men and women of every rank and status, compelled by this disaster rushed out of the church. Only the bishops and clergy along with the monks stayed, terrified, in front of the altar and only just managed to complete the consecration rite over the king who was trembling violently. Nearly everyone else ran towards the raging fire, some to fight bravely against the force of the flames, but more hoping to grab loot for themselves amid such great confusion. The English, believing there was a plot behind something so completely unlooked for, were extremely angry and afterwards held the Normans in suspicion, judging them treacherous.

After this fiasco, it was not surprising that William was not prepared to take the formal acts of homage offered at his coronation at face value. The fort that would become the Tower of London – a stone castle of unprecedented strength – began to be constructed right after Christmas.

The debacle of his coronation was the only time anyone would get a glimpse of William 'pale and trembling'. More often he appeared as the god-like victor: tall – 5 feet 10 inches – red-haired and potent. Around Easter 1067 he felt confident enough to return to Normandy for a triumphal progress through the towns and churches of the duchy. It was an elaborately planned spectacle, with the king departing from Pevensey where he had first set foot on English soil and taking with him, as if the captives of a Roman triumph, a few tame specimens of the Saxon elite: Edgar the Atheling, and the earls Edwin and Morcar.

The euphoria in Rouen must have made it seem as if the contest for England was over. It was not. William would spend virtually his entire reign stamping on one brushfire rebellion after another – and on both sides of the Channel. During that time almost anyone who had reason, principled or opportunistic, and who had the chance to take up arms against William I, did so: 'Eadric the Wild' of Wales, who was said to have married a fairy princess and introduced her to the king ('Beauty, say hello to Beast, Beast, say hello to Beauty') but who was more concerned in the real world with holding on to his lands, stolen by a Norman lord; Harold's sons, who mounted serious raids from Ireland in 1068 in Devon and Somerset; the citizens of Exeter, who held out for eighteen days against a Norman siege and desisted only when allowed to keep their old civic privileges; even some of those who had fought *with* William at Hastings, such as Eustace of Boulogne, the ravager of Dover, who this time crossed with a troop of knights to *defend* the town; and Sweyn II of Denmark, who had certainly not abandoned his claim to the throne and who landed with an enormous invasion fleet of 200 ships, occupying large tracts of what had been Viking England in East Anglia and Northumbria.

By 1069 William was, in fact, facing almost as many headaches as Harold had three years before and, like Harold, had to make pell-mell dashes from one end of the realm to the other. What he must have realized, in these years of grim campaigning, was how much of the British island had remained unconquered with the disposal of the Saxon aristocracy. Wales was so endemically rebellious (as it had been in Godwine's day) that it needed years of brutal subjugation and colonization with the castles of the Marcher lords before the borderlands were dependably pacified. The long-lived king of Scotland, Malcolm III, was even more audacious, marrying his sister to Edgar the Atheling and treating the fugitive Saxon prince as an honoured guest at his court. At one point William was facing, simultaneously, Danish landings in the east and a Scots invasion from the north. York had opened its gates to Sweyn, greeting him as a liberator, so when William mobilized a formidable army and took it north in 1069, his campaign went well beyond the usual punitive treatment and turned, instead, into a merciless, calculated exercise in slaughter and starvation. Thousands of men and boys were gruesomely butchered, their bodies left to rot on the highways; fields and livestock were destroyed so completely that any survivors of the massacres were bound to die in the great famine and pestilence that followed. 'I fell on the English of the northern counties like a raving lion,' the Norman historian Orderic Vitalis has William confess on his deathbed, 'subjecting them to the calamity of a cruel famine and by so doing…became the barbarous murderer of many thousands, young and old, of that fine race of people.' At the time, though, William's sentiments did not run to compassion. At Christmas the king made a point of celebrating the nativity amid the burned ruins of York.

After the apocalypse came the castles. William built large numbers of them – some still the timber-and-earth-mound structures, others permanent stone buildings – sited especially inside towns thought to be trouble-spots, such as York, Chester and London. They were citadels of authority in peacetime, engines of terror if need be in times of civil war. Others were erected, in emulation of late Roman Britain, at crucial entrances to the kingdom, at Dover and at Rochester on the Medway. There were, however, some places where the terrain was unsuitable for castles of any kind – the fenland around Ely in East Anglia, for example – and there, in conjunction with the Danish penetration of the waterways, some sort of resistance was possible. Although the legend of Hereward the Wake – the outlaw-thegn who returns to find his family destroyed and his lands in the possession of Normans and becomes the guerrilla of the fens – is, indeed, largely a myth, there was, for a while, an 'Isle of Refuge' at Ely, sheltering not only Hereward but also Earl Morcar of Northumbria. Once Sweyn decided to cut his losses, however, and revert to Viking type by being bought off by William, the rebellion was doomed – although not before the rebels had burned down Peterborough Abbey and had had the satisfaction of seeing a causeway built to take Norman troops collapse under its own weight into the bogs. And since there is a Hereward who appears in the Domesday Book as a landholder in the west Midlands, he, too, seems to have come to terms with the Conqueror.

Piece by piece, then – with terror or with bribery – William was bringing the country into obedience. The last piece fell into place when, in a strategically astounding pincer movement in 1072, he moved against King Malcolm from the Clyde in the west and the Tay in the east, cutting Scotland in two and forcing the Scots king to ditch the Atheling and accept William as the lawful monarch of England. William's charisma as warlord was potent enough to bring over to his side some of the surviving Saxon nobles like Eadric the Wild, who served him in Scotland and had his lands reinstated. *The Anglo-Saxon Chronicle* even records that Malcolm delivered hostages and swore to be William's 'man' – although whether this meant the crown of Scotland did homage to the king of England was a point that would be debated with blood and for centuries to come.

Most of the voices describing these events – as those of the events leading to 1066 – belong to the victors: the boastful William of Poitiers or, in a later generation, Wace, sketching the starkest possible contrast between the deceitful, perjured Harold and the noble, betrayed William; the one a felon, the other a paragon. But among the rather nauseating chorus of self-congratulation there is at least one voice that sings off-key and that dares to criticize William and describe the Conquest as it surely was: a ruthlessly calculated, brutally executed act of aggression. The voice is all the more credible because it belongs to someone with a special perspective on the Conquest, having a Norman father and an English mother: the monk Orderic Vitalis. His father had come with William but then had sent the boy back to Normandy, where he had grown up feeling estranged from what was supposed to be his homeland. In the early twelfth century he wrote an account of the war, which in contrast to all the other versions has the reality of blood and ash on every page. And Orderic never minced his words about what he thought of as a colonization. 'Foreigners,' he wrote, 'grew wealthy with the spoils of England while her own sons were either shamefully slain or driven as exiles to wander hopelessly through foreign kingdoms.'

In other words, Orderic saw what had happened as a trauma. Of course, the trauma was a decapitation rather than a deracination. Not everything in Anglo-Saxon England disappeared after 1066. There were still shires and hundreds and public courts for each of them. If the *witan* had gone, the Norman king still turned to a council for advice (although in William's case he was just as likely to ignore it). Unfree peasants – the villeins – continued to labour the required number of days for a lord as the price of being permitted to till a strip of land or keep animals on it. What difference did it make if those lords now went by French rather than Anglo-Saxon names? What was in a name after all?

A great deal, as it turns out. For the most part the Anglo-Saxon thegns didn't use surnames at all. When a place-name was added to a Wigod or a Cedric, it simply told you where the man came from. But when the Normans incorporated place-names into their names it was an act of occupation and of possession. They were Roger Beau-Mont or Mont-Gomery, because the place was them and they were the place: they owned it – knights, peasants, mills, woods, swine-pastures, fords and bridges – lock, stock and barrel. And once they got their hands on this nicely packaged property, it was not going to be chopped up again by accidents of death or survival in the family. The Anglo-Saxons thought of their landed estate as just one piece of the thegn's assets, which might also include precious gems, fine weapons and armour. Taken together, the assets were considered the property of the 'big' family: brothers and sisters, aunts and uncles, even cousins. When the thegn or his widow died, the assets would be parcelled out among them, a practice that was useful for preserving family peace but bad for preserving its property empire. Preserving the estate intact was an obsession for the Norman nobility. There would be no more sharing the dovecotes with Aunt Aelfrida. Instead, everything would go to a single heir. The kingdom itself was just the largest of these estates. In the old way, a successor would get the nod from a dying king, provided the *witan* consented to his choice. In the new way, the king gave his realm to his son. End of debate.

The replacement of a ruling class by foreign-speaking conquerors was not, then, a trivial substitution. The old system of lordship had rested on chains of connection as well as on obligation. A thegn had owed the Saxon king military service because of his status as a landholder. Under the new order, the count was *allowed* to hold land only on condition that he appeared in arms. Service was, in effect, his rent. And the Anglo-Saxon thegns, whether 'royal' or not, were seldom loftily removed from their tenant farmers, especially the most prosperous *ceorls*, who might well hold and farm a hide or two. Differences in the timber house, in dress and in speech habits were all a matter of degree rather than kind. In some circumstances the *ceorl* might even imagine that he could rise, through wealth and marriage, into the class of the thegns themselves. After the Conquest, however, proximity and familiarity were replaced by alienation and impotence and, in all likelihood, a sense of fearfulness, of having the protection of custom ripped away, of being helpless in the face of the exercise of force. It was the difference between the wooden hall and the castle; between the intimate scale of the Saxon chapel and the immense, fortress-like scale of the great Norman cathedrals.

The great castles and churches that were the visible imprint of the Conquest on England are deceptive in suggesting its monolithic character. Although William had certainly delivered on his promises to transfer the entire estate of the English land-holding classes to his own vassals, this did not preclude the greatest of them from challenging his rule. As conqueror and king he was no more immune from family conspiracies than he had been as duke. At one point, his own eldest son Robert was in rebellion; at another, his half-brother, Odo of Blois, the Bishop of Bayeux, for whom the tapestry had been made, his closest companion and the man he unhesitatingly appointed regent when he travelled abroad, was also involved in a plot, reputedly going so far as to attempt a march on Rome to make himself pope. The Count of Flanders and another Cnut of Denmark all continued to harbour ambitions on his new realm.

None of this prevented the king from carrying on the business of the kingdom, however. At Christmas 1085 he held court at Gloucester and launched what may be the most extraordinary campaign of his entire reign: the campaign for information. His immediate need was to impose a geld – the land tax he had inherited from the Anglo-Saxon kings, which would pay for the defence of the realm – but the compilation of Domesday Book was much more than a glorified audit. It was a complete inventory of the kingdom up to the Tyne, shire by shire, hundred by hundred: who owned what on the eve of the Conquest and who owned what now; how much it had been worth then and how much it was worth now. Beyond the

immediate pragmatic need for money, William's instinct – remarkable for someone
usually thought of as more or less continually in the saddle – was that knowledge was
also power. William the Conqueror was also the first data-base king.

His servants got him that knowledge at what, in the eleventh century, passed for
warp speed. The king, wrote Orderic Vitalis:

> sent his men all over England into every shire and had them find out how many
> hundred hides there were…or what land and cattle the king himself had in the
> country or what dues he ought to have from the shire. And he had a record
> made of how much land his archbishops had and his bishops and abbots and
> earls…so very narrowly did he have it investigated that there was no single hide
> nor indeed (a shame to relate but it seemed no shame to him)…was one ox or
> one cow or one pig left out that was not put down in his record.

At Old Sarum on Lammas Day in 1086 William was presented with reams of
densely packed, cross-referenced information, material that had been gathered first at
the local level, then brought to the hundred, and finally compiled by a commission
of the shire before being made into the books. Some of that material was taken orally
from villeins or priests. But much of it must have been taken from pre-existing
written documents like geld-books, and what we usually think of as a monument to
the brisk efficiency of Norman government probably owed as much to the advanced
information-retrieval machinery left in place by the Anglo-Saxon state. So the world
of the older England lingers on, captive ghosts, recorded on the pages of Domesday
Book: the thegns, the sheriffs, the hides. And when William was presented with
the books, it was as if he had reconquered the kingdom all over again, this time
statistically, and thus in a form that no disgruntled motte-and-bailey barons would
ever overcome.

So although they were distinct events, the two ceremonial moments at Old
Sarum defined post-Conquest England and its monarchy in a perfectly complemen-
tary way. First was the oath, taken by all the magnates, nobles and gentlemen (on the
eve of yet another campaign): 'and all the people occupying land who were of any
account whatsoever in England, whosoever's vassals they might be…all submitting to
him and swore oaths of allegiance that they would be faithful to him against all other
men.' But then there was The Book, from which, should it ever be necessary, William
would have the information to coerce, fine or confiscate, should any of his own
vassals waver in their loyalty. For centuries afterwards the strength of government
in England was this partnership (never easy or uncomplicated) between the power

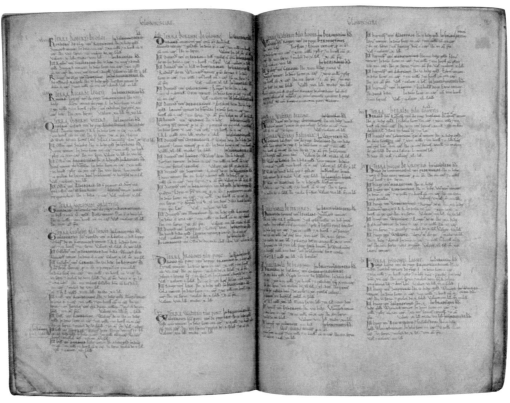

Top: Pages from Domesday Book.
Above: Ely Cathedral – Norman architecture at its most imposing.

of the landed classes and the authority of the state; the guardians of the green acres and the keepers of the knowledge. And between them, posing as a neutral, professing to understand each of their concerns, was the eternal umpire: the sovereign.

One might suppose that William would now be satisfied to let this hybrid system of 'Anglo-Norman' governance work of its own accord, especially since the perennial threat of a Danish invasion had ended with the murder of Cnut IV in 1086. Ironically, the last coinage that he minted bore the same hopeful inscription as Harold's: PAX (peace). And William was much given to long crown-wearings, sitting in silent regal splendour, the image of majesty – very much the way Harold is shown holding court in the Tapestry. But William's threshold of irritation still remained, as it always had been, extremely low. All the king of France had to do was to cross the border between his kingdom and the duchy of Normandy, into disputed territory, to invite a fierce response. William, now in his late fifties and run to fat, rode again and burned again with an enthusiasm undimmed by the advancing years. The town of Mantes, near the Norman-French border, was so comprehensively torched that it is archaeologically impossible to find any building that dates from before William's wrath, which was visited on it in 1087. But perhaps this last devastation was one too many. He was riding through the smouldering wreckage of the town when, according to one chronicle, something hot – a piece of beam perhaps – fell away from a roof in front of the king's horse, making it buck and throwing William violently against the high pommel at the front of the saddle. The corpulent William's girth now presented a large soft object to the puncturing pommel. Some internal organ – probably the spleen – was ruptured. The Conqueror began to haemorrhage.

William was taken to the priory of St Gervais in Rouen. His chancellor and councillors arrived post haste, some in consternation, some already in vulture mode. Of William's old campaigning circle only Robert of Mortain, his half-brother, was among those who expressed their concern. The other half-brother, Odo of Bayeux, was in prison. The king's oldest son, Robert Short-Hose (Curthose), was an enemy, even though William had given him the duchy of Normandy. England had been awarded to his second son, William Rufus, who, probably on his father's unsentimen- tal advice, returned at speed to England to secure his inheritance. The third son, Henry – who would become Henry I – got something to which he was especially partial: money.

At the very end Orderic Vitalis puts into William's mouth an extraordinary deathbed confession, so completely out of character that it seems, on the face of it, utterly incredible. But Orderic, then in Caen, was in a position to know. So perhaps

William did, *in extremis*, have a qualm of conscience if not the all-out spasm of guilt that Orderic gives him as he refused to appoint any heir:

> for I did not attain that high honour by hereditary right but wrested it from the perjured King Harold in a desperate battle, with much effusion of blood, and it was by the slaughter and banishment of his adherents that I subjugated England to my rule. I have persecuted its native inhabitants beyond all reason. Whether noble or commons I have cruelly oppressed them; many I have unjustly disin-herited…Having therefore made my way to the throne of that kingdom by so many crimes I dare not leave it to anyone but God alone.

If he did say anything remotely like this, no one paid any attention, any more than they had attended to what Edward the Confessor had to say on his deathbed. Once he had gone, in the early hours of the morning of 9 September 1087, the great bell of Rouen Cathedral tolling, a scene of shocking indignity took place. 'Some of the attendants,' Orderic wrote, 'behaved as though they had lost their wits. Nevertheless the wealthiest of them mounted their horses and departed in haste to secure their property. While the inferior attendants, observing that their masters had disappeared, laid hands on the arms, linen, plate and royal furniture and hastened away leaving the corpse almost naked on the floor of the cell.'

As for his old antagonist, Harold Godwineson, he certainly did not remain buried on the beach facing the Channel. Rumours abounded in the years after the battle that he had actually escaped and was living out his days as a hermit – some said in Cheshire or in the remote fastness of ancient Britain, Wales – but another story is much more likely to be close to the truth. At some point when it was safe, the female survivors of the family took his remains and had them interred at one of the many religious houses of which Harold had been patron: Waltham Abbey in Essex. If the accusations of being a 'despoiler of the Church' and a grievous perjurer had been enough to persuade the pope that Harold was notorious enough to be cast out and overthrown, they did not seem to have much effect on the monks of Waltham, who secretly buried him and prayed for his soul. Somewhere, then, beneath the columns and arches of the Romanesque church, a handsome specimen of post-Conquest architecture, is the last Anglo-Saxon king, literally part of the foundations of Norman England.

3

The idea of Britain was born in a fabulous reverie. The dreamer was Geoffrey of Monmouth – *Galfridus Monemutensis* as he signed himself – who, around 1136, completed his *History of the Kings of Britain*. Like Britain, Geoffrey was himself a hybrid: probably a Breton, but born in Wales and raised in the aggressively Norman culture of the Marches, the borderlands that were colonized by the Norman nobility. But Geoffrey was also a cultural product of medieval Oxford, where, he claimed, an archdeacon Walter had given him 'an ancient book in the British [meaning Welsh] tongue' on which he based his own Latin history. Geoffrey's ambition was to plant the roots of Britain deep in the worlds that mattered most to him: classical antiquity and Celtic mythology. So, according to his history, Britain, 'the best of islands', a country of five races, had been first civilized by Brutus, the grandson of Aeneas, the Trojan prince who had founded Rome. Brutus's northern Tiber was the Thames, and on its banks he had, apparently, established *Troia Nova*, New Troy, destined to be the capital of a great multi-national empire. After his death, Brutus's sons, Locrinus, Kamber and Albanactus, had divided the island among them, creating, respectively, Loegria (England), Kambria (Wales) and Albany (Scotland).

Much of Geoffrey's *History*, however – and by far the most famous part – was devoted to the epic of a British hero, prophesied by the Welsh magician, Merlin. That dauntless champion had liberated the country from the plague of the barbarian Saxons, invited into Britain by the tyrant Vortigern following the departure of the Romans. Vortigern had built a tower, which repeatedly subsided, baffling his counsellors until Merlin enlightened them that the tower had been precariously constructed directly above a subterranean pool in which slept two dragons. Thus sank the state of Britain, its roots gnawed by monsters, until Arthur, the son of Utherpendragon, arose to rebuild the country on the firm foundations of Christian chivalry and martial courage. Once the Saxons were expelled from the length and breadth of England, Arthur turned his attention to the Picts and the Irish, who were subdued in short

SOVEREIGNTY UNBOUND?

Detail of a manuscript illumination showing Becket arguing with Henry II.

order. York, the target of their devastation, was rebuilt to the greater glory of God. Men of distinction now flocked to his court, where 'even a man of noblest birth thought nothing of himself unless he wore his arms and dressed in the same way as Arthur's knights. At last, the fame of Arthur's generosity and bravery spread to the very ends of the earth.' At the height of his reign, Arthur extended his power to encompass an entire northern empire, stretching from Scandinavia to Gaul and out into the wide, chill sea to Iceland. At Caerleon-at-Usk, in the most ancient heart of Britain, a thousand ermine-clad noblemen assembled before Arthur and Guinevere and celebrated in tournaments and feasting the Britain that had become the centre of the world, a country that 'reached such a sophistication that it excelled all other kingdoms in its affluence, the richness of its ornaments, and the courteous behaviour of its population'. Such idylls, Geoffrey the expert fabulist knew, are beautiful because they are mortal. In the end, Arthur's golden age must be ended by the treachery of his nephew, Mordred, and Britain thrown back into the murky misery of paganism.

The *History of the Kings of Britain* was, of course, an outrageous fantasy, but by the time its author, now known as Geoffrey *Arthur*, became the second Bishop of St Asaph (in what is now Flintshire) in 1152, his manuscript had already reached the wide readership that would endure for centuries. Geoffrey had learned about Arthur from his patron, Robert, Earl of Gloucester, who, in turn, had been told the story by another protégé, the librarian of Malmesbury Abbey. The librarian had visited Glastonbury Abbey, where the Benedictine monks were convinced that the hero's body lay somewhere on the premises, although just precisely where they could not say. Geoffrey understood that the times called for heroic romance and an epic of wise governance, not least because Robert of Gloucester was a combatant in the civil war that was then tearing the country apart. That war was bitterly and unrelentingly fought for nearly twenty years between rival grandchildren of William the Conqueror. On the one side (supported by the Earl of Gloucester) was Matilda, the daughter of William's son, Henry. On the other side was Stephen of Blois, the son of his daughter, Adela.

When William I died in 1087 it might have seemed, on the face of it, that the Anglo-Norman state created by the Conquest had settled down. Theoretically, post-Domesday government had the potential to be a finely tuned tool of sovereignty: Anglo-Saxon administrative and legal experience married to Norman military force. In reality, the exercise of power could be shockingly crude. Between the death of the Conqueror and the accession of Henry II in 1154, no monarch could hope for acceptance without first seizing the royal treasury at Winchester, and the ostensibly dignified process of succession was reduced to a smash-and-grab operation: smash your rival and grab the gold. This is why William I's designated heir, his second surviving son, William Rufus, rode at high speed from Rouen once he decided his father was not long for the world. Likewise, coronations were high-speed affairs, cobbled together under the auspices of whichever senior cleric happened to oblige. But even with the loot under lock and key and the head duly anointed, securing the throne and running the government required political skills that William II (Rufus) in particular conspicuously lacked. Much of his reign was spent in attempting to extract taxes from his tenants-in-chief to pay for wars on the Welsh and Scottish borders and in alienating the Church by promoting court favourites into bishoprics. When he was killed in a hunting party by a stray arrow in 1100 (as his oldest brother, Richard, had died before him), not everyone thought his death was accidental.

Accompanying William II on the hunt was his brother Henry, the youngest of the Conqueror's sons, who, at the fatal moment, found himself nicely placed in the New Forest, a conveniently short gallop from the treasury at Winchester. A few days later the Bishop of London had crowned him Henry I, thus denying the throne (again) to the oldest surviving brother, Robert Curthose. To shore up his shaky claim, Henry did something even cleverer. Six days after his coronation, on 11 August, he married Matilda, the daughter of Malcolm III, king of Scotland, whose own queen was directly descended from the royal house of Wessex. Their children, then, would have both Saxon and Norman blood in them and so, Henry must have hoped, would have a double claim on the allegiance of the English. But although he managed his Anglo-Norman inheritance expertly for thirty-five years and fathered twenty illegitimate children, Henry's hopes for posterity came to grief. His first wife died in 1118. His sole surviving legitimate son, William, was drowned in the wreck of the *White Ship* in 1120, together with the flower of the Norman nobility, silks amid the seaweed. A late second marriage produced no heirs, which left Henry's daughter, Matilda, as his only possible direct heir. At his royal council of Christmas 1126 Henry bound the leading bishops, abbots and lords to honour her as his successor.

Needless to say, after Henry died in Normandy in 1135, eating the lampreys his physician had expressly forbidden, the first-to-Winchester axiom superseded any of those promises, and the first-to-Winchester was not Matilda but Henry's nephew, Stephen of Blois, the son of William the Conqueror's formidable daughter, Adela. Although Dover and Canterbury refused to admit him as king, London opened its doors to Stephen. Many of the nobles who rallied to him excused their disavowal of Matilda by claiming that Henry I had changed his mind before he died and that, in any case, their allegiance had been conditional on the princess not contracting a

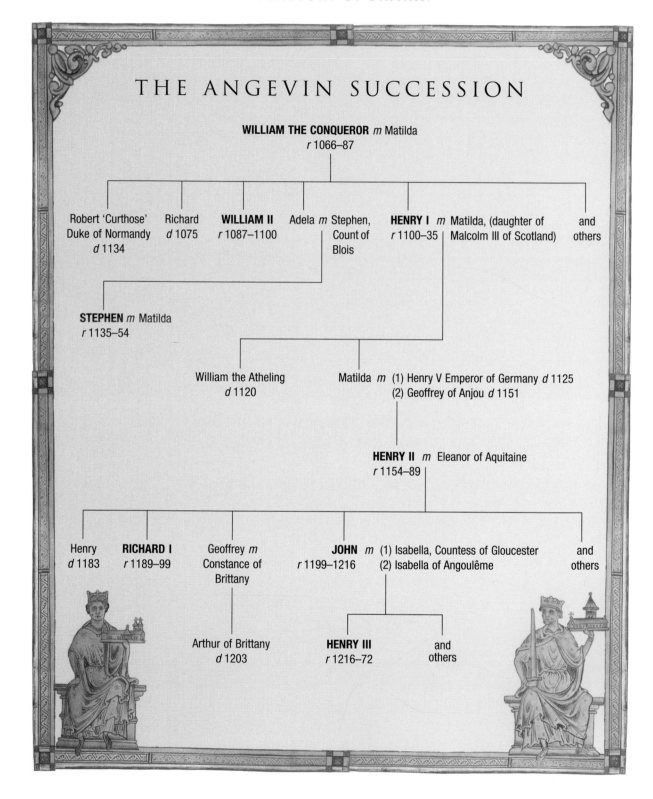

THE ANGEVIN SUCCESSION

WILLIAM THE CONQUEROR *m* Matilda
r 1066–87

Robert 'Curthose'
Duke of Normandy
d 1134

Richard
d 1075

WILLIAM II
r 1087–1100

Adela *m* Stephen,
Count of
Blois

HENRY I *m* Matilda, (daughter of
r 1100–35 | Malcolm III of Scotland)

and
others

STEPHEN *m* Matilda
r 1135–54

William the Atheling
d 1120

Matilda *m* (1) Henry V Emperor of Germany *d* 1125
(2) Geoffrey of Anjou *d* 1151

HENRY II *m* Eleanor of Aquitaine
r 1154–89

Henry
d 1183

RICHARD I
r 1189–99

Geoffrey *m*
Constance of
Brittany

JOHN *m* (1) Isabella, Countess of Gloucester
r 1199–1216 (2) Isabella of Angoulême

and
others

Arthur of Brittany
d 1203

HENRY III
r 1216–72

and
others

Henry I mourning the death of his only legitimate son, William the Atheling, in the wreck of the *White Ship*, from a fourteenth-century manuscript.

foreign marriage. But Matilda, who had been the wife of the German Holy Roman Emperor Henry V, had been remarried after his death in 1125 to Count Geoffrey of Anjou. This, too, was meant as a diplomatic masterstroke on Henry I's part, uniting the traditionally hostile duchies of Normandy and Anjou. But many of the Anglo-Norman nobility remained more hostile than reconciled. Matilda had one great champion in England, the most powerful and politically intelligent of Henry I's many bastards, Robert, Earl of Gloucester. Without doubt, the timing of the appearance of the *History* a year later (in 1136), with its cautionary tale of the anarchy that followed the division of the kingdom by old King Leir, was not fortuitous. No one reading that famous story could possibly have missed the analogy between Matilda and the good daughter Cordeilia who, unlike Shakespeare's tragic heroine, survived, after fighting great battles, to reign over the kingdom.

Matilda, who made it known that, as long as she lived, she should be addressed as 'Empress', had little of Cordeilia's winning humility. After slogging her way to London, she managed to alienate almost everyone of importance in the kingdom, opening a long, gruelling period of siege and counter-siege. And while the monarchy was losing authority, the barons were taking it. Dependent on local support to tilt the balance against their rival, each side in the civil war was prepared to let the magnates of the shires do what they wished – build castles, create private armies, carry out vendettas against personal enemies, torch their manors – as long as it hurt the other side. *The Anglo-Saxon Chronicle* remembered this as the *tempus werre*, the 'time of war'.

> Every great man built himself castles and held them against the king…they sorely burdened the unhappy people of the country with forced labour and when the castles were built, they filled them with devils and wicked men…By night and by day they seized those whom they believed had any wealth to get their gold and silver, they put them in prison and tortured them…they hung them up by their feet and smoked them with foul smoke…when the wretched people had no more to give, they plundered and burned all the villages…the wretched people perished with hunger…never did a country endure greater misery.

This, in the end, was the legacy of William the Conqueror: chaos, carnage, famine, extortion; every jumped-up baron a kingling in his own shire; William's grandchildren banging away at each other while the realm fell apart. Somehow, however, this mayhem generated a line of rulers who, for better or worse, redefined sovereignty in England. War was their vocation and power their obsession, but in the course of pursuing it they managed to re-invent government. That reinvention was so forceful that it provoked, in turn, furious campaigns of opposition that would set the limits on the power of the medieval state. The Angevins – the children and grandchildren of Matilda and Geoffrey of Anjou – were the alpha and omega of English history: at once insatiably ambitious and ostensibly in control of a vast empire, stretching from the Pyrenees to the Cheviots, but also vulnerable to family jealousies and territorial over-reach. What their intelligence and energy built, their passions and their immoderation destroyed. To their many enemies they were, literally, fiendish. A story was told about an earlier Count of Anjou whose bride, Melusine, had flown, shrieking, out of the window, thus unmasking herself as the daughter of Satan. But demonic or not, for a generation the Angevins were the masters of everything that counted in Christendom.

The marriage between Matilda and her second husband, Geoffrey of Anjou, was famously unhappy. She spoke German, retained her imperial airs (and honorific title of Empress) and was twenty-six. He had been reared as the flower of chivalry, spoke French and was fifteen. But it didn't need happiness to produce heirs, and in 1133 Matilda bore her husband a son, named Henry after both her father and first husband. The red-haired child, running about among the hounds, was the living embodiment of Henry I's strategic vision: of the creation of a cross-Channel superstate beside which the kings of France would be reduced to puny impotence. As this boy Henry 'Plantagenet' (known for the Counts of Anjou's chivalric badge of the yellow broom, the *Planta Genesta*) grew, it became evident that he had inherited steely physical courage and a foul temper from his mother, and razor-sharp political intelligence from his father. But the quality that everyone who ever met Henry II remembered most vividly – his fidgety energy – was all his own. As both child and adolescent he showed up in England on his mother's behalf no fewer than three times – when he was nine, fourteen and sixteen – to show the Anjou-Plantagenet flag of the red cross on a white field. At Carlisle on Whit Sunday in 1148 Henry was knighted by David I of Scotland, submitting to rituals of Arthurian solemnity: a purifying bath, the laying on of a golden tunic, the presentation of a shield painted with his personal device and the acceptance of a sword, preferably very old and curiously engraved.

Now that he was dressed to kill as the new Arthur, it was imperative that Henry's apprenticeship be completed by a fitting Guinevere. As it happened, the perfect candidate had just become available in the person of Eleanor of Aquitaine. She had been recently divorced by Louis VII, the king of France, the official grounds being given as 'consanguinity' (too close a kinship for the Church to tolerate), but the truth was that she had failed to produce a male heir. The fruitlessness of the union, Eleanor let it be known, was none of her doing. Being married to Louis, she had

Geoffrey, Count of Anjou, the second husband of Henry's daughter Matilda;
enamelled grave plate from his tomb in Le Mans Cathedral.

complained, was more like being married to a monk than a king. It was rumoured that Geoffrey of Anjou had personally verified Eleanor's appetite for passion before recommending her to his son. Still, the match was a gamble. She was thirty; he was eighteen. He was relatively inexperienced; she had seen as much of the ways of the world as it could offer. But something surprising apparently happened between the teenage Arthur and the dangerously mercurial Guinevere, something unusual in a marriage of political expediency: the parties concerned appeared to desire each other.

Barely eight weeks after Eleanor's divorce, in May 1152, Henry stood at the altar beside a considerably older woman, whom all contemporary accounts describe as a dark-eyed beauty: disconcertingly articulate, strong-minded and even jocular, and not at all the modestly veiled damsel in the tower. For her part, perhaps Eleanor could see beyond her husband's stocky frame, the barrel-chest, the boyish freckles and the fair complexion that reddened easily, like all his Norman ancestors, to someone who was an intriguing peculiarity: an unlikely combination of the bookish and the horsy; scruffy informality and arrogant self-possession; buzzing with febrile adolescent energy yet also somehow cerebral and inwardly intense; the rare prince who looked right with a falcon on one hand and a book at the other. In fact, their native worlds were not all that far apart: bloody-minded gangs of knights astride brightly caparisoned chargers, thudding into each other in the lists or obliging their overlords by burning down the opposition's manors. If anything, Eleanor had grown up in a world even more besotted with the knightly ideal at the same time as it was violating it with habitual brutality. Her grandfather, Duke William IX of Aquitaine, had been a crusader but also the 'first troubadour', happiest in his *cansa* songs when celebrating the joys of adultery. The pious Louis VII of France might have known when he married Eleanor that he was not getting Griselda the Meek. A thousand innocents had been burned alive in the church of Vitry-le-François in an ugly little war she had had the king fight on behalf of her sister, Petronilla. When Louis took the cross to atone, Eleanor went with him to the Holy Land, in a magnificent, rather than penitential, style. Dismayed to discover that crusading was an arduous, pious business, she quickly developed an unhealthily warm relationship with her uncle, the slightly impious Raymond of Toulouse.

Divorced from Louis, Eleanor was damaged goods. So it was to Geoffrey of Anjou's credit that he could see the brilliant possibilities of the match with his son, Henry, and he doubtless put them to Eleanor. Instead of being the cast-off queen of France, she would be the new queen of England and duchess of both Aquitaine and Normandy. In 1153 Henry Plantagenet, now twenty years old, crossed the Channel yet again, this time with arms and money supplied by his bride's feudal levies as well as his own. Faced with this formidable army and the loss of his surviving son, Eustace, Stephen was pessimistic enough to come to terms. In November 1153 a deal was struck at Winchester. Stephen would be allowed to die on the throne (as seemed to be imminent) on condition that he named Henry his sole and legitimate heir.

Henry and Eleanor were crowned together in Westminster Abbey on 7 December 1154. When they emerged from the *vivats* and the incense, they were the sovereigns of an enormous realm, which stretched from the Pyrenees, through the vineyards of Gascony and the bustling Atlantic port of La Rochelle, across the Loire and Seine into orchard-dotted Normandy and over the Channel to England, all the way to the Welsh marcher hills and the Cumbrian moorland abbeys. It was a good time to come into this inheritance. The mid-twelfth century was, literally, a gentler climate. Harvests were more abundant, and land was being taken from swamp, forest and moorland and put under pasture or even made arable. Technological innovations were making the land more productive. Nailed shoes, horse collars and tandem harnesses had made it possible for the first time for horse-drawn ploughs to replace oxen, expanding the acreage that could be worked in a day. Machine-based processing, in the shape of watermills and even the occasional windmill, was appearing on the landscape. Markets and fairs were multiplying. Long-distance travel was safer, and commercial connections between west and east, north and south, made more dependably profitable.

Although he must have been all too aware of its discomforts and dangers (the drowning of the *White Ship* had, after all, engendered a civil war), Henry II made the Channel crossing twenty-eight times in the thirty-five years of his reign and is more likely to have thought of the sea as an inconvenience than an elemental divide between two utterly unlike halves of his lands. The two sides, after all, were joined by a common language of polite culture and government – medieval French. And while Westminster was, increasingly, the heart of administration, this did not make London an imperial 'capital'. It was natural and necessary for Henry to think of other centres of power – Rouen in Normandy, Chinon on the Loire, Eleanor's city of Poitiers in Aquitaine – as equally vital in holding together the disparate territories of his realm. On both sides of the Channel his Francophone administration faced the same challenges to its authority: the unreliable loyalty of local feudal magnates; and a clergy, both monastic and secular, fast developing the autonomous doctrines encoded in the canon law codified in Rome. In the rapidly burgeoning towns immigrant populations, Flemings and Jews, each speaking their own tongues, were encouraged to settle under the direct protection of the Crown, a protection that included their vulnerability to the extortion of forced loans and levies.

Beneath all these social layers, the vernacular cultures survived, both in speech and in written literature – English, Breton, Occitan, Brythonic Welsh and perhaps even some traces of Danish and Norse in East Anglia – and Henry would have been made enough aware of the different traditions and customs in each of these territories to avoid ever imagining he could impose some sort of uniformity on them. When he eventually (and reluctantly) delegated power in Normandy, Brittany and Aquitaine to his three oldest sons – Henry, Geoffrey and Richard – he assumed they would, as he had, respect the local customs and conventions of their respective territories, if only from a sense of political prudence. What they were supposed to be governing was not, in any sense, a common empire of language and law but rather a multi-national family firm.

England was, however, undoubtedly the trickiest case to master. At the outset, Henry, who was brought up almost entirely in Anjou, might not have had much of a clue about the peculiarities of its governance. His mother, Matilda, who had botched the job when given the chance, was not an auspicious model. His father, Geoffrey, had spent his crucial years in the dogged conquest of Normandy. Henry spoke only very basic English, and although accompanied by a translator when in England, of the abstruse and esoteric institutions of law and government bequeathed by both the Saxon and Norman monarchies, he could have comprehended very little. What, after all, did Huntingdonshire know of Henry Plantagenet or Henry know of Hunting-donshire? What he would have grasped, however, if only from the coronation oaths handed down from Edgar and Edward the Confessor, was that kings of England were supposed to be judge and warlord, theocrat and potentate. The basic obligations were four: to protect the Church, to preserve the patrimony of your ancestors, to do justice and (most sweepingly) to suppress evil laws and customs. No one would have any reason to fault Henry II on counts two and three. The crop of castles that had sprung up during the civil war was mown down, along with the petty tyrannies entrenched within their walls. The barons were given the opportunity to surrender gracefully or see their walls smashed and the lord branded a traitor. Not for nothing was Henry II known as 'castle-breaker'. Within the British isles, Henry turned out to be a true imperialist, pushing English power, for the first time since the Conquest, across its old borders, across the Irish Sea to Leinster and reducing the king of Scotland into a humiliated vassal.

Henry would prove to be a zealous dispenser of justice. During his reign there was a decisive and irreversible shift away from baronial courts to royal courts. Any freeman might appeal from the lord's local jurisdiction or simply demand that their case be heard before the king's justice. A 'jury' of twelve, begun informally and

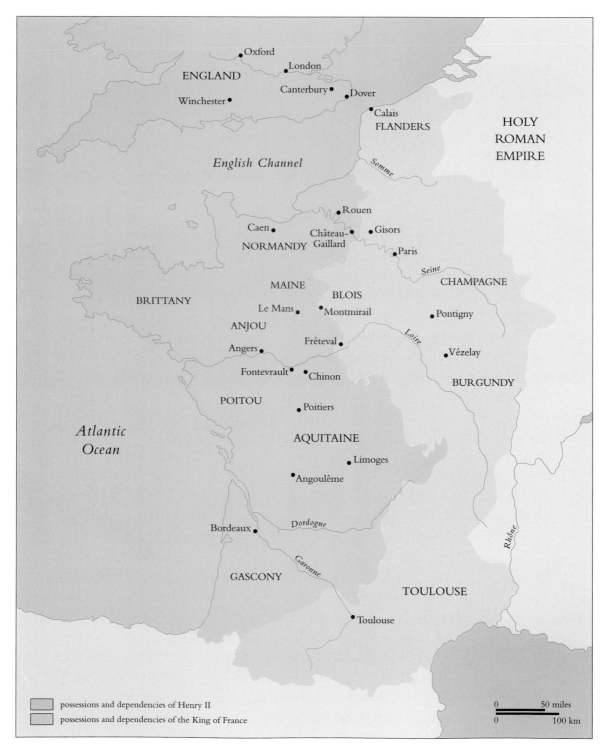

The Angevin Empire in France.

selectively in Aethelred II's reign, now became the norm for trying many such cases, so that justice ceased to be an extension of the unequal social order and was, instead, an obligation of the king's state. That was the principle, at any rate. In reality, of course, the criterion of 'freeman' necessary to have access to this 'common law' excluded the vast number of those peasants – villeins and cottars – who were legally tied to the lord of their manor and subject to the law of his court. Nonetheless, it was still an immeasurable advance on the feudal monopoly of justice common elsewhere in baronial Europe.

It was because Henry II was so determined that his writ should run supreme through England that he failed to avoid a collision with the Church. Deep in the throes of his bitter quarrel with Thomas Becket, Henry would discover, to his dismay, that he had pacified one kind of civil war only to inaugurate another, spiritual conflict, which was every bit as destabilizing. This was particularly ironic since at the beginning of his reign it was the Church that supplied him with the literate and numerate personnel who staffed the Chancellery and who initiated Henry into the complicated mysteries of English government. It was the venerable Archbishop of Canterbury, Theobald, who talent-scouted for the king, pushing his way bright, well-travelled and internationally schooled young men, who were perhaps better suited for work in the world than the cloister. One of his recommended protégés, quickly appointed as chancellor, was Theobald's archdeacon, Thomas Becket. Until he transformed the office, being chancellor was a good deal less important than it sounded. It involved running the spiritual side of the royal household – a combination of personal chaplain and (much more significant) a secretary-general, keeper of the archives and guardian of official knowledge.

Becket was the first Londoner to make a serious mark on English history. The fact that a merchant's son could rapidly become the king's closest adviser said something about the potential of the swarming city itself, its population grown by the mid-twelfth century to around 25,000. At its heart, then as now, was the great church of St Paul's and around it, upriver from the grim pile of the Conqueror's Tower and on both banks of the Thames, were wharves, thick with ships, wool going out, wine and silk coming in. And in the midst of them was the pride of London, the original river café, a public cook-shop and eatery, catering to all pockets, open twenty-four hours day and night: 'coarser meats for the poor, more delicate for the rich such as venison and big and small birds…those who would cater for themselves fastidiously need search no further for the sturgeon, or for the Ionian godwit.' In this noisy, jostling, swilling and swaggering place, Gilbert Becket, Thomas's father, lorded it, not just a merchant but a construction baron, sheriff of the city, owner of one of the biggest houses in Cheapside, with a 40-foot frontage and 110 feet deep. So Thomas was born and raised in flashy confidence. We think of him, with good reason, as an austere man, but the truth is that he was a real Londoner, with an instinctive flair for the things that Londoners have always cared most about: display and costume; the getting and spending of money; theatre, private and public; and (even though his stomach was delicate) fine food and drink. He was street smart and book smart. He was, from the get-go, a Player.

Henry seems to have noticed this right away, for during the six years of his chancellorship, Becket was seldom out of the king's presence. They were a match of opposites: Becket, the older by thirteen years, had the mastery of administrative minutiae that Henry was happy to leave to someone else. The king was packed with edgy energy; the chancellor, taller, his pale face crowned with dark hair, was more studiously self-contained. From his years in the cathedral schools in Paris and Auxerre he seemed to know the Church, doctrinally and (a boon this) economically. His personal seal seemed shockingly pagan: a naked, helmeted figure, perhaps Perseus, slaying a monster. And he could keep pace with the king. Medieval courts were always itinerant, travelling 20 or 30 miles a day, eating in a royal forest or by the roadside. But Henry, who made a fetish of exercise for fear of growing fat like his great-grandfather William, never slowed down, hawking as he rode, barely arriving at one of his favourite places, like Clarendon near Salisbury, or Woodstock near Oxford, before chasing off again. As one of his courtiers, Peter of Blois, wrote:

> If the king has said he will remain in place for a day, he is sure to upset all the arrangements by departing early in the morning. And you see the men dashing around as if they were mad, beating packhorses, running carts into one another, in short giving a lively imitation of Hell…I hardly daresay it but I believe in truth he took delight in seeing what a fix we were in. After wandering some three or four miles in an unknown wood and often in the dark we thought ourselves lucky if we stumbled upon some filthy hovel.

Becket understood Henry's game of studied informality and his aversion to the formal crown-wearings that William the Conqueror had so much enjoyed; his affectation of ordinary riding clothes; his volatile behaviour towards his entourage; the way in which he cultivated friendship, the better to have courtiers eating out of his hand, only to inflict on them frosty withdrawals of affection to be followed by terrifying explosions of full-throttle Norman-Angevin rage. It was Becket's own pseudo-sibling relationship with the king that may have given him the confidence later to take him on as a virtual equal – with catastrophic results for all concerned. Time and again Becket must have told his faltering band of followers, in effect: 'Look, I *know* this man. This is the way he works, trust me.' But even in the glory days of the chancellorship there were telling signs of tension. When the king and Becket rode through London, Henry pointed to the numberless destitute and, eyeing Thomas's scarlet and grey cloak with its edging of miniver, let it be known how charitable it would be to cloak a poor beggar's nakedness. 'Well yes,' responded Becket. 'You should attend to it right away.' An undignified wrestling match on horseback followed, with the chancellor finally allowing the king to pull the cape from his back and give it to the deserving indigent.

But Becket was always more than a sparring partner. More than any other medieval councillor he understood the hypnotic power of spectacle. The Norman kings had achieved authority with brute force. Becket thought he could dazzle his way to allegiance, so he orchestrated jaw-dropping displays of animals, music and armour, shrewdly understanding that against that gaudy backdrop Henry's genuine preference for simplicity would appear even more majestic. So Becket became the royal impresario and was never more in his element than in the embassy to France in 1158, designed to impress Louis VII enough to allow his infant daughter, Margaret, to be betrothed to Henry's little son. What Becket organized was an immense, calculated display of Englishness. There were 250 footmen singing *English* anthems, followed by English bred mastiffs and greyhounds, followed by eight carts with iron-rimmed wheels bearing Real English Ale, each pulled by teams of five horses. Each of the horses had a groom and a monkey (not English, but dressed in English livery) riding on its back. And then there were twenty-eight packhorses, the gold and silver plate, the squires and falconers and, finally, Becket himself with a few friends, bringing up the rear with studied casualness. The best compliment paid to this strategy of numbing ostentation was Louis VII's desperate attempt to deprive the train from being supplied from French villages, hoping it would arrive in Paris famished and bedraggled, a tactic pre-empted by Becket, who had bought up everything on the route well in advance.

When Archbishop Theobald died in 1161 Becket must have seemed the perfect replacement: savvy in the ways of the world, yet learned in the ways of the Church. For Henry needed someone who would put the Church in its place. This was never meant to be a lowly posture, grovelling and servile at the feet of the glamorous warrior-king, but a place, nonetheless, firmly *within* what Henry kept referring to as 'the laws and customs of the realm' as he imagined they had been at the death of his grandfather, Henry I. This was not just a matter of dynastic nostalgia. It was the fact that the authority of twelfth-century temporal rulers, especially in the crucial matter of appointing bishops, had, of late, been infringed by the pretensions of the papal Church. Kings took it as axiomatic that they were the directly anointed of God, so when Henry II restored the remains of Edward the Confessor to Westminster, carrying the coffin on his own shoulders, he was as good as saying: 'Behold a king – both saint and monarch. And I, by the way, am his true successor.'

But this idea of the sacred autonomy of kings had never been accepted by the papacy. They held the keys to salvation and the supreme power over Christendom. They crowned the Holy Roman Emperor and allowed archbishops to crown kings as a recognition that these temporal rulers were the servants, not the masters, of the Church, and that their authority was upheld on condition that they understood the Church's independence. In the eyes of the Church, then, royal sovereignty stopped at the cathedral porch. In the eyes of the Angevin king, sovereignty was absolute within his realm. So from time to time, this fundamental difference of conviction, a medieval cold war, was bound to warm up.

In England there were two flashpoints: first, whether bishops had the authority to excommunicate royal officials or nobles without first consulting the king; second, whether the clergy could be judged by the king's courts and whether, if so judged, they could appeal to Rome. Both of these issues boiled down to one critical matter, which cut to the heart of sovereignty. Was the Church an institution of the realm or was it, by virtue of its ministry, separate from it? For Henry II the answer was straightforward. Just as the long years of civil strife had given local barons the occasion to usurp or ignore the king's law, so too the Church had taken advantage of a power vacuum to assert a greater degree of immunity from royal law than had been the case under the earlier Normans or, indeed, the Saxon kings. Under his Norman ancestors, Henry learned, bishops had been required to swear homage to the Crown prior to, and as a condition of, their investiture. That was the old way and, he supposed, the right way.

By making Becket Archbishop of Canterbury (over much muttering of disapproval among the clergy) Henry evidently believed that he would be able to depend on someone who would share his view of the subordinate relationship of Church to state. But a story was told of Becket's own premonition of what might actually happen. Recovering from sickness in France, he was playing chess when an old friend informed him that he was being spoken of as the next Primate. After some jokey banter Becket turned serious, saying that he knew of three poor priests he would rather see elevated: 'for if it should come about that I am promoted I know the king too well, indeed inside out, [not to] realize that I would either have to lose his favour or, God forbid, neglect my duty to the Almighty.'

Becket before Henry II; stained-glass window in the Trinity Chapel, Canterbury Cathedral.

Outwardly, it seemed as if little had changed. The archbishop's table was as heavily laden with fine food as the chancellor's had been, and he surrounded himself as always with the bright young cosmopolitan scholars of the Church – the *eruditi*. At dinner there would be a reading and, afterwards, witty debate on the text. But all was not what it appeared. Becket ate none of the feast and beneath his grand garments he may have already begun to wear the hair shirt and monk's habit that were found on his murdered body eight years later.

Once Becket began to oppose, in public, the king's demands for a new tax, which was to be levied on barons and clergy alike, Henry saw with stunned disbelief that a mysterious transformation had taken place in his friend. That Becket had been (as he often reminded him) raised from the ranks of commoners by his special favour and now was repaying him with presumptuous opposition only added to his rage. The king found it especially difficult to understand Becket's objections to his treating clerical malefactors like any other criminals. In royal courts rapists, thieves and murderers would have been executed or mutilated; in Church courts they were evicted from office or subject to a penance. The inequity of sentence struck Henry as a slight on his sovereignty and a fundamental violation of the premise of a common law: that all free subjects should be treated alike. To Becket, though, the efforts of royal prosecutors to re-open cases already judged in Church courts was the beginning of the end of the independence of the clergy and a failure to recognize that their ministry was not just another profession but a truly separate estate, ordained by God and accountable only to the successor of St Peter. In a series of cases Becket went out of his way to re-assert that autonomy, ruling in one case that priests should never face the death penalty.

The dispute came to a head at Henry's hunting lodge at Clarendon near Salisbury. In January 1164 Henry summoned all the principal barons and earls, bishops and archbishops to an extraordinary royal council at which he demanded unconditional assent to what he called 'the customs of the realm' as they had been observed in the time of his grandfather, Henry I. Becket knew that this meant a formal affirmation that the clergy was, indeed, subject to royal jurisdiction. He had seen it coming and for months had been urging resistance. While he was getting an abusive roasting from the likes of the Earl of Leicester, his fellow clergy must have assumed that he would stay true to his word. Instead, and without warning, Becket caved in, leaving Gilbert Foliot, the learned Bishop of London, to complain, with understandable bitterness, that 'only the leader fled the field'. But Becket then compounded his inconsistency by reverting to his original opposition. At Clarendon he had ordered general submission to the 'Constitutions' of the king, but he changed his mind days later when he looked at the details: the excommunication of royal officials was to be conditional on the king's consent; the Crown was to control all communications between the English clergy and Rome; clerics who had been convicted in Church courts were to be re-arrested and re-tried in royal courts. Becket, finally, ordered all-out resistance. This didn't mean that abbots donned chain-mail (although they certainly had it to wear if need be). The Church's greatest weapon in these wars of the will was the threat of excommunication, a shut-down of spiritual services. There would be no more baptisms, weddings or deathbed absolutions; the 'no Plantagenets or English need bother to apply' sign would be posted at the gates of paradise.

For the moment, however, it was the state that could bring more obvious force to bear on the argument. When Becket tried to see the king at Woodstock, the doors were slammed in his face. Fearing the worst, he attempted to leave the country but was recognized by the sailors, who returned him to the shore and the king's tender mercies. 'Why do you want to leave?' asked Henry. 'Don't you think the country is big enough to hold both of us?' The king knew he had the upper hand. By attempting to flee without royal permission, Becket had already fallen foul of the law, but Henry brought him to trial at Northampton in October 1164 on two other charges: failing to answer a summons in a dispute over archiepiscopal lands and accusations of improper use of funds when he had been chancellor. The charges were deadly serious. If he were found guilty, the punishment would be the confiscation of all Becket's personal and movable property. The bishops were in an even more frightening predicament. If they went against Becket they risked excommunication. But many of them, like Foliot, had never liked him in the first place and had not believed that he was the right choice for Canterbury. Why should they have to pay for his extravagance as chancellor or his erratic behaviour at Clarendon? So when Becket was seen on his way to court, dressed up in full archiepiscopal rig as the defender of the Church, carrying the great silver cross of Canterbury himself rather than have it borne by a cross-bearer, Foliot was incensed by the play-acting and tried, in vain, to seize it from him. Episcopal grappling ensued. 'A fool he always was, and a fool he'll always be,' was the bishop's judgement on the histrionic tomfoolery.

By the time Becket got to Northampton another very serious accusation had been added to the charges against him. In violation of the promises made at Clarendon he had attempted to appeal to the pope over the head of the king. This opened him to charges of treason, and at the trial Henry's barons hardly minced their words, shouting 'perjurer' and 'traitor' at him, while Becket, for his part, gave as good as he got, replying 'whoremonger' and 'bastard' at the particular lords for whom the labels were most apt. Convicted on the charges, he was now in dire peril. But one of his most loyal followers, Herbert of Bosham, found a key to a normally locked gate. With no time to saddle two horses, Becket swung Herbert up on the saddle behind him and the two galloped away from captivity. For days they led the life of fugitives, changing disguises, sleeping behind altars in friendly churches, finally reaching the Channel. In November 1164 Becket and a small group of die-hard followers landed on the coast of Flanders; they were demoralized, penniless, exhausted and frightened at what they had done.

They ended up at the Cistercian abbey of Pontigny, about 100 miles southeast of Paris. The undecorated white limestone of the church was a conscious choice to emphasize the austerity of the order, and it was a perfect place for Becket's single-mindedness to harden, untroubled by the outside world's need for compromise. His mind-set is vividly illustrated by the Bible that he commissioned at this time and that includes a self-portrait set immediately below the figure of the enthroned Christ. He had Pope Alexander III send him a specially designed monk's habit, and beneath it he wore a shirt of goat's hair for maximum discomfort. Becket naturally assumed he would receive unequivocal support from Alexander, who was, after all, in much the same position as himself, having been evicted from Rome and forced into a French exile by a ferocious secular ruler, the Emperor Frederick Barbarossa, who had appointed a more malleable antipope to the see of Rome. The snag was that in order to survive, Alexander was dependent on the goodwill and money of the kings of France – and England! So when a delegation of bishops (including Gilbert Foliot) came to see Alexander in Sens to put Henry's case, he greeted them with calculated ambiguity: 'I am happy [to hear] the king is so good. May God make him even better.' And when Becket's party denounced the Constitutions of Clarendon, he did no more than agree that they were indeed very shocking and very wicked.

Forced back on his own devices, Becket established at Pontigny what was, in effect, a government in exile, complete with his own pan-European spy network, his own letter-smugglers, who knew how to get through Henry's blockade, and his own tireless department of propaganda. He was sustained, always, by his unwavering sense of righteousness. What better place than a Cistercian abbey, devoted to re-asserting the *difference* between the religious and the secular life, for Becket to reiterate his own impassioned belief that the English Church ought never to be a mere appendage of the Angevin state.

In England Henry peeled back the velvet glove from the mailed fist. Anyone who was reported as saying a good word for Becket risked, at the very least, banish-ment. Innocent relatives – nieces and nephews – were incriminated by family associ-ation and turned into exiles. Becket's property was seized and handed over to the

Top: Becket consecrated as Archbishop in Canterbury Cathedral; from the
fourteenth-century Queen Mary's Psalter.
Above: Becket pronounces the sentence of excommunication on his enemies
and argues his case before the king; from the Becket Leaves, *c.* 1220–40.

knight Ranulf de Broc as 'steward'. This was a licence for de Broc to do what he wanted with the archbishop's estates: his forests, his deer, his cellars and his rents. And by no means all the English clergy rallied to Becket's support. The Bishops of London and York – Gilbert Foliot and Roger of Pont l'Évêque – remained bitter enemies, believing that Becket's own vanity and egomania had needlessly destroyed a reasonable and pragmatic working relationship with the monarchy and had actually made it harder, not easier, to secure the proper liberties of the Church. To a solemn reproof from Becket, Foliot retorted witheringly that, in fleeing like a thief in the night from the consequences of his own erratic confrontations with the king, the archbishop had abandoned the ordinary clergy whom he purported to defend.

But in the cloisters of Pontigny Becket listened only to his own adamant convictions. Tired of the temporizing pope, on Whit Sunday 1166, after celebrating mass at the abbey of Vézelay, to general shock, not least the abbot's, Becket 'unsheathed the sword of the Church' against those he named as its enemies, pronouncing anathema and excommunication on those who, like Ranulf de Broc, had created 'tyranny', perpetrated 'heresy' and had made off with the property of the Church. Henry II was conspicuously omitted from the list of the damned, but if by so doing Becket supposed he was leaving an opening for a rapprochement with the king, the sentences at Vézelay had the opposite effect. Henry now counter-threatened that all Cistercians would be expelled from his lands unless they evicted the treacherous archbishop forthwith. Tearfully, the abbot of Pontigny complied. In November 1166, discharging his followers, Becket settled into a Benedictine abbey at St-Colombe. Just before he moved, he dreamed that he was being murdered by a company of four knights.

Shaken by Becket's independence and worried by its implications for his own relationship with Henry II, Pope Alexander was now stirred to action. Henry, he knew, had one crucial incentive for reconciliation. Obsessed by anxieties about the succession, the king had decided to take a leaf from Charlemagne's ceremonial book and have his eldest son, Henry the Younger, crowned king of England at Westminster during his own lifetime. The premature coronation carried no implication of the senior king's abdication. Rather, it was a pre-emptive device against disaffection and a way to bind all the nobles who would swear homage to the designated successor. But precisely because it was such an alien innovation, Henry needed the Archbishop of Canterbury to do the honours if the ritual was to have any semblance of legitimacy. For two years specially appointed papal legates shuffled back and forth between Henry's travelling court and Becket. It was not rewarding work. Becket refused point-blank to concede that Henry was entitled to attempt to restore the customs of his grandfather's time; Henry refused to abandon the Constitutions of Clarendon.

Rebuffed on principles, the legatine diplomacy fell back on pragmatism. Neither side would be asked to abandon their convictions, only to be less intemperate about their expression. That way, Becket would restore peace to the realm, end his exile and have his property returned, and Henry would get his coronation.

In January 1169, in a wintry meadow at Montmirail, on the border between the kingdom of France and the Angevin lands, on the day after the feast of Epiphany – the feast of the kings – Henry and Becket met. The two former bosom companions turned deadly enemies had not seen each other for four years, since the archbishop's traumatic arraignment at Northampton. Henry was now thirty-six, more manically energetic, acutely intelligent and explosively temperamental than ever. Becket was forty-eight, middle-aged by the standards of the Middle Ages. His beard was grey and his face lined, set in the flinty manner of the apostle of truth and justice he believed he was. The encounter had been scrupulously prepared. Becket had agreed not to say anything to upset the king, although as he approached the field where King Louis of France and Henry were astride their horses, conferring, Becket's most die-hard follower, Herbert of Bosham, tugged his sleeve and urged fortitude, not reconciliation on him. Becket seemed, at first, to stick to the agreed script, falling to his knees before Henry, who raised him from the ground. The archbishop then announced: 'I now submit the whole case between us to your clemency and judgement.' But the general relief turned to horror when, after a meaningful pause, Becket added the words: 'saving the honour of God.' This meant, in effect, that Becket was 'reserving my position on any matters concerning the Church'! It was Clarendon all over again: concession followed by contradiction. Louis VII and Henry were appalled and then livid, and Henry reverted to his own hard line, demanding assent to the 'customs of the realm'. Becket duly refused. As dusk closed in and the crows gathered on the field, the archbishop was left alone with his righteousness.

If anything, after Montmirail Becket became more militant, passing sentences of excommunication on the Archbishop of York and the Bishop of London. He was convinced that, with the king reportedly still desperate to have his son crowned before he himself died (for no man knew when that might be), time was ultimately on his side. And sure enough, his toughness seemed to be paying off. Reports came back that Henry would agree to restore Becket's title and property and drop the charges of chancellery corruption. Emboldened, Becket asked, finally, for the kiss of peace. Such medieval kisses were not given lightly, as airy cheek pecks. They were oaths of good faith. Your kiss was your bond. Asking for it implied unworthy suspicions. Henry balked. It was a kiss too many.

So when the two met again on 22 July 1170, in another grassy meadow, this

Scenes from the Becket Leaves: (top) Becket departing after his
disastrous meeting with the king at Montmirail; (above) Becket arriving at
Sandwich, while Ranulf de Broc and his henchmen wait on the shore.
Left: The Cistercian abbey church at Pontigny where Becket spent the first
two years of his exile.

time on the east bank of the Loire, near the village of Fréteval, there was, inevitably, a certain air of wariness along with the expectation that, this time, at last, an accord could be reached. Herbert of Bosham thought the site auspiciously beautiful; only later did he discover that it was known locally as 'Traitor's Field'. Henry and Thomas rode out to each other. The king removed his hat in greeting. The two men embraced and then sat for hours talking, the archbishop's irritation with Henry increased by the chafing of his goat's hair underwear. He had discovered that, tired of waiting, the king had gone ahead without him and in June 1170 had had his son crowned by the Archbishop of York (still under Becket's anathema). For once, however, Henry bridled his own anger, and he agreed to Becket's conditions and to treat his enemies as the king's. When all the talking was done and Thomas appeared to have everything he wanted, a dam broke. A flood of tearful emotion swept through Becket, who dismounted and flung himself at the feet of the king's horse. Henry, in turn, got off his own mount, walked to his old friend, took hold of him bodily, set one foot in the stirrups and hoisted him back into the saddle. He then rode Becket over to the royal tent, at the end of the field by the water, and announced that they were reconciled and that henceforth he would be a most kind and generous lord.

It seemed that nothing could now break the restoration of goodwill. But Becket found a way. When Henry, wanting to hold the moment in the palm of his hand for just a little longer, asked his old friend to ride further with him Becket declined, saying he needed to thank all those who had supported his cause in France. Then, when the king had pardoned Becket's loyalists, including Herbert of Bosham, he asked Becket to reciprocate with a pardon for his own royal officers and was ungraciously refused. 'It's not the same,' retorted the archbishop. This did not bode well. 'If he chooses to love me,' said one of the unpardoned knights, Geoffrey Ridel, 'I'll love him back. If he hates me, I'll hate him.' The sour aftertaste of Fréteval was not lost on Becket. He wrote pessimistically to the pope that he was returning to England, although whether to peace or punishment he could not surely say.

The last meeting between Thomas and Henry took place at Chaumont-sur-Loire, where Henry let off a little steam (though without ever blowing a gasket) at Becket's impolitic lack of magnanimity. 'Why don't you [ever] do what I want?' one chronicler records him as complaining. 'For if you did, I would entrust everything to you.' No response ensued. One imagines a sigh. 'Well, go in peace,' said the king. 'I will follow you as soon as I can and we will meet either in Rouen or England.' To which Thomas replied: 'Something tells me, my lord, as I leave you on these terms that I shall never see you again in this life.' 'Do you take me for a traitor then?' said Henry. 'Heaven forbid,' answered Becket.

The archbishop did not have to wait long for his forebodings to be realized. When his ship, bearing the archiepiscopal cross, came into the harbour at Sandwich in Kent in the first week of December 1170 a great throng prostrated themselves in front of Becket. But as soon as he stood, for the first time in six years on English soil, Becket was confronted, as if he were a criminal, by three royal officials, in full coats of mail and conspicuously armed. One of them was Ranulf de Broc, the 'steward' of Becket's seized estates. The sheriff of Kent, Gervase of Cornhill, roundly denounced the archbishop for coming not to make peace but to start a fire in the kingdom, to uncrown the young Henry and to punish the bishops and barons who had stood by their sovereign. It must have been immediately clear to Becket that he faced a coalition of all those who now felt threatened by his return. His response was not to reassure them. Those who had been excommunicated could, he said, be pardoned only by the pope. While technically true, this was disingenuous. It had been Becket who had decided on the sentences, and everyone knew that if he so recommended, the pope would be only to eager to revoke them

But Becket did not so choose. There was already something ominously mystical about his manner. When Canterbury came into sight, he got off his horse, took off his boots and walked barefoot the rest of the way through anthem-singing crowds of ecstatic devotees. Much of December was spent attempting to get the terms of the Fréteval agreement duly executed, but when he tried to get de Broc to restore Saltwood Castle, what he got instead was an archiepiscopal packhorse with its tail chopped off, sent bleeding back to Canterbury. The English clergy acted with similar coldness and trepidation. Henry the Younger refused to see Becket, and reports went to Henry II in which the archbishop was described as being consumed by a desire for retribution, as being impatient to de-throne the young Henry and as parading about England with a private army. The truth was that, after the frightening encounter at Sandwich, Becket had a small armed entourage – no more than five – to protect him. But it was also true that he was deaf to appeals to be reconciled with the royalist bishops. On Christmas Day 1170 he did exactly what he had said he would do: he hurled the candles to the stone floor of Canterbury Cathedral and shouted the dread anathema against Foliot and Roger of Pont l'Évêque for their part in crowning the young Henry: 'May they be damned by Jesus Christ.'

But the bishops were not in hell. They were at Henry II's court near Bayeux, delivering venomous reports into Henry's ears about Becket's incorrigibly treasonous arrogance. On the same day that Becket pronounced the anathema, Henry raised his reddened neck from the pillow of his sickbed and let out a roar of rage, the kind of sound that had knights turning to water inside their chain mail. It was not 'will no one rid me of this turbulent priest?' but the much more alarming outcry: 'What miserable drones and traitors have I nourished and brought up in my household who allow their lord to be treated with such shameful contempt by a low-born cleric!' To anyone present, the king's outburst could mean only one thing: that he wanted the interminable, insufferable Becket problem to go away. Not necessarily as in six feet under. But if that's what it took, so be it.

The four knights who would kill Becket had no doubt about Henry's meaning, and they rushed to the Normandy coast to take ship for Kent. But even had they not done so, Becket was now in grave peril, for Henry had mobilized an official mission to order the archbishop to desist from recrimination or suffer the consequences.

At Saltwood Castle (where Ranulf de Broc was still enjoying Becket's venison) de Broc met with the four knights on 28 December. As much as they despised the low-born, jumped-up Becket, their idea was to arrest, not kill him. But they planned the raid on Canterbury as if it were a small-scale military assault. At dawn the next day, 29 December 1170, Reginald fitzUrse, William de Tracy, Richard le Bret and Hugh de Morville, all of whom had drunk heavily the previous night and may still have been fortifying their resolution, gathered a platoon of twelve more knights and set off for Canterbury. At three they burst into the archbishop's palace, where they found Thomas with his advisers after dinner. When he studiously ignored the interruption, fitzUrse announced he had an important message from the king: that Becket should go forthwith to Winchester to young Henry and give an account of his conduct. Becket replied that he had no intention of being treated like a criminal. The exchanges got ugly, quickly. FitzUrse declared that Becket was no longer under the king's peace and arrested two of the archbishop's own knights.

At this point Becket might still have temporized, if only to buy time, but he told his follower, John of Salisbury: 'My mind is made up. I know exactly what I have to do.' 'Please God,' responded John, obviously unconvinced, 'you have chosen well.' Instead of escaping to fight another day, as he had at Northampton in 1166, Becket proceeded calmly to the cathedral for vespers, his cross carried before him. Instead of bolting the door, he made sure to open it to receive the congregation. If he was to die, it would be in the sight of his flock. But before they could enter the church in any numbers, the knights caught up with Becket in the north transept. Becket must have known what they intended since they had now dressed themselves in the standard gear of terrorism: their heads and most of their faces were covered. Naked swords glimmered in the candlelight, and there were axes to smash in resisting doors. They were shouting, 'Where is the traitor?' 'Here I am,' said Becket. 'No traitor but a priest of God. What do you want?'

He was defenceless. All but two of his attendants had disappeared into the shadows of the church. Even now Reginald fitzUrse still thought he could apprehend Becket and attempted to strong-arm him on to William de Tracy's back and carry him off. But the fifty-two-year-old Becket was a cockney, a street-fighter and as tough as old boots under the cowl, and when he stood his ground, he became physically, as well as theologically, immovable. In extremis, his Cheapside lingo came back. 'PIMP, PIMP,' he yelled at fitzUrse, who must suddenly have felt impotent, ridiculous. A sense of ridicule is itself dangerous; a burst adrenaline-pump. Down went a sword, cutting the arm of Edward Grim, Becket's attendant, and then slicing through the top of the archbishop's head. The crown hung by a thread of flesh as Becket sank to the floor, murmuring rather lengthily (according to his hagiographers): 'For the name of Jesus and the protection of the Church, I am ready to embrace death.' The *coup de grâce* followed. Another slash severed the head completely, striking so hard that the blade broke in two on the stones. To finish the job, a third warrior stood on the severed neck, stuck the point of his sword into the open cavity of his skull, scooped out the brains and spread them about the floor. 'Let's be off, knights,' he shouted. 'This fellow won't be up again.'

It was around four thirty in the afternoon. The cathedral door was still open. Frightened people who had come for vespers now emerged from the darkness, some of them gathering about the body. But it was not a flock that unanimously regarded what they saw as a martyrdom. The chroniclers even describe some of the aspersions that were voiced: 'He wanted to be a king; so let him be one.' But then it all changed. Becket's chamberlain tenderly reattached the bloody crown to his head using a strip of material torn from his own shirt. The monks and priests began to prepare the body for burial – the departing knights had ordered them to do this unless they wanted the corpse thrown on a dunghill – and as they went about their business they discovered what no one had, until that moment, known: the hair shirt close to Thomas's body, with the lice moving busily through the fibres. Becket the entertainer had been Becket the self-mortifier; Becket the proud had also been Becket the humble.

He was allowed to lie, washed in his own blood. Over the bespattered body were laid the archiepiscopal garments. By chance, in the crypt, a tomb had been prepared for another person's burial and was waiting. Down into its receiving coldness went Becket, arrayed in the full rig: the dalmatic and the pallium, the cope and the chasuble, the orb and the ring. He had always thought that kit mattered, had Thomas Becket.

And for what, exactly, had he laid down or thrown away his life: a fantastic notion, already outdated by the time he became archbishop, that the Church could, in the last resort, lay down the law to the state; that kings were no better than the obedient sword-bearers for Christ? All our modern instincts assume the futility of that insistence. Henry's world and his work is intelligible to us – the smasher of anarchy and the guardian of the common law – while Becket seems to be off in some theocratic fairyland, which was not even plausible to the pope. But this is to sell the archbishop short. For the infuriating, theatrical, arrogant Becket did make a huge difference. His view of the proper relationship between Church and state lasted. The omni-competent sovereignty of the Angevin empire did not. Until the Reformation, three centuries later, there were Church courts and the clergy could appeal to Rome against a royal verdict. While the secular power could do little to interfere with the spiritual, the great prelates of the Church – rich, powerful and literate – continued to be indispensable to effective royal government. To an extra-ordinary extent Plantagenet England would be run by administrator-prelates like Hubert Walter, justiciar, papal legate and Archbishop of Canterbury from 1193, and Stephen Langton, who was the Archbishop of Canterbury imposed on Henry's youngest son, John, and virtually the architect of the Magna Carta. These were the kind of men – politically shrewd, intellectually subtle and administratively tireless – for whom Becket might have been a perfect prototype had he not become consumed with a vision of himself as a latter-day St Paul: the uncompromising prosecutor of the unrighteous.

In the days, weeks and months after the murder, power rather than piety seemed to get the upper hand. The assassins made for Yorkshire, where they lived untouched for a year. Eventually excommunicated, they were sentenced to take the Cross, and some of them died *en route* to the Holy Land. But Becket's most violent enemies sur-vived and prospered. The de Brocs became lords of a Suffolk estate; Gilbert Foliot, Bishop of London, and Roger of Pont l'Évêque, Archbishop of York, were absolved of blame and took part in Becket's canonization and the care of his shrine! As for the king, aware that he was denounced throughout France, he was reported to be so pros-trate with grief and horror that fears were expressed for his sanity. In 1172 the pope ordered him to take the Cross for three years as penance. He never went. But in 1174, in the midst of a terrible war launched against him by his own son Henry the Younger and his now-estranged wife, Eleanor, the king may have felt in special need of atonement. He made a pilgrimage to Canterbury, by this time the site of innu-merable miracles at Becket's shrine. 'Canterbury water', made rosy with droplets of Becket's blood, was said to cure the blind and the crippled. Over the last miles Henry walked barefoot in a hair shirt (as Thomas had done four years earlier). At the tomb he fell on his face, confessed his sins and was given five lashes by each of the attend-ing bishops. The king lay all night on the bare ground, fasting and surrounded by throngs of ordinary pilgrims. When he left Canterbury the next day, scourged and purged, he heard that one of his most powerful enemies, King William the Lion of Scotland, had been defeated and taken prisoner. Perhaps Canterbury water had worked its miracles for the king.

In November 1176 an emissary from the Byzantine emperor, Manuel Comnenus, arrived in England to see the man called 'the greatest and most illustrious ruler of the world'. A glance at the map of Angevin power, which now extended beyond even the lands Henry had inherited on his accession, into the kingdoms of Scotland, Ireland and Wales, seemed to suggest this was not an exaggeration. But appearances can be misleading. Henry's 'empire' was not a unitary state in anything like the sense that would have been understood in Constantinople. It was a shaky federation of Norman- and French-dominated colonies, the presumptive ruler of each of which, even when he had knelt in homage to Henry as his overlord and sovereign, would still be suspected, with good reason, of unreliable loyalty. The Byzantine traveller, riding from one region to another, would not have noticed very much difference. The country, from Yorkshire to the Loire, would have been dotted with grand Cistercian abbeys, under the patronage of the king or an earl. There were parish churches subject to the central control of a bishop rather than a local patron; river valleys were dominated by steeply walled castles, built increasingly of stone and mortar rather than of timber and earth. Royally chartered towns and burghs, with quarters settled by immigrant merchants and moneylenders, Flemings and Jews, were under Crown or aristocratic protection so that the licenser could enjoy the proceeds from commercial tolls. Comnenus's emissary might also have encountered the travelling retinue of a new species of grandee – the royal official, more often than not a cleric, but with a whole cartload of scribes and clerks, carrying the king's sealed writ and accountable to one of the great men of the court: the chief royal law officer, the justiciar or the keeper of the exchequer. At one of the larger shire towns – Lincoln or York – he may even have witnessed one of the monthly sessions of the travelling general 'eyre' court, in which royal judges heard cases brought to them by any freeman said to have access to the 'common law'. And if he were mystified by this, he could have been shown a new book, possibly edited by Ranulph Glanvill, Henry's justiciar (or chief legal officer), which anthologized the body of legal conventions and customs to which freemen who judged their rights to have been violated might have recourse in the king's courts. The cases so heard might even be judged not by a single royally appointed arbiter but by a panel of twelve. It was not, the traveller might have gathered, even unheard of, in such disputes, for royal officers themselves to be brought to book by such means!

The earliest version of Becket's martyrdom from a Latin psalter, *c.* 1200.

The burial of Becket from a Latin psalter, *c.* 1200.

The Byzantine would have noticed, however, that this law, deemed 'common', was not for everyone. The vast mass of toiling villeins, bound to their land and lord, were deprived of it and were, instead, still subject to the local law of the manor. Knights and barons, descendants of the Norman colonists, could still summon an antagonist to trial by arms. And in vast tracts of the country – some genuine woodland, some much more open and populated areas of the shires – had been declared 'royal forest', where there was another entire system of law and penalties in operation, with especially brutal sentences of mutilation and death intended to prevent the local population from touching the king's game, working the woods or pasturing their animals, as their ancestors had done, time out of mind.

As he approached the far reaches of the Plantagenet lands, the traveller would have noticed that the writ of the king gave way to other, more local powers. At the northern margin of England, the barons of the north had been able to exploit Anglo-Scots rivalry to entrench their own autonomy from either state. For twenty years the Scottish kings played a tug-of-war game with the Angevins over their claim to Cumbria, Northumbria, Westmorland and even part of Lancashire. When they could exploit an embarrassment or weakness in England, they extracted concessions or launched military raids. But in 1157, although he himself had promised David I on his being knighted that he would uphold the Scots claim to the north, Henry II took it all back and made King Malcolm IV swallow the retrocession. In 1173, in yet another effort to reverse this, the young Scottish king, William I (later called the Lion), made the mistake of joining the side of the Angevin sons in their war against their father. When William was captured at Alnwick in 1174, Henry made sure that he arranged an elaborate humiliation. William was paraded as a captive, feet tied below his horse, incarcerated at William the Conqueror's native castle of Falaise and released only on condition of his doing unequivocal formal homage to Henry, both for his Scottish kingdom 'and any lands elsewhere'. The treaty was later abrogated in 1189 by Henry's son and successor, Richard I, but from it derived the perennial claims of the Plantagenets that they were indeed the feudal suzerains of the Scots, an assertion that would be made with much blood and misery for all concerned.

In one of the more unnoticed ironies of Angevin-British history, the Angevin colonization of Ireland began as an answer to the *Welsh* problem. The difficult topography (especially the lack of anything like north–south roads) had meant that Wales remained divided in Henry's time, much as it had been in William the Conqueror's. With the border country occupied by opportunist Marcher barons, 'Englishry' was established in forbidding castles at Chepstow, Brecon and Monmouth, and the barons held the frontier as well as much of south Wales, all the way to the coast at Swansea and Gower. In return for keeping their territories free of native Welsh control, the Marcher lords were legally considered to be masters of their own lordships, unbound by royal or common law. Further west and north, *pura Wallia*, 'Welshry', was divided into three kingdoms: Gwynedd in the mountainous north, Powys in the centre and Deheubarth in the south. Every generation or so a powerful king – in Henry's time it was Rhys ap Gruffydd – tried to unite two or more of these kingdoms and expand into the Marches. In response to one such alarm in 1165, Henry sent a massive army of knights into Wales. But Wales (as Harold Godwineson had learned a century before) was no country for mounted knights, and the army became bogged down in rain and mud. The ignominious failure of coercion cut off the Marcher lords from Angevin help and made Rhys ap Gruffydd confident enough to dictate terms to some of the most powerful of the Anglo-Norman lords of the Marches. Instead of remaining an anomaly in Wales, it was suggested, why did they not respond to appeals from the king of Leinster in Dublin, Diarmait MacMurchada (Dermot MacMurrough), for help against his own Irish rebels. Diarmait had already asked Henry II for assistance, so the extrication of the Marcher lords from Wales and their transplantation into Ireland as auxiliaries of King Diarmait seemed a neat solution for all concerned. On paper, at least, the Anglo-Normans did not come to Ireland as imperialists but as mercenaries. Needless to say, matters did not quite work out as planned.

In 1169 a small company of knights landed at Bannow Bay near Waterford. They were followed a year later by a much more formidable group, which was led by the Earl of Pembroke, Richard de Clare, known as 'Strongbow'. The subtlety of de Clare's general approach to Irish politics can be gauged from the way in which he ordered seventy citizens of Waterford to be thrown into the sea after their legs had been broken. Terror worked. In short order, Strongbow and his knights had recovered Leinster, at which point, in 1171, Diarmait conveniently died, leaving Strongbow, who had married Diarmait's daughter Aoife, as his successor. It was now that Henry II woke up to the fact that what had begun as an expedition of assistance to an Irish ruler had turned into the creation of a virtually autonomous Norman colony. He took decisive action, crossing to Ireland itself where, in the wattle palace at Dublin, he received the homage of most of the native Irish kings as well as of the Norman knights. Henry's policy (like that of countless generations who crossed the Irish Sea after him) was intended as damage containment, and he was unquestionably seen by the indigenous Irish nobility as an arbitrating overlord, not a conqueror. But the consequences of the Anglo-Norman presence in eastern Ireland were anything but limited. Temporarily stopped in their tracks, the Norman colonists still managed to push west, deep into Gaelic Ireland, halted only by the most powerful of the resisting Irish kings, Ruaidri Ua Conchobair (Rory O'Connor). But in a generation or two, within their new 'pale of settlement' (the area of English rule), they created a feudal Ireland, complete with castles, manors, walled towns, monasteries and a French-speaking knightly caste, utterly unlike the cattle-droving, kinship-based clans of the indigenous Gaels. Ancient kingdoms were treated like Midhe, which was granted to Hugh de Lacy and transformed into the 'Liberty' of Meath – 'liberty' meaning something like its precise opposite, a holding granted by the king conditional on the acceptance of his overlordship.

An expanded realm was, in fact, the last thing Henry II needed. By the third decade of his reign, no matter how hard and how far he rode, it was apparent to the king that it was increasingly difficult to keep his over-extended territories as a coherent dynastic estate, much less any kind of unified polity. There was a bitter irony that his endless travels and travails had all been on behalf of the Angevin family firm; but it was precisely from within the family that the most serious threats arose. He and Eleanor had had eight children, four of whom were sons, which was an astonishing asset in a time when male heirs were notoriously hard to bring to maturity. But a mural at Winchester Palace of an eagle viciously attacked by its own young (another of Becket's ominous dreams) better summed up the relationship between the king and his brood. For that hostility Henry was, himself, at least partly to blame. Suspicious of their ability and their integrity, he delegated power to them only grudgingly, and then, quite as often and abruptly, withdrew it again, leaving them to smoulder with humiliation. The eldest son, Henry, 'the flower of chivalry', was much doted on by his father, but just as the king fretted over his son's vanity and addiction to idleness and gaming, he compounded the problem rather than solved it, by ostentatiously keeping him from access to power or the purse. The coronation in June 1170 only increased young Henry's sense of the emptiness of his dignities as 'king' of England and Duke of Normandy and drove him into rebellion. Crushingly defeated in the rebellion against his father, he was, astonishingly, pardoned by Henry II and given more responsibilities, but he died of dysentery in 1183. The second son, Geoffrey, as bright and as devious as his grandfather, Geoffrey of Anjou, was given charge of Brittany but was trampled to death by a horse in one of the tournaments his father so despised as foolishness. This moved the third and fourth sons, Richard and John, up the waiting list, where their impatience was encouraged by the one member of the Angevin household who was evidently most eager to see Henry II's power and pretensions receive their comeuppance: his long-estranged, long-suffering wife, Eleanor.

Matthew Paris's map of Britain, c.1250, with Hadrian's Wall and the Antonine Wall clearly visible. 'Scocia' is shown as virtually an island north of the Firth of Forth.

Early in the reign, it had looked as if Eleanor would, indeed, be the consort for which she was so richly qualified. When Henry travelled to Normandy or Anjou, she often acted as regent in his absence. Her own court attracted troubadour poets and musicians, the cult of love transported from southern France to southern England! Bearing Henry eight children, she aged as gracefully as she could but not gracefully enough to keep her husband from the arms of mistresses, above all Rosamond Clifford, *Rosa mundi* (the rose of the world), for whom he built a love bower at Woodstock. After 1163 Eleanor and Henry spent less and less time together. The queen went back to Aquitaine, re-establishing her troubadour court in Poitiers and devoting all her energies to educating her sons (especially Geoffrey and Richard) and encouraging them to prise their inheritance from their father's grip. If this meant they had to ally themselves with Henry II's natural enemies – even the Capetian kings of France – so much the better. In 1173 Eleanor took the drastic step of fomenting the war of the sons against the father and managed to escape Henry's besieging army only by dressing in man's clothes and fleeing for asylum to her ex-husband, Louis VII of France. Recaptured, she was kept under strict surveillance in England, her household was reduced to a bare minimum, and her travels were closely monitored by the understandably suspicious Henry II. This quasi-imprisonment was to last for ten years.

The death of young Henry in 1183 seemed to bring about a temporary reconciliation. Eleanor was released from captivity, allowed to tour Aquitaine and to see her daughter Matilda. But this greater freedom also gave her greater liberty to plot a revenge. In the second serious round of hostilities, in 1189, she was again a major instigator of trouble. The king was now fifty-six, and his relentless life in the saddle had finally taken its toll. Eleanor encouraged her surviving favourite, Richard, to demand from Henry that he be publicly and immediately acknowledged heir in England, Normandy and Anjou. But Henry suspected that this would only quicken, rather than satisfy, his son's impatience and balked, thus triggering the revolt he had meant to prevent. One rumoured explanation was that Henry was sleeping with the French princess, Alais, whom the king had designated as Richard's bride. Perhaps Richard's sense of dishonour and humiliation became unbearable when Alais bore Henry an illegitimate child, for then Richard was prepared to take the same road as his brother Henry had done sixteen years before: kneel at the feet of the king of France, Alais's brother, Philip Augustus, and swear to be his vassal.

The war went disastrously for Henry II. Watching his birthplace, Le Mans, burned by the armies of Richard and Philip, the king agreed to terms, humbling himself before the two younger men. To onlookers he appeared to embrace Richard in the kiss of peace, but what he really said as he took his son in his arms was: 'God spare me long enough to take revenge on you.' Worse followed. Henry asked to see a list of all those who had conspired against him so that he might pardon them. The first name was his youngest son, John. This must have been deeply wounding, since Henry had provoked Richard in the first place by attempting to wrest some lands from him and transfer them to the under-endowed John. Two days after seeing that John was a treacherous ingrate, he died, his chroniclers said, of shock and heartbreak. The only child present at the deathbed was his illegitimate son, Geoffrey, whom Henry had made his chancellor. 'The others,' he said, before he expired, 'are the real bastards.' After the usual vulture-like picking-over of the king's jewels and clothes by his attendants, Henry's body was re-costumed in the kind of finery he had shunned in his life, and in Arthurian style he was carried on a black-draped barge down the river Vienne to the abbey of Fontevrault. When Richard eventually came for a cursory visit to his father's tomb, it was said that blood poured from the nostrils of the corpse. There were other alarming portents. Just before the king's death, according to Gerald of Wales, the fish in a certain pool in Normandy, near the castle of Exmes, had engaged in a nocturnal aquatic battle that was so violent that scarce any survived to the next morning.

There were many, however, like Eleanor, who was now in her seventies, who greeted the death of Henry II quite dry-eyed. For her, as for many, it was an occasion for uninhibited rejoicing. With Richard, the *preux chevalier* (gallant knight), with his intensely blue eyes and red-gold locks, a character formed by Eleanor's educated passions, finally seated on the throne, she could assert herself again in the business of the state. In England, Richard lost no time in proclaiming that he would be his mother's, not his father's, son. Henry's most unpopular high officers of state were shown the door, and a flamboyant, crowd-pleasing show was orchestrated for his coronation. The Westminster ceremony in 1189 (the first to be reported in detail) dripped with gold. Emulating Charlemagne, Richard picked up his own jewel-encrusted crown and tendered it to the Archbishop of Canterbury, a clear gesture of precedence. In addition to the usual regalia, he was invested with a golden sword and spurs and a golden canopy held by four barons above his head. The only ill-omen was a bat that flew, unnervingly in daylight, about the throne, striking the superstitious assembly with consternation. More seriously, the gift presented by the Jews of London was suspected of being the token of a sinister plot. Rumours spread. A general massacre ensued, described by the chronicler Richard of Devizes as a *holocaustum*, adding, irritably, that it took so long to 'send them to the devil, that the work had to be continued a second day'. To his credit Richard, who, like his father had taken the Jews under his protection, attempted to outlaw this first wave of English pogroms. But he was in a hurry to fulfil his coronation oath to take the Cross, and a few months after he had left for the Holy Land the mass murders began again. In York, rather than surrender to the doubtful neutrality of the local authorities, the Jews holed up in the old Norman castle, slit the throats of their women and children and died in their own fire.

But the king had to be off. For Richard's passion for the crusade was not some idle piety. It defined him. He had been brought up in Poitiers, in his mother's world of chivalric idylls and Arthurian poetry. In all likelihood he heard directly from Eleanor heavily embellished stories of the Christian war in the Holy Land, and he could hardly have failed to notice when, after a convenient fire at Glastonbury Abbey, excavations prior to reconstruction revealed two bodies, widely believed to be Arthur and Guinevere. Also found was an ancient sword, immediately taken to be Excalibur. Once equipped with it, Richard was ready for God's work. He may also have wanted to atone for Henry's failure to respond to the pleas of the aged Patriarch Heraclius of Jerusalem, who, in 1185, had brought the keys of the Holy Sepulchre in the forlorn hope of persuading the Plantagenet to become the next king of Jerusalem.

There was no question, then, that (unlike Henry II) he would make good on his coronation vow to take the Cross. Equally, however, there was no question what the result would be. As one chronicler put it: 'As the earth shudders at the absence of the sun, so the face of the kingdom was changed by the departure of the king. Nobles became busy; castles were strengthened, towns fortified, moats dug.' In other words, it seemed that the long era of predictable, secure Henrician government, in which over-mighty barons or officials could be kept in check by the threat of a royal visitation, was now in jeopardy. Those fears were confirmed by Richard's entrusting government largely to William Longchamp, Bishop of Ely, who swiftly colonized its offices with his own dependents and made the royal administration an instrument of favouritism rather than its monitor. When Richard's younger brother John, Count of Mortain, set himself up as a rival focus of loyalty, the barons alienated by Longchamp flocked to him.

Not that John was motivated by a budding sense of the interests of the realm. Richard had anticipated that, in his absence, his brother would make trouble and also that he might be bribed to keep his hands off England. So John was assigned the revenues of six English counties on condition that he stayed out of England for three years, by which time Richard assumed that he would have returned from the crusade. Unwisely, Eleanor persuaded him to rescind the agreement. John swiftly returned and even more swiftly began to act as if he already had the keys to the kingdom, travelling with his private army. Longchamp and his men were turned into fugitives, leaving John to establish a virtual state within a state, complete with his own court. When news came, in 1192, that Richard had been captured on his way back from the Holy

The tomb of Henry II in Fontevrault Abbey.

Land, John lost no time in proclaiming his brother dead and himself king. Richard was, of course, very much alive, but incarcerated in Austria, where his fate had become the trophy in an undignified bidding war between prospective ransom-hunting princes. His predicament drew from Eleanor, in a letter beseeching the intervention of the pope, a heartbreakingly poignant reflection on her turbulent life:

> *Moi Aliénor, par la colère de Dieu reine de l'Angleterre* [by the wrath of God, Queen of England], duchess of Normandy, unhappy mother, pitied by no one, the wife of two kings, I have arrived at this miserable old age which plunges me into ignominy. I was also the mother of two kings. The Young King and the Count of Brittany lie in dust and their unhappy mother is doomed to be incessantly tortured by their memory. Two sons remain but they exist to add to my miseries. King Richard is in irons; his brother John ravages the kingdom with fire and sword. I know not which side to take. If I leave, I abandon the kingdom of my son torn by civil war, the country bereft of wise council and consolation. If I stay I may never see the dearly beloved face of my son again. No one will work fervently for his deliverance. O Holy Father draw the sword of St Peter against the wicked…

But the sword of St Peter was not much help. The king's ransom was set at 34 tons of gold – three times the annual revenue of the Crown and a punishing burden that would lie heavily on England for a generation. When Philip Augustus of France (who had encouraged John in his ambitions) heard that Richard was finally at liberty in 1194 he sent a friendly message: 'The devil is out. Look to yourself.' Richard eventually caught up with his terrified, treacherous brother at Lisieux in Normandy and then took a leaf straight out of his detested father's book by deciding to crush the traitor with condescension. Raising the prostrate, terrified John to his feet, he gave him the kiss of peace and said: 'Think no more of it, John, you are only a child [he was twenty-seven at the time] who has been led astray by evil councillors.'

Much of Richard's authority was based, in fact, on the cavalier gesture, the code of honour, the full-tilt charge. But although sustaining the chivalric charisma of the Crown was important, it was only half the practice of sovereignty as reinvented by Henry II. The rest was political intuition. And in this department, too, Richard developed his own psychological edge over his adversaries. To look at the colossal ruin of Château Gaillard, the 'saucy château', is to see Richard's energy translating itself into strategic intelligence. Built above the banks of the Seine, north of Paris, it was sited deliberately as close as possible to the border between Plantagenet Normandy and the territories of the king of France. Defensively impregnable, supplied by both water and land routes, it was a base for harrying offensive operations when needed; the last word in military engineering, it was meant to make a statement and the statement was, in effect, don't even think about it. 'Were its walls made of butter,' Richard is reputed to have said, 'they would still stand.'

Richard died in 1199, besieging a castle near Limoges that belonged to a rebellious vassal. Exasperated by the prolonged resistance and bent on punishment, Richard refused a surrender to the outnumbered occupants. After a hard day's battering, he took archery practice, displaying his contempt for the defenders by going unarmoured, protected only by an esquire walking in front and holding a small shield. On one occasion he noticed a solitary defender on the battlements reduced to using a frying pan as a shield, whose quixotic bravura both amused and touched the king. He was less amused, however, when a bolt from the lone archer's crossbow struck him at the join of shoulder and neck. The wound turned fatally gangrenous. Knowing his end was near, the dying king magnanimously ordered that the bowman be spared the general hanging that would follow the surrender of the castle. And so he was. After the king's death, he was flayed alive instead.

Nothing remains of Richard in England, save the Victorian statue outside the House of Lords, which gives the utterly misleading impression that he was, somehow, a quintessentially English king. But barely a year out of the nine and a half of his reign was spent in England. The heart of Lionheart was buried in Rouen, and the rest of him was interred in the family mausoleum at Fontevrault near Chinon; both perfectly apt places for a sovereign who evidently assumed that the centre of his realm lay on the far side of the Channel. His brother John, who succeeded him, however, was buried in England, mostly in Worcester Cathedral, although the monks of Craxton Abbey took care to secrete away the entrails (which, in the medieval way of things, needed swift burial), leaving the king as gutless in death as, it was said, he had been in life.

Not only in every Robin Hood romance but even in their own day, the two brothers were thought of as the embodiments of the good and wicked ruler. Richard was lauded as a paragon, who was courageous, magnanimous, pious and disinterested; John was reviled as shifty, rapacious, cruel, vindictive and self-serving. But they had much more in common than the cartoon stereotypes allow for. They were both violent. John was detested for his cold-blooded execution of twenty-eight sons, taken as hostages from the Welsh princes and nobles with whom he was warring. But Richard slaughtered 2700 hostages at the siege of Acre to express his displeasure at Saladin's tardy payment of their ransom. They were both rather vain and given to ornamental excess. Richard's taste for oriental-Poitevin splendour ran to gold brocade. John was

Top: Effigy of Richard I from his tomb in Fontevrault Abbey.
Above: Château Gaillard, the 'saucy château'.

fond of jewels and plate, and one of the most intriguing items listed on the baggage he would lose in the Wash just before his death were pieces of glass, which, it has been suggested, were window-pieces carried around on his travels so that they could be fitted into apertures, custom-cut, wherever he happened to lodge. Depending on how much aversion John provokes, his travelling windows might equally be thought of as the refinement of a cultivated prince or the peep-holes of a paranoid. Neither cared for England so much that they balked at making it the fiefdom of another ruler if personal survival dictated. Richard handed the realm over to the Holy Roman Emperor to get out of prison; John delivered it to the pope to escape excommunication and win an ally in his war against the king of France. Above all, both worked the Angevin system of spoils and extortion for all it was worth (and it was never worth quite enough to get either of them out of trouble). Barons were forced to cough up scutage (shield-money) to avoid personal military service, while heirs and widows paid 'relief' before being allowed to succeed to their father's estate or to remarry. During both reigns the power of government and the scope of the law that might support, or resist, it expanded immensely as it had during the time of their father. Yet both kings, when the mood and the need took them, were quick to abandon the forms of legality for purely arbitrary acts of coercion. Richard, the absentee, could offload the odium for taxation and vexation on to his minions and ministers; John, the ubiquitous, neurotically hands-on interventionist, got all the blame for his government's excesses.

It was as a politician, rather than as a governor, that John was most obviously a failure. The Angevin empire under Henry had been sustained by a shrewd combination of charisma, feudal loyalty, appeals to self-interest and, when necessary, intimidation. The trick of the thing was so to distribute rewards and punishments among the barons that the inevitably aggrieved few would always be outnumbered (and outcastled) by the preferred many. John's problem, however, was that he had great difficulty in believing that any of those professing loyalty would ever be more than fair-weather friends. (And it must be said that the example of the way his own brothers had treated their father was itself unlikely to do much to shake this pessimistic cynicism about the value of allegiance.) By projecting his own low valuation of the bonds of loyalty on to the baronial class as a whole, John supposed that when he rewarded baronial service with grants of land, he had made not a friend, but a future conspirator. So, instead of creating the kind of loyalist coalition that, until almost the end, had bolstered Henry's survival, John preferred to rely on men and measures about which he had no illusions at all: mercenaries, hostages, blackmail and extortion. Assuming disloyalty, he ended up by guaranteeing it.

John's pathetic sense of insecurity is not a surprise. The runt of the Angevin litter, he had been ridiculed by his father and virtually ignored by his mother in favour of her darling Richard. But once he was king in his own right and with his mother Eleanor, an octogenarian tigress, her claws sharpened against the enemies of her last son, John still failed to grow into his throne, the agitated sense of vulnerability habitually making him opt for fear rather than persuasion to get his way.

Nowhere did the king manage to snatch defeat from the jaws of victory so damagingly as in Normandy. Attacked from the east by the army of Philip Augustus and in the west by supporters of Geoffrey's son, his nephew Arthur, Duke of Brittany, John showed himself (in contrast to his nickname 'Softsword') to be a formidable general. He mobilized a lightning forced march overnight to the castle of Mirebeau, where Eleanor, his mother, was being besieged. The dawn attack was a complete surprise and a phenomenal success. The twelve-year-old Prince Arthur was taken prisoner. But perhaps he had been reading too much Geoffrey of Monmouth, for in a startling encounter Arthur not only refused to acknowledge his uncle as rightful king but threatened him with the consequences of his 'usurpation'. John's panicky response was to make little Arthur disappear. The most plausible account of what happened to the youth is from the hand of an annalist monk at Margam Abbey, Glamorgan, who was patronized by William de Briouze, then John's faithful follower (although later his enemy and victim), who was with him at Rouen and in a position to know exactly what happened. According to the annalist, John, when drunk after dinner on the Thursday after Easter, 'slew him [Arthur] with his own hand and tying a heavy stone to the body cast it into the Seine. It was discovered by a fisherman in his net, and being dragged to the bank and recognized, was taken for secret burial in fear of the tyrant to the priory of Bec.'

So Geoffrey of Monmouth's legend in which Arthur was betrayed by an evil nephew was reversed, with the wicked uncle this time the villain. Whatever the truth, the rumours of Arthur's murder had an even more potent effect on politics than Becket's had had for Henry II. John's Norman loyalists fell away, both in dismay and disgust, and John himself slunk back to England, as one by one the major castles and cities of ducal Normandy fell to the king of France, Philip Augustus. After a long, nightmarish siege (in which the citizens of Les Andelys who were caught between the two camps virtually starved to death), the untakable Château Gaillard was taken.

Insular historians might find the stripping away of Normandy from the Angevin lands a blessing in disguise, which would allow the Plantagenets to fulfil their proper destiny as mighty English kings. But no one saw it that way at the time. It was, rather, a catastrophe: it was both the breaking of the ducal-royal patrimony that William the

Conqueror had put together and a failure to live up to the first of the coronation oaths. Without either the revenues of Normandy or Henry II's habit of parsimony, it meant that revenue – desperately needed to defend England from a feared French invasion and to beat back the Scots – now had to come from John's island subjects alone. John found himself in precisely the opposite position from his father. Under Henry the immense expansion of Angevin-controlled lands and his success in fending off attacks had created a myth of martial potency and a rational incentive for land-hungry barons to flock to his banner. But although John attempted to compensate for his losses in France by expeditions to Ireland and Wales, at some point he began to give off a kind of negative charisma, in which attachment to his cause seemed to promise more grief than satisfaction, and the allegiance that had snowballed with Angevin successes now began to melt away in the glare of defeat.

It didn't help that in 1208 John chose to pick a fight with the formidable and learned Pope Innocent III, which he couldn't possibly win. Doubtless he imagined he was replaying his father's axiom that the Church owed its first allegiance to him and not to Rome. But when he refused to accept Stephen Langton, the pope's nominee for Archbishop of Canterbury (and a compromise between John's candidate and the Canterbury chapter's choice), he took the country down a disastrous road. An interdict was placed on England, which in effect meant a spiritual lock-out. No subject of the king could receive the sacrament of marriage or be buried in consecrated ground. John responded by seizing Church property, which led to his excommunication and eventual capitulation, in 1213, when he surrendered England itself to be a fiefdom of the pope. In its way this improbable strategy was an adroit move, for it transformed John overnight from the most cursed to the most blessed of Christian rulers. Armed with the papal blessing, he made a final run at the aggressive Philip Augustus, but failed to be present in person at the battle of Bouvines in 1214, where his armies went down to disastrous defeat, sealing the doom of the Angevin empire.

Had John won the battle of Bouvines, in all likelihood there would have been no Magna Carta. For the famous 'charter' signed by John at Runnymede in mid- June 1215 was conceived, in the first instance, opportunistically by a coalition of barons who were resolved to take advantage of the king's defeat and to push back the centralizing power of the Angevins. Bouvines had given the green light for a full-scale rebellion to break out in the north. The barons, who, if the chronicler-monk Roger of Wendover is right, met at Bury to consider the 'charter', meant it to be some sort of golden mean, around which both contentious parties might find agreement, thus sparing the realm a return to the miseries of the *tempus werre*. And as was invariably the case in movements of reform, the language in which the barons presented their demands was nostalgic rather than revolutionary. The Angevin kings were always harking back to the 'customs' they insisted had obtained in the time of Henry I. Well then, they would out-hark John, requiring that he reinstate the 'good laws of Edward the Confessor' (whatever they were). No one should read the Magna Carta as if it were some sort of primitive constitution. It was not, as has been aptly said, a charter of liberty but a charter of liberties, in the medieval sense of exemptions: a catalogue of things that the king would not henceforth be permitted to do.

Inevitably, many of these prohibitions amounted to tax relief for the landed and armoured classes. Much emphasis was put on the most glaring abuses of feudal sovereignty: the power, for example, to force a baronial widow to remarry purely in order that the king might collect an arbitrarily set fee for remarriage, a fee that, depending on the family's conduct towards the king, might be lenient or deliberately ruinous. Once conveniently ruined, the king could then move in and collect on the estate. This was the sort of thing that had to stop. But if the main driving force behind the charter was the narrow interests of the baronial classes, the *form* in which they expressed those grievances, and their rights to have them addressed, does indeed deserve all the historical significance conventionally attached to it. Paradoxically, it was the ambitious, restless Angevin monarchy itself that had inadvertently schooled the barons in just what it was they were missing. By granting towns 'charters of liberties' in return for tolls and taxes paid on commerce, the Angevins established the idea of such charters as contracts made between the king and his subjects. By taking law out of the hands of baronial courts and putting it into courts of royal justice, the government made the more alert barons acutely aware (especially when members of their own class were arbitrarily imprisoned, harassed, ruined or even killed) that they had nowhere to go to obtain redress for their own grievances. Astonishingly, then, the legally minded but equally bloody-minded Angevins turned out to be the schoolmasters of their own correction.

So, if the Magna Carta was not the birth certificate of freedom it was the death certificate of despotism. It spelled out for the first time, and unequivocally, something with which the Angevins themselves, as the highest justices of the realm, could not conceivably quarrel: that the law was not simply the will or the whim of the king but was an independent power in its own right, and that kings could be brought to book for violating it – that they should, for example, show due cause why a person's body might be confined (*habeas corpus*) and not just declared to be detained at the inscrutable pleasure of the prince. All this, in turn, presupposed something hitherto unimaginable: that there was some sort of English 'state' of which the king was a part (albeit the supreme part) but not the whole. And it was, in the name of that state, that

Top: Detail of a fresco in the chapel of St Radegonde,
Chinon, thought to show Eleanor of Aquitaine (on the right).
Above: Effigy of King John in Worcester Cathedral.

the barons added something startling to the charter: a proposal that a body of twenty-five of them would be instituted to monitor compliance with the charter and, if necessary, to act as collective ombudsmen, hearing cases in which Crown officials were themselves accused of infringing the charter.

John, of course, had no intention of putting the Angevin monarchy into commission. Had London not fallen to the rebel army in the spring of 1215, he might not even have felt the tactical need to consent to the charter as a way of dividing the moderates from the hard-core rebels among his opponents and giving himself time to rally his own loyalist forces. But it was significant that the ante had been so much upped by mere talk of a charter of liberties that John felt he had to issue it himself, so that it would appear, at least, to be a free grant of the king and not (as has been traditionally assumed) something imposed on him.

Needless to say, this was all a sham. John had no intention of abiding by the charter a minute longer than he had to. He lost no time in appealing its illegality to his new and staunchest ally, the pope, and Rome duly obliged by damning it as the work of traitors and rebels against their anointed lord and annulling it outright. It had lasted less than three months. Freed from its constraints, John now launched an all-out war in the autumn of 1215, personally directing the siege of his father's castle at Rochester in Kent, which had opened its gates to the rebel army. John oversaw the battering and may have thought up the tunnel into which the fat of forty pigs was poured and set alight, bringing down one of the corner towers. Through much of 1216 the king fought a war on two fronts – against a French invasion, the first successful incursion since 1066, which was led by Philip Augustus's son, Louis VIII, who now claimed the throne of England, and against his own barons. At first, John seemed to be fighting a losing battle. By May 1216 Louis and his English allies had taken London and it looked very much as if the next king of England would be Lewis I. But the more experience the barons had of French power, the less they liked it. And perhaps John knew this, for he fought a dogged rearguard action, harried and threatened but showing the authentic Angevin strain of animal ferocity when cornered.

Fighting gave him an appetite. At Lynn in Norfolk, facing the wind-swept waters of the Wash, John ate a meal so hearty that he was stricken with a violent and unceasing spasm of dysentery. A fever took hold. On 11 October, while he was attempting to reach Wisbech, a wind got up that disoriented horses, carts and riders, trapping them in blowing quicksand. Some (not all) of the baggage carts – those containing John's precious jewels and his household effects – were lost.

It was as if Merlin's warning to Vortigern in Geoffrey of Monmouth's *History*, that his tower of power was built on subsiding foundations, had again come true.

A week later, after making a solemn will asking that he be buried (unlike his father and brothers) in England, in the abbey church at Worcester, John died on 18 October. His nine-year-old son, the 'pretty little knight' Henry, was quickly crowned at Gloucester and almost immediately the baronial opposition disintegrated. The barons' conflict, after all, was with the father not the son. And even those who had fought temporarily alongside Louis of France much preferred to see a Plantagenet boy on the throne, guided by the veteran regent William Marshal, than to become a satellite of the king of France.

More had been lost than King John's baggage. The loss of Normandy ripped the heart out of the great Angevin realm that Count Geoffrey of Anjou had constructed, even though Gascony remained (for the time being) under English suzerainty. Along with the unbroken territorial span of the empire that never was, went myths of Plantagenet invincibility and their pretensions to be treated as the dominant power of western Europe. By way of compensation, English power had been projected more forcefully than ever in Britain itself, especially in Wales and Ireland. In massive fortresses, like Dover Castle (which resisted the French invasion), its presence continued to dominate the margins of the island state. In the end, however, the impact made by the Angevins should be measured less by mileage or masonry than by magistrates. For in re-issuing the Magna Carta in 1216, 1217 and again, with amendments, in 1225, the barons of England were, in effect, paying the Angevins a backhanded compliment. By pressing so very hard on their kingdom, the dynasty had produced in necessary counter-response a generation of men who educated themselves in the business of the state. The dynasty left behind not just castles and churches, not just ceremonies and tournaments, but tribes of busy justices, sheriffs, burgesses and knights of the shire, whose understanding of the law would be as important for them as their knowledge of battle.

So the best thing that can be said about the Angevins is perhaps that they left behind an England that no longer needed them. They had been rough parents. But the unlikely result of their way of doing things had been that their subjects had developed their own brand of feisty truculence. When, on the death of John in October 1216, William Marshal proclaimed with typical chivalry that, if everyone else abandoned the boy he would carry the young king, Henry III, on his shoulders, 'step by step, from island to island, country to country and I would not fail him even if it meant begging my bread', he sounded like some sweetly superannuated Lancelot. But for once, England didn't want an Arthur. It had the Magna Carta instead. And that, it was hoped, would be Excalibur enough.

CHAPTER
4

In the second half of the thirteenth century the nations of Britain found their voice. Their speech is defiant, and angry enough to warn their own princes never to betray their homeland to the English.

In 1282, in the northern Welsh kingdom of Gwynedd, a proclamation drawn up by the 'lords of Snowdonia' declared: 'the people of Snowdon assert that even if their own prince should give overlordship of them to the King [of England] they themselves would refuse to do homage of any foreigner of whose language, customs and laws they were ignorant.' In Arbroath in 1320 the barons and earls of Scotland warned their king that: 'as long as but a hundred of us remain alive, never will we, on any conditions be brought under English rule.' Two years earlier, in Ireland, the king of England had been put on notice that: 'on account of the endless perfidy of the English and to shake off the harsh and insupportable yoke of servitude to them and to recover our native freedom, the Irish princes are compelled to enter a deadly war.'

Historians are professionally fretful about reading the story backwards rather than forwards, projecting the languages and institutions of our own time into a past quite innocent of them. Nationalism, we are trained to assume, is a modern invention. But what then do we make of these utterances with their passionate attachment to territory and local memory? They document, unmistakably, if not nationalism, then at least 'nativism', a politics of birthplace, of land and language. After these voices were heard, Britain would never be the same.

The inadvertent midwife to this native assertiveness was an English state that itself had been twice reborn: first in the years between 1258 and 1265 as a 'community of the realm' when a powerful movement of reform, the most radical until the seventeenth century, had forced the monarchy to make itself accountable to the representatives of the wider nation. Then, after that cause perished on the battlefield of Evesham along with its fervent, charismatic leader, Simon de Montfort, Edward I overcompensated for the humiliations of the Crown by trying to establish, in the

ALIENS AND NATIVES

The walls of Conwy Castle.

British isles, the first English empire. In England itself Edward was hailed as the heir to the empire-building King Arthur, the heralded restorer of an ancient British unity. The Chronicler of Bury St Edmunds wrote, jubilantly, if prematurely: 'England, Scotland and Wales are under his sway. He has thus acquired the former [Arthurian] monarchy of the whole of Britain, for so long fragmented and truncated.'

There was only one way to turn this fantasy into reality: coercion. Before he was done and England's imperial presence stamped on the face of the island, Edward would leave an enduring legacy of bitterness, not least in the massive fortresses with which he studded the landscape of conquered territory. In the eighteenth century English tourists and painters visited Wales to sketch the piles of granite as exercises in the picturesque. But to the Welsh of that time and earlier they were 'the magnificent badges of our subjection', the architecture of colonial domination. Set against the sea to choke off the country from the outside world, should resistance ever dare raise its head, they remained hulking, alien presences in the native heartland.

The wars of the British nations were not just trials of brute strength, though. They were also a battle of ideas about sovereignty: a contest of allegiance between empire and nation, mastery and memory, the omnipotent prince and the community of the realm.

In 1774 the tomb of Edward I in Westminster Abbey was opened by a circle of antiquarians, curious about his fearsome reputation. On the side of the austere marble sarcophagus was just one inscription: *Hic est malleus Scottorum* (Here lies the hammer of the Scots). When the lid was lifted the tomb revealed a recumbent figure every bit as imposing as thirteenth-century reports suggested. 'Longshanks' lived up to his nickname, measuring a full 6 feet 2 inches in his coffin. He was, in contrast to his image in effigies and statues, clean shaven and wearing a delicate crown. He was dressed in the purple cloth of a Roman emperor, a jewelled clasp at his right shoulder. Placed in his right hand was the sceptre, crowned with the crucifix; on the left was the rod of virtue, topped by a little dove (an emblem of Christian appointment), which initially must have appeared to be pecking at his cheek. The eighteenth-century onlookers were struck by the majesty of the figure, intact after four and a half centuries, although one of them attempted to make off with a royal finger before he was stopped by the vigilant dean of Westminster. Edward, it was also recalled, had been the first king of England since 1066 to bear an expressly English name. His eleventh- and twelfth-century predecessors, whether they thought of themselves as primarily Norman or Angevin, had been essentially French in language and culture, but Edward spoke English, had imbibed Geoffrey of Monmouth's myth of origins with his mother's milk and was aggressively self-conscious about the historical destiny of the English realm.

It began with the name. Henry III called his eldest son after the predecessor whom he believed had personified the highest ideals of kingship: Edward the Confessor. To say that Henry was obsessed with the last of the Anglo-Saxon kings, who was canonized in 1161, would hardly be an over-statement. He had a mural painted in his bedchamber so that he could turn to the Confessor for inspiration last thing before closing his eyes at night and on opening them in the morning. Told that Edward dressed austerely, Henry took to imitating him, wearing the simplest robes. During the coronation mass arranged for his queen, Eleanor of Provence, in 1236, Henry and the queen both partook of the blood of the Saviour from the Confessor's own chalice. The vividly illustrated history commissioned by the king and dedicated to Queen Eleanor, the *Estoire de St Aedwaerd le rei*, presented Edward's reign as dedicated less to battles than to peace and piety and punctuated by a succession of miracles and prophetic visions.

This may have suited Henry very well. For although he may have wished (somewhat desultorily) to recover the French territories of Normandy and Anjou lost by his father, John, he was seldom in a position to do much about it. His minority was dominated by baronial guardians who ensured that when he asked for taxation grants, the condition of their being granted by the council was Henry's reaffirmation of the validity of the Magna Carta. In any case, he seemed unsuited to the life of relentless itinerant campaigning that had been characteristic of his Angevin forbears, preferring, for the most part, seats to saddles. When he kept some of Henry and John's hunting lodges – at Clarendon, for example – he turned them into Plantagenet design statements, heavily influenced by Eleanor's Mediterranean culture, gorgeously decorated with polychrome tiles and ceilings painted with stars and the crescent moon.

To be a sedentary rather than a peripatetic monarch was not simply a matter of pampered indolence, however. It was meant to be a concentration of power. The new English monarchy, in both its secular and spiritual forms, would have its proper seat in the place Edward the Confessor had designated: Westminster. Although Henry was not responsible for building Westminster Hall, it was in his reign that it became the great ceremonial space of the Crown, both for his personal household and the court, acting as the highest institution of justice in the land. It was also where the council met, which, in the years after the Magna Carta, became increasingly bold in asserting its right to judge the propriety and wisdom of the policies for which the monarchy would require funds. The council was not quite yet a recognizable parliament (although the term came to be used first in the 1230s), but it was certainly more than the pliant instrument of the royal will.

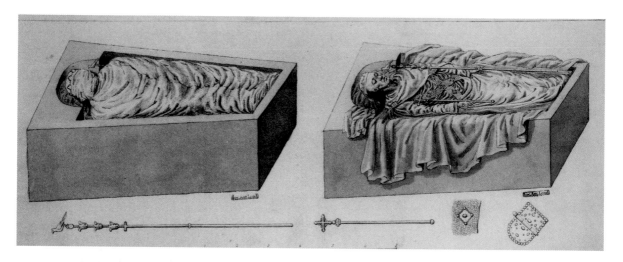

Top: Eighteenth-century engraving of Edward I in his tomb.
Above: Henry III supervising building works at St Albans,
from Matthew Paris's *Chronica Majora, c.* 1250.

The shrine tomb of Edward the Confessor in Westminster Abbey.

In keeping with his lofty vision of a restored and emphatically English monarchy that could command awe and reverence, Henry demolished the Romanesque basilica of Edward and the Norman kings and replaced it with an immense Gothic church, comparable to the greatest of the French cathedrals and designed by an architect from Rheims, where the kings of France were crowned. Henceforth, this would be the symbolic heart of the kingdom, the place where all English monarchs themselves would be crowned and buried. At its mystical centre Henry III planned an astounding shrine to the Confessor. It was to be inlaid with Purbeck marble, decorated with gold and set high above the altar, like the Ark of the Covenant, while around its base would be a pavement of glittering Italian mosaics. In preparation for the re-entombment, Henry had the bodies of Edward and his queen, Edith, moved to the sanctuary (thus inadvertently smuggling one of the Godwines into Westminster). The first phase alone of the abbey rebuilding took thirty-nine years and some £46,000 – an immense sum that did nothing to endear the king to those who shouldered the burden of the taxes. Even so, we may be sure that Henry III had not a shred of doubt that it had been (other people's) money well spent. 'O man,' read his proud inscription at the Confessor's tomb, 'if you wish to know the cause. The king was Henry, friend of the present saint.'

So while his ancestors had battled, Henry of Winchester, with the droopy eyelid and the stolid manner, was content to build (especially after a failed expedition to Poitou in 1242). At the opposite end of London from Westminster he constructed the powerful enclosing wall around the Tower, and inside it the 'Wakefield' Tower and a number of smaller buildings, including the menagerie. Out in the country he encouraged projects of enormous magnitude, such as the building of St Alban's Cathedral and the removal of the Norman cathedral and bishop's palace of Old Sarum to the new and less exposed site that became Salisbury. Henry is the first English king to be depicted in contemporary images, where he is seen as a master-builder, conferring with masons and architects and men busy with pulleys and plumb-lines.

But because architectural campaigning cost almost as much as the military version, it was seen by the keepers of purses and guardians of the charter, for all its ostensible veneration of the English Confessor, as a suspicious extravagance. Their suspicions were strengthened by the conspicuousness at court of men who were now, tellingly, described in opposition rhetoric as 'foreigners'. There were two groups: the Provençal and Savoyard kin of Queen Eleanor, and Henry's own half-brothers (the children of his mother's second marriage), the Lusignans, who came from the western French region of the Poitou. A generation or two before, the presence of newcomers from continental Europe in the royal household or lodged in some of the principal offices and bishoprics of the land would hardly have been any kind of occasion for comment, since they were scarcely more foreign than the king himself. But in the post–Magna Carta decades of the early thirteenth century the definition of what served and what compromised the interests of the English realm had become much more explicitly nativist, in the literal sense of discriminating on the grounds of where one was born. In the literature of protest the phrase *natus est* crops up for the first time with heavily loaded significance.

The institution that began to regard itself as the co-protector of England was parliament. Before the crisis of 1258 it was still largely indistinguishable from the royal council of ecclesiastics and barons that had advised or cajoled the Angevins. But even though clause 61 of Magna Carta, which had proposed a supervisory body to oversee the conformity of royal government with its provisions, had not survived the amendments, the spirit of that shockingly audacious initiative had lived on. Through the years of Henry's minority the councils-become-'parliaments' had grown accustomed to considering the propriety or irresponsibility of projects needing hefty supplies of money and to threatening to withhold sums if they disapproved. As the English earls and bishops watched while Henry III doled out castles, offices, bishoprics and land on demand to his foreign courtiers, the baronial parliament began to assert a quite different and much more ambitious claim: the right to approve, veto or even dismiss the king's choice of officers and advisers. Pushed to its logical extreme in the late 1250s and 1260s, this claim would be tantamount to making the exercise of royal sovereignty conditional on its accountability to those who said they represented the *communitas regni* (community of the realm). Needless to say, this interference in the king's choice of councillors was taken by Henry as a grave infringement of his sovereign prerogatives, and he resolved to resist it. The resulting conflict led, in the end, to a civil war, the captivity of the king and a revolutionary crisis every bit as momentous for the fate of the nation as the civil wars of the seventeenth century.

Although the pressure for reform came from many of the highest nobles and clerics of England, the figure who ultimately came to personify its uncompromising resolve, both on and off the battlefield, was the aristocrat Simon de Montfort. Never has there been a less likely leader of an opposition movement claiming to speak and act on behalf of the English community of the realm. For although de Montfort came to be Earl of Leicester, in his origins and early career he was every bit as 'foreign' as the pernicious courtiers he and his allies sought to evict from power. His father, also called Simon, whose home estate lay about 30 miles west of Paris, had put his Christian zeal to work by organizing the 'crusade' (in effect a mass slaughter) against the Albigensian heretics and the expulsion of the Jews from the south of France.

On his mother's side, though, the senior Simon had inherited the earldom of Leicester. When Simon junior came to claim it in person in 1229 he was just eighteen years old and must have seemed to the older nobles another self-serving French adventurer with a purported claim on an English fortune, who needed to be kept as far as possible away from the king. But there was something oddly compelling about the young man – an eloquent intelligence and a peculiar air of confident self-assertion that made his presence forcefully felt. Yet when Simon secretly married Henry's sister, Eleanor, in 1238 (a matter affecting the succession and therefore within the council's right to consultation), the suspicions of opportunism must have been confirmed. It did not help that after her first husband died, the sixteen-year-old widow had, in the presence of the Archbishop of Canterbury, taken a solemn vow of perpetual chastity. When Simon and the king subsequently became sharply estranged, the arguments were personal rather than political. Frustrated in his attempt to have Simon repay a debt to his own father-in-law, Henry let it be known that he had consented to de Montfort's marriage to his sister only after discovering she was pregnant. Correctly suspecting that he was about to be arrested, Simon took the swelling Eleanor and fled by boat downriver and across to France.

In the 1250s the periodic bickering between the brothers-in-law took on much more serious implications. Simon and Henry were now both in their forties. De Montfort had been a crusader in the Holy Land for two years, fighting alongside the Hohenstaufen emperor, Frederick II, and he returned in the mid-1240s very much the seasoned traveller and cosmopolitan aristocrat. More importantly, he had become deeply pious, rising at midnight to spend the rest of the night in silent vigil and saying the Psalter by heart. He began to wear a hair shirt and, although munificent in his hospitality to others, was frugal in his own habits, dressing in what for an aristocrat were the ostentatiously modest hues of 'burnet and bluet'. He had also become close to, and corresponded with, some of the most articulate and thoughtful clerics of the day: Robert Grosseteste, Bishop of Lincoln; Walter de Cantilupe, Bishop of Worcester; and the Franciscan scholar, Adam Marsh. All three were committed to the mission of converting lay rulers to the reinstated ideals of Christian government: charity, justice and clemency. Just before he died in 1253, Grosseteste had written a treatise distinguishing between just rule and tyranny, and this was a document that was evidently to have a profound effect on the intense and temperamentally dogmatic de Montfort. Henceforth his political convictions were held religiously.

Simon believed he already had direct experience of what Grosseteste meant by tyranny, petty or otherwise. In 1247 the king had made him lieutenant of the last Plantagenet territory in France: Gascony, with its priceless wine trade centred on

Bordeaux. De Montfort proceeded to conduct his government with such uncompromising rectitude that it triggered rebellion among the local Gascon nobles, the last
thing Henry needed. To pacify them, in 1252 the king agreed to the drastic step of
putting de Montfort on trial, in effect a form of impeachment for overstepping the
bounds of his authority. Sparks flew between them, kindling a fire of mutual recrimination. Henry accused Simon of provoking insurrection and made it clear that he
would not 'keep covenant with a traitor', but de Montfort spoke back to the king as
if he were a peer, upbraiding and even threatening him, and reacting to the accusation
of treason by replying: 'That word is a lie and were you not my sovereign it would be
an ill hour for you when you dared utter it.' At another point Simon glared furiously
at Henry and asked him if he had been confessed, since he seemed no Christian at all.

Acquitted – and popular with most of the nobility, who felt that he had been
subjected to a show trial – Simon was sent back to Gascony for another tour of duty.
The king and de Montfort even became sufficiently reconciled for Henry to give
Simon and Eleanor two royal castles, one of them the immense and grandiose
Kenilworth in Warwickshire. It quickly became something more than just a baronial
fortress; it was, rather, a centre of courtly and even scholarly life, which completely
overshadowed any other noble residence in the country. But when he returned from
Gascony in 1253, Simon began to treat his own personal grievances (often monetary,
in the form of arguments over his wife's unreleased dowry) as part of the larger public
malady afflicting the kingdom. By the time the next major crisis arose in 1258 Simon
had begun to speak and act as if he, the cosmopolitan, had nothing dearer to his heart
than the interests of England. In common with some of the most important
magnates, like Richard de Clare, Earl of Gloucester, and Roger Bigod, Earl of
Norfolk, de Montfort believed that Henry had finally begun to reveal himself as the
true son of his father, King John, and that unless he were restrained as John had been,
the king was quite as capable of political mischief. The proof seemed to be Henry's
irresponsible acceptance, in 1254, from the pope, Alexander IV, of a kingdom in Sicily
for his second son, Edmund. But this was not a free gift. England would pay for the
liberation of the island from the hands of one of the pope's Hohenstaufen enemies, a
commitment the king had made without consulting the council, although he must
have known there was little chance of this being sanctioned. Henry had got himself
into an unenviable position: if he reneged on his sworn promise to the pope, he (like
his father before him) would face an interdict on the country or even personal
excommunication. So he persevered, with increasing shortness of temper, and
demanded that he receive the necessary funds to prosecute the Sicilian 'crusade' and,
in due course, levies of men from his tenants-in-chief.

What Henry got instead on 28 April 1258 at Westminster was an armed confederacy of seven barons, including Gloucester, Norfolk and de Montfort himself. The fact that they had left their swords at the entrance to Westminster Hall did little to reassure the suddenly frantic Henry: 'What is this my lords, am I wretched fellow, your captive?' The barons, led by the Earl of Norfolk, responded that they came not in rebellion but, on the contrary, in all due loyalty to liberate the king from wicked and corrupt foreign counsel. 'Let the wretched and intolerable Poitevins and all aliens flee from your face and ours as from the face of a lion and there will be glory to God in the heavens and peace to men of goodwill.' Henry had little choice but to agree and, according to the chronicler Matthew Paris, 'acknowledged the truth of the accusations…and humbled himself declaring that he had too often been beguiled by evil counsel and…made a solemn oath at the shrine of St Edward that he would fully and properly amend his old errors and show favour and kindness to his native born subjects.' Specifically, Henry agreed to the establishment of a committee of twenty-four (half appointed by himself, half by the parliament) to draft reforms for the government of the realm and report back to the council.

On 11 June that council meeting was convened in Oxford. Its deliberations were so momentous for the long-term future of English politics that 1258 ought to be one of the dates engraved on the national memory as having far more immediate significance than 1215. The town had been chosen as the mustering place for an army destined for a fresh campaign in Wales, where Henry's recent efforts had met with abject failure. Because of the crowd of men in arms, the leaders of the reform movement knew that in Oxford they could call on representatives from a broad cross-section of the aggrieved: knights of the shire, sick of being put upon by sheriffs who knew nothing of their county; barons who hated the Lusignans and wanted them out of English castles; and clerics and scholars, who had, from the beginning, been the brains and the soul of the campaign for reform. The fact that the Oxford assembly took place against a backdrop of terrible distress in the country only heightened the sense of urgency. The harvest of 1257 had been a disaster, and by the following summer much of the country was suffering from near famine conditions. Matthew Paris wrote that: 'owing to the shortage of food an innumerable multitude of poor people died and dead bodies were found everywhere, swollen through famine and livid lying by fives and sixes in pigsties and dunghills in the muddy streets.'

The barons would not be able to fill those empty bellies, but they certainly fulfilled expectations of a radical change in the government of the country. Essentially, they abolished the absolute monarchy of the Anglo-Norman state. The council of twenty-four was now replaced by a council of fifteen, with the royal delegation reduced to three. It was appointed for an indefinite period and was charged to deal 'with the common business of the realm and of the king'. What had happened at a stroke was the transfer of sovereign powers from the Crown to a standing committee elected by the barons and the Church. That committee, rather than the king, was to have the final say in the Crown's choice of ministers and councillors and also, evidently, in proposing and disposing of funds to make war or peace. No less radical was the devolution of power to the counties, where four knights in each shire, elected by an elaborate process, were to be made responsible for collecting complaints and grievances and delivering them to the justiciar. There had been no justiciar for several generations in England, but under the Angevins he had been the king's chief legal officer. Now the role was transformed into something like an ombudsman for the nation. Sheriffs, who had for so long been the bane of local landholders, were henceforth to be recruited exclusively from the county community and were to be salaried and appointed for one year only at a time. The Lusignans and other foreign undesirables (de Montfort excluded, of course) were to be expelled forthwith from their castles and, indeed, from the kingdom. 'You will either lose your castles or your heads,' the implacable Simon told his arch-enemy, William de Valence, Earl of Pembroke.

The climax of this startling revolution took the form of a collective swearing of an oath to observe these 'Provisions of Oxford'. When they were finalized the following October, the documents were written, for the first time, not only in Latin and French but in Middle English, the native tongue. As such, the Provisions became something akin to a political canon and a touchstone of allegiance for all those professing disinterested concern for the good government of the realm. England may not have become a republic, but it was no longer an autocracy.

The king, doubtless roiling in impotent chagrin, took the oath, holding a burning taper along with rest, as the Archbishop of Canterbury threatened damnation on the heads of all those who violated the Provisions.

The impulse to reform had come so far, so fast, that it inevitably overtook some of its original promoters, who, once the complaints that the Provisions had invited began to pour in, took fright at their own creation. The precarious unity of the reformers came to grief over questions of whether or not plaintiffs were entitled to pursue grievances against *them* and their own manorial regimes. It was one thing to bring the king and his men to book; quite another to have some jumped-up villein with a little book learning grousing about the ills he had suffered at the hands of the manorial bailiff or reeve. Predictably, de Montfort thought this was absolutely right; equally predictably, the great earls, especially the Earl of Gloucester, were much cooler. When Gloucester balked at the 'Ordinance of the Magnates', which had been drawn up by Montfort, who vowed to put his own class under the same restraints as the king, Simon barked: 'I do not want to live or have dealings with men who are so fickle and deceitful.'

At the height of the reforming campaign, the position of Henry's oldest son, the 'Lord Edward', was anything but clear. For a time in 1259–60 the spell cast by de Montfort and the popularity of their anti-foreigner programme inclined him towards the reformers. He, too, was impatient to be free of his father's control and saw the crisis as an opportunity to promote his own claim to come into possession of castles. There was something about Simon that simply mesmerized people, even someone as self-assured as Edward. But the prince's dalliance with the barons had its suspicious aspects. A breakfast negotiation with the Earl of Gloucester and his brother turned sinister when William de Clare died the next day with excruciating abdominal pains, while the earl awoke to discover that his hair, fingernails and toenails had fallen out. Edward was, in fact, discreetly building up a third party, composed of young bachelor knights, 'vavasours', free of the odium associated with Henry's court, but still independent of baronial control. Ultimately, though, Edward knew that the fate of the monarchy as an institution was at stake. So once the detested Lusignans had been got rid of and the struggle became polarized between the Crown and its challengers, Edward not only threw in his lot unequivocally with his father but was often all there was between the king and ignominious defeat. While de Montfort was away in France Henry had taken advantage of the crumbling unity of the opposition to restore his fortunes, largely financed by the king of France and at the price of renouncing all further claims to Normandy and Anjou and accepting that Gascony would be a fiefdom of France. Reinforced by mercenaries, the king gradually recovered many of his strategic castles, and by late 1261 he had renounced the Provisions and had secured a special papal bull absolving him from his Oxford oath.

But in 1263 Simon belatedly returned, to discover that the reform movement was in perilous disarray. It took him no time at all to conclude that it must now fight or perish and that to prevail would require unswerving and resolute leadership, namely by himself. He also knew that he was coming back to a country in the throes of an immense upheaval that had gone well beyond Westminster and the castles of the mighty and had rippled out into the remote shires and hundreds. For the first time since the Conquest the political fate of England was completely fluid, its eventual outcome uncertain. The royalist restoration had thrown out the locally appointed sheriffs and replaced them with dependable court men, but that had engendered a backlash among the knights and gentry of the counties. While Simon's harsh fierceness and loftiness had alienated some of the great nobles who had been part of the reforming party in 1258, he was now so intoxicated with the righteous certainty of his cause that he could appeal over the heads of the magnates to the citizens of London (to whom he addressed public 'letters'), the Church (which for the most part saw him as a loyal son), and even to the free peasantry: in short, to all those who constituted, as he thought, the true, just and honest people of England. It did not escape notice that while he voiced these lofty sentiments, he was also busy building up a family empire from the seized lands of his enemies. When Simon rode, he rode with a train of 160 knights, far more numerous than either the king or his son. But despite this Caesar-like grandeur, in his own mind – and in the minds of those who were devoted to him – Simon de Montfort was, indeed, a crusader for England. 'He loves right and hates wrong,' said one typical panegyric. If he was not quite God, he certainly seemed to have a direct line to Providence.

It seems pointless to debate which was the 'real' Simon – the vainglorious adventurer or the messianic reformer – for he himself was incapable of disentangling the two roles. Few charismatic leaders have ever amounted to anything without a streak (at least) of selfish ambition and vanity. And Simon certainly had his share. But equally there is no doubt that he believed that what was good for the de Montforts was good for England. For a while, at least, he had a significant part of both the nobles and commons believing it too.

In the summer of 1263 the situation became critical. De Montfort and his allies had captured most of southeastern England. Henry had retreated in fright to the Tower of London, doubtless relieved that he had added those new walls to its defences. To raise money to pay the mercenary troops in the royal army the queen had pawned her jewels to the Templars. On the pretext of inspecting or possibly redeeming them, Edward talked his way into the New Temple, where he proceeded to stage a bank robbery, smashing the treasure chests and relieving the Templars of their gold and silver. It was a classic Edwardian stunt, but its effect was to convert the mayor and burgesses of London from cool sceptics of the Montfortians into unreserved allies. What, after all, was the point of supporting the forces of order if they were themselves the leading criminals? Taken off their leash, the citizenry expressed its displeasure against the royalists in the usual ways. The fact that the queen was not only the patroness of the hated 'foreigners' but also enjoyed the proceeds from several prime tolls in the city made her an especially choice target. Fearing the worst, Eleanor attempted to break out of London by river and get to Edward's army at Windsor. But her boat was recognized and pelted with stones and ordure from the crowds standing on London Bridge, the site of her most lucrative toll stations. Mortified by the humiliation, she was forced to take refuge in St Paul's. It was an affront that neither she nor Edward would ever forget or forgive.

Now styling himself 'Steward of England', Simon de Montfort was virtually sole and supreme governor of the country. But none of his titles could do anything to prevent England from spinning into civil war.

The issue was decided in two great battles. The first took place near Lewes on the Sussex South Downs in May 1264. De Montfort had broken his leg in a riding accident and was forced to travel to the battlefield in a cart, but this seemed to have no effect on his decisive generalship. Although his side was badly outnumbered, especially in cavalry, it had seized the high ground above Lewes through a daring night march. Before the battle Simon spoke to his troops, some of them untested Londoners, pledging that he and they were fighting for the kingdom of England, for the honour of God and for the blessed Virgin Mary, the saints and the Holy Church. The soldiers – knights, archers, foot soldiers – prostrated themselves on the ground, their faces pressed into the wet spring meadows, their arms stretched out, praying for victory. Then they got up, absolved by the bishops of Winchester and Chichester, and put on their armour with the white crosses of crusaders. Many were there, of course, because whoever was above them in the social pecking order commanded their presence, but there must have been some who truly believed that Simon de Montfort, for all his solemn piety and irascibility, was indeed a kind of political messiah. In a Canterbury manuscript he is even described as 'Simon Bar-jona', the name given by Jesus in Matthew 16:17 to St Peter, the keeper of the keys of heaven. No wonder his soldiers called themselves the 'Army of God'.

At first, God did not seem to be on their side at all. Encouraged by the greater numbers of the royalist side, including a substantial number of Anglo-Irish and Scots knights – among them Robert Bruce (1210–95) – Edward launched a full-tilt charge at the opposing troops, who were mostly from London, and when they broke, he pursued them, cutting them down. Assuming that the royal army had won the day, Edward made his way back to the battlefield to look for his father. A rout was, indeed, in progress, but it was the reverse of what Edward had supposed. The commanders of the royal side had been killed or captured, the Earl of Cornwall was hiding in a windmill, and the king had fled to a priory in the town of Lewes. Although his victory was incomplete without the capture of the king and the prince – which would have meant sacking the priory (not a good move for the Army of God) – de Montfort laid down terms, which included Edward's becoming a hostage for the good conduct of the king's forces.

The eighteen months that followed were a brief but extraordinary episode in the history of the political nation and the closest that England came to being a republic before the seventeenth century. In July 1264, when there was a serious threat of invasion from France, de Montfort's government sent sealed writs (this was a particular source of fury to the king, whose prerogative this was) to each shire, 'to bishops, abbots, earls, knights and freemen', asking them to provide 'men, lances, bows, arrows, axes and crossbows' – in short, a people's army. The response was extraordinary. A huge throng of all ranks and classes gathered at Barham Downs between Dover and Canterbury to repel the invasion, which, needless to say, never came. But Pandora's box had most definitely been opened. In the populist euphoria, the mayor of London could summon the audacity to speak to Henry III like a schoolmaster dressing down a naughty child – 'Lord, as long as you will be a good lord we will be your faithful and devoted men' – with the implication that if not, well not. On 8 August 1265, four days after the battle of Evesham, a royalist esquire, Peter de Nevile, was apprehended by the villagers of Peatling Magna (who evidently did not know that the king had won) and accused of 'treason and other heinous offences because he was against the community of the realm'. Some of the popular emotions and prejudices unleashed by the civil war were unappetizing and violent. The category of 'undesirable foreigner' provided de Montfort with a useful whipping boy to drum up anger, and he was certainly prepared (if not eager) to use it against the Jews, whom he had expelled from Leicester in 1231, much to the delight of the Church. During 1264–5 Jewish communities in many of the commercial towns of the country suffered horribly from violent attacks on their property and persons.

Nineteenth century historians, celebrating the epic of English parliamentary liberalism, imagined de Montfort's assemblies as calmly deliberative institutions – the Victorian reform acts in medieval dress – but in fact Simon's revolution took place amid immense social uproar, which, as the crisis deepened, threatened to get completely out of control. It was true, however, that the parliaments of 1265 were utterly unlike the old royal councils, both in their composition and the topics they deemed proper to debate. Not only barons and churchmen deliberated on the business of the kingdom, but also knights of the shire, elected by assemblies of their peers, and even burgesses from the towns. So a cloth merchant or a Suffolk knight with a few acres now got to judge the terms on which the son of the king might safely be released from captivity! This was not yet anything like a House of Commons, but it certainly represented an enlargement of the political community that, by the standards of feudal and absolutist Europe, was breathtakingly radical. Without any question it changed England. It inaugurated the union between patriotism and insubordination.

Like many quasi-revolutionary bodies, however, the parliaments of 1265 were more emergency war councils than permanent institutions. The neutralizing of Edward's political and military influence was on everyone's mind, and Edward himself was probably aware that his value as a hostage was limited by the fact that de Montfort would probably not dare lay hands on him (although with Montfort's blazing temper no one could be quite sure). Once he had done the necessary by pledging allegiance to the Provisions of Oxford, had submitted to the expropriation of a large part of his estates (and their transfer to the de Montfort family) and had even agreed that the council might judge the acceptability of his own followers, Edward was formally released. But although he was out of prison, he was still, together with his father, kept in a kind of travelling custody, along with Simon's own moving train. Because so many of de Montfort's erstwhile supporters were now deserting him, angry at the apparent greed and rapacity of his family, and because Edward had never quite been identified with the follies of the king, some of these men were conveying intelligence to the prince about the movements of potential supporters, including the powerful Marcher earls, like Roger Mortimer, among Simon's bitterest foes. From some of his friends, whom de Montfort had rashly allowed to travel to the prince under safe-conduct, Edward was in a position to know that Mortimer's troops were just 40 miles away and closing. On 28 May, while outside the gates of Hereford and pretending to examine the quality of a batch of horses brought for his inspection, he rode all of them save one into the ground. At the right moment he dug his spurs hard into the flank of what was now the only fresh mount and at a furious gallop easily outdistanced his pursuers. News of the prince's daring escape was electrifying. At liberty, he instantly became a magnet for all those who felt that the sanctimoniousness of the de Montforts had become just a pretext for a naked seizure of power.

Simon was now as much hated as he was adored and feared. The Marcher lords of Wales hated him for making an agreement with Llewellyn, the prince of Gwynedd; the Anglo-Irish Normans hated him for his presumptuousness. And many of those earls and barons who had felt that he had indeed spoken for England in 1258 and even in 1263 now began to look on Simon as a somewhat suspicious oddity, as, in fact, a foreigner, passing himself off as the salt of the English earth. In a month or two Edward ran a dazzling campaign, seizing Gloucester along with a good part of the Montfortian army and cutting off Simon's own forces, which were divided by the Severn from his son Simon's garrison at Kenilworth. A surprise raid on Kenilworth caught many of the garrison actually lodged in town, doubtless taking their ease in baths and stews, and forcing Simon junior to escape (naked, some chronicles said) by swimming across the castle lake. Following the disastrous failure to join with his son's army, it was with a badly depleted force that de Montfort had to engage Edward's army at Evesham. Watching from the tower of the abbey, his herald at first believed

Bronze gilded effigy of Henry III by William Torel, in the chapel of St Edward the Confessor, Westminster Abbey.

that the advancing troops he saw carrying the Montfort colours (another Edwardian ruse) were those of Simon's long-awaited son. But when their true identity was discovered, de Montfort spoke prophetically: 'God have mercy on our souls for our bodies are theirs.' He was right. The battle was a slaughter. Told that his son Henry had been killed, Simon replied, 'Then it is time to die' and charged into the fray. Many of his oldest and most devoted knights, men from his home *patria* of Leicestershire and Warwickshire, went down with him. Simon was unhorsed and died fighting on his feet. 'Thank God', were said to be his last words. In the fury of his vindication, Edward was not interested in obeying the conventions of war. While he went to rescue his wounded and confused father, Simon's hands, feet and testicles were cut off, the genitals hung around his nose. Thirty of his knights were killed by stab wounds as they lay wounded and helpless. Anyone personally associated with de Montfort was mercilessly hunted down, and his great castle at Kenilworth was subjected to a five-month siege – it yielded only after a tremendous pounding, when the defenders were perishing of famine and cold. When the royal army finally got inside what had been the greatest and grandest of all English castles, they climbed over stinking corpses, gagging at the foulness.

Henry III gave thanks for the salvation of his crown in the only way he knew: by completing the shrine of Edward the Confessor and finally, in 1269, by seeing the saint's remains translated into the darkly glowing sanctuary. In 1272, with Edward on crusade in Palestine, Henry III was himself laid, temporarily, in the tomb of the Confessor, pending the creation of his own ornately Italianate sarcophagus, set at a respectful distance from that of his hero. (Dante, rather unkindly, placed him in the portion of purgatory reserved for simpletons.) It was against this background of Roman magnificence that Edward I was crowned in August 1274.

Like the hybrid English 'nation', Edward was an intriguing mixture of inherited and culturally acquired characteristics: he was ruthless in war, yet capable of falling apart when the queen who had borne him fifteen children died. In his youth he would have seen the three leopards, which had been sent to his father, Henry III, by the Holy Roman Emperor and which he kept in the Tower of London (along with a polar bear, a porcupine and an elephant). So perhaps he might not have minded the unflattering comparisons with a leopard: fierce and fleet, but also notorious for changing its spots. The hostile writer of The Song of Lewes, for example, warned: 'when he is cornered he promises anything you like…but once he has escaped he soon goes back on his word. The lying by which he gains his ends he calls providence …and whatever he wants he calls lawful and thinks there are no legal bounds to his power.' But Edward did what it took to survive and triumph. His mettle had been tested early and often, by bungled military campaigns in Wales, by disingenuous flirtations with the opponents of his father and by falling hostage (literally) to a great civil war. While he was on crusade he had to be tough enough to withstand the poisoned dagger of an assassin and to be patient while the venom was sucked from the wound (possibly by his wife) and while the surgeons made a butchery of his wounded limb. By the time he was crowned in 1274 Edward had seen pretty much everything that medieval politics and warfare could put a prince's way, which was just as well, since Edward Plantagenet had, from his childhood, been the bearer of impossible dreams.

But where was his empire to lie? In England he was sensible enough to leave some of the reforms of 1258 temporarily untouched, even while he hounded the de Montforts themselves to ruin and oblivion. The experience had taught Edward never to make his father's mistake of appearing to be the pawn of foreign courtiers; rather he would make himself and his monarchy the personification of the community of the realm. In the hectic weeks between his escape from Hereford and the battle of Evesham, Edward had quite deliberately presented himself as the true custodian of the great reforms of 1258 and Simon de Montfort as a power-crazed nepotist. Needless to say, he had no intention of abiding by a political regime that reduced the real power of the Crown to a nullity, but he could easily imagine a working relationship with the barons and bishops in which rather than treating parliament as the perpetual adversary of the Crown he could co-opt it as a partner in the enterprise of England. And if that didn't work, he would be free to exploit the natural divisions separating barons from knights of the shire and burgesses. It was characteristic of the future king that after the initial vindictiveness had passed, the proclamation disinheriting all barons associated with the rebellion was changed so that they could buy back their seized estates: the appearance of clemency with the reality of profit.

In essence, Edward I revived the basic axiom of his great-grandfather, Henry II: that allegiance depended on the expectation by the great magnates and barons that they were part of an ever-expanding enterprise. But while Henry II's Angevin enterprise had taken as its field of expansion most of western and northern France, Edward reconceived his empire as Britain. As with Henry, Edward had no particular wish (at the beginning at any rate) to impose standardized English institutions and law on the several disparate parts of his empire. What he wanted from the rulers of Ireland, Wales and Scotland was an unconditional admission that he was their feudal overlord, and, with that admission, their obligation to provide him with men and money where and when he chose. As the acknowledged emperor of Britain he would then be able to try his strength, blow for blow, with the king of France.

Was Edward, from the beginning, deluded in his mania for sovereignty? Could he not see that Ireland, Wales and Scotland were, in fact, independent realms, inhabited by peoples of different cultures, steeped in a sense of their own history and accustomed to utterly different systems of law and government? It is certain that he could not, but in many ways his myopia is understandable. For the civil war had amply demonstrated not the separateness of the ruling clans of the British into neat national compartments but their complicated and unavoidable interconnections. The royalist army at Lewes had contingents from both the Anglo-Norman Irish knights (who themselves, remember, had originally been settlers in Wales) and from some of the major Scottish dynasties, like the Bruces, who possessed land on both sides of the border and who acknowledged Edward as their feudal lord, at least for their English manors. De Montfort had made an alliance with Llewellyn ap Gruffydd, the prince of Wales; while Llewellyn's enemies, the Marcher lords such as the Mortimers and de Clares, had sealed his doom at Evesham.

Edward might, in fact, be forgiven for not thinking of Ireland, Scotland and Wales as discrete, cleanly demarcated nations and realms. Their relationship was sometimes personal and familial. His own sister, Margaret, was married to the Scottish king, Alexander III, and the prince of Gwynedd was descended from Joan, the bastard daughter of King John. All three realms were sub-divided into an ancestral, indigenous, non-English-speaking core, with their heart and home in the highlands and islands, and a much more densely populated, culturally hybridized lowland region. In the remoter upland areas the customary laws of kinship and the allegiance of the clan cut across the authority of the ruler's laws. Traditional rituals such as the blood-feud survived, and in *pura Wallia* (deep Wales) the laws of Hwel Dada, which had been codified in the tenth century and which, for example, pardoned a theft if the culprit had passed ten houses and failed to obtain anything to eat, still obtained. Most often, too, these regions were pastoral and hunting worlds, living off native cattle, horses and goats. Between the upland and the lowland zones, in dales and valleys, Cistercian abbeys (like Melrose in Scotland or Strata Florida and Valle Crucis in central Wales) ran flocks of sheep so enormous that they arguably constituted the single most important industry in the British isles. The lowlands – Carmarthen and Glamorgan in Wales, the area between the Tweed and the Firth of Forth in Scotland, and the eastern half and centre of Ireland – had all been colonized by varieties of Middle English tongue (together with Latin for the clergy and French for the aristocracy) along with the baronial magnates who built the castles that signified their staying power. Gaelic and Celtic had been pushed back into the highlands. As the language zones shaded down into a hybrid mix at the edges of these worlds, so did the landscape. In the

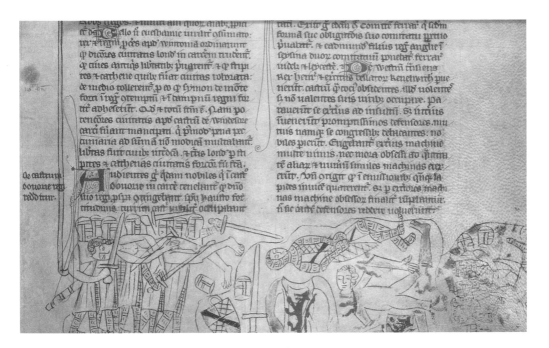

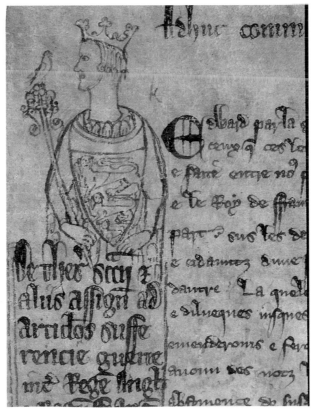

Top: The dismemberment of Simon de Montfort's body after the battle of Evesham, from an early fourteenth-century chronicle.
Above: Drawing of Edward I from an Exchequer roll, *c.* 1297–8.

lowlands peasants worked scattered strips of land within open fields just as they did in England, pastured their animals on the village's designated common land and supplied either personal labour or a sum of money in commutation to their lord in return for the privilege of being where they were. It was in these lowlands (or gently hilly regions, like the Cheviots and the Black Mountains) that the frontiers were most unstable and shadowy, moving back and forth across hills and rivers according to which ruler could, for the time being, command the greatest power.

In many respects, Wales, Scotland and England were becoming more, not less, alike. In the middle to late thirteenth century all three were subject to the strenuous policies of aggressive, intelligent and dynamic princes who sought to impose a single law and a single rule on the disparate pieces of their jurisdiction. In Scotland Alexander III, who reigned from 1249 to 1286, presided over a flourishing kingdom, with its ceremonial centre divided between Scone, the place of royal inauguration, and Dunfermline Abbey, the necropolis of the House of Canmore. The prosperous maritime port cities of Scotland, from Aberdeen in the north to Berwick-upon-Tweed in the south, shipped hides and wool and housed the same mix of local artisans and foreign merchants and bankers – especially the Hansa Germans and the ubiquitous Flemish – and had established a place in the dynamic trading economy of the North Sea.

None of this is to say that what was in progress in the thirteenth century was some sort of spontaneously developing common British economy and society. Quite the opposite was, in fact, the case. Similarity does not necessarily make for affinity. The more alike these regions became, the more determined they were to remain apart. In Wales the great power was the ruler of the northern, mountainous kingdom of Gwynedd, Llewellyn ap Gruffydd. He was the grandson of Llewellyn ab Iorwerth, 'Llewellyn the Great', who had successfully resisted all the efforts of the Angevins to subdue Wales and who had married John's bastard daughter, Joan.

Llewellyn's son by Joan, Daffydd, had died childless, and his elder half-brother, Gruffydd, had been taken hostage and incarcerated in the Tower of London from where he fell to his death on St David's day 1244, attempting to escape down a knotted sheet. Llewellyn II, his son, made up for this misfortune by breaking out from Gwynedd into the neighbouring kingdoms to the south. By 1257 he was master of two-thirds of the territory of Wales and was writing to the Scots as 'the prince of Wales'.

Even though his core territory was the mountain fastness of Snowdonia, Llewellyn was the opposite of a primitive 'tribal' king. His court had the full complement of falconers, harpists, bards and even a 'silentiary', whose job it was to silence a rowdy company at table when things got out of hand. Llewellyn was also responsible – like Alexander in Scotland and Edward in England – for trying to standardize the law or at least for demarcating clearly the boundaries between customary and manorial law and the laws of the realm. Llewellyn II, as much as de Montfort, Edward and Alexander III, was a conscious state-maker, attempting to bring law and custom, language and history, together in a new polity. He was also enough of a general to withstand the armed expeditions that came his way whether they were launched by the Marcher lords or Henry III. In 1265 he had made an alliance with Simon de Montfort, sealed by the promise of marriage between himself and Simon's daughter, Elinor, which pushed the frontiers of *pura Wallia* much further east and south than they had been for centuries. Two years later, in 1267, the Treaty of Montgomery recognized his title as 'prince of Wales', while he in turn acknowledged the king of England as his feudal overlord. Wales was not, then, regarded as a completely independent state, but within its territory a Welsh prince, not the Marchers or any other colonist, was to be recognized as supreme.

Twenty years of success may have made Llewellyn over-confident, however, for in 1274 he failed to perform the basic obligation incumbent on a feudal vassal, no matter how grand he might be: to kneel at the feet of a new king, place his hands in the hands of his liege lord and pledge fealty. Certainly, Llewellyn had his reasons. He was angry that his Welsh enemies (including his elder brothers) were being given refuge in England and argued, reasonably, that this was a violation of the Treaty of Montgomery. Edward had already stated, however, that he would not recognize the validity of the treaty, so Llewellyn may well have feared for his physical safety should he venture into England. After all, his betrothed, Elinor de Montfort, was being held prisoner in Windsor Castle on the groundless suspicion of reviving a Montfortian plot. Between 1276 and 1277 he wrote Edward three letters stating that he was not ignoring but merely postponing his act of homage until the differences between them were resolved. But Edward, who had experienced years of political upheaval turning precisely on issues of allegiance, was not interested in discussion. When Llewellyn failed to answer not one summons but five, the king declared him a rebel.

In the summer of 1277 Edward mobilized the biggest army Wales had ever seen – some 800 knights and 15,000 foot soldiers (9000 of them Welsh, raised from all those who had been offended by Llewellyn's pretensions: the Marcher lords and the princes of Powys and Deheubarth) – and marched on Gwynedd. Going south from the stronghold of Chester, Edward took Anglesey, cutting off Snowdonia's grain supply from the sea. With winter approaching and starvation a serious possibility, Llewellyn capitulated in November. Although Llewellyn finally performed the overdue act of homage at Worcester in 1278, when he also married Elinor in the king's presence, Edward was not inclined to be magnanimous. Not for the last time, his appetite for territories and sovereignty had grown with the eating. All the territories Llewellyn had governed at the height of his powers were stripped away, leaving him with a rump state in Gwynedd alone.

As they apprehensively watched new royal castles go up at Aberystwyth, Flint, Builth and Rhuddlan, forward bases for English garrisons, Llewellyn and his younger brother, Daffydd, suspected with good reason that the reduction of their state was just a prelude to what, sooner or later, would be a complete and outright annexation. Llewellyn now attempted to suggest a 'federal' solution to Edward, declaring that:

> each province under the lord king's dominion – the Gascons in Gascony, the Scots in Scotland, the Irish in Ireland and the English in England – has its own laws and customs according to the modes and usage of those parts where they are situated, [and that this] amplifies rather than diminishes the Crown. In the same wise he seeks to have his own Welsh law and be able to proceed by it especially as the lord king had, of his own free will in the peace made between them, granted this law to him and to all Welshmen.

But when clashes of jurisdiction arose, English justices (especially the justiciar of Chester) made it clear that they would hear cases in the royal courts referred to them from plaintiffs adversely judged under Welsh law and if necessary overrule them, thus further reducing the prince of Wales's dignity and power. In this, the royal officers were, in fact, faithfully reflecting Edward's own increasingly imperialist instincts.

Something bad was in the offing. The choice for the prince of Wales seemed to be either to submit to gradual but inexorable subjugation or to resist, perhaps hopelessly, perhaps not. Kings of England, after all, had been repelled before. Taking a leaf from Edward's own ruthless book, Daffydd, Llewellyn's brother, struck first, attacking an English garrison at Hawarden Castle on Palm Sunday 1282. Edward threw at the Welsh everything he could: another huge army, led by himself, moving by land and sea and abundantly supplied with weapons, provisions and even clothes, from materials sent from all over his dominions. The army of repression was once again a mixed coalition, including once again Robert Bruce senior, the Scots Earl of Carrick, the Marcher lords and Llewellyn's Welsh enemies. But after some initial successes in taking strongholds in the north and east, the offensive faltered as so many others had before. The Marchers in the south lost ground and fortresses, and in Anglesey, at the beginning of November, an army of knights sent to secure a connection between the

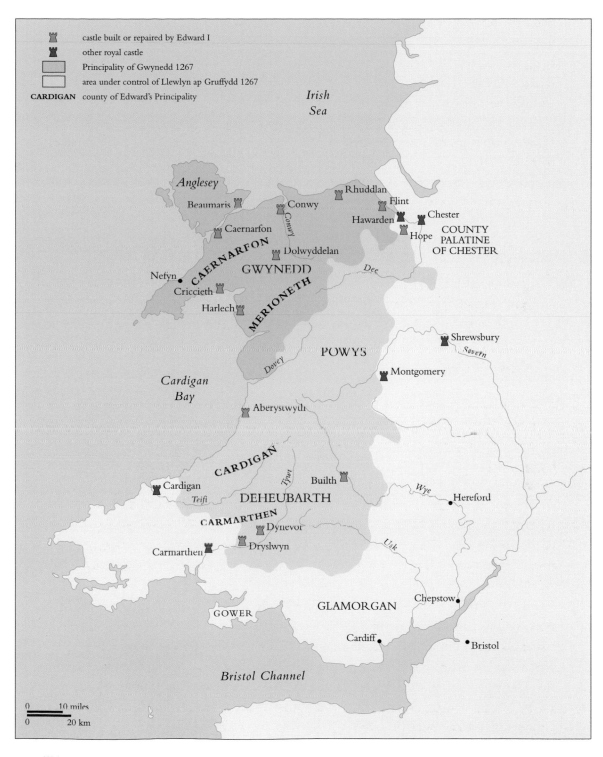

Wales in the thirteenth century.

island and the mainland was cut to pieces by the Welsh, and many of the knights drowned in the Menai Strait.

It was at this point, during a truce, that John Pecham, Archbishop of Canterbury, attempted some sort of arbitration. Might Llewellyn consider a lordship in England worth £1000 a year in return for handing over Gwynedd to the king? Pecham might not have been the ideal negotiator, considering that he had also let it be known that the traditional laws of Wales were contrary to the Bible. Back came Llewellyn's unequivocal reply that the country was not his to give: 'Let it be known that since Snowdonia is something that pertains to the principality of Wales which he and his ancestors have held since the time of Brutus, his council does not permit him to renounce that land and take in its place a land in England to which he has less claim.' More trenchantly, it was Pecham's proposal that provoked in counter-response the stirring declaration drafted by Welsh lords that insisted that, even if Llewellyn or some other prince 'should give overlordship to the King, they themselves would refuse to do homage to any foreigner of whose language, customs and laws they were ignorant'.

In mid-November, perhaps mindful of the difficulty of surviving a winter with his supply routes cut off, Llewellyn broke out of Snowdonia and marched south into Powys. It was a bold and literally fatal move because on 11 December Llewellyn was killed near Builth by a Shropshire soldier who failed to recognize his opponent. (Had he done so he would, in all likelihood, have kept him alive as a valuable prisoner.) His severed head was sent to Edward and with it went the organizing genius that had sustained Welsh resistance. The war went on well into 1283, but there was a flurry of desertions on the Welsh side, hurrying to make their peace with the king before his vengeance overtook them. Their haste may have been indecent but it was understandable. In areas of the country that held out against Edward's huge force, large numbers of the population saw their villages burned to the ground and their men marched off into captivity as hostages. But the king of England was unforgiving. When Daffydd had been turned in by some of his own men, Edward raved to his barons: 'The tongue of man can scarcely recount the evil deeds committed by the Welsh against our progenitors…but God wishing, as it seems to put an end to these evil proceedings has, after the prince had been slain, destined David [Daffydd] as the last survivor of the family of traitors…to be the king's prisoner after he had been captured by men of his own race.' Daffydd was made an example of in the most hideous fashion, quadruply punished: sentenced to be dragged by horses to the scaffold (as a traitor), hanged alive (as a homicide), have his bowels burned out as a violator of religion (since he had attacked at Easter) and his body quartered (as he had plotted the king's death). At Shrewsbury, where the sentence was carried out, a brawl broke out between Londoners and Yorkshiremen over which should get the prime body parts. Needless to say, the cockneys got the head.

Early in 1284 Edward presided over an Arthurian-style court at Nefyn in north Wales, complete with elaborate tournaments and round table. The weight of the new Camelot was such that the floor collapsed during the festivities. In the Welsh epics, Arthur had been, of course, a true western Briton, a Celt, in fact. Geoffrey of Monmouth, the borderer, had begun the process of anglicization, and Edward had now completed it. The British hero was now an English emperor, an emperor, more-over, to whom, in the words of the Statute of Rhuddlan that formalized the annex-ation of Wales, 'divine providence has entirely transferred under our proper dominion the land of Wales along with its inhabitants'. This was just the beginning of a com-prehensive exercise in cultural demolition and imperial control. Just because Edward had himself witnessed his father's creation of a sacred mystique of princely rule (and was its first beneficiary), he knew exactly what to rip out from the Welsh tradition to maximize their demoralization. At Aberconwy, the Cistercian monastery that had been the burial place of Llewellyn the Great – the equivalent to the Westminster sanctuary of the Confessor – was demolished (its monks moved eight miles away) and replaced by an immense castle, one of a stone ring of fortresses interposed between Snowdonia and the sea. The relic of the Croes Naid, the fragment of the True Cross which had been in the safe keeping of Llewellyn's house, was taken away to England along with Llewellyn's coronet. And since a son, Edward, the eleventh child to be born to Edward and Eleanor, had been born at Caernarfon in 1284, the title that had defined Welsh autonomy – the Prince of Wales – would now be bestowed on the most English of princes, the heir-apparent, the emperor in waiting. Edward of Caernarfon was formally invested in 1301 – in Lincoln, which was about as far as one could travel from Wales and still be in Britain.

Edward's Welsh conquest gave him the chance to play Roman emperor, an ambition that may well have been stimulated by his experience of Latin Christendom in arms on the crusade. While the excavations for Conwy Castle were under way, bones were unearthed which were said to be the remains of Magnus Maximus, the father of the first Christian Roman Emperor, Constantine the Great. Edward had the bones taken to the nearby site of the ancient Roman city of Segontium and re-interred with great pomp and ceremony. The king may not have had much time for book learning, but he often behaved as if he were an heir to the Caesars: formidable on the battlefield, a stickler for homage in triumph, and all the while trumpeting the belief that he was creating an empire of law. The Welsh and Irish (whose traditional laws Edward had decreed were 'detestable to God and so contrary to all law that they ought not to be deemed law at all') were to be deprived of their traditional practices but would gain the immeasurable satisfaction of being enfolded within the king's law. To cap it all, the greatest warlord of the century kept harping on about 'Pax'. Come to my peace, he would say, like some latter-day Trajan, and all will be well. Choose otherwise and you will regret it. In *The Mabinogion*, the cycle of early Welsh tales, there is mention of a king who had dreamed of a castle with high, coloured towers. That dream had been translated into reality at Constantinople, and at Caernarfon Edward created a Byzantium by the sea, with banded octagonal towers copied slavishly from the Theodosian walls of Constantinople. On top of the battlements he set the eagles of imperial Rome.

The scale of castle-building, the most ambitious exercise in colonial domination ever undertaken anywhere in medieval Europe, was likewise Roman-crusader in its colossalism. The construction of Conwy was organized like an imperial military campaign. Between the spring of 1283 and late autumn of 1287, when most of the work was done, there were on site some 1500 *minuti* (semi-skilled labourers) and around 500 specialized artisans shipped in from wherever it was that they did things best: the forested west Midlands for the carpenters, the boggy fens of Lincolnshire for the *fossatori* (the excavators who made water defences) and stony Devon and Dorset for the *cementarii* (masons). First, the skilled craftsmen were shipped to posting stations (just like soldiers) in Bristol or York and then to regimental headquarters at Chester. From Chester they arrived on site, along with the stone and timber, to be assigned to their tents and work places. It must have been at places like Conwy and Harlech that West Countrymen and Midlanders and men from Yorkshire and Lincolnshire would have had their first encounter with each other, just like the many nations that found themselves bonded together in the legions of Rome. There, beneath the lion standard of Edward Plantagenet, they were made to understand what it meant to be part of the great Britannic realm.

Over all this presided Edward's master-builder, an architect of consummate genius and versatility, Master James of St-George, a Savoyard whom Edward had met on his way back from the Holy Land and whose work he had seen in southern France. Master James was someone who understood how to build not just great crusader fortresses (the closest thing to the Welsh castles), but what were actually entire walled colonial cities, controlling supply routes, fitted out with modern conveniences like bath-houses and with flexible defences: towers that could be manned or abandoned, connected or isolated as circumstances required. The last time that anything like this had happened in Britain was the construction of Hadrian's Wall.

Harlech Castle, Gwynedd.

As for the natives themselves, they were now second-class citizens in their own country, treated like naughty children down in the satellite towns and villages built at the feet of the stone monster. They were forbidden to carry arms or to have strangers stay overnight without permission. They were allowed to keep some of their more esoteric laws, as long as they understood that they could be superseded at any time by the king's laws. And the sheriffs responsible for administering royal law, were, for several generations, overwhelmingly English, as befitted the government of a colony. Worst of all perhaps, in the mind of the conquerors they were doomed to a kind of patronized quaintness – permitted to retain (for the entertainment of their colonial overlords) their quaint blind harpists, bards and choirs. As for those who wanted to do something more serious with their lives and get aboard the Plantagenet gravy train, Edward's army awaited.

It could have been worse. And for the Jews of England it was. In 1290 England acquired the distinction of becoming the first country in Christian Europe – or anywhere else for that matter – to expel its Jews as if they were a contagious disease. It is sometimes supposed that this enormity was perpetrated as a financial expedient to meet the huge bills falling due as a result of the Welsh wars. Certainly, the costs of empire were staggering – probably a third of a million pounds or ten times the annual revenue of the treasury – and Edward certainly wished to avoid the imposition of heavy taxes, which might provoke the same kind of opposition in and out of parliament that had been his father's and his grandfather's ruin. But he also had the banking house of the Riccardi from Lucca ready and willing to advance substantial sums, albeit at equally substantial rates of interest. The three thousand Jews, on the other hand, had been so exhaustively bled by earlier forced loans and penal taxes that they were in no condition to yield much at all to Edward's needy coffers. Throughout their history in England they had always been treated as property rather than humanity; something to be used and disposed of once that usefulness had been exhausted.

Prodded by the Church, Edward had already abolished usury in his kingdom, immediately depriving the Jews of the only form of livelihood to which they had been allowed access. At the same time he required that they wear yellow badges of identification, the better to be recognized as the subspecies of humanity he undoubtedly believed they were. In 1285 he took the further disingenuous step of requiring them to abandon money-lending for other pursuits while doing nothing to make those alternative occupations available. Five years thence he was able to ask the Church and parliament for an enormous grant of taxes, the quid pro quo for which would be the expulsion. The measure, as Edward well knew, was immensely popular, as attacks on the Jews always were. Edward's mother, Queen Eleanor of Provence, had been an enthusiastic anti-Semite and piously believed (along with countless others) the obscenities of the blood libel that claimed that, because Jews needed blood to bake their Passover matzo (unleavened bread), they regularly took the lives of innocent Christian children to ensure a supply. The boy Hugh of Lincoln, whose body had been found in a well in 1255, was assumed to be one such martyr, much mourned over by the Plantagenet court and given his own shrine in Lincoln Cathedral. Whenever a child went missing a hue and cry went up that the diabolical Jews had claimed yet another victim, so their elimination would merely remove from the body of Christianity a particularly offensive toxin.

Edward's modern biographer, Michael Prestwich, describes this ethnic cleansing – the violent uprooting of entire communities in York, Lincoln and London – as an 'operation [that] went surprisingly smoothly', congratulating the king and his officers on carrying it out without unseemly massacres. But there were ways to avoid the messiness of public bloodshed and still see the Jews off with a satisfying degree of loathing for the crucifiers of the Saviour. One ship's captain devised a method that doubtless gave him, his crew and all those who heard about it enormous amusement. When the ship was beached at low tide in the Thames estuary at Queenborough, he suggested that his Jewish passengers might like to stretch their legs. When the tide came in they were barred from re-embarking. Vastly entertained, the captain told them to beseech their God to part the waters as he had done for their ancestors in the Exodus. But there was no miracle this time. The Jews drowned.

Not long after the expulsion of the Jews Edward I had his own loss to mourn. In that same year, 1290, Eleanor of Castile died in Lincoln. Like his father before him (and in stark contrast to the libidinous Angevins), he had been tied to his wife by what seem to have been bonds of real affection. Most of their life had been together. She had been twelve when they married, had given birth to fifteen children of which only one boy and five daughters survived into adulthood and was still comparatively young when she died. Edward, normally so thick-skinned and emotionally coarse, was torn apart by her death, plunging into deep mourning. He ordered two tomb effigies be made in gilt bronze, one for her entrail tomb at Lincoln, the other for Westminster. And between the place of her death and the place of her interment he created a monument unique in medieval kingship: a series of elaborately carved stone crosses – at Waltham, Charing and Cheapside among other places – all marking the journey of her body.

There was another royal death in 1290, and its implications were dramatic enough to pull Edward out of his mourning and back into the chess-game of politics he played so wickedly well. In September the six-year-old Maid of Norway died at Kirkwall in Orkney. She had been the granddaughter of Alexander III of Scotland, and with her the house of Canmore became extinct. Her death was only the last of a series of mortal misfortunes that had created the succession crisis in Scotland. Alexander's two sons had both died young and childless, and his daughter, Margaret, the wife of the king of Norway, had died while giving birth to a baby girl, also called Margaret. But Alexander was only in his early forties, and by his marriage in 1285 to the young French noblewoman, Yolande of Dreux, he could reasonably expect a decent chance of producing more heirs. On the tempestuous night of 18 March 1286 he was in too much of a hurry to get on with the succession project for his own – and Scotland's – good. Eager to reach his manor on the far side of the Firth of Forth, Alexander was twice told in no uncertain terms to turn back, first by the ferryman and then by the baillie who met him on the north shore. Ridiculing their fears, he rode off with a small company towards the manor along the coast road. In the morning his body, neck broken, was discovered on the shore.

The completely unexpected death of the forty-four-year-old king was an immense disaster for Scotland. Alexander had presided over a long period of prosperity and had managed to keep the country out of the civil and foreign wars that had done such damage in Ireland, Wales and England. If Alexander had not managed to keep the thirteen great earls from pursuing their perennial clan vendettas and land and cattle feuds with each other, he had at least prevented the disputes from turning into anarchy. Now this long peace was in jeopardy, thrown by a horse and its rider too impatient for the marriage bed to wait for a storm to pass. An anonymous poet mourned:

> Sen Alexander our king was deid
> That Scotland left in luve and lee,
> Away wes sonse of aill and breid,
> Of wine and wax, of gamin and glee.
> The gold wes changit all in leid,
> The fruit failyeit on everilk tree…

[Since Alexander our king was dead/That Scotland left in love and peace/Away fled abundance of ale and bread/Of wine and wax, of pleasure and glee/The gold it was all changed to lead/The fruit it fails on every tree…]

There was an heir, Margaret, the infant whose birth had caused the death of her mother, Alexander's daughter. But she was in Norway and reputedly sickly. So while 'the damsel' was in her infancy, government was entrusted to a body of senior nobles

Top: Edward I with bishops and attendants, *c.* 1285.
Above: Persecuted Jews at the time of their expulsion in 1290.

and clerics known as the Guardians of the Realm. The mere fact that there was such a body presupposes a sense of the national community in Scotland (much as in England in the 1250s) that existed independently from the prince who happened, at any time, to personify it. And the Guardians believed that they had found a practical solution to the dangers of a long period of minority. The child Margaret would be betrothed to Edward's infant son, Edward of Caernarfon. It was specified that in this marriage of realms, Scotland was to keep its independent identity, laws and customs. But Edward I doubtless assumed that he could now count, without fail, on Scotland's loyal support in war – especially in conflicts with France.

The death of the child-queen amid the dark red sandstone of Kirkwall wrecked all those finely tuned calculations. It was now unavoidable that the royal presence looming to the south would have something forceful to say concerning Scotland's destiny. Edward, however, did not interfere unbidden in Scottish affairs. He was invited, first by letters and then by a delegation, to act as arbitrator in deciding the claims of the contenders for the Scottish throne. It was a priceless opportunity and Edward seized it with alacrity. The Scots needed something from him. Very well, then he would take something in return, an acknowledgement that he was their feudal overlord. An assembly of magnates and prominent churchmen from England and Scotland was called to the border, on the river Tweed, in May 1291. The English gathered at Norham Abbey on their side of the frontier while the Scots, judiciously, remained at Upsettlington, north of the beautiful, winding river. Edward then duly invited representatives of the Scots to cross the Tweed to join him. But the meeting that then transpired was not exactly a union of minds (though the proceedings took place, as usual, in French). As the price of settling their affairs, Edward summarily, and shrewdly, asked the Guardians to produce documents showing why he should not be recognized as their feudal overlord. What he got, instead, was an equally astute contradiction. 'The *bons gents'* – the responsible men – 'who have sent us here say they know full well you would not make such a claim if you did not believe you had a good right to it. Yet of any such right made or used by your ancestors we know nothing.' This was as good as saying that the king might not be completely off his head to make such a demand, but it was for him, not them, to come up with the substantiating document. For good measure they added that they were unauthorized to answer any questions that would commit, in advance, a king who had not yet been installed on the Scottish throne and who (it was implied) might well have his own notions on the matter.

In the end, of course, the liberty of the discussions at Norham was seriously circumscribed by a small but significant fleet of warships anchored at the mouth of the

Tweed, not to mention the armed following of sixty-seven English magnates. Despite the epic of national resistance which would follow in the years ahead, in 1290 the leading contenders were so anxious to have succession settled (preferably in their favour) that they were prepared to take individual oaths of homage to Edward in June 1291. But as a group the Guardians had extracted some crucial conditions: Edward was to promise to maintain the 'laws and liberties' of Scotland during the period of his adjudication, and, once a king was decided on, he was to return the realm, and especially its castles, no later than two months after the new Scottish sovereign's installation. Should he violate that agreement, Edward was to be penalized to the tune of £100,000!

Edward, one suspects, took good note of these conditions and perhaps even found them inoffensive, for in 1291 he had no plans to colonize the kingdom to the north as he had Wales. What counted for him was that ceremony in the meadows on 13 June when the Scottish lords and Guardians had placed their hands in his and recognized him as 'superior and direct lord of the kingdom of Scotland'.

With that satisfaction, the beauty contest could begin in August 1291 at Berwick, then, of course, still a Scottish city. Nor was the occasion just a charade allowing Edward to pick the stooge of his choice. A hundred and four 'auditors' were to hear the claim (modelled on the 105 *centumviri* of the Roman Republic), just twenty-four nominated by the English and eighty by the principal Scots competitors. After a small army of monks had sifted and sorted a dense body of ancient documents, the competition rapidly boiled down to two candidates, both claiming descent from the daughters of Henry, Earl of Huntingdon, the brother of King William the Lion: Robert Bruce of Annandale (the grandfather of the future King Robert I) and John Balliol, Earl of Galloway. Although no love was lost between the families of the Bruce and the Balliols (who were allied to the great clan of the Comyns in the southwest), they were very much the same kind of Scottish aristocrat – not at all unpolished dwellers of the glen but well-travelled Francophone families of Anglo-Norman ancestry, boasting several scattered manors in England and France. Both had, in fact, served Edward on his campaigns in Wales. Bruce had even been Edward's governor of Carlisle – a crucial strategic posting – fortified *against* the possibility of Scottish incursions into England. By Roman law Bruce had the better claim, being closer in degree to the last ruling dynasty. But by feudal law, which emphasized the succession of the eldest son, it was Balliol who had the edge.

At first the English king honoured his side of the pact. John Balliol was inaugurated at Scone (by both Scots and English bishops), and duly got his castle back. Was his succession, as some Scots historians have always maintained, a carefully sprung

Above: Gilded bronze tomb effigy of Queen Eleanor by William Torel, in Westminster Abbey.
Left: The Eleanor Cross at Geddington in Northamptonshire.

trap, the weaker candidate chosen to play the part of a puppet? No one believed this at the time. Balliol was not shoved down the throats of the Scots as the pro-English candidate He was the clear and free choice of the vast majority of the 'auditors'. Nineteen of *Bruce's* nominees at Berwick actually ended up voting for Balliol. None of this is to say, though, that Edward was blithely prepared to hand over the keys to the Scottish kingdom after a mere pro forma recognition of his overlordship. He had kept, after all, the four pieces of the broken Great Seal of Scotland carefully in his treasury in Westminster. And from the beginning of the reign of King John Balliol, Edward let it be known that he meant to test it in practice, early and often. As with Wales, those tests were, in the first place, legal. Edward hardly needed to invent cases brought to him as a supreme royal arbiter; he was almost immediately besieged by a host of plaintiffs who didn't much like judgements they had received from Scottish courts: Manxmen and Hebrideans, who were not at all pleased to be incorporated into greater Scotland; feuding Macdougalls and MacDonalds in the western isles; most of all Macduff, Earl of Fife, who had been sentenced to a term of imprisonment by the new King John.

As in Wales, the issue of adjudication was the issue of sovereignty. By being so obliging to Scottish suitors, Edward was, of course, rubbing King John's nose in the inferiority of his status and in effect demoting him from a judge to a defendant! As such, he was summoned to appear before the King's Bench towards the end of 1293. After initially declining, John eventually showed up at Westminster Hall, where he was treated to abuse and ridicule. At first, well briefed by his Scots advisers, he held his ground and invoked the agreement of 1290 by which Scotland's laws and customs were to be preserved intact. He was then subjected to one of Edward's blood-curdling tirades, threatened with the confiscation of his castles and (at least) imprisonment should he persist in this contumacious nonsense. Inevitably John – like so many who faced Edward's wrath – crumbled and grovellingly renewed his submission.

In Scotland the reaction was a mixture of fury and dismay. A council of twelve – akin to the Guardians – stripped the king of his powers and, much like the council of fifteen established at Oxford in 1258, transferred them to themselves. They were now Scotland, and they were of a mind to resist Edward's demand for feudal levies to accompany him on a war expedition to France; not only to resist, in fact, but to switch sides, for a delegation in the spring of 1295 travelled to France to conclude an alliance, promising to cement it by a marriage between the daughter of John Balliol and the son of Philip IV. Given what was about to happen, this might look like suicidal folly. But the Scots must have taken heart from believing they were joining a long-overdue anti-English coalition: France, Scotland and Norway in alliance and, most hearteningly for them, a huge uprising in Wales which had actually succeeded in taking the supposedly impregnable royal castles, including Caernarfon, the biggest of them all.

It was, nonetheless, a colossal miscalculation. When the Scottish army mustered near Selkirk, the troops had not gone into war in any serious fashion for two generations. Edward, now almost sixty years old, with a great mane of white hair flowing down over his shoulders, still tall, bony and upright, remained very much the warlord without peer. His tactics were unsubtle. The Scots needed, quite simply, to be smashed. The army to do the job put even the Welsh campaign in the shade: some 25,000 foot soldiers and almost a thousand knights. The first target was Berwick, the richest and most populous city in Scotland. The actual military work of taking the castle was, in fact, just a prelude to the real job at hand, which was to inflict on the unfortunate inhabitants of the town a slaughter of such horrific dimensions that it would instruct the rest of the country on what to expect if it continued to resist. Over three days an immense massacre – at least 11,000 souls, including countless women and children – took place. One chronicler grieved: 'Blood streamed from the bodies of the slain so copiously that mills could be turned by its flow.' What was left of Berwick was burned to ashes, reduced to ground zero. It would be made over as an English city and colonized with Northumbrian settlers; the border between the two kingdoms would always run to the north of it.

From Berwick, ignoring Scottish raids into Northumbria (which English chroniclers claimed took the lives of 200 children at Corbridge), Edward's juggernaut proceeded to roll over the Scottish feudal army at the battle of Dunbar. The entire campaign of destruction took less than three weeks, and at the end of it, Edward seemed to be standing on the neck of Scotland's freedom. One by one, the great earls made their submission, including the elder Bruce. At Kincardine Castle in July King John was made a mockery of once more, forced to confess his rebellion and to dress in the white surcoat of a penitent, while his royal insignia was torn from his chest like a court-martialled subaltern. He was now, in both England and Scotland, a pathetic object of derision – 'Toom Tabard' (the 'empty coat') – and was taken off to imprisonment in the Tower of London. The humiliation was once again, as in Wales, a calculated exercise in demoralization. The royal treasures of Scotland, including the Black Rood of St Margaret, were hauled off to Westminster as was the Stone of Destiny, on which Scots kings had been inaugurated at Scone Abbey and which was now to be presented to (who else?) Edward the Confessor. A special coronation chair was custom-designed to hold it, which became, in effect, the first identifiable 'throne' of the monarchs of England, who, from Edward I to Elizabeth II, have been crowned sitting upon the most precious emblem of Scottish sovereignty. When the great seal of Scotland was handed to Edward, he set it aside with a facetious profanity, commenting that 'a man does good business when he rids himself of a turd'.

The separate kingdom of Scotland was not eliminated, however, for Edward had never been interested in ruling it directly as king. He continued to style himself as 'lord', while introducing a colonial administration run, of course, by Englishmen – William de Warenne (who disliked the Scottish weather enough to stay, for the most part, south of the border on his estates in Yorkshire) and the more effective treasurer Hugh Cressingham. To formalize the country's dependence, every freeholder in Scotland was now required to come forward and swear an oath of fealty to the conqueror.

The vast majority did just that. But there was one who did not, and that was a tenant of James the Stewart called Malcolm Wallace. And this Wallace had a brother, William, whose intervention in the Anglo-Scots wars, though brief, was extraordinarily dramatic. Celebrated by historians of the nineteenth century as a national hero, debunked by professional historians as a self-serving renegade and immortalized once more courtesy of Mel Gibson and the big-screen *Braveheart*, Wallace is one of those larger-than-life figures whose epic romance refuses to go away. In fact, much of what is known or imagined about Wallace comes from two histories, the *Scotichronicon* and the bardic poems of 'Blind Harry', both of which date from the fifteenth century. What we do know with more certainty does nothing to strip Wallace of his heroic importance, but makes him much less of a people's champion and even less of a solo act. Far from being the homespun-wearing, oatmeal-eating man of the glens of Hollywood's imagination, Wallace grew up in the genteel manor house owned by his father in Strathclyde in southwest Scotland and attached to the following of the great aristocrat James the Stewart. But there is also no doubt that if he was not the 'runaway from righteousness' of English propaganda, he did, at some stage, cross the line into outlawry. This was precisely the period, throughout Britain, when wronged knights, gone to the greenwood (or the highlands and islands) were cropping up in popular culture like mushrooms after the autumn rain. And even after cutting through the dense thickets of mythology surrounding Wallace, there is still enough substance to see how he became set on his career of patriot-avenger. His father was certainly killed by an Englishman. And though we don't know for sure if he had been goaded to fight in the city of Lanark by an English soldier who tried to take his shortsword saying, 'What's a Scot need a knife like that, as the monk said who last screwed your wife?' But whatever it was, Wallace didn't like it and started a riot. He managed to escape but left behind his betrothed, Marion, who was taken by the sheriff as a

Top: Norham Abbey, on the borders of England and Scotland.
Above: King John Balliol with a broken crown and sceptre.

hostage for the outlaw and summarily killed. Wallace returned, killed the sheriff, an Englishman called Haselrig, and went on the run and the rampage, collecting myths and men with every stop along the way.

It may be that in the years before 1297 Wallace had been a fugitive, carving his way through the English in southwest Scotland, the line between freedom-fighting and out-and-out thuggery becoming increasingly blurred. But his hit-and-run exploits would not have made much difference had not the whole of Scotland been close to the boil in the spring and summer of 1297. It is certainly true that word of Wallace's exploits spread like wildfire, along with the rumour that he was physically some sort of giant among men and the saviour of the old realm. Men of all sorts and conditions flocked to his camp in the traditional mustering place of Selkirk forest, armed with Lochaber axes, spears and claymores. If he was declared outlaw, so much the better, since it was the *English* law he was defying, and the quarrel of the two laws had been at the heart of the unequal dispute between kings Edward and John. Throughout his entire fiery rebellion Wallace never ceased to profess himself King John's loyal man.

Wallace's was never a one-man campaign. North of the Forth, Andrew Murray matched or surpassed Wallace by leading a guerrilla campaign that made the highlands effectively ungovernable for the English. It was when Wallace marched north to the Firth of Forth and Murray marched south that a wildfire rebellion turned into something like a serious military operation. By this time, some of the most powerful men in Scotland had come on board, including James the Stewart and the violent and bloody-minded William Douglas, who had kidnapped the Englishwoman who became his wife when she had come north of the border to visit relatives! Many of the magnates were moved by a sense of their country's humiliation: their king was a pathetic prisoner in the Tower. The younger Robert Bruce, Earl of Carrick, repudiated his oath to Edward, saying: 'no man holds his own flesh and blood in hatred and I am no exception. I must join my people and the nation into which I was born.' Many others had less lofty motives, mainly the settling of local scores, while others stayed loyal to the English king for the same reasons, preferring a distant to a nearby lord.

But by the time that Wallace laid siege to Dundee Castle in August 1297 something like a national crusade was well under way, blessed by the fathers of the Scottish Church, Bishop Wishart of Glasgow and Archbishop Fraser of St Andrews. It was their aggressive participation that finally gave the uprising its moral legitimacy. Armed with both men and faith, Wallace and his allies later that month caught an English army at the river in front of Stirling Castle. Confident of their superiority, the English commanders – the most important of Edward's officers in Scotland, de Warenne and

Cressingham – sent out a feeler to see if Wallace wished to treat. His famous reply was: 'Tell your commander that we are here not to make peace but to do battle, to defend ourselves. Let them come on and we shall prove this in their very beards.' The taunt was meant to provoke the English out from their position by the castle and across the river to deal with the Scots. It worked like a dream. Wallace and Murray waited, the majority of their men concealed at the wooded top of Alton Craig, until a portion of the heavily armoured knights were obligingly packed on the narrow bridge. They then swooped down to attack. The result was a bloody traffic jam of catastrophic proportions for the English. With nowhere to go, some attempted to turn about, others to swim for it, a bad idea for those in chain mail. Thousands of the trapped English and Welsh were cut down where they stood – Wallace himself swinging an immense battle sword – or drowned in the muddy river. After Cressingham, the treasurer, was killed, his skin was flayed from the body and turned into a belt for Wallace's broadsword.

Elated with triumph, Wallace now described himself in letters as 'the commander of the army of the kingdom of Scotland', although he was, in fact, still acting on behalf of the forlorn King John imprisoned in London. Taking advantage of the shock inflicted at Stirling Bridge, Wallace led an army across the border into Northumbria, committing the usual atrocities as he went, but neither there nor in Scotland itself was he able to take any of the royal castles other than Stirling. As so often happened in Scotland's history, a great victory was followed by an even more stunning defeat. Wallace's posthumous reputation for irregular warfare is belied by the fact that his natural element (like most Scots gentlemen) was the all-out battle rather than the guerrilla escapade. At Falkirk, in July 1298, Wallace was facing not Edward's deputies but the king himself, and yet another army, swollen with recruits from subdued regions of the Plantagenet empire: from Gascony and Wales (2000 from Gwynedd alone). They had all been fed stories of the monstrous Wallace, who was said to have skinned Englishmen wholesale, and forced nuns to dance naked for his barbarian pleasure. Badly outnumbered, Wallace packed his men into the defensive formation of four *schiltrons*: circular hedgehogs of 2000 men bristling with 12-foot spears to gore advancing cavalry. 'I have brought you to the ring,' he is reputed to have said, perhaps over-merrily. 'Now let us see if you can dance.' Dance they did, or at least they stood their ground for hours, as wave after wave of knights punctured themselves on the *schiltrons*. But eventually the weight of massed troops, especially the rain of arrows from Welsh and Gascon archers, took a fatal toll, the *schiltrons* were forced open and Wallace's men went down by the thousand. 'Bodies covered the field,' wrote one lamenting chronicler, 'as thick as snow.'

Calamitous as it was, there was no immediate capitulation after Falkirk. Although the English controlled southern and eastern Scotland, the experience of Murray in particular had educated the Guardians in the possibility of a flexible defence, advancing and retreating from highland and backcountry fastnesses as circumstances allowed. So what followed for five years was an equally sombre war of attrition. Realizing that he could not afford another round of imperial castle-building to subjugate the natives, Edward committed himself to taking them from the Scots and either garrisoning them or destroying them. For year after year, with grim resolution, Edward returned to Carlisle and Berwick to assemble his armies, and he trudged up through Scotland, implacable and relentless, taking the country abbey by abbey, castle by castle. The royal armies were built for stamina, micro-cities on the move, supplied by fifty or sixty ships brought to the Tweed or the Clyde. His devastation left behind long, bitter memories. In Galloway in the southwest, when the castle of Caerlaverock was destroyed, 300 of its defenders were hanged from the battlements. At Bothwell 7000 English soldiers dragged an immense siege engine across the Clyde and smashed their way through the fortress walls. The war became a murderous academy of siege warfare. The Roman treatise of Vegetius was consulted to come up with ever bigger and more monstrous devices to hurl projectiles at the masonry; some of them were given affectionate nicknames as if they were pet hounds. At Stirling in 1304 the garrison, desperate to surrender, ash on their heads, wanted to do so before Edward had had a chance to try out his latest toy called, ominously, 'the war wolf'. Needless to say, the king refused to permit the capitulation until the machine had done its work with who knows what dreadful results. At Dunfermline in 1303 the abbey itself, the royal necropolis, was put to the sack so that the Scots should have no illusions about the posterity of their kings.

By 1304, understandably, many of those who had originally committed themselves to resistance had had enough and came to what was called the king's peace at Strathmore. They knelt and were pardoned. In victory Edward was shrewd enough to be selective in his punishments. The lords who abandoned the Scottish cause had their lands restored. William Wallace, on the other hand, who was betrayed in 1305 by some of his own countrymen, was made to undergo a hideous show trial. Accusing Wallace of violating his feudal oath was particularly grotesque, since he (unlike virtually all of the other leaders of Scotland) had never shown the slightest sign of pledging allegiance to Edward. But the king brushed aside these technical niceties to get on with the real business of making a spectacle of the presumptuous rebel. Made to wear a laurel crown, Wallace was dragged to his execution where live disembowelment awaited him.

With Wallace dead and many of the most prominent Scots fighting for, rather than against, his authority, Edward must have surveyed the results of his long war of repression with satisfaction. That was that. On with the next item on the imperial agenda. France perhaps. Except, it wasn't. Just as he supposed the fires of resistance were dead, they burst back into flame, and they were set alight by someone whom Edward could never have tipped as a saboteur, much less a leader of a war of liberation: the young Earl of Carrick, Robert the Bruce.

By some measure the most politically intelligent and militarily successful of all Scotland's kings, Robert the Bruce must have seemed (mistakenly) to Edward his kind of Scotsman. He'd had a polished education, spoke French and was the holder of the Honour of Huntingdon and estates in Tottenham, and his brother, Edward, had been a student at Cambridge. Because he had done the sensible thing in 1302 and submitted to the king, he had seemed to be the sort of person bright enough not to waste his time and his life on a sentimental lost cause. This was a disastrous misjudgement. To understand the real Bruce, Edward might have done worse than look in the mirror. For sheer wily ruthlessness, this particular Scottish lion needed no tutorials from the leopard. In 1306 he did exactly what Edward had done – took care of his enemies at home before turning on the foreigner, and he did it in shocking Macbethian fashion, murdering his principal rival, John Comyn of Badenoch, at the very altar of Greyfriars Abbey in Dumfries. The murder is neither explained nor extenuated by its being a case of a patriot knocking off a quisling, for Comyn had been a lot more consistent in his opposition to the English than Bruce. But the Comyns had long fought with the Bruces for mastery of southwest Scotland, and they were allies by marriage with the Balliols. With King John Balliol still alive and actually boasting an heir – named, with doubtful taste, Edward – the Comyns refused to have anything to do with Bruce's whispered proposal of an uprising led by himself as Scotland's new king. What was more, Comyn was one of many of Scotland's nobles who had been surprised by Edward's leniency when, following his submission, the king had restored his ancestral estates and given undertakings that Scotland's own laws and customs would be preserved.

Barely six weeks after he had murdered Comyn, Bruce was inaugurated king at Scone by the inveterate old thorn in the side of the English, Bishop Wishart of Glasgow, who not only absolved Robert of the killing but unblushingly demanded that the flock now rally to his cause! Instead of unifying the Scots behind a single leader, Bruce's murder of Comyn only intensified what was already a Scottish civil war. The Lanercost chronicler in 1311–12 recalled that: 'in all this fighting the Scots were so divided that often father was with the Scots and his son with the English or

William Wallace monument, Glasgow.

one brother was with the Scots and another with the English, or even one individual was first on one side and then on the other.' And initially it was hard to see what Bruce had gained. The loser in a battle against the Comyns, he was forced to take flight, travelling north and west.

In all likelihood he went to the Hebrides, and perhaps across the Irish Sea, but wherever he went, Bruce vanishes for a while from any kind of reliable historical record. This vacuum of knowledge was filled by heroic mythology: the fable of the cave and the spider, whose exemplary patience and industry gave Robert the resolution to persevere. But what happened to Bruce in the period he went missing was, in fact, much more remarkable – the transformation of the polished aristocrat and machiavellian conspirator into a guerrilla warrior. For it was Robert the Bruce not William Wallace, the battlefield enthusiast, who truly wrote the book on partisan warfare in Britain. Bruce used what have since become the classic tactics of hit-and-run: small groups of swiftly moving attack raiders, mounted on horses or ponies, unencumbered by not having to carry their own provisions or cooking pots and pans and subsisting instead, as Froissart described, on 'the water of rivers, underdone meat cooked in cattle hides' or, if 'their stomachs feel weak and hollow, they lay stones of a fire and mix a little of their oatmeal with water, sprinkling the thin paste on the hot stone and make a small cake like a wafer' – the military origin of the oatcake. Bruce's lightning-strike forces struck fast and deep across the border to make their point: laying ambushes; using rope ladders and grappling hooks to force their way into enemy castles; wreaking havoc and disappearing again into the night. And the more damage he did, the more infuriatingly elusive he seemed to be. With every month that went by without his capture or defeat, he picked up allies.

In the end Bruce out-foxed, out-fought and outlived his nemesis, Longshanks. In the preamble to an ordinance for the government of Scotland Edward had written that he had spent sleepless nights 'tossed about by the waves of thought', but now he wished to promote 'pleasantness and ease and quiet for our subjects dwelling in our realm, for in their quiet we have rest and in their tranquillity we are inwardly cherished'. He died the following year, 1307, at Burgh-by-the-Sands near Carlisle, on his way to yet another grim campaign of siege and destruction. Before expiring, according to the chronicler Froissart, he ordered his son to boil his bones away from his body so that they might be carried with the English armies in Scotland. Without them he evidently feared for the military prospects of Edward II should he ever have to face Robert the Bruce on the field of battle.

The father's opinion of the son had long been notoriously low. Although he did not actually throw one of Edward's boyfriends from the battlements, Edward I was sufficiently provoked by his son's refusal to abandon companions he deemed deplorable to attack him physically, tearing out large chunks of the prince's hair. But in 1306, he had nonetheless celebrated Edward's knighthood in the New Temple (the site of his bank heist forty years before) with lavish festivities, featuring golden swans and the usual tournaments, in which at least two knights were killed. So in 1307, when Edward of Caernarfon came to the throne, no one wrote him off as some limp-wristed playboy hopelessly unfit to fill his father's shoes. In many ways they must have seemed quite alike – tall, blond-haired and sinewy – and Edward II's temper was certainly hot enough to remind anyone of his paternity. His favoured choice of pastimes, it's true, raised eyebrows, although they tended more to the Boy Scout than the lounge lizard: rowing, ditch-digging and thatching. In the end, however, it was not Edward's rustic pastimes, his fancy clothes, his racehorses, his creepy boyfriends or even his extreme fondness for amateur theatricals that got him into big trouble. It was rather that somehow he personified neither of the models for leadership of the English nation. He was neither the second Caesar of Britain nor the princely embodiment of the community of the realm.

Robert the Bruce, on the other hand, was just that. Although the Comyn murder showed that he was capable of striking out with unscrupulous independence, Bruce drew on the experience of his embattled country since the death of Alexander III by making the most of its tradition of collective leadership. He knew that he was in for a civil, as well as a national war and that there were some Scottish families who would never forgive what he had done to John Comyn. His task was to reconcile all but the most alienated and to do so by emphasizing that his enterprise was not for himself or his own family but for Scotland. In this way Bruce avoided de Montfort's worst mistakes after Lewes, when even the best disposed of his supporters suspected him of personal, dynastic empire-building and resented his aloofness. Bruce, on the other hand, went out of his way to consult with his nobles and especially the bishops who had, from the beginning, been his fervent supporters. By 1309 he had succeeded in establishing his own legitimacy, as much as a guardian-protector as a prince, and was able to call his own Scottish parliament to raise money for an army of national defence. Over the next five years, Bruce went systematically from stronghold to stronghold, moving by water as well as land, until all of the north, west and south-west of Scotland were firmly under his control. But this still left the southeast and the crucial castles of Berwick and Stirling in English power. Finally, by the summer of 1314, the commander of Stirling was close to capitulation but managed to foist Bruce off for a while in the hope that his plight might finally spur action from Edward II. The disgrace of losing Stirling was indeed enough to prompt an expedition from

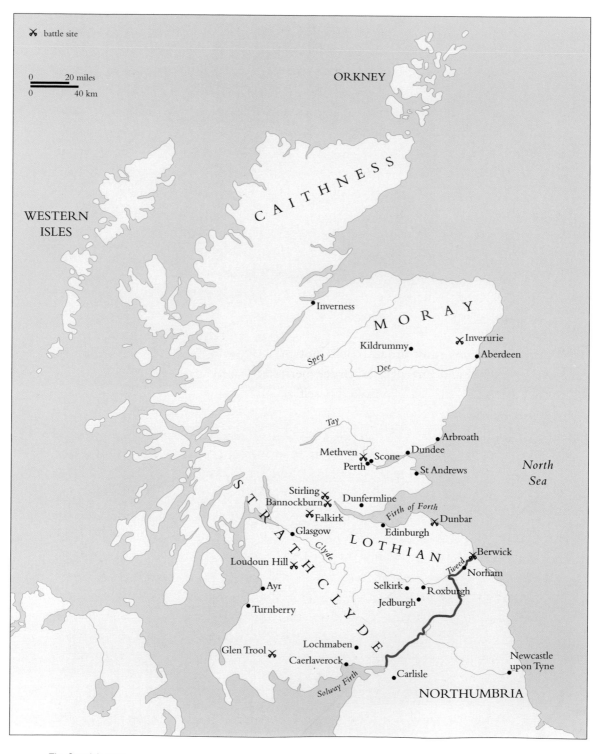

The Scottish wars.

Edward II, who moved north with yet another Anglo-imperial army of thousands.

It was the usual formidably equipped Plantagenet war machine that faced Bruce on the Forth plain outside Stirling on 23 June, but war machines don't work well in wet ground, and, outnumbered as he was three to one, Robert had carefully chosen the site of the engagement to box the English army in between the river and the boggy ditch of the Bannockburn. For Bruce himself the battle was very nearly over before it had begun, when one of the English knights, Henry de Bohun, caught Bruce unawares on his little mount some way off from his soldiers and charged directly at him with his lance. Bruce turned matador, keeping absolutely still until the very last minute, when he swerved to the side, simultaneously bringing his axe down on de Bohun's head with such force that it went cleft through helmet and skull, burying itself in his attacker's brains. Bruce sat alone on his horse, holding the shaft end of the axe. The army that had been momentarily aghast was now euphoric with relief. Providence had obviously armoured their king against destruction. It was a good sign.

The battle got serious on the second day with an unsparing, head-on collision between the *schiltrons* and the horsemen. According to his friend the Abbot Bernard, Bruce made an extraordinary speech to rally his men before the moment of truth. Shakespeare at his most ardent could not possibly have done better. Addressing both 'my lords' and 'my people' Bruce personalized the past trials in ways that perfectly captured the need to make himself, simultaneously, one of his brother Scots and their captain:

> For eight years or more I have struggled with much labour for my right to the kingdom and for honourable liberty. I have lost brothers, friends and kinsmen. Your own kinsmen have been made captive and bishops and priests are locked in prison. Our nobility's blood has poured forth in war. Those barons you can see before you, clad in mail, are bent on destroying me and obliterating my kingdom, nay our whole nation. They do not believe we can survive. They glory in their war-horses and equipment. For us the name of the Lord must be our hope of victory in battle. This is a day of rejoicing: the birthday of John the Baptist. With our Lord Jesus as commander Saint Andrew and the martyr Saint Thomas shall fight today with the saints of Scotland for the honour of their country and their nation. If you heartily repent for your sins you will be victorious under God's command.

So as they emerged from the woods into the sight of the English, the Scots soldiers knelt to pray. Seeing this, amidst general merriment Edward asked his entourage: 'What! Will those Scots fight?' On being assured they would, the king assumed they were kneeling for mercy and was told by one of his Scots allies that they did, indeed, seek mercy, 'not from the king but from God'.

From the beginning it was apparent that this was to be no repeat of Falkirk. Under the impact of the first tremendous charge, led by the Earl of Gloucester, the *schiltrons* stood fast, inflicting enormous damage by aiming their spears first at horses, then at the fallen riders. The formations were impenetrable to the mounted knights. Only the archers might have been able to break the tight cohesiveness of the *schiltrons*, but they were kept in the rear of the English attack until the battle was well under way. Perhaps it was hard to believe that, sooner or later, the repeated charges of the knights would not take their toll, as they had at Falkirk. When it became evident that this was not going to happen, the archers were belatedly moved up into firing position, but their passage was blocked by the debris of fallen horses and men, giving time for the small, mobile troop of Scottish cavalry to attack them headlong. Scattering, the Welsh and Gascon bowmen were taken out of the battle, and the conflict turned into an elemental hacking between the spears and axes of the Scots and the swords and lances of the knights. 'Many a mighty splendid blow was struck by both sides until blood burst out of the coats of mail and ran streaming down into the earth.' Gradually, the English vanguard became unhorsed, lost its coherence and turned into a disorganized mass, trapped between the now slowly advancing *schiltrons* and the deep, muddy ditch of the burn. At some point in the afternoon an irregular crowd of Scottish peasants and yeomen, whom Bruce had kept in reserve sensing that the English were on the defensive, and who were armed with flails, hammers and pitchforks, charged down towards the fray. In the confusion the English commanders might well have imagined this to be a second and fresh Scots army. More to the point, they were certain that the king was now in personal peril and urged flight before he was captured or killed.

Edward II, who had certainly not shrunk from combat and who had had horses killed under him, was finally persuaded to depart. He left behind on the battlefield his personal shield and seal (later gallantly returned by King Robert), his personal belongings and clothes, what was left of his reputation as a battle captain and 4000 dead – English, Welsh, Gascon and Scots enemies of the Bruces. The burn was 'so choked that men could pass over it with dry feet on the bodies of horses and men'. 'Maydens of Englonde, sore may ye morne,' wrote the Scots author of Fabyan's *Chronicles*. 'For your lemans ye have loste at Bannockisborne.' But what was also lost at Bannockburn was the Plantagenet dream of the Anglo-Roman empire.

Understandably, Robert the Bruce wanted it to stay dead. So instead of resting on his laurels, in 1315, a year after the battle, he did something quite remarkable: he took the attack to the English across the North Channel to Ireland in the person of his younger brother, Edward. To smooth Edward's way, he invited 'our friends, the kings of Ireland, the clergy and the inhabitants' to join a pan-Gaelic alliance. The Scots, he promised, would come not as invaders, but liberators. Together with the Irish, they would rid Caledonia and Hibernia of the detestable English, and the two Bruces, Robert in Scotland and Edward in Ireland, would rule the free peoples of *nostra natio*, our nation:

> Whereas we and you and our people and your people, free since ancient times share the same national ancestry and are urged to come together…by a common language and common custom, we have sent over to you our beloved kinsmen …to negotiate with you in our name about permanently strengthening and maintaining inviolate the special friendship between us and you so that with God's will our nation may be able to recover her ancient liberty.

The rhetoric was stirring but the timing unfortunate. For 1315 also saw the worst famine in living memory. Very soon, Edward Bruce's army became indistinguishable from any other disorderly gang of knights, using force to extract the provisions they desperately needed for their men and animals and not choosing to distinguish with any care between Gaelic friends and English foes. Famished and desperate, the Scots soldiers took what they needed from the Irish villagers and finally resorted (so it was said) to digging up fresh graves and eating the cadavers. Month by month the Bruces' war of liberation turned into something remarkably like an occupation.

Not all the Irish nobility and kings opened their arms to embrace their Scots liberators. A bitter civil war broke out between native Irish supporters of the Anglo-Normans on one side and the Scots on the other. In Dublin, many of the population tore down their own houses to use as walls against the Scots rather than surrender the city. A climactic battle took, according to contemporaries, no fewer than 10,000 lives. In 1318 Edward Bruce was himself killed, and before the end of the year the Scots had left. Perhaps the experiment in collaboration across the North Channel deserved to fail because, from the beginning, Robert the Bruce had his own, rather than his Irish brothers', interests at heart, needing a second front which might divert critical English military resources from Scotland to Ireland. Not for the last time the Irish were being used in someone else's quarrel. All the same, the Scots did leave something behind in Ireland other than widows and ballads. They had managed to complete what Bannockburn had begun and finish off the Plantagenet myth of invincibility. The proclamation of the Irish princes that they were compelled to 'face the dangers of warlike men in defence of our right rather than go on bearing outrages like women' hit a note of righteous belligerence that would, for better or worse, echo down the centuries.

The failure of the Irish expedition and Robert's correct assumption that Bannockburn had by no means finished off English efforts to recover their power over Scotland prompted him to look abroad for support. In the end, it was Scottish self-reliance rather than dependence on the French that fended off Edward II's repeated probes across the border. But an appeal to the pope to recognize the holiness of their cause did produce, if nothing else, the most eloquent statement to date of Scottish (or, for that matter, any nation's) right to self-determination that had yet been uttered in medieval Europe. At Arbroath Abbey fifty lords and bishops of Scotland attached their seals to a 'declaration', which, although coming from an unknown hand, undoubtedly reflects both Robert's and his peers' passionately held convictions about their shared history, culture and liberty. The Declaration of Arbroath was, in the first instance, the product of the usual antiquarian digging amid unreliable chronicles and myths. Needing a myth of origins that did not depend on Geoffrey of Monmouth's story of a Trojan settlement, an alternative fable in which the ur-Scots were traced back to Scythia in the Balkans where St Andrew had converted the locals in AD400, significantly *before* the Angles or the Saxons.

But the heart of the document was something much more powerful and especially extraordinary in that, although very much the instrument of the king and his government, it actually took pains to present the native homeland as not merely distinct from, but potentially in *conflict* with, its temporary royal personification. The claim, as in Snowdonia, was that the nation was its own sovereign. This had been heard before – in Oxford in 1258 – but never so eloquently as at Arbroath where the image of the free patriot is represented as one of a band of brother-survivors, the Maccabees bound to a leader, but never unconditionally. For if ever the lord Robert:

> should give up what he has begun and agree to make us and our kingdom subject to the king of England or the English we should exert ourselves at once to drive him out as our enemy and a subverter of his own rights as well as ours, and make some other man who was well able to defend us our king; for as long as but a hundred of us remain alive never will we, on any condition, be brought under English rule. It is in truth not for glory nor riches nor honours that we are fighting but for freedom – for that alone which no honest man gives up but with life itself.

The battle of Bannockburn, from the Holkham Bible, 1327–35.

In the mid-fourteenth century John Barbour's poem *The Bruce* sounded the same powerful note:

A! Freedom is a noble thing!
Freedom makis man to have liking;
Freedom all solace to man givis:
He livis at ease that freely livis!

In the England of Edward II, however, liberty and sovereignty seemed unnatural partners, and the possibility that a king might commit himself to a manifesto of national self-determination that might envisage his own overthrow should he betray the interests of his compatriots was wholly inconceivable. The lessons of Simon de Montfort had long been forgotten. Instead of the Provisions of Oxford, Edward II may have been wont to gaze for inspiration at the great gilt effigies in Westminster Abbey, which enshrined not just the bodies of his ancestors, but the fantastic infallibility of the imperial crown. At any rate, his entire disastrous reign was marked by a wilful disregard of anything that could remotely be considered the shared interests of the community of the realm. By heaping power, riches and favour on men who were transparently abusing government and justice for their own unscrupulous personal ends, Edward was, in effect, making himself not native but alien to his own country. The abhorrence of his homosexuality merely completed the sense in which, somehow, he was foreign to the kingship of England. The attempts to overthrow him, the first by Earl Thomas of Lancaster in 1321, which failed, and the second by his estranged wife Isabella with her lover Roger Mortimer, which succeeded, should not be taken as a reassertion of the Montfortian insistence on the primacy of the realm over the person of the prince. Isabella and Mortimer merely replaced one regime of selfish opportunism by another. But Edward's deposition in 1327 (and his hideous death in Berkeley Castle, probably from a hot iron thrust up his rectum, a punishment sadistically calculated to match his crime), the uprising of London citizens that preceded it and the uninhibited glee at the dismemberment of the Despensers and the overthrow of their hated administration, all presupposed that a king could now be removed, even physically disposed of, if he appeared to the custodians of the community of the realm to be incompetent to protect it or viciously indifferent to his duties.

So when Edward III, at the age of seventeen in 1330, shook off the guardianship of his mother and Mortimer, having the one made captive and the other beheaded, England seemed at last to have a Plantagenet who was conscious of the need to identify himself, publicly and unequivocally, with the community of the realm. His murdered father was encased in another golden tomb, but it was diplomatically placed, not in the sanctuary of the Confessor at Westminster, but at a decent distance in Gloucester Cathedral. Beyond his mother and her immediate associates there would be no vindictive witch-hunt for culprits in the overthrow of his father's regime. Instead, the young Edward seemed to offer what the nobles, the Church, the burgesses, knights and free yeomen of England had long wanted to hear: the voice of a ruler who understood that effective government depended on consultation and consent rather than on force. It would be in Edward III's reign that the Commons would assume they could petition the king on their grievances with the expectation they would be answered in statute law. And it would be in Edward's reign that parliament asserted its right to be consulted on matters of war and peace and to consent to any special subsidies or taxes before they could be levied. In a proclamation issued the day after the seizure of Mortimer at Nottingham, the young king let it be known that 'the affairs that concern him and the estate of his realm shall be directed by the common counsel of his realm and in no other wise'.

This must have been good news. Not for the last time, it seemed, it had taken the rest of Britain to remind England how to be a nation.

The Eve of St John, 23 June 1348, was a festival of fertility in Dorset, as everywhere else in medieval England. The wheat was ripening, and on this one night, lit by a great bonfire, the unmarried women of the village, flowers in their hair, could flirt with impunity. But in Melcombe, on Weymouth bay, death, not life, was having its way. The first Englishmen were dying of the plague. The bacillus *Yersinia pestis* had disembarked at the port along with some Gascon sailors from the Plantagenet province that was already riddled with the infection. It was carried to Melcombe in the guts of fleas. They might have been the human flea (*Pulex irritans*), or they might have been the rat flea (*Xenopsylla cheopsis*), getting a free ride on the bodies of the rodents that lived with ships and their cargoes. The fleas passed on the bacillus, either through their faeces, expelled into the air for humans to inhale, or through their bite, regurgitating the organism into the bloodstream before settling down to a hearty meal. It took no time at all for the bacillus to make itself at home in southwest England. The Melcombe casualties would have died within four days after detecting the beginnings of the swellings at groin or armpit that signalled the contamination of their lymph nodes. If they had drawn the disease into their lungs, they would have hacked bloody sputum for two days before expiring. Anyone close enough to catch the plague from droplets of coughed-up blood or mucus would be well on their way. Within eighteen months almost half of the population of Britain would be dead.

The king of England was supposed to be a doctor. More than any other of his predecessors, Edward III liked to 'touch for the king's evil', using his sacred magic to heal thousands of sufferers from scrofula at a time. But this was not a malady but a plague, and in the high summer of his long reign Edward III's mind was on other matters: the inaugural ceremonies of the Order of the Garter, for example. Edward founded the order, which was bestowed on knights and nobles who had distinguished themselves as valiant companions-in-arms, imagining it as a pious company, the

KING DEATH

The burial of victims of the plague in Tournai,
from a fourteenth-century Flemish manuscript.

reincarnation, of course, of the knights of the Holy Grail. So a new chapel, a place of devotion and beauty, had to be built for its solemnities at Windsor. It would be dedicated to St George, the late third-century dragon-slayer who had been the patron saint of the Byzantine armies and whose cult had been adopted by the English crusaders. For the reredos screen at the back of the altar alone, immense quantities of pure white Nottinghamshire alabaster were used, transported to Windsor on ten enormous wagons, pulled by eighty horses. On the feast of St Lawrence, 10 August 1348, the founder-knights, Edward's Bediveres and Percivals – in fact, Sir John Grey and Sir Miles Stapleton, Sir Bartholomew Burghersh and Sir James d'Audeley, together with twenty-two more – all clad in blue robes and sporting their badges, filed into the chapel in pairs, the lines parting to seat themselves behind either the king or the Black Prince. They faced each other across the chapel like the opposing tournament teams they were and attended to the anthems, the pieties and the blessings. As they looked at the stone carving of St George, they must have inwardly rejoiced that he had proved too strong for the likes of the opposition, the patron saints of France and Scotland, St Denis and St Andrew.

The king, too, could not have been entirely immune to a beguiling sense of his invincibility. The previous decade had witnessed military marvels so stupefying that they could have come about only with God's express sanction. In 1329, summoned by Philip VI, the new Valois king of France, to do homage for his province of Gascony or else forfeit it, Edward knelt at the feet of his liege lord. Eleven years later he had thought better of the obedient gesture, proclaiming himself king of France instead and adding the fleur-de-lis to his arms to make the point heraldically. The claim was not as preposterous as it might now seem. In 1328, the Capetian line of kings had died out. Through his mother, Isabella, Edward was the grandson of Philip IV, who had reigned from 1285 to 1314, but the French succession traditionally passed through the male line only, which had given the Crown instead to the son of one of Philip IV's younger brothers. The ensuing war, which would last *more* than a hundred years and bring untold misery to both sides, opened therefore with the usual exchange of parchment but proceeded quickly to lances and arrows. The arrows had the better of it. In 1340, at the mouth of the river Zwijn, off Sluys (L'Écluse), in Flanders, English and French ships locked together while their archers and men-at-arms slaughtered each other on a floating battlefield. Two hundred French ships were captured, thousands of men were killed, wounded and drowned, so many that if the fish could speak, went a favourite jibe, they would have learned French. Six years later an even more comprehensive annihilation was visited on an enormous French army at Crécy in Normandy. There the English faced not just the French but Flemish and

German knights as well as Genoese crossbowmen. But they were all pierced like pin-cushions by lethal downpours of arrows from English and Welsh longbowmen.

As if this were not sweet enough, in the same year, King David II of Scotland, the son of Robert the Bruce, was captured, wounded in the head by an arrow at Neville's Cross in Northumberland, abruptly halting a Scots invasion, launched in support of the French. David remained a captive, intended to be ransomed back north were it not for the unflattering reluctance of the Scots to come up with the necessary funds. It seemed just a matter of time before Edward III became, in fact if not in title, the master of three kingdoms. No wonder, then, at the Christmas revels in Guildford in 1347, the court indulged its taste of the fantastic, with men and women disguised, head to foot, as dragons or swans, complete with pairs of wings.

There was one sovereign, though, to whom Edward was forced to yield and he was King Death. A few weeks after the Garter ceremonies in St George's Chapel, the king heard that his daughter, Joan, had died of the plague in Bordeaux on 2 September. She had been travelling, together with an immense red silk bed, to Spain where she was to marry the Infante Pedro of Castile. Edward's personal motto at this time was 'It is as it is', a stoical device that must have sounded all very fine when surveying the grim carnage of the battlefield, but did not serve him well when faced with such heartbreak. For although he wrote to Alfonso XI that he consoled himself with the thought that Joan had 'been sent ahead to heaven to reign among the choirs of virgins where she can intercede for our own offences before God himself', and that she had been his 'dearest daughter (whom we loved best of all as her virtues demanded)', the king's brave pieties were mixed with confessions of sorrow. 'No fellow human being could be surprised if we were inwardly desolated by the sting of this bitter grief for we are human too.'

The glow of his triumph cooled by the hand of death, Edward asked the Archbishop of Canterbury to organize penitential prayers in Kent, since the areas around the southern ports were most immediately stricken by the plague. But the archbishop had himself died of the infection on 23 August. The prior of Canterbury, who now had to pass on the royal command, began his letter to the Bishop of London with the word *Terribilis*: 'Terrible is God towards the sons of men and by his command all things are subdued to his will.' Just how terrible, few in the first weeks of the plague could scarcely have had an inkling.

It had not been unexpected. The Italian mercantile and banking community in London had heard, through their correspondents at home, horrifying stories of cities in the grip of pestilence in the summer and autumn of 1347. In Venice alone 100,000 were said to have died, the cadavers dumped on the outer islands of the lagoon. Siena,

Florence, Padua and Piacenza had all become hecatombs of the dead. The Genoese in London must have been especially alarmed, since it was their ships that had originally brought the disease to the Mediterranean from the Near East. According to Gabriele de Mussis, a Piacenza lawyer, the Mongol army of Kipchak Khan Janibeg, besieging the Black Sea port of Caffa in the Crimea in 1346, had brought the bacillus with them from the wild-rodent-infested steppes of Central Asia and had resorted to catapulting their own plague victims over the walls of the city, which was held by the Genoese: the earliest case of intentional biological warfare. 'What seemed like mountains of dead were thrown into the city and the Christians could not hide nor flee nor escape from them although they dumped as many of the bodies as they could into the sea. And soon the rotting bodies tainted the air and poisoned the water.' By the spring of 1348 the plague had crossed the Alps into northern Europe and was moving inexorably through France and the Low Countries towards the Channel.

It must have seemed that God had decided the human race had been a mistake. 'What are you thinking of, merciful God, thus to destroy your creation…and to command its sudden annihilation?' de Mussis asked in stricken bewilderment. As the scythe moved steadily through Europe, reaching into cities and remote villages alike, there seemed no getting out of the way. You knew when the plague was coming in your direction. Riders would report it and suddenly fall sick themselves. A customer minding his own business, who broke into a sudden, hacking cough in the middle of a crowded alehouse, would empty the place in seconds. Waiting for his own infection (which, sure enough, came), the Welsh poet Jeuan Gethin wrote feverishly, multiplying similes like spots breaking out on the skin:

> Woe is me of the shilling in the armpit; seething terrible wherever it may come, a head that gives pain and causes a loud cry, a burden carried beneath the arms, a painful angry knob, a white lump. It is of the form of an apple, like the head of an onion; a small boil which spares no one. Great is its seething like a burning cinder, a grievous thing of ashy colour…an ugly eruption. They are similar to the seeds of the black peas, broken fragments of brittle sea coal…a grievous ornament…the peelings of the cockle-weed, a black plague like half-pence, like berries.

The Black Death was a knock-out blow to a world that was already hurting. Paradoxically, fourteenth-century England (and the rest of Britain) was a victim of its earlier success. The humming economy of the twelfth and the thirteenth century had triggered a population explosion, nearly trebling the post-Conquest population of

Top: Edward III grants Aquitaine to the Black Prince.
Above: English troops with the Black Prince on their way to France;
from Froissart's *Chronicles*, 1460–80.

England to around 4 million by 1300. Much of the land that could be reclaimed had been reclaimed – from forest, heath and marsh – and now there were simply too many bodies and not enough acreage to support them. At least 90 per cent of the population still made a living from the soil. For centuries people had lived in the same village world: a one- or two-room house, framed by timbers cut from nearby trees and filled in with a curtain of twigs and mud, the whole thing covered with lime-wash. The floors were dirt or clay, covered with straw to take the mud tracked in from the yard and the droppings of the chickens, geese and pigs that wandered freely through the house. The windows, if there were any, were unglazed. Food was cooked over an open hearth. Out beyond the 'croft', the little yard, beyond the huddle of houses gathered around the church, were two or three big, open, unfenced fields, which were divided into countless narrow strips – *selions* – each of them worked by the peasants of the village, free and unfree. The better off among them might have held many of these strips (seldom contiguous); the worst off would have had just a few, scarcely enough for subsistence. In return for the right to till them, to pasture their animals on the village common land or to have a share of animal feed from the common hay meadow, the unfree peasants would be required to work a day or two for the lord's own farm or to pay a substitute rent in money or kind. There were countless other burdens and extortions associated with unfree status. When someone in the family died, the best animal was due to the lord; when a marriage was made, yet another fee was liable. To make ends meet, most of these families needed an extra source of income. So the women brewed ale or carded fleece; the men resorted, when they could, to woodcutting or carting. It was, at best, a society on the edge of disaster.

And in the decades before the plague, it seemed already to have dropped over that edge. A succession of catastrophically bad harvests leading to the great famine of 1315–16 had been followed by cattle murrain and sheep disease. (No wonder, when it too came to pass, the plague was greeted as another of God's chastisements visited on the iniquitous.) The endless wars of the Plantagenets had sent the tax collectors into the villages more frequently than at any time in the previous century to lean on the reeves and the manorial courts so that they would fulfil their village quotas for the king. They, in turn, leaned on those who could least afford to give and were least able to resist. But with population pressing on resources, land and grain prices going through the roof, landlords were tempted to fence off their increasingly precious real estate, taking more land out of the manorial economy. With manual labour forced to sell itself so cheaply, farming their own lands directly suddenly looked like good business for the owners. When neither manual work nor strip farming could make ends meet, the worst-off peasants had no choice but to sell off their holdings, hoping to regain them when better times allowed. But always the prices seemed to go up and the prospect of returning to the way things had once been became ever more remote. The differences between the village fat cats – the men who were jurors and ale-tasters, who worked for the reeve and owned many rather than few strips and who now pounced on their opportunity – and the poor village mice became more and more marked. The reduction in alms-giving by the lords made this already difficult situation still worse, and as the many became poorer, their willingness to abide by the rules governing the collective management of resources and labour (ploughing, allocating strips, harvesting) even in deferential England, came under increasing strain. All sorts of little anti-social transgressions, neighbourhood spats – which in a world this tight amounted to high crimes – were becoming common. Gleanings reserved for the very poorest were being taken at night by villagers who just needed them. Animals were being pastured illegally in fields supposed to be left fallow. Ploughmen were caught 'accidentally' trespassing on their neighbours' strip. Communities that had, as long as anyone could remember, worked through the shared acceptance of common rules, were now splintering into collections of self-interest.

If all else failed, of course, there was begging or crime. It was in Edward III's reign above all that the reality, as well as the legend, of the forest outlaw entered the national culture. Then, for the desperate or the adventurous, there was the lure of the towns, especially the great ant heap of London, its population perhaps numbering as many as 100,000 on the eve of the Black Death. If the migrant was not quite so bold, there were less remote centres like Norwich, York or Bristol, none of them with populations greater than 10,000 but, compared to a village of fifty or a hundred souls, a metropolis of unimaginable numbers. Bristol was the first major town in England to fall to the plague, and it was the kind of place that was a perfect factory for the reproduction of the bacillus, a hospitable port of entry to cargoes, crews and rats coming from already infected regions of Europe. Its narrow, tightly packed streets were home to much the same animal population as in the villages – backyards full of pigs, chickens and swill – while the alley ways (despite the king's campaign to have them cleaned up) were running with open sewers and refuse from noxious trades like tanning and dyeing.

Stuck inside these lousy, busy commonwealths in the summer of 1348, few would have noticed the nibble of the flea until it was too late and the dread buboes appeared. The bodies began to mount up as hundreds died every day; those with least resistance – the youngest and the oldest and the poorest – were the earliest victims. In a town ripe for infection, almost one in two people – about 45 per cent of the population – perished within the year. Fifteen of Bristol's fifty-two councillors died within six months, their names struck through with a cross as they passed away. Henry Knighton, the chronicler, wrote that in Bristol: 'virtually the whole town was annihilated. It was as if sudden death had marked them down beforehand for few lay sick for more than two or three days.' In Knighton's own town of Leicester 700 died in a single parish in a matter of days. 'The pestilence grew so strong,' wrote Thomas Burton, a monk in Yorkshire, 'that men and women dropped dead in the streets.' These provincial towns were abruptly cut in two, between a city of the living and a city of the dead and dying. Families — and contrary to many myths about medieval England, these were all basic nuclear families of two parents and their children — would have been poignantly split, the healthy moving away from the sick. Whatever their remorse, parents might be forced to abandon some children for whom they could do nothing to save others still clean of the disease. 'There was in those days,' wrote a monk of Westminster, 'death without sorrow, marriage without affection, want without poverty, flight without escape.'

Everything that had been taken for granted became suddenly questionable. Where could one find bread now that there were no bakers, for the open hearths in most houses would not make it? Where might one find physic now that none seemed to work? And who would take away the bodies before their putrefaction caused yet more contagion? In Rochester, Kent, William Dene wrote:

> Alas this mortality devoured such a multitude of both sexes that no one could be found to carry the bodies of the dead to burial, but men and women carried the bodies of their own little ones to church on their shoulders and threw them into mass graves from which arose such a stench that it was barely possible for anyone to go past the churchyard.

The bigger the town, the greater the trauma. When the first wave of the plague hit London 300 people died every day within the square mile of the city itself. As fast as people died, new cemeteries were dug with mass pits. At East Smithfield they were stacked in haste, five rows deep. While the ancient hospital cemetery at Spitalfields was being excavated in 1999 the archaeologists discovered close by something quite different: a mass burial pit, strongly suggesting the panic of a sudden epidemic, with thousands of bodies, many of them very young. Instead of being carefully interred with their feet facing east, so that the dead might stand upright facing Jerusalem on the Day of Judgement as in a regular graveyard, the bodies had been flung in the pit pell-mell, like so much human junk. One of these impromptu burial grounds was sited on land given by the Bishop of London. Enclosed by walls, it rapidly acquired

Skeleton from a late fourteenth-century burial pit
in Spitalfields, east London.

the nickname 'No Man's Land'. When he wrote his survey of London in 1598, John Stow claimed to have read a document from the reign of Edward III listing 50,000 bodies that had been dumped in these pits; the figure was almost certainly an exaggeration but nevertheless a shocking reminder of the enormity of the disaster.

Inevitably, some of those bodies went to their maker without benefit of clergy, as the supply of parish priests was itself dwindling. In January 1349 the Bishop of Bath and Wells wrote to his clergy: 'Priests cannot be found for love or money...to visit the sick and administer the last sacraments of the Church – perhaps because they fear they will catch the disease.' If none can be found, the bishop went on, the laity need to be told that it was proper to confess their sins to a lay person or even (a really radical step) 'to a woman if no man is available'. But bishops were often also aristocrats and like the rest of the rich they could choose the luxury of flight, doubtless justifying their behaviour in terms of the necessity of saving the princes of the Church. Bishop Bateman of Norwich, in one of the worst-hit areas, damp and boggy East Anglia, spent most of the summer of 1349 in the saddle, trying to outrun the plague, ending up on his own estates at Hoxne, where he hunkered down, fearing the worst. By this time, the pestilence had penetrated the length and breadth of the British isles. Courting hubris, the Scots had decided that the prostration of England was a perfect time to mount an invasion and recoup their losses against Edward. An army of many thousands duly gathered at the traditional mustering place of Selkirk forest. But before it could march, the plague struck the camp. The army disintegrated, 5000 died, the remainder fleeing home taking the Black Death with them.

Those who had nowhere left to run became resigned to their fate. As enclosed communities, monasteries were especially hard hit. Of the forty-two monks in the Cistercian abbey of Meaux, Yorkshire, just ten survived the first hit of the plague. In August alone Thomas Burton, later abbot and one of the few survivors, recorded twenty-two deaths among the monks and six lay brothers. Six were buried on a single day. In Kilkenny in Ireland the Franciscan monk John Clynn set down the horrors he had seen and then, as if measuring his shroud at the end of the world, wrote: 'Seeing these many ills and that the whole world is encompassed by evil, waiting among the dead for death to come, I have committed to writing what I have truly heard...and so that the writing does not perish with the writer or the work fail with the workman I leave parchment for continuing it in case anyone should be alive in the future.' At which point, a second hand writes: 'Here, it seems, the author died.'

When the survivors recovered from the shock of the first brutal wave of the Black Death, they asked, inevitably, why us, why now? For many in Europe the answer was obvious: the Jews had poisoned the wells and rivers. So there were the usual slaughters that made the Gentiles feel better but did nothing to halt the buboes. In England, where there were no Jews, men of learning and men of faith had different answers to give, although both communities believed the answers lay in the heavens. Many of the learned believed that there had been a fatal three-way conjunction of the planets. Benevolent, moist Jupiter had come into conjunction with hot, dry Mars and the mysterious, malevolent force of Saturn. Others thought that filth had been responsible. The muck of men and beasts, offal and sewage, rising from lakes, swamps and ditches, had vaporized into a dank, smoggy curtain – the fatal miasma – which hung over the earth, bred contagion and then dropped its poisoned seeds back on to the ground. Those who wanted to improve their chances of survival were well advised to steer clear of noxious resorts where the polluted air might form a mass – tanneries and butchers' shops and even brothels (for the pungent fumes of lust were said to be a major source of the miasma) – and if dangerous odours were unavoidable (as they were for most people in the fourteenth century), their effects might be prophylactically resisted by wearing little packets of sweet-smelling herbs about the neck or body: dittany, lavender or thyme. Herbalists even offered antidotes to those already stricken. One herbal advised:

> If it be a man take five cups of rue, and if it be a woman leave out the rue, five little blades of columbine, a great quantity of marigold flowers, an egg, fresh laid, and make a hole in one end and blow out all that is within, and lay it to the fire and roast it till ground to powder but do not burn it, and take a good quantity of treacle and brew all these herbs with good ale but do not strain them – and make the sick drink it for three evenings and mornings. If they hold it in their stomach [a tall order in the best of circumstances], they shall have life.

If God decided otherwise, though, there was no potion in the world that could stay his judgement. Many had already come to the conclusion that it was human behaviour, rather than a disorder in the air, that had called down divine wrath. In 1344 John of Reading had warned that shameless dress, a symptom of vanity and debauchery, would certainly invite punishment: 'Women wearing clothes so tight that they wore a fox tail hanging down inside their skirts at the back to hide their arses.' Monks like Henry Knighton and Thomas Burton of Meaux believed that the shameless tournaments of the 1340s had provoked retribution. Burton remembered women coming in droves to the spectacle, not with their husbands but with paramours, who 'used them to satisfy their sexual urges'. Even worse, Knighton thought, was the habit of women dressing as men at these gaudy shows, 'in parti-coloured tunics with short

Ploughing and sowing; two scenes from the
fourteenth-century Luttrell Psalter.

hoods and liripipes like strings wound across the head, and belts thickly studded with gold and silver slung across their heads, below the navel with knives called daggers suspended from pouches beneath them'. The great Benedictine preacher Thomas Brinton took a good look at the face of concupiscent, complacent, Edwardian England and found it utterly abhorrent:

> We are not constant in faith; we are not honourable in the eyes of the world, on the contrary of all men we are the falsest and in consequence unloved by God. It is undoubtedly for that reason that there exists in the kingdom of England so marked a diminution of fruitfulness; so cruel a pestilence, so much injustice, so many illegitimate children – for on every side there is so much lechery and adultery that few men are contented with their wives but each man lusts after the wife of his neighbour or keeps a stinking concubine.

The long-term remedy, then, would not lie in potions or the kind of street-cleaning measures that Edward III ordered to be undertaken in London. Rather, what was needed was a moral sanitation campaign, beginning with the processions, fasts, penances and prayers for the intercession of the Virgin that erupted all over the country along with the plague. Those who had the means attempted to escape from the places where moral as well as physical pollution was most concentrated – the cities and towns – and followed the advice of the poet John Lydgate, whose *Dietary and Doctrine for the Pestilence* recommended that the prudent take themselves off to the countryside where they might have supposed both the air and the manners were sweeter and the contagion less virulent.

If that was their expectation, they were in for a shock. Scenes of ruin and neglect would have greeted them. A third of the houses would have been empty, scythes and sickles were going to rust, and anvils and looms were gathering dust. Sheep and cattle wandered about amid the unharvested fields. 'For want of watching,' Henry Knighton wrote, 'animals died in uncountable numbers in the fields and byways and hedges.'

Historians are supposed to take the long view and detach themselves from the emotions of the moment. Looking beyond the immediate trauma, many have concluded that in the villages the plague was not so much the great reaper, obliterating rural life from top to bottom, as a winnower, sorting viable from unviable communities, killing off hamlets that had already been weakened and thinned out by the hard times of the early fourteenth century. But to those hit brutally hard – in the villages around Bury St Edmunds in Suffolk, for example, where 60 per cent of the population perished in a year — the information that this was all part of a structural change from a manorial to a cash economy would have been little comfort. All the villagers could see were the bodies of infants; orphaned children, dirty and wandering; crops bolting into weeds; missing parish priests; and cows, swollen and lowing for want of being milked.

The manorial rolls vividly document precisely what happened in the first year or two after the plague struck. On the Bishop of Winchester's manor in Farnham, fifty-two households — a good third of his villagers — died in the first year of the plague. At first, the bishop's reeve had no difficulty finding takers to move into the empty lots and was pleased to take their entry fee. But by 1350, when the plague struck again, the situation became much more serious. By the time that the Black Death in Farnham finally receded, fully 1300 had died, and the rolls humanize that calamity by putting names to numbers: Matilda Stikker, who perished along with her family, and the serving girl, Matilda Talvin, who was put out of work when her master died along with his entire household. But while the plague at Farnham took, it also gave. John Crudchate, then a minor, was left an orphan, but an orphan with assets since he inherited the lots of both his father and another relative, perhaps an uncle. The consolidation of all those strips would have been the making of a small but serious village fortune, and it pulled young Crudchate up from the poorest to among the best endowed of the village. He could now afford geese.

A momentous change was under way in the villages of England, Wales and Scotland. The balance of economic power was shifting dramatically and, for once, it favoured the people not the lords. Before he, too, died from the plague, the reeve of Farnham complained that the harvest was costing twelve pence an acre to bring in — double the pre-plague rates. Labour was thin on the ground now, and it was beginning to charge accordingly. Farnham's story could be repeated all over the country. Whether the Black Death was the prime cause of a great rural transformation or whether it merely completed a process that had been under way for generations, the countryside of late medieval Britain was unquestionably an irreversibly altered world. For one thing, it had no more serfs. For some time it had been getting harder to force unfree peasants to do unpaid work for their lord — to cart hay or plough fields, for example, merely in recognition of a legal right to occupy their house and yard — but now, when the laws of supply and demand so obviously favoured the survivors, it was virtually impossible. To a lord's or a reeve's demand that certain tasks be done, the peasant could respond by demanding to be paid, or paid at a higher rate than before. If a deserted holding was on offer, it would now be the tenant not the lord who could set the terms of occupancy. And if the lord found this new economic assertiveness insolent, the peasant could simply up sticks and find a manor where the owner had a more secure grip on the new economic reality. It had long been a legal axiom that 'town air makes free' – a year of residence in a city could change legal status – but in the new world of the plague, where disappearances of all kinds were commonplace, there were precious few ways to discover where exactly an errant peasant had gone and what he was doing. Following the labour market hundreds of thousands migrated to wherever their economic and social prospects were best served. And there was nothing anyone could do about it.

Matthew Oxe was one such fellow who said goodbye to serfdom and to the village of Staverton, Suffolk, where his family had been unfree peasants. Around 1430 Matthew disappeared for parts unknown, possibly entering the service of the Duke of Norfolk at Framlingham Castle. Twenty-five years later he returned in triumph to Staverton, showing off to the manorial court the document that certified his freedom. Matthew paid six pence to have a copy of this 'charter of manumission' put into the court roll, declaring that henceforth he and his heirs were freemen. He added that henceforth he and his heirs were no longer to be called Oxe, like some beast of burden, but Groom, a more fitting name for someone who obviously had aspirations to join the riding classes.

King Death was, then, an unlikely liberator, shaking up the old social hierarchy in the countryside and rearranging the relationship between the powerful and the powerless. The onslaught of his scythe cut to the heart of what, for centuries, had been the heart of feudalism: the contract between submission and protection that had said 'do what you're told, stay where you are, and you will be protected from those who may wish you harm'. But in the middle of the fourteenth century, with those who were supposed to make good the promise – the lord's reeve and his bench on the manorial court, the county knights and their fellow jurors, and even the lord himself, his family and esquires and servants – following each other to the boneyards, this promise must have rung hollow.

This was not yet a world of individualists, cut loose from the inter-connected obligations of feudal society, but it was a world in which, suddenly, self-help seemed not just desirable but urgent. And this was as true for the structures of belief as it was for the structures of social power. Despite all the prayers and processions and penances, it seemed that God's wrath was not yet assuaged by gestures of tearful contrition, for the plague came back in 1361 (and after that in twenty- to twenty-five-year cycles), taking not a half but certainly a quarter of an already shrunken population. From the beginning, a disproportionate number of its victims had been priests, whose oblig-ations to minister to the sick and dying had put them in the front line of the epidemic. The decision in 1349 that the last rites could be received from the laity when there were no priests around to do the job, although strictly temporary, must already have made inroads into the clergy's absolute monopoly on the sacraments, and it may well have encouraged those who were understandably fearful of being struck down to prepare themselves as best they could against the day when they might be struck down in their prime. Increasingly, salvation seemed a do-it-yourself project. For some of the boldest, this sense of having been left bereft by the institutional Church led them dangerously (or excitingly) close to heresy. The Oxford scholar John Wyclif taught that the priesthood was not indispensable for salvation and that, in the words of scripture, each Christian might find the true way. His gospel 'mumblers' or Lollards were initially saved from formal charges of heresy only because Wyclif himself had powerful protectors, especially Edward III's third son, John of Gaunt, whose enthusiasm for Lollardy was passed on to a small but influential group of knights.

For less audacious souls, however, it was possible to pursue the personal road to salvation in ways that were sanctioned, rather than proscribed, by the Church. For the humble this might be a pilgrimage to the shrine of a saint like Becket, whose intercession might be implored for the sins of the pilgrim. But those who had the means could take out an insurance policy against being struck down by King Death without having had adequate time to prepare themselves to be properly commended to God's mercy. This was a chantry. It was based on the idea, widespread for the first time after the Black Death, that pending final judgement, souls did time in the stony limbo of Purgatory where they atoned for their transgressions. The chantry was a sum of money, which was given in advance of one's death either to establish a special chapel or simply to designated clergy to chant masses for the soul. So much money would pay for so many monk-hours of chanting, and the time spent in Purgatory would shorten accordingly. If in doubt, give big was the rule – the conspicuously pious Henry V, for example, left enough money for 20,000 masses to be said within a year for his soul and another 5000 for the Joys of Mary!

Even as they shelled out in advance for a reserved space in heaven, the mighty and the moneyed were acutely aware that King Death was apt to laugh at the pretensions of rank. The years of the Black Death saw the popularity of the story of the Three Living and the Three Dead, in which a trio of handsome young kings out for a day's sport are abruptly confronted by three cadavers, each in a different state of decomposition. The three living pipe up, in turn, 'I am afraid', 'Lo, what I see' and 'Methinks these devils be'. Back come the other three, 'Such you shall be', 'I was well fair' and 'For God's love beware'. The furthest gone of the gruesome threesome continues with a little homily:

King Death from the *Book of Hours* of Marie de Brabant.

Know that I was head of my line
Princes, kings and nobles
Royal and rich, rejoicing in wealth
But now I am so hideous and bare
that even the worms disdain me.

This was one invasion that Edward III's realm had not prepared for: the invasion of the space of the living by the dead. There was a chilling sense, peculiar to the world of the Black Death, that the borders between backyards and boneyards had collapsed and that perhaps one might not, after all, as the skeletons warned, be able to buy one's way to salvation. Tomb effigies that proclaimed (as in the case of Christ) a triumph over death were, perhaps, premature. So another kind of tomb that positively revelled in the idea of death as the great leveller became fashionable in Europe in the late fourteenth century. They were called 'transi' tombs (literally, and appropriately, meaning 'gone off'), and they were meant to advertise the tomb-dweller's redeeming awareness of his own reduction to a heap of dust and maggots. The most elaborate of the 'transi' tombs were double-decker affairs, designed to contrast, as shockingly as possible, the way we might like to imagine ourselves remembered with the way we really are after death. The top deck would display the deceased in the splendour of his bishop's robes, but beneath the grandeur would lie the truth, a pathetic cadaver, carved to show the flesh eaten away and the skeleton brittle and frail. The 'transis' were meant to provoke those who saw them not only to timely penance but also to offer prayers for the soul of the departed. Archbishop Henry Chichele, who designed the first 'transi' tomb in England for himself, made sure it was finished and conse-crated in 1425 (twenty years before he actually died), so he got to show it off to admiring visitors to Canterbury. 'I was pauper born,' reads the inscription, 'then to Primate raised, now I am cut down and served up for worms…behold my grave whoever you may be, who will pass by, you who will be like me, after you die, horrible in all things, dust, worms, vile flesh.' And just in case the 'transi' didn't do the trick, Chichele founded All Souls College as an academic chantry where the Fellows were obliged to pray for the founder's soul and to keep the tomb painted and spick and span. They still do.

The fervent insistence on the equality of death did not, of course, prevent some of those tombs from being more equal than others. The tomb of the Black Prince, who died – to great and general sorrow – in 1376 at the age of forty-six, has the usual cautionary inscription warning admirers:

Such as thou art, so once was I/As I am now, so thou wilt be.

But the sombre modesty of the sentiment is somewhat belied by the prince's having commissioned the tomb from his architect Henry Yevele and ordering that it be carved from the finest Purbeck marble, with 'our leopard helm placed beneath the head', a painted wooden canopy or tester above him, with a picture of the Holy Trinity as if receiving him into paradise, and a complete set of fake armour, including gauntlets and shield, so that the prince could embark on his last campaign: the march out of Purgatory.

The death of the Black Prince, 'the comfort of England', whose martial fame represented the continuity of the Plantagenet warrior state, cast a long shadow over a political landscape that, through all the social and religious disruption triggered by the Black Death, had remained remarkably stable. Learning from the mistakes of his predecessors (and his own errors, earlier in the reign), Edward III made sure to co-opt the 'community of the realm' represented in parliament as a partner in the spectacular expansion of the dynamic, multi-national empire that was Plantagenet Inc. Just as rural England had adjusted to the changing realities of the land and labour market by making property and money, rather than birth, the determinant of status, so the military enterprise of the realm had also become a matter of business rather than honour. The king and his great nobles no longer seriously expected their tenants-in-chief to supply them with soldiers as a matter of pure feudal obligation. Instead, mobilization of knights, foot soldiers, archers and siege machinery was put on a contractual basis, with a tariff specified for the different kinds of military personnel (two pence a day for a foot soldier), animals and hardware and for a specific period of time. Theoretically, such sums might be payable in advance, which meant that the king might have to go to parliament to ask for a 'subsidy' (for which read tax) or levy a sum on the wool trade or go to the Italians again. But often enough, the campaigns were self-financing, with built-in bonus-incentives for success, since the aristocratic captains knew that in the event of victory they would be able to lay their hands not only on plunder but on the immense sums needed to ransom their prisoners. Even after the crown took its hefty 33⅓ per cent cut from the proceeds, there was still ample to go round, as the great fortunes left by Edward's principal commanders testify. The Earl of Arundel, for example, who fought both at Sluys and Crécy, left £60,000, most of it gained from the fortunes of war. And one of the founder members of the Order of the Garter, Sir Bartholomew Burghersh, got £6000 from the king for handing over his prisoner, the Count of Ventadour. Many of the great Edwardian castles – both redoubtable moated fortresses and architectural works of art, such as Bodiam in Sussex, which was built by Sir Edward Dalyngrygge – were entirely funded from military enterprise.

Top: Effigy from the tomb of the Black Prince in the Trinity Chapel, Canterbury Cathedral.
Above: The Three Living and the Three Dead, from the fourteenth-century Psalter of Robert de Lisle.
Left: The 'transi' tomb of Archbishop Henry Chichele in Canterbury Cathedral.

The Black Prince, vigorous, intelligent and charismatic, was the symbol of this happy state of affairs, give or take a few million bodies in the ossuary. Even before he joined them, though, there was a creeping sense among the stakeholders of Plantagenet Enterprises that their years of unlimited expansion might be coming to an end along with the life of the chief executive. Edward I's French conquests had been reversed by a resurgent French monarchy. Attempts to take money for new campaigns by taxing the wool and wine trades – already badly hit by a new outbreak of the plague in 1374–5 – were not well received in the country. The king himself was old and ailing and generally thought to be the captive of his mistress, Alice Perrers. His only option was to go to parliament and ask, rather than demand, the necessary funds. This Edward hated to do and, as it turned out, with good reason. For parliament was in a feisty temper, as it often was when the monarchy failed to deliver uninterrupted good fortune. What made the Good Parliament of 1376 (as it called itself) different from earlier challenges to the Crown was the assertiveness of the Commons. Instead of the usual cap-doffing gathering, for the first time the knights and burgesses elected a Speaker, Peter de la Mare, who presided over what we would recognize as a genuine debate. Even the seating arrangements suggested something other than passive obedience. Instead of forward-facing ranks, seats were set around four sides of a lectern – in effect, a primitive dispatch box – and one after another, members came to this lectern and delivered unsparing attacks on the chosen councillors of the king. Alice Perrers, her husband, William Windsor, and the London merchant Richard Lyons, who dominated the court, were, they said, neither 'loyal nor profitable to the kingdom'. The Commons also let it be known in no uncertain terms that henceforth they expected the king to 'live off his own' – that is, that he should trim his ambitions and expenses to his revenues. John of Gaunt was outraged by this insolence but was forced to accept an inquiry into the conduct of the government and the impeachment of the most heavily criticized councillors as the price of securing revenue. The parliamentary purge was duly carried out, but in the end, on 10 July, parliament had the temerity to decline the government's request for funds!

By the time that a new parliament convened early in 1377, the Black Prince, who had let it be known that he endorsed the reform programme, was dead and the king's own days looked numbered. The *de facto* regent in waiting, John of Gaunt, exploited the sense of national crisis and persuaded or bullied parliament into co-operation, and it obliged by undoing much of the reforming programme of its predecessor. But for the moment, the great engine of English ceremonial suspended politics. Edward III died of a stroke in June, the mark of the paralysis faithfully depicted on his tomb effigy. His body, carried on a bier by twenty-four knights dressed in black and walking to a slow march, was the last great Arthurian show of the Plantagenets. 'To witness and hear the grief of the people; their sobs and lamentations on that day, would have rent anyone's heart,' wrote the chronicler Froissart.

Edward's successor was a child of ten, Richard of Bordeaux. Although the poet William Langland warned 'woe to the land that has a boy for a king', Richard II's accession was greeted with jubilant expectation rather than apprehension. England needed a saviour, even if he was ten years old. The last wave of plague in 1375 had made it certain that the Black Death had not gone away, and the country's sense of imperial invincibility had been abruptly thrown into reverse by the losses in France. Now it was less a matter of taking the war across the Channel than in preventing the French from landing at Dover. The passing of the Black Prince had robbed England of its expected captain, so Richard's coronation became an occasion for a demonstration of faith in the future realm. After all, there had been no coronation in England for fifty years. Knights of the shire rode in from all over the country to be present at the spectacle. The conduits in Cheapside ran with Gascon wine, and a fake castle was built at the western end of the city, from which white-robed virgins threw golden scrolls at the yellow-haired boy as his procession passed by.

As soon as it had been apparent that his father was dying, the emotional investment in the Black Prince had been transferred to his son. He, not his father, would usher in the reign of gold. His guardian and uncle, John of Gaunt, and his other uncles, Gloucester and York, had been preparing the boy for the weight of all these expectations. On 25 January 1377 they had orchestrated a great entertainment at the west end of the city, near Gaunt's great palace at the Savoy, and 130 masked mummers paraded through the streets as emperors and popes for the public to hiss at. At dusk torches were lit and the villains met their match: John of Gaunt and his brothers, and little Richard, richly dressed for the fantasy that, in his case, was going to be real. Up came the chief mummer, grinning, and gave the boy a set of dice. They were loaded. He threw, he won, and his arms were heaped with golden prizes.

In Westminster Abbey for his coronation the overture to the golden age continued. Richard had his shirt taken off him behind a golden screen, and his face, hands and chest were touched with holy oil. Perhaps as they listened to his little voice replying that he would, indeed, protect the Church, do justice to his people and respect the laws and customs of his ancestors, the assembly of nobles and clergy imagined that Richard would grow to fill the throne of his great-great-grandfather, Edward I, and the legs, now dangling over the Scottish Stone of Destiny lodged beneath its seat, would before long touch the ground and the boy would stand upright as a man. For now, though, while the bells tolled, he had to be carried from the abbey, and as he was borne along, one of his slippers came loose and fell off. But only the most nervous could have worried that this might be an ill omen. He was, after all, only ten.

How was the child marked by all this and by the public deaths of his grandfather and father? Did he later recall the moment of his anointing as an apotheosis, his transformation from a little man to a little god? If early on Richard somehow became so accustomed to all the ceremonies and solemnities that he mistook himself for a junior messiah, perhaps this was just as well, since only someone with that inbred self-confidence could have managed to face down, at the tender age of fourteen, the most violent upheaval in the history of medieval England.

It happened with terrifying swiftness, and it began in the corner of England one would least expect a rural uprising to explode – not in some destitute mud hole in the back of beyond, but in the most economically developed region of England, the belt of fertile country stretching from Kent over the Medway and Thames into Essex and East Anglia. The 'Peasants' Revolt' of 1381 was, in fact, conspicuous for the absence of peasants. From the arrest records we know that most of the leaders in the southeastern counties were actually yeomen, the village elite, who served as reeves, constables, ale-tasters and jurors; the men who ran manorial courts and saw to the military musters. The beneficiaries, not the victims, of the crisis of the Black Death, these were the men who had moved into lots vacated by the plague-dead, who had driven hard bargains with their lords to contract for lower rents and had done well. Some of them, like Sir Roger Bacon of Norfolk, were knights. The Good Parliament of 1376 had been, they imagined, their cause. They had cheered the Commons when it clung to the nation's purse strings and rejoiced when the court favourites had been sent packing. Now that John of Gaunt seemed to be running the country, they were damned if they were going to stand idly by while they were robbed of their little fortunes to line the pockets of his hangers-on, including Joan of Kent, the Black Prince's widow, or the treasurer, Sir Robert Hales. Listening attentively to these angry village notables were their natural constituents, the blacksmiths, alewives, fullers, sawyers and carters – the sort of people, in fact, who knew everyone's business, had a bit of money and sometimes even a smattering of book learning. Their trades put them in touch with worlds beyond their parish, and they knew how to make an army out of those one rung down on the social ladder, the families barely above the poverty line, who had had to sell their labour to make ends meet and whose efforts to profit from the labour shortage of the Black Death had been stymied in 1351 by the Statute of Labourers, which had pegged wages at pre-Black Death levels. Even though the statute had proved of limited effect in a sellers' labour market, the memory of it rankled.

In their different ways, all these sections of the rural community thought of themselves as up and coming. Not surprisingly, it was in the second half of the fourteenth century that the legends of Robin Hood, with its message of injustices put right by a fellowship of equals under the leadership of a 'true' royalist, first became genuinely popular.

The immediate provocation for the revolt was, naturally, a new tax, the poll tax of 1380, the pretext for which was the defence of the realm against another threatened French invasion. But John of Gaunt's government made the serious mistake of imposing a tax that, for the first time, took no account of wealth and was levied at the flat rate of three groats (a shilling a head) per household. The response was predictable: fury and mass evasion, as entire families, sometimes entire villages, disappeared on to the roads or into the woods, where temporary encampments of tax-fugitives established themselves while they waited for the levy-men to go away. The usual corrective, of course, was to beef up the enforcers and collectors and to recruit local sergeants at arms, who knew the alehouses where they could winkle out the frauds and the runaways. But it was those men who went down to the woods who were in for a really big surprise.

In south Essex in the spring of 1381 the tax commissioners had ordered the men of villages around Brentwood to appear there before a certain date and make their payments. The commissioners were a formidable group, four justices and the sheriff, but on 30 May they found themselves engulfed by a hostile crowd led by a Thomas Baker from the village of Fobbing. Baker was accompanied not just by his own villagers but by Essex men from a wide sweep of countryside — from Rainham, Billericay, Goldhanger and Mucking. The numbers were sufficient for the rebels to feel brave enough to threaten physical harm to one of the commissioners if he persisted. Instead, he got on his horse and spread the news. The stakes escalated. Heavily reinforced, the Chief Justice of the Court of Common Pleas descended on the insurgent area, but he, too, was taken captive by a still bigger throng and made to swear he would never repeat the effort. When the rebels discovered the identity of informers who had named names, their heads were hacked off in short order. By 2 June something extraordinary had happened. At Bocking the leaders of another uproarious crowd had it swear an oath not just against wicked impositions but against feudal lordship itself. They would, they vowed, 'have no law in England except only they themselves moved to be ordained'.

Even as it began to kill those who claimed to be the officers of the king and make statements of astonishing radicalism, the rebellion professed fervent loyalty to the person of the fourteen-year-old king. Richard was still seen as saviour not oppressor, and they would liberate him from his captivity at the hands of evil men, like Gaunt, the Archbishop of Canterbury Simon Sudbury, and the treasurer Hales. And like many of the uprisings of the common people that broke out in Europe at the end of the fourteenth century, the English rising was fired by a sense that the world of the Black Death was a time of reckoning. If the hand of God struck down the mighty, reached through the walls of their castles, levelled their vanity and pulled them into their graves, why should they imagine they should escape the hand of the long-suffering people? The people would now do the work of God and his anointed king; they would be the rod of his punishment and inaugurators of a golden age of justice and Christian equality.

This is what was being said at the gatherings, mobilized by flying pickets riding through the countryside. By the first week in June the revolt had gone beyond Essex into Kent, where another army, thousands strong, descended on Rochester Castle, where they found a perfect symbol of their cause: a man imprisoned for his failure to come up with the 'manumission' money needed to change him from serf into free man. In Maidstone Wat Tyler, originally from Colchester in Essex, was elected as their general and captain. In Canterbury, John Ball, a priest from Colchester who had been excommunicated and then imprisoned for defying the ban, told the crowds to rid the world of all bishops and lords save only one Bishop of the People: John Ball. The priesthood, loaded with wealth, was an abomination that stank in God's nostrils. Once purged, the country could be made a kingdom of the Lord, returned to the innocent state of long, long ago. 'Things cannot go right in England and never will until goods are held in common and there are no more villeins and gentlefolk but we are all one and the same,' Froissart has Ball tell his flock:

> Are we not descended from the same parents, Adam and Eve? And what can they show or what reason can they give why they should be more masters than ourselves? They are clothed in velvet and rich stuffs ornamented in ermine and other furs while we are forced to wear poor clothing. They have wines and spices and fine bread while we only have rye and refuse of the straw and when we drink it must be water. They have handsome manors...while we must brave the wind and rain in our labours in the field and it is by our labours that they...support their pomp. We are called slaves and if we do not perform our services we are beaten and we have no sovereign to whom we can complain...Let us go to the King and remonstrate with him; he is young and from him we may obtain a favourable answer, and if not we must seek to amend our conditions ourselves.

So they marched, Wat Tyler, John Ball and Robert Cave, the baker from Dartford, the Three Dead, confronting the rich and the mighty with their day of judgement.

June 12th, 1381 was a warm Wednesday. In the fields of Blackheath overlooking the Thames the rebel army was camped in what, to Londoners, must have seemed alarming force. If it was not the 50,000 described by Froissart, the army was certainly between 5000 and 10,000 strong. They were emphatically not a rabble. Many of them had got to the edge of London on horseback, and others in carts and wagons. *En route* their targets had been carefully selected: estates belonging to tax collectors or prominent members of the royal council and anything belonging to John of Gaunt. The sheriff of Essex, Sir John Sewale, had seen his house pillaged before the insignia of his office were torn from his clothing. Any document bearing the green wax seal of the Exchequer was marked for destruction. The manor house of the treasurer, Sir Robert Hales ('Hob Robber' as John Ball called him), at Highbury was ransacked and demolished. It was an army that knew what it was doing. And it believed itself patriotic. No one living within 12 miles of the south coast was permitted to join the march lest the French be tempted to attempt a landing. This paradoxical obligation on the part of a popular movement to demonstrate its loyalty, its responsibility and its political maturity would return time and again in British history to undo the most powerful weapon of any potential revolution: the refusal of deference. No crowd that forms itself into a line to petition a sovereign is ever going to make a revolution.

None of this was apparent to the authorities in June 1381. Their immediate reaction to the appearance of the rebels on the outskirts of London was panic. John of Gaunt headed for his castles in Northumberland, was refused admission and was obliged to seek shelter in Scotland. His son Henry Bolingbroke ran for the Tower along with Archbishop Sudbury, Sir Robert Hales and Joan of Kent, the king's mother, who took Richard with her. Confused arguments broke out over whether to show the rebels a hard line (as the Lord Mayor of London, William Walworth, consistently proposed) or to make at least a show of tactical negotiation. In the midst of all this chaos, Richard himself seems to have kept a composure astonishing in a fourteen-year-old. Perhaps he believed in the professed loyalism of the rebels; perhaps he even allowed himself a secret touch of sympathy with their hostility towards his guardians. At any rate, when the council asked him to see the leaders of the rebels, he showed no hesitation.

To avoid capture, he travelled by barge downstream on the morning of 13 June from the Tower towards Blackheath in the company of Archbishop Sudbury and the earls of Warwick and Arundel. At some point between Rotherhithe and Greenwich the barge came close enough to the bank to hear the rebels, who demanded the head

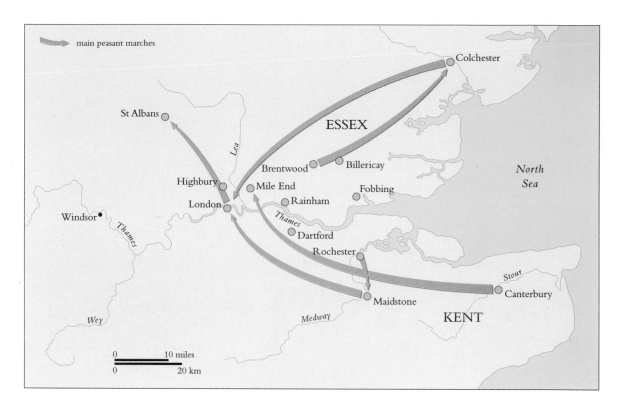

Top: Map showing areas of activity during the Peasants' Revolt.
Above: The Great Seal of John of Gaunt.

Scenes of the Peasants' Revolt from Froissart's *Chronicles*, 1460–80.
Top: John Ball, on horseback, preaching to the rebels. Above: The death of Wat Tyler.

of John of Gaunt and fifteen other 'traitors' as a precondition of negotiations. Suddenly it did not seem a good idea to disembark. The barge returned to the Tower. Assuming that they had been rejected, the rebels unleashed the crowds on the city. The prisons were opened, beginning with the Marshalsea and the Fleet. Legal and financial records, the key, the rebels thought, to their tax assessments, were destroyed at the Temple and Lambeth Palace. A brothel on London Bridge, staffed by Flemish whores and owned by Walworth, burned down, and finally the crowd got to their choice target: the Savoy. First, John of Gaunt's impressive cellars, full of Bordeaux wine, were drained; then his gold and silver plate was seized, but rather than steal it, the attackers dropped it from the Savoy terrace into the Thames. Emptied of its grandeur, the palace was burned to the ground.

As the June sky was darkening, Richard climbed one of Henry III's towers and looked out at the city. The sky over London was red with flames, while the Savoy, Clerkenwell hospital and the houses of many other rich and powerful merchants were falling in smoking ruin. Many in his position, and a good deal older than fourteen, would have collapsed in terror. But somehow Richard seemed to understand that the only way out of the desperate situation was to confront it head-on. Walworth suggested that to get the rebels out of the centre of the city, a meeting should be proposed at Mile End, then a rustic village well beyond the eastern gate. So, on the next day, Friday, 14 June, Richard rode on his palfrey, together with his mother and most of the court, through the jostling crowds to meet Wat Tyler and the rest of the leaders. The people on the highway spoke to him with startling familiarity and directness, demanding restitution for whichever officers had done them injury. As the milling throng closed in, some of Richard's knights thought better of their body-guarding assignment and turned back to the city. At Mile End Tyler asked Richard's permission to deal with the traitors as they deserved. Richard responded with calm intelligence that those who had already been sentenced by due process of law would, indeed, be punished. This was not the licence to lynch that the rebels had in mind. When they pressed him for an end to serfdom and a flat-rate rent of four pence an acre, he consented. If, however, Richard and his councillors imagined these tactical concessions would take the sting out of the revolt they were wrong. Richard's apparent endorsement of the revolt had the effect of unloosing further retribution. Anyone marked as 'foreign' was hunted down, and perhaps 150 were killed. Thirty-five Flemings, who had replaced the Jews as the scapegoat of choice – the personification of money – were dragged from sanctuary in St Martin in Vintry and decapitated on the same block, one after another. At the Tower the crowd was big enough and in an ugly enough mood to persuade the garrison to open the gates. The armoury was plundered, and the royal beds tried out. Richard's mother, Joan of Kent, was made to kiss one of the rebels. In the chapel of St John the crowd found Sudbury and Hales preparing for death. Before he was beheaded on Tower Hill, Sudbury made a speech to the crowd, warning them that if he were killed the country would be put under interdiction. The threat provoked only laughter, followed by grim resolve. Eight blows were needed to finish him. The heads of both men were stuck on the spikes reserved for traitors to the Crown. But it was the likes of Wat Tyler who now decided who was true and who was treacherous.

Richard must have felt that there was a chance he might not survive, but he agreed nonetheless to a second face-to-face meeting at Smithfield on the Saturday morning. Before he left, he went to the great shrine that Henry III had built at Westminster and prayed to the king whom the Plantagenets had made their guardian saint, Edward the Confessor. When he reached Smithfield, he saw that the rebel leaders were on the west side of the field, the royal party on the east. Wat Tyler rode over to Richard, dismounted, briefly and unconvincingly bent his knees, but then rose, shook the king's hand and called him 'brother'. 'Why will you not go home?' Richard asked. Tyler is said to have responded with a curse and a demand for a new Magna Carta, this time for the common people, formally ending serfdom, pardoning all outlaws, liquidating the property of the Church and declaring the equality of all men below the king. As revolutionary as all this sounds (and undoubtedly was), all the demands, other than the pardon for outlaws, would, in fact, return as elements of English royal policy in the centuries to come. But that was for the future. When Richard replied in the affirmative (with the crucial loophole, 'saving only the regality of his crown'), it was hard to know who was more flabbergasted – the rebels or the royals.

Perhaps taken aback by the unexpected concession, for a moment no one did anything. A silence fell over the field, broken by Wat Tyler calling for a flagon of ale, emptying it, then climbing back on his mount, a big man on a little horse. And it was at that moment that history changed.

Someone on the royal side was evidently unable to take the humiliation a moment longer. It was a royal esquire, a young man of the king's own age, who shouted that Tyler was a thief. Tyler turned his horse, drew his dagger and rounded on the boy. The spell was broken. A mêlée broke out, and Walworth, who must have been beside himself with mortification, attempted to arrest Tyler. There was fighting, Tyler striking the mayor with his dagger, Walworth cutting Tyler through the shoulder and neck. He rode his horse a little way back, blood pouring from him, then fell to the ground where the king's men were on him, finishing him off.

It was the moment of truth. Once they had discovered Tyler's fate, the rebel side might have attacked then and there. But before they could, Richard himself pre-empted the action with a show of astonishing courage and resourcefulness, riding straight to them shouting, famously: 'You shall have no captain but me.' The words were carefully chosen and deliberately ambiguous. To the rebels it seemed that Richard was now their leader just as they had always hoped. But the phrase could just as easily have been meant as the first, decisive reassertion of royal authority. In any event, it bought time for Walworth to speed back to London and mobilize an army that, just the day before, had been much too scared to show itself. At Smithfield the process of breaking the now leaderless army began cautiously and gently, with promises of pardons and mercy. Once back in London and Westminster, though, the king and council acted with implacable resolution. On 18 June, just three days after Smithfield, orders were sent to the disturbed counties, commanding the sheriffs to do whatever it took to restore the peace.

In selected cases and places this meant swift, summary justice: gibbets and swing-ing bodies were soon on display. In London the man said to have beheaded Archbishop Sudbury was himself decapitated. But there were many local authorities that preferred to pacify with relative leniency, imprisoning rather than executing offenders. Only where there was continued resistance did the government show itself ferocious. At Waltham on 22 June the king faced another group of rebels who were asking for a restatement of his Mile End concessions. But they found a very different Richard, who turned on them with authentic Plantagenet rage:

> You wretches, detestable on land and sea; you who seek equality with lords are unworthy to live. Give this message to your colleagues. Rustics you were and rustics you are still: you will remain in bondage not as before but incomparably harsher. For as long as we live we will strive to suppress you, and your misery will be an example in the eyes of posterity. However we will spare your lives if you remain faithful. Choose now which course you want to follow.

Astounded by this new voice, many of the rebels did, indeed, decide to cut their losses and accept the king's mercy. Others determined to fight. At Billericay on 28 June a force took on the royal troops and were routed. In Essex a special commission hanged nineteen of the leaders, and another twelve were executed by hanging and drawing. When the new Archbishop of Canterbury, William Courtenay, asked for men who loved the king to appear in arms in his defence, one source records 40,000 as answering the call. It was all over.

It's never healthy for a teenager to get a premature sense of omnipotence, but in the circumstances how could Richard have avoided it? His father had won his spurs in France when he had barely been out of his adolescence, and all his young life Richard had been hearing about the *preux chevalier* (valiant knight), the flower of chivalry and so forth and on and on and on. Now that he had faced his first battle – one that, moreover, had called on great reserves of mental and physical courage – and had come through the firestorm a hero, it was understandable if he were a little carried away with the wonderfulness of being King Richard II. Equally understandable was the king's lingering sense that it was the 'official' guardians of the realm – his uncle Gaunt and the great nobles of England, the men pressed on him by his mother as his political tutors and councillors – who had got him into the hideous mess of the rebellion in the first place. After the revolt was finished off, the Commons actually voiced their own sense that some of the rebels' grievances were, in fact, not without substance. So they, too, evidently felt the Gaunt regime to blame for the crisis. What was more, amid the general meltdown of the magnates, their scurrying back to their estates, he, Richard, had kept his cool while they had lost theirs. So why should he not trust his own judgement when it came to choosing his companions and councillors?

We have been conditioned by Shakespeare's portrait of a feckless, wilful and petulant prince, designing his own disaster, to think from the beginning of Richard's court and his councillors as a reflecting pool of his own vanity and the fish swimming in it as prize specimens of the ornamental, the greedy and the parasitic. In fact, they were not a bunch of orchidaceous nonentities but an interestingly mixed and able group, representing many of the communities that counted in late fourteenth-century England. The much-execrated Simon Burley had been the Black Prince's choice of tutor for his son. Robert de Vere, who was absurdly suspected of homosexual affection for the king, was not only a notorious womanizer but came from one of the most ancient baronial families in the country. Michael de la Pole, who became Richard's chancellor, represented the new social reality, coming as he did from a family of ennobled wool merchants. Thomas Mowbray, Richard's boyhood boon companion, was a famous champion of the tilts and tournaments.

The real sin of Richard's court was that it paid insufficient attention to the ancient and powerful aristocracy – the Gloucesters, Arundels and Warwicks. As they began to smart at being set aside in offices and favours for Richard's inner circle, so the impression began to be circulated that there was 'something wrong' with the king, and that he was, somehow, not a 'give-'em-hell' native Plantagenet but rather a fancy, nancy boy with foreign, if not actually deviant, tastes. Never mind that Richard was built like all the rest of his forebears – 6 feet tall with long, flowing, blond hair. The late unlamented Edward of Caernarfon boasted the same Plantagenet features, too, and in crises Richard was already being ominously reminded by his enemies of the fate of Edward II. Somehow he wasn't the real Plantagenet stuff. Real Plantagenets built fortresses. Richard was more interested in beautifying the great ceremonial space of Westminster Hall with a stunning hammerbeam roof, the better to display the mystique of his royalty. Real Plantagenets smelled of the battlefield. Richard apparently liked to bathe, and worse, to bathe *frequently* in bath-houses decorated with coloured tiles and walls. Real Plantagenets tore at their meat and slurped the drippings. Richard not only insisted on using spoons but also inflicted them on his nobles. A real Plantagenet would not have commissioned the first royal cookbook with 186 recipes packed with suspicious foreign spices like cardamom and spikenard. Real Plantagenets brought you blood-soaked victories over the ancestral enemies, the Scots and the French. Richard II brought you the handkerchief.

Which is, of course, only to say that Richard II was very much an early Renaissance prince in the European mode: someone who prized civility and the patronage of the arts as much as feats of arms and the hunt. And none of his courtly or mystical self-indulgences, nor even his notorious mood-swings between lordly euphoria and manic depression, would have mattered – at least not fatally – had he managed to conduct policy with any kind of sensitivity as to what it took to keep a supportive coalition together. Personal access to the king, even for the most senior nobles, now had to be directed through the gatekeepers, whom the magnates detested as jumped-up parvenus. Still more seriously, Richard's determination to pursue peace, rather than war, with France seemed to be a unilateral liquidation of the great Plantagenet joint-stock enterprise of conquest, which had so enriched the great dynasts. Had Richard managed to compensate both his military reputation and his nobles by a brilliant campaign in Scotland in 1385 all might still have been well. But unable to lure the Scots to battle in the classic Edwardian style and sensibly reluctant to pursue them north of the Firth of Forth (given the problems with logistics), Richard was reduced to meaningless marches and burnings without ever bringing the war to a decisive resolution.

The smarting sense that someone had to be made accountable for these expensive failures brought together in parliament sections of the political community that normally would have disliked each other much more heartily than any of them disliked the king. At their core were the great magnates of the realm – the Duke of Gloucester, the king's uncle, and the Earls of Warwick and Arundel. They called themselves the 'Lords Appellant', but their 'appeal' was a euphemism for the prosecution of men they believed had made Richard deaf to their own counsel – especially to renew the war with France. But their animosity was shared by younger nobles like Gaunt's son Henry Bolingbroke. Creating so broad a coalition of the exasperated was, on Richard's part, quite an achievement, and in the autumn of 1387 he reaped the consequences of his obtuseness. Faced with the demand by both houses of parliament that he remove his most unpopular councillors – among them de Vere, de la Pole and the Chief Justice, Robert Tresilian – Richard's reply was that he would not dismiss so much as a scullion at their request. Very well, was the response, in a tone calculated to remind the king that he was still a minor, a 'Council of Government' would now rule, and the three highest officers in the land would be appointed by parliament until the king came to his senses. It was a replay of the mid-thirteenth century conflict between Henry III and the 'community of the realm', but this time there would be no great civil war. Bolstered by his lawyers' advice that the parliamentary attempts to dictate his choice of councillors infringed his royal prerogatives, Richard attempted to arrest his major adversary, the Earl of Arundel. Instead of cowing the opposition, it solidified it, and Richard's small royalist army under de Vere disintegrated on contact with the much bigger body of troops put together by the lords. Defenceless, Richard was back where he had been in the crisis of 1381 – in the Tower of London, a virtual captive. The 'Merciless Parliament' that followed rubbed salt in the wounds of his hurting pride by dealing brutally with his friends and councillors. Accused of 'abusing the king's youth' and turning him against those who should have been his wise councillors, de Vere and de la Pole managed to escape before they could be taken, but Burley was tried and executed, despite a plea for mercy by Queen Anne on her knees before the Lords Appellant.

This was the second great ordeal of Richard's reign, and in many ways it was much more damaging to the king than the Peasants Revolt. In 1381 he had emerged from the crisis with his authority enhanced. The coup of 1387, on the other hand, was a crushing humiliation. So when Richard, to whom so much had happened, so fast, declared his own majority in 1389, the question he had to be asking himself was, what kind of king could he be? And the answer he came up with would, in the end, ruin him.

Between 1389 and 1397 Richard evidently decided to lead a double-life. To the power-brokers in parliament, especially his uncle John of Gaunt, he promised to be a good boy, to behave, to listen to the sage counsel offered by his elders and betters and to be prudent where he bestowed his patronage. In 1390 a three-day tournament held at Smithfield to mark his coming of age (with stands built by the royal clerk of works Geoffrey Chaucer) was designed as an allegory of harmony. The lances and maces of the competing knights were blunted *à la plaisance* to signify an entertainment. But to students of signs and symbols, there were already signs of the other Richard, the Richard whose obsession with his own divine appointment would feed on itself. For the first time, the king's own team of knights appeared in identical livery, all sporting badges with his newly chosen personal device, the white hart. Against them were foreign knights arrayed in a multitude of liveries. But these team badges were something new. Richard's 'affinity' looked for all the world like a miniature private army.

The white hart reappears, significantly crowned and chained, in a mural in Westminster Abbey, as if the king still felt restive about his constraints. Inwardly, though, there was nothing at all inhibited about Richard's vision of his kingship as the lieutenancy of God, an intercessor and protector of his realm, a saviour in a plague-smitten world of the fallen. English kings could, after all, be saints, and in the Wilton Diptych Richard appears in the company of two of them – St Edmund, the martyr-king of East Anglia, and Edward the Confessor – as well as St John the Baptist. He is directly addressing the choir of angels and the Virgin Mary as a donor. And what he is giving the Virgin, as her dowry no less, is Britannia – the 'island set in the silver sea', just visible in the banner. With this special relationship between Richard and the Virgin securely established, the king and the kingdom need fear no harm.

The realm was not in Richard's gift, however. When Shakespeare put the famous hymn to insularity in the mouth of the dying John of Gaunt, it was to emphasize the God-given autonomy of the island kingdom. It was the *land* that was sceptred and blessed, not the person of the monarch. But any notion of the sovereign identity of the nation separate from his person would have been incomprehensible, if not heretical, to Richard. What he wanted was reverence, making it clear for the first time in the history of English kingship that he should rather like to be known as 'majesty' and 'highness'. The first *self-conscious* designer of a royal identity, Richard understood as none of his predecessors had done that ceremony was not just the dressing of royalty; it was at the heart of its mystery and the secret of its power to make men obey. For long periods between vespers and dinner, he sat alone in silence, wearing his crown. Anyone whose eyes met the royal gaze was required directly to cast them down in respect and bend the knee. After Queen Anne, his 'little scrap of flesh', died in 1394, Richard became even more rigid in his ceremonial pieties. A great portrait panel of the king, unique hitherto in English history, exactly expressed this autocratic solitude: the formidable, unsmiling god-king, his purple-blue tunic decorated with monogrammed Rs, stared down at the lowly subjects. No wonder Richard found time for 'geomancy' and commissioned a book on it, part alchemy, part philosophy, part science. He wanted, apparently, to be England's magus.

The Wilton Diptych, 1390s. Richard II presented
to the Virgin by his patron saint, St John the
Baptist, and Sts Edmund and Edward. The detail
of the white hart comes from the reverse.

In 1397 the barrier between fantasy and reality broke down in an extraordinary storm of revenge. The pretext was an aristocratic 'plot' that Richard claimed to be nipping the bud. He was thirty years old and childless, and in those circumstances the ambitious did indeed begin to mutter deviously in the shadows. But the necks that Richard was after were old and scrawny – Arundel, Warwick and Gloucester were all political back numbers. The real power in the land belonged as ever to John of Gaunt, Duke of Lancaster, and his son Henry Bolingbroke, Earl of Derby. Occasionally Richard let fly with tantrums of royal displeasure, such as when he gave Arundel a bloody face with the back of his hand when he failed to show up to Queen Anne's funeral, but the witch-hunt of 1397 was more than a tantrum. Warwick and Arundel were arrested, and Richard descended in person, together with a small army, on the Duke of Gloucester's castle to take the old man into custody. Before the trials began the Bishop of Exeter preached a sermon on the scripture 'there shall be one king over them all', and during its proceedings Lancaster, Richard and his Speaker of the Commons, Sir Richard Bushy, interrogated Arundel, who bravely refused to concede any wrong-doing yet undercut his own case by taking refuge in an earlier pardon granted by the king. Richard now decided that the pardon had been revoked. Arundel was executed. Warwick was exiled to the Isle of Man, and when a messenger was sent to Gloucester's cell in Calais, he was discovered dead in suspicious circumstances, almost certainly suffocated in his feather bed on Richard's orders.

The old scores had been settled, and one would imagine that Richard would manage to contain his sense of triumph, if only in the interests of political survival. But now that Richard II discovered that people seemed to be rather frightened by him, he also discovered that he rather liked it. When John of Gaunt took to his sick bed, the remaining restraints on Richard's delusions of omnipotence disappeared and the autocrat of his imagination became the real thing. He took to eating, sleeping and travelling surrounded by his own praetorian guard, like a Roman emperor. The lieutenancy of Cheshire was turned into his personal satrap, and the Welsh castles close by were fortified under his own command. Feeling militarily strong, he began to lay hands on the sheriffs of the counties, in violation of the principles established after the civil war of the thirteenth century that drew their personnel from the community of the shire. Anyone now suspected of less than absolute loyalty to Richard was purged and replaced by a dependable hack. At court, too, the king cultivated a new circle of yes-men, ready to pander to his sense of imperial infallibility. And this was, in any case, a period when treatises like Dante's *De Monarchia* ('On Monarchy'; *c.*1313) were making the case for the authority of a single, absolute princc, answerable directly to God. Doubtless there was no shortage of scholars willing to give Richard the gist of the argument, and doubtless he recognized himself in their encomia.

But philosophy would be unable to protect Richard from one of the swiftest, steepest falls in English history: from autocracy to abdication in less than two years. The brutal disposal of the Lords Appellant had left all those not inside the charmed circle of Richard's immediate entourage understandably jittery. There had been no warning when he had struck against Arundel. Who knew when he might lash out next and against whom? John of Gaunt and his son, Bolingbroke, were acutely aware that as long as Richard remained childless they were, presumptively, next in line to the throne, and that was both an opportunity and an enormous danger. Their worst fears were realized after a bizarre episode involving mutual accusations of treason levelled by Thomas Mowbray, the Earl Marshal and Duke of Norfolk (Richard's childhood friend), and Henry Bolingbroke. The issue was to be settled by combat in the lists at Gosford, near Coventry, and, with the antagonists commissioning special suits of armour for the occasion, expectations for the extraordinary, Arthurian spectacle were sky-high. They plummeted when, just before the riders prepared for the gallop, Richard rose from his seat shouting 'Hold!' as he did so. As the royal judge and arbiter, he was perfectly within his rights to halt the proceedings and perhaps he was suddenly aware that, whatever the outcome, he would be the loser. Should Mowbray win, the whispered accusations that he had helped the king dispose of the Duke of Gloucester would suddenly become shouted accusations. Should Bolingbroke win, his status as king-in-waiting might be even more intolerable. But the penalties Richard imposed satisfied no one and outraged many. Mowbray was banished for life, but Bolingbroke, judged innocent, was nonetheless given ten years in exile. At the time of his banishment there seems to have been no thought in Richard's mind of dispossessing Bolingbroke. For years, Gaunt had been an ally, not an enemy. And old as he was, Richard assumed he would be around for some time to back the king's interests. In the winter of 1398–9, however, Gaunt became gravely ill and he died in early February. With his passing the immense and fortune of the House of Lancaster became the property not of a friend, but an ex-Appellant, a rival, an adversary. Doing nothing about this was dangerous. Doing something about this proved fatal. Richard changed Bolingbroke's sentence to banishment for life, and parcelled out his inheritance to loyal supporters of the Crown. He held out the remote prospect that one day Bolingbroke or his son Henry might recover their lands. But in the furore no one noticed this small concession.

Laying hands on an inheritance – especially the greatest in the country – was seen by many of the great magnates as a direct violation of the coronation oath. If Richard could do this to Bolingbroke, they must have thought, he could do it to anyone. He needed to be stopped. Deaf to these ominous murmurs, Richard took the opportunity of what he must have thought was the acme of his power to lead an expedition to Ireland in May 1399. The plan was to bring the Irish princes, who were led by the intelligent and elusive king of Leinster, Art MacMurrough (Art Caomhánach Mac Murchadha), into line as vassals. The timing was dreadful; the execution worse. The king took just enough troops to leave him defenceless at home and not enough to intimidate the Irish. So by the time that Richard returned from another miserably inconclusive campaign, Bolingbroke, now Duke of Lancaster, had already landed at Ravenspur in Yorkshire to claim his inheritance with an army thoughtfully provided by the king of France. In a matter of weeks Henry had command of most of southern and eastern England.

Even now, had Richard been determined to play to his strengths and hold out in the near impregnable Welsh castles together with his fighting force of Cheshire archers and foot soldiers he might have had some chance to rally resistance. But Shakespeare's haunting portrait of a man whose inner resolve crumbled is strikingly close to the mark. Richard seemed one step ahead in pessimism. When he got the bad news that many of his most trusted allies had defected to Bolingbroke, his reaction was not to dig in his heels and make a stand, but to flee across country at night, disguised as a priest, bewailing his misfortunes and, as usual, blaming everyone else.

Initially, it wasn't at all a foregone conclusion that he would be forced off the throne. Henry III and his son Edward had survived their crisis by making tactical concessions while building themselves a royalist army. When the Earl of Northumberland came to Richard at Conwy as Bolingbroke's emissary, the demands were simply that Lancaster have his rightful inheritance returned and that Richard repeat the concessions of 1387 and remove a list of undesirables. At some point during his uncontested march through England Bolingbroke's ambitions changed, however. Given the experience of the Appellants, he could hardly be sure that if Richard did make concessions they would not be followed, some day, by sudden, savage acts of retribution. There was also the matter of the king's newly arranged child bride, Isabella, who might yet produce an heir for him. So when nudged further by the lords and bishops, who wanted a pragmatic, rather than an erratic, mystically self-absorbed king, a king who would understand that it had been men, rather than God, who had put the crown on his head, Henry allowed himself to be steered towards the throne.

Top: The hammerbeam roof of Westminster Hall.
Above: Richard II; portrait from Westminster Abbey, *c.* 1395.

At this point, Shakespeare has Richard paralysed by fatalism, declaring, as he sees Bolingbroke's army approach Flint Castle: 'Now I can see my end.' But this resignation was, in fact, a convenient piece of Lancastrian–Tudor propaganda, neatly disposing of the embarrassment of a deposition by claiming that Richard resigned the throne rather than having it snatched from his desperate grip. Only when the throne was vacant, Lancastrian propaganda histories insisted, did Bolingbroke very decently agree to volunteer his services. What actually happened was a month of painful negotiations, with Richard a prisoner in the Tower of London. Three times he was asked if he would abdicate and three times he refused, before he finally bowed to the inevitable and became plain 'Sir Richard of Bordeaux'.

As for the reasons given for the change in regime, Henry was extremely nervous about listing categories of misconduct, which might compromise the future authority of the Crown and be used against himself and his heirs. So he fell back instead on obscure arguments about genealogy, arguing that the crown rightfully belonged to him as a descendant of Henry III's son, Edmund Crouchback, whom, it was absurdly alleged, had actually been the oldest of the brothers and who had been illegitimately set aside in favour of Edward I on account of his physical deformity! Even Henry and his immediate backers realized this was too far-fetched to win general assent, so when Richard's 'Renunciation' was read to parliament on 30 September 1399, the deposition was said to be based on 'vengeful sentences given against the lords'. When parliament was asked to approve Henry Bolingbroke, Earl of Hereford and Duke of Lancaster, as king, cries of 'yes, yes, yes,' echoed around the chamber. But not loudly enough apparently, for Bolingbroke himself asked for another hearty round of acclaim.

This surprising insecurity nagged away at Henry IV, just as Shakespeare depicted him: an insomniac, deeply troubled by a bad conscience. The man who had been made king as a result of discontent at Richard's imperial pretensions immediately appropriated them for himself. Richard had been interested in imperial crowns (and commissioned a special book on the regalia of England), but it was Henry IV who was the first to have the closed imperial-style crown (still in use) set on his head. As if to advertise his impeccable Plantagenet pedigree, Henry chose the saint's day of their favourite patron, Edward the Confessor, for his coronation. And assuming you couldn't have too much of a good thing, Henry had himself anointed with the oil said to have been given to Becket by the Virgin, Richard's own, but apparently not dependable, protectress.

All this was still not enough to make Henry IV feel secure. There were risings in support of the deposed king, and as long as Richard was alive he could expect them to continue. In all likelihood, 'Sir Richard of Bordeaux' was starved to death in Pontefract Castle, a truly horrible way to die but one that ensured there would be no compromising marks on his body. For the whole point of Henry's elimination of his predecessor was that his body should be publicly displayed as a pre-emptive strike against hard-core Ricardian supporters. So the long, slow journey south from Pontefract Castle was orchestrated by Henry in a display of staggeringly disingenuous concern. In London the body was borne on a black bier with the arms of St Edward and St George on the side. But it was not, of course, destined for the mausoleum at Westminster. A requiem mass was said in St Paul's and the body was taken to the Dominican abbey at King's Langley in Buckinghamshire, where it remained for the rest of the disturbed and unstable reign of Henry IV.

Even more peculiarly, it was his son Henry V (who had served with Richard in Ireland, where he had been praised by the king) who had Richard's body exhumed and re-interred in Westminster in the gilt-effigy grandeur Richard had already planned for himself before his deposition. Perhaps Henry V had inherited his father's guilty conscience. Perhaps he hoped, in vain as it turned out, that somehow the wounds of the contending parties might finally scar over and heal.

And during his brief reign it looked, for a while, as if this might happen. With Shakespeare's gorgeous rhetoric forever ringing in our ears, it's impossible not to think of Henry V first and foremost as a warlord. But the lesson he took from the mistakes of his predecessors was that to survive and prosper, a king of England needed to be both messiah and manager. And in the managerial department, Henry was undoubtedly chief executive, knowing when to stamp on the inevitable quarrels of the magnates and when to stroke them into assent. To the Church he was the most assiduous and consistent patron since Henry III, and he possessed, in spadefuls, the critical psychological skill of making everyone in his immediate circle, beginning with his brothers, feel trusted and honoured. Unlike Richard, who seemed to conceive of the realm as an extension of his own persona, Henry evidently made the political community confident that the king's business was also the country's. So he managed without too much difficulty to extract from parliament taxes that were, in fact, far heavier than those that had triggered the Peasants Revolt! Of course, the stunning victory over a much larger French army at Agincourt, the annihilation of much of the French military nobility and the humiliation of their king did help. The streak of native pugilism that Shakespeare catches was not, in fact, missing from Henry's campaign. The dispatches from France were written and publicized, for the first time, in English, and the London Company of Brewers noted that: 'our most excellent King Henry hath procured the common idiom to be recommended by the exercise of writing and greater part of the Lords and Commons have begun to make their matters noted down in our mother tongue.' When Henry came home after Agincourt, an immense 'joyous entry' was staged in the streets of London. Hosts of angels, prophets and apostles rained hosannas on the dark-haired, pale-faced, unnervingly sober king, the personification of the *miles celestis* (the anointed knight of heaven): a king perfectly capable of lecturing abbots on their proper Christian duties, a St George and a Galahad wrapped up in one unbeatable package.

Unbeatable, of course, except by King Death. For Henry's premature death from dysentery in 1422 at the age of thirty-five was every bit as disastrous as all the histories now and then lamented. Of course, it is entirely possible that even had Henry V lived, he would eventually have run into the same troubles experienced in the disastrous reign of his son, Henry VI. There would have come a time when the French, smarting from a treaty imposed under duress, would have rejected the son of Henry V and Queen Katherine and would have gone to war, Joan of Arc or no Joan of Arc, to recover their lost provinces. The king – whoever he was – would then have been obliged to come to parliament for yet more subsidies and taxes, and without an unbroken string of victories would have met the inevitable resistance. That being said, it was plainly a poor prospect for the realm to have yet another child on the throne. And as Henry VI grew, it became evident that his child-like naïveté was not going to go away. So there came again all the old miseries – waves of the plague; a huge debt, partly incurred by the king's irresponsibility; a peasant rebellion in 1450; and the conspiracies of magnate factions determined to capture the king for their own ends.

The chaos and anarchy of the period known as the Wars of the Roses was (as many of Shakespeare's characters in the history plays argue) the poisoned fruit of Bolingbroke's *coup d'état*. He had shown that a junior branch of the royal family could overthrow the legitimate king, and once the precedent had been set, the English aristocracy went at it with a will.

There are only two ways to feel about the Wars of the Roses. Either the endless chronicle of battles, of the entries and exits of kings, of hasty shipboard departures and even hastier coronations seems one of the great epics of English history, or the same story leaves the reader slightly numbed. If the latter, the temptation is to write off the entire sorry mess as the bloody bickering of overgrown schoolboys, each with their miniature armies or 'affinities', whacking each other senseless on the fields of Towton, Barnet and St Albans; a dance of death to a tune played by the Earl of Warwick, 'the Kingmaker'. But there was something at stake in all the mayhem, beyond the bruisings of toughs and toffs, and that was the need to make the English monarchy credible again and to re-solder the chain of allegiance that had once

Henry V by an unknown artist; late sixteenth/early seventeenth century.

stretched from Westminster to the justices of the shires and the jurors of the villages and that had been snapped by the fate of Richard II. The major players in the wars were, of course, only too acutely aware of this, wanting their survival to depend on something more than cheques made out to Warwick and the temporary possession of coercive force. But they divided into managers and messiahs rather than uniting them in the same personality like Henry V.

Edward IV was emphatically a manager, who believed he could finesse his authority through patronage, some of it conveyed to the Lancastrian family of his wife, Elizabeth Woodville. But there were also petty messiahs: Edward's father, Richard, Duke of York, who seemed to believe he had been called by the Almighty to restore England's dignity, and his youngest son, Richard of Gloucester, whom we have been conditioned to think of as either the incarnation of a godless villain or (by impassioned devotees) as a northern hero vilely defamed by Tudor propaganda.

In reality, Richard III was much more interesting but also much more sinister than either of those stereotypes allow, being not a godless but a godly fanatic, devoted to wiping out the unworthy, beginning with Edward IV's in-laws, and his own inconvenient nephews, so that he might institute the reign of piety and justice in England: Henry V in a crazy-castle mirror. It was Richard who took improbable offence at what he thought was his brother Edward's gross immorality – insisting that he was living in sin with Elizabeth Woodville – and who forced Edward's mistress, Jane Shore, to parade through London as a common harlot. When Richard was killed at Bosworth Field, the country was saved not from a monster of corruption and depravity but from a puritan martinet.

The historians who began to busy their quills with apologias for Henry Tudor and his dynasty were at pains to represent the Wars of the Roses as one long nightmare, from which only the Tudors could release a grateful nation, a country torn from top to bottom, a pitiless field of carnage in which, as in Shakespeare's histories, fathers were capable of killing their own children and vice versa. But in the middle of it, an intelligent French observer, Phillipe de Commynes, could claim in the 1470s (a decade in which the crown changed hands three times) that of all the countries he had known, England was 'the one where public affairs were best conducted and regulated with the least violence to the people'. Commynes grasped an essential fact about the fifteenth century: that the battles affected only a small part of the country. Remarkably for medieval warfare, there were almost no protracted sieges and few dreadful marches in which the helpless countryside was put to the torch. While the peerage of England slaughtered each other, the rest of the country got on with living.

Yet perhaps, as in so many instances in British history, we have over-corrected. For while the Black Death was still more of a terror for most people than the Earl of Warwick, the humiliation of the Crown and its impotence in the face of the over-mighty and the over-armed did filter down to conditions of local lawlessness. A petition of parliament to Richard III complaining of the perversion of government under Edward IV is not, of course, a disinterested document, but there was still something authentic about its lament that 'this land was ruled by self-will and pleasure, fear and dread'. Great holes certainly *had* been torn in the fabric of authority, both by plague and by anarchy, and the spaces that opened up could be seen either as exciting opportunities or as frightening voids.

No family typified this high-risk, high-gain, knife-edge world of late medieval England better than the Pastons of northeast Norfolk whose letters – the earliest such surviving correspondence in English – have miraculously been preserved in brilliant vividness. They document the extraordinary change that could transform a single family against the backdrop of local anarchy, distant battles and the plague, which returned with a vengeance in the 1460s and 1470s. The founder of the Paston fortunes was Clement, mentioned in village records as a plain 'husbandman' – in other words, a peasant. But before he died in 1419 Clement had been able to profit from the labour shortage to make the kind of bargain with the lord of the manor that ensured his small prosperity. A power in the village, he might have served as ale-taster or constable, but his great achievement was in getting enough money to buy his son William a legal education and having the shrewdness to understand that it was through education as much as land that the family fortunes would be advanced.

William Paston did indeed become a lawyer, married into money and moved into Oxnead Hall, one of the grander houses in the county. In short order, he became the king's man in his parish and indispensable to absentee landowners in the management of their local estates. His son, John, followed his father in the law and was now sophisticated enough to befriend Sir John Fastolf, alas, neither plump nor jolly but a wealthy veteran of Henry V's wars and rich enough to leave a hoard of gold plate and jewels, including a 'great diamond' in a white rose, and lord of Caister Castle. Before long, John Paston was a trustee running Fastolf's little East Anglian empire of manors in Suffolk as well as Norfolk. When he became Sir John Paston and inherited Caister, he had completed the family's meteoric rise from peasant to knight of the shire in just three generations.

Nothing is ever quite this easy. As long as the Pastons were obscure nobodies, the bloody carnage of the Wars of the Roses was someone else's problem, but as soon as they became rich and influential, they also became targets for the heavies, and no

Houses of the Paston family in Norfolk: (top) Oxnead Hall; (left) Caister Castle.
Above: The Paper Mill, Benenden — a fine example of a fifteenth-century Wealden
hall-house in Kent, built *c.* 1480.

one was heavier than the Duke of Norfolk. One of the countless thugs of his 'affinity' who was running a small private army, the Lord Moleyn, drove John's redoubtable wife, Margaret Mautby, out of Gresham Manor while her husband was away in 1449 – 'myned down the walle of her chamber where she was and bare her out of the gates'. 'Please it Your Highness,' John wrote to Henry VI, 'if this great insurrection, riot and wrongs and daily continuance thereof so heinously done against your crown's dignity and peace…should not be duly punished it shall give great boldness to them and all other misdoers to make congregations and final destruction of your liege people and laws.' In 1469 Norfolk himself, who had always coveted Caister, came to get it. Margaret wrote in anguish to her eldest son: 'I greet you well, letting you know that your younger brother and his fellowship stand in great jeopardy at Caister.' She was clearly desperate. But she was also very angry and, a few lines on, let her son, John, have the rough edge of her tongue: 'Every man in this county marvels greatly that you suffer them to be…in so great jeopardy without help or other remedy, the greatest rebuke to you that ever came to any young gentleman.' John the younger, it seemed, had other fish to fry since he was busy trying to find an even grander heiress at court, a woman 'right nigh of queen's blood'. In the meantime, however, Margaret had no alternative but to surrender the castle to the greedy Duke of Norfolk. It took a seven-year legal battle, including direct appeals to Edward IV, before the family was reinstated at Caister. And the vindication did John little good. In 1471, in the midst of a terrible plague epidemic, he wrote home fearfully asking for news: 'This is the most universal death that I have ever witnessed in England. For by my troth I hear from pilgrims who travel through the country that no man who rides or goes in any country or borough town in England is free from the sickness.' No more was he. Later that year he too died.

The Pastons survived all those setbacks to settle down as a well-to-do power in their corner of Norfolk. And that would have been true for countless other Englishmen and women like them. They were, above all, survivors. They somehow managed to survive the plague, dethronements, civil war and local outrages. They became accustomed to the nerve-wracking knowledge that affairs of high state were in constant commotion. But they also knew that the courts at Westminster (in whoever's name) still dispensed justice in Common Pleas and King's Bench, Chancery and Exchequer. Twice a year, when the assize came through, they could, if need be, still air their grievances. They could still expect marks of consideration, to serve time as justices and to send their sons as esquires, preferably to less embattled households; and when times were easier they might even be called to court to bathe in the affable smiles of Edward IV.

The first century of the plague had seen the country turned upside down. In the twilight years of Edward III it seemed that nothing could damage the greatness of the Plantagenet royal estate. But the world of the village went from impoverished claustrophobia to traumatized infection. A hundred years later, everything had been up-ended, courtesy of King Death. Although some historians have thought the fifteenth century a 'slump', characterized by depressed trade and shrinking agricultural incomes, the evidence of fine country houses, like the Wealden houses in Kent, built not for great magnates but for local gentry and yeomen, hardly seems to bear this out. Kings came and went, but the men of the village, the same kind of men who had marched on London in 1381 and who had burned the Savoy to the ground, were now on their way to becoming squires. They knew what the worst was – an outbreak of the plague that would carry off the babies and the children or a rampage by the knights from over the next hill. But they also knew that with equal measures of prudence and prayer they would get through it.

So a visitor to an English village around 1480 would see what we now expect to see in such a place but that had never been there before: a church handsomely rebuilt in the solid, economic elegance of the Perpendicular; for the first time an alehouse with a name, such as 'the Swan' or 'the Frog'; and at the heart of the cluster of houses a grand and handsome dwelling for the biggest tenant farmer in the area. This was no longer just a glorified wattle-and-daub single-bay hut but a miniature manor house, with its own hall and servants to wait on the master and mistress, a buttery at the back, a cellar below and private retiring chambers.

Out of the fires of pestilence and bloodshed had come, then, that most unlikely example of survival: the English country gent.

CHAPTER

6

You don't notice the ghosts, not right away. At first sight Binham Priory looks much like any other East Anglian country church: limestone and limewash, plain and simple. But then you look again and sense something else lurking behind the innocent façade. The multi-storied arcades and the round window high on the west wall seem much too grand for a parish church. And then you begin to see things that are no longer there: stained-glass windows, wall paintings, a great rood crucifix. The emptiness fills. The vaulted space becomes a forest of faith. An ardent, coloured, noisy world begins to press in, a world of monks and masses, of plainsong and pictures: the world of Catholic England.

For centuries this phrase didn't sound strained. 'Catholic England' was just another way of saying Christian England. But then, in two generations, it stopped being a truism and started being treason. Images of the Virgin, the saints and the apostles, once glorified and cherished, were mocked and vandalized. At Binham the rood screen supporting the hanging crucifix was decorated with graceful pictures of the apostles. Come the Reformation, those images were expunged and covered up by texts from the English Bible. But time can work miracles. The lost souls sent wandering by the obliterators have returned, peeping through the letters of the Gospel like prisoners on the other side of a barred window, trapped, but not yet disposed of.

It's no good reaching out for ghosts. If you were so inconsiderate as to try to touch them, the Binham apostles would flake away into nothing, just as the world in which they were at home resists restoration. But it is because the death of that world was so unexpected, so shocking and so improbable, and because the Reformation and the religious wars it triggered cut so deep a mark in our history that the surviving fragments need to be reassembled into a big picture. Only then might it be possible to answer one of the most poignant questions in the nation's history: whatever happened to Catholic England?

BURNING
CONVICTIONS

Illustration from the opening of Chronicles 2 showing Solomon
making an offering to God; from the Great Bible of 1539.

In the 1950s, when I began to learn something about the mysteriously bitter wars of the Gentiles, there was no question of the inevitability, nor indeed of the rightness, of the Reformation. It seemed one of the fundamental building blocks of the English nation state, as self-evidently necessary as the development of parliamentary statute law with which it was evidently linked. If the Reformation had been regrettably brutal in execution, this was just a matter of putting an obsolete institution out of its misery. But a visit to a church like St Mary's in Fairford, Gloucestershire, would have swiftly put paid to those jejune assumptions. Right on the eve of the Reformation, when the Church was supposed to be in a state of lethargic stagnation, St Mary's was, in fact, at the height of its busy piety. The church had had a long tradition as a specially favoured place, patronized by Warwick the 'Kingmaker' and the Yorkists before ending up in the hands of the victor of Bosworth, Henry Tudor. Always happy to see someone else's money being spent, Henry VII leased the church to one of the richest cloth manu-facturers in the country, John Tame, who responded by funding the building of a hand-some new tower over the crossing. Bishop Richard Foxe was then brought into the planning of the decoration of St Mary's, completing a three-way partnership between money, monarchy and the priesthood. The results can be seen in some of the most spectacular stained-glass windows in Britain. The undeniable splendour of the project may even have prised loose some funds from Henry's own treasury, and in return he and the rest of the righteous royals are featured in transparently obvious disguises: Queen Elizabeth as the Queen of Sheba; Arthur, Prince of Wales, as one of the Magi; his older sister, Margaret, as the presenter of doves, and his younger sister, Mary, as one of the Marys. Henry VII himself appears, crowned and haloed, yet another reincar-nation of the perennially venerated Edward the Confessor. There was, in fact, just one member of the family conspicuously missing, and that was Arthur's younger brother Henry, who would, as king, without even meaning it, begin the process that would doom windows like this to the evangelical hammer. But as those windows were being stained and set within their lead armatures, an impending clash between Crown and Church seemed utterly inconceivable.

From the start, Henry VII's mind was very much on his heavenly, as well as his earthly reward. Acutely conscious of the tenuousness of his claim to the throne (as a descendant of an illegitimate line of the Lancastrians), Henry needed to invoke the support of the Church to sanctify his title and to demonize the posthumous reputation of Richard III. The new king knew very well that a number of the bishops, in particular John Morton, Bishop of Ely, had suffered personally for refusing to rally to Richard, and so Henry lost no time at all in offering himself as a committed patron of the Church.

His models were the genuinely pious Lancastrians: Henry V, who had built a lavish chantry shrine in Westminster Abbey and had attacked the Benedictines in 1421 for their worldliness, and his son, the saintly fool Henry VI. Henry Tudor made sure that he sustained Henry VI's great foundations at Eton and Cambridge and was liberality itself when it came to the most spectacular project of all: another great royal shrine in Westminster Abbey, a chapel the likes of which had never been seen before in an English church, a marvel of Renaissance carving and gilt decoration. The shrine was originally meant to house the remains of Henry VI, but when it became apparent that he was not to be moved from Windsor, the king decided instead to make it the mausoleum — with tombs designed by the Italian sculptor Pietro Torrigiano — of the founding trinity of the Tudors: himself, his queen Elizabeth, and his mother, the formidable Lady Margaret Beaufort.

Lady Margaret, the Duchess of Richmond, personified the high end of the Tudors' ostentatious zeal for the welfare of the Catholic Church. But this did not imply complacency. Lady Margaret put her prestige and power at court behind those who, like John Fisher, Bishop of Rochester, and John Colet, Dean of St Paul's, thought of themselves as reformers, not with an aim of weakening the Church but of strengthening it. The aims of reform were exactly those that had been voiced for generations, not least by Henry V: fewer and more austere monasteries and convents, and more schools and colleges — like my own Cambridge college, Christ's, for example, established by Fisher and Lady Margaret as 'God's House' to produce schoolmasters. Colet in particular felt it necessary to lead the charge against a whole litany of evils, including absentee clergy and the excessive deference shown by priests to lay patrons. But the reformers' pessimism was, in fact, largely groundless. Repeated visitations to the dioceses revealed a picture not of a venal, absconding and irresponsible clergy but of something very nearly its opposite. Of 500 livings in the diocese of Canterbury, for example, only twenty-six parish priests were recorded as at all absent and then mostly on administrative business. No doubt the record of the Church was not spotless, but it was hardly the sink of indolence and ignorance the critics supposed.

The reformers spent a lot of time holding their noses at what they considered to be the cheapening of belief and practice by popular superstition. Their hero, Erasmus of Rotterdam, for example, visited one of the two most famous miracle-working shrines, Our Lady of Walsingham in Norfolk (the other was Becket's shrine at Canterbury), expressly to jeer at the credulous, getting a rise out of the pilgrims who worshipped the sacred milk of the Virgin or believed the founding legend of the place, which had the chapel transported by direct flight from the Holy Land to East

Above left: Stained-glass windows from St Mary's, Fairford; on the right, Elizabeth of York as the Queen of Sheba kneels before Solomon.
Above right: Panel from the medieval rood screen in Binham Priory, showing a painting of Christ as the Man of Sorrows superimposed with text from Cranmer's Bible of 1539.
Opposite: The tomb of Henry VII and Elizabeth of York by Pietro Torrigiano in the Henry VII Chapel, Westminster Abbey; completed c. 1518.

Anglia. It's true that Walsingham was a mixture of hucksterism and holiness, the sort of place one might expect to find in Naples rather than Norfolk. But Erasmus's view was that of the scholarly critic, safely expressed in Latin and not necessarily endorsed by his aristocratic and royal patrons. For the Henrys were regular and earnest pilgrims to Walsingham. Henry VII went at least three times in his reign, and in 1511 Henry VIII walked there as a barefoot penitent, offering the Lady a ruby necklace in thanks for the birth of his son. Prince Henry died within weeks, but the King's Candle (thanks to the 48 shillings and 8 pence he supplied) continued to burn for many years to come.

Catholic England was, certainly, a peculiar world, with the Walsingham pilgrims co-existing alongside the sceptical Erasmus and his sober friends Fisher, Colet and More; the urge for renewal and reform beside a deep attachment to the venerable, the hallowed and, occasionally, the fraudulent. But all these apparent inconsistencies could be accommodated within the capacious skirts of the Catholic Mother Church.

Holy Trinity Church at Long Melford, Suffolk, for instance, is an extraordinary example of both spectacle and sophistication. Built as a hymn of glory to the county's wool trade, massively outsized, no expense spared, it's an example of what happened when money, lots of it, was sunk into piety. When that investment was made, so the gentry and merchants of Long Melford calculated, what they would be getting in return was a secure reservation on the trip to paradise. And in its prime, early in the sixteenth century, Long Melford was just that: the closest one could get to a vision of heaven and still be in Suffolk. Only fragments of that vision survive, but thanks to an account left by Roger Martyn, a lawyer and churchwarden at Long Melford during the reign of Queen Mary, we know what Holy Trinity Church was really like in its glory days, just before the Reformation struck. Writing in the very different time of Queen Elizabeth and dismayed by the monochrome thing called the Church of England, Martyn, with a palpable mixture of pride and regret, set out to inform future generations what they would be missing. 'The state of Melford Church and Our Lady's chapel at the east end as I...did know it: at the back of the high altar there was a goodly mount carved very artificially with the story of Christ's passion all being fair gilt and lively and beautifully set forth.' Martyn wrote of a roof painted like the vault of heaven with gold stars; gilt horsemen watching a golden Christ raised behind the altar, normally concealed but on feast-days opened to dazzle the eyes of the flock; brilliantly painted tabernacles with images of Jesus and the Virgin; a rood loft that was a virtual miniature church high in the air and painted with images of the twelve apostles; the entire building crammed with statues, carvings and relics, all glowing with candlelight reflecting off silver and gold chalices.

Martyn's church, though, was more than just a building. He describes processions and festivals, ceremonies and rituals, which made Holy Trinity not only a centre
of spiritual illumination but also (although it seems sacrilegious to say so) entertainment and spectacle.

> Upon Palm Sunday the Blessed Sacrament was carried in procession about the
> churchyard under a fair canopy borne by four yeomen…at which point a boy
> did sing standing upon a turret, *Ecce Rex Tuus Venit*, Behold thy King Cometh
> …and then all did kneel down and then rising up went and met the Sacrament
> and went singing together into the church and coming near the porch a boy did
> cast among the other boys, flowers and cakes.

The church at Long Melford was the heart of a wraparound world which spilled
over from the church porch into the streets along time-honoured processional routes
towards the little halls – the ancestors of village halls – which were the assembly
places of religious guilds and confraternities. Their spending power had made them
an essential element of the social fabric of Catholic England. Part club, part miniature
welfare state, they paid for local schools and almshouses, cared for the sick and paid
for the burials of their poorer members. They hired extra priests to say masses for the
dead, kept stores of candles, ordered vestments and altar cloths to dignify births,
marriages and deaths, and bought silver shoes for the feet of the crucified Christ on
the great rood that dominated the church, hanging between the nave and the chancel

There was no hard-and-fast border between the secular and the spiritual here,
no embarrassment about calling on the saints to do you a good turn when you
needed one. You might invoke one saint from the plough gallery to ensure a good
harvest or summon the help of St Catherine of Antioch (who had erupted from a
dragon's belly) to guard over a childbirth. If you couldn't quite remember which saint
it was you needed for a particular job and on which day to call him, you could
consult the perennial bestseller and vade-mecum of early Tudor England, *The Kalender
of Shepherdes*, part farmer's almanac, part horoscope, part prayer book. The wider
Church, then, was school and theatre, moral tutor and local government and, not
least, magic and medicine.

None of this, however, would have made sense without The Management: the
clergy, the guardians of the mystery at the heart of traditional Catholic belief – the
redeeming sacrifice of the Saviour. Every time the priest held the Host (the communion wafer) high at mass that mystery became overwhelmingly real and the flock
would have felt Christ crucified physically present in flesh and blood among them.

On weekdays in a big church like Long Melford several masses could be celebrated simultaneously at side altars, long since gone. The timing of those 'low masses' was carefully choreographed so that the 'sacrings' (the highly charged moment when the Host was raised) did not overlap. As that moment approached, members of the congregation would rush from altar to altar in a state of fervent excitement, calling out to the priest to 'hold up, hold up'. And no wonder, for to see the Host was to see your own salvation.

So the priest, then, was the indispensable man, and there was no getting to heaven but through his hands. Only the priest's hands could touch the bread and wine and consecrate them, changing them through the sacrament into the flesh and blood of Christ. Only the priest's hands could make the sign of the cross giving absolution from sins. These were the hands that gave meaning to 'good works', whether that meant buying wax or founding a college. They made the difference between salvation and perdition.

But it was precisely this claim, devolved from St Peter, that priests were necessary for salvation, that the apostles of the new Christianity – the Christianity of the word, not of spectacle – found so offensive, even blasphemous. Following Martin Luther, they attacked the received wisdom that only the priest could consecrate the Host as an unlawful usurpation, and they launched that attack with startling vehemence. How could a priest have the power to undo what God had already decided? The decision on the fate of a poor sinner was the Lord's alone, and the notion that masses, chantries, pilgrimages and penances could do anything about it was the height of sacrilegious presumption. All the good works and alms-giving in the world would cut no ice with the Almighty if in his infinite mercy he decided to save the most miserable transgressor. All that was asked, as St Paul had insisted, was that the sinner surrender himself to the inscrutable but infinitely compassionate grace of God. Faith in that mercy, faith in the Bible and faith that the sacrifice of Jesus had been sufficient (without the intercession of the saints) were enough. *Solus fides*. Faith alone.

The prophets of this new faith called themselves evangelicals, from the Greek word for scripture, *evangelion*. Their aim was to replace the monopoly of wisdom claimed by the Church of Rome with the gospel truth available in their own tongue. Once in possession of this indisputable truth, the need for the clergy as instructors, guardians and busybodies would go away. The flock would, henceforth, be self-shepherded. There would be a priesthood of all the faithful. The demotion of the priesthood from gatekeepers of salvation to spiritual counsellors suddenly made their special legal status moot. If they were, after all, just men, why did they need their own courts, their own taxes, their own government? Chantries now seemed a nice little

Long Melford church, Suffolk.

racket. Perhaps purgatory itself was part of the scam? If all the money left for chantries worked as it was supposed to, said one sceptic, purgatory must be empty, no matter how congested it might once have been at peak hours of admission. In the 1520s it is possible to hear these kinds of things being said in England. William Bankes of Loughborough (who was on trial in 1527 for fathering two children by his own niece) had the effrontery to tell a Church court ordering a penance: 'I will not do penance for you nor shall ye be my judge for I intend to go to a superior judge.' Some, like the London merchant tailor Richard Hunne, had gone much further, refusing to pay the 'mortuary' due to the Church on the burial of his infant child in 1514. Instead of submitting to the Church court, Hunne had the cheek to counter-sue in the king's court under the statute of Praemunire, which covered infringements of royal prerogatives by the Church. Hunne was arrested by the Bishop of London's men, who ransacked his house for heretical literature. Two days after his imprisonment he was found hanged in his cell. Shockingly, the coroner balked at bringing in the convenient verdict of suicide and found instead that Hunne had been strangled. Unrepentant, the Church still branded the dead man a heretic and had his corpse burned. The case provoked a tremendous hue and cry in parliament (especially in the Commons, where a number of lawyers sat), and for the first time, almost since the reign of Henry II, Church courts were beginning to be thought of as infringing the equity of the common law.

Anti-clericalism was nothing new, of course. In time gone by the Church could simply have brushed off occasional scandals like the Hunne affair. But the panicky search for incriminating materials in his house suggests that they knew they were up against something infinitely more dangerous than one man's obstreperousness, and that something was the printing press.

The printed vernacular Bible had the potential to turn the 'priesthood of all believers' from a heretical fantasy into a true religion. English Bibles had been around since the days of Wyclif and the Lollards in the late fourteenth century, but they had been circulated in the form of manuscripts, which were hard to find and relatively expensive. A printed Bible, on the other hand, could be made much more widely available and for but a few shillings. The man who devoted his life to seeing it off the presses was William Tyndale. He is an immediately recognizable historical type – austere, unswerving, a little fanatical, but tireless in the pursuit of his mission, which was easily stated: 'It was not possible to establish the lay people in any truth except [that] the scriptures were so plainly laid before their eyes in their mother tongue.' Like all revolutionaries, Tyndale was an astute tactician. When the Bishop of London refused him funds to print an English Bible, he secured money from a rich merchant sympathizer who sent him abroad to get the job done. In 1526 3000 copies of Tyndale's translation of the New Testament were eventually printed in the German city of Worms. When the format was reduced from quarto to octavo and the price to four shillings, they became portable enough to be smuggled into England through the Lutheran-Lollard underground that flourished especially in port cities, which had regular contacts with Protestant northern Europe. Sailors from Hull, who had visited Bremen and had been astonished by a place where priests married, brought back the Bibles hidden in casks of wax or grain.

Nervously aware of the clandestine import trade in Tyndale Bibles, the guardians of orthodoxy resolved to root out the 'most pestiferous and pernicious poison', no matter how ugly the means needed to do it. The most zealous enforcers were not from the most reactionary wing of the Catholic Church at all, but were men whom we usually and wrongly think of as liberal, martyrs for the freedom of conscience: Thomas More and John Fisher. Both reserved for themselves and men like them the luxury of debating niceties of scripture, but in the prospect of 'each one man to be a church alone' they saw the collapse of all theological authority: a time when every man or woman, no matter how ignorant, would be presumptuous enough to judge doctrine for themselves. The ranks of the horrified included Henry VIII, who in 1521 had allowed a treatise attacking Lutheranism as an abominable heresy to be published under his name. His most trusted servant, Cardinal Thomas Wolsey, was likewise eager to muffle what Tyndale had called 'the noise of the new Bible' before it became a cacophonous din. And he went about it with systematic determination, infiltrating cells of Bible readers and staging show trials at St Paul's, where the monsters were forced to recant, carry faggots for the fire and kneel in abject supplication as their writings were fed to the flames. They were solemnly warned that should they be tempted to stray from the straight and narrow (as some inevitably did) it would be their bodies, as well as their books, that would be the next to burn.

All this delighted Henry VIII. There was not the slightest reason to imagine, as the king entered his thirties, that he would ever be anything except the loyal *Fidei Defensor*, Defender of the Faith, the title a grateful pope had given Henry for writing against Luther. He was, after all, the Walsingham pilgrim, and his queen was the impeccably Catholic Catherine of Aragon, the sister of Ferdinand, the king of Spain. She had originally (if very briefly) been married to Henry's older brother, Arthur, Prince of Wales, since through most of Henry's youth there had been no thought that he would ever be king. The marriage between Arthur and Catherine had been Henry VII's attempt to piggyback the Tudors to dynastic respectability by allying themselves with the great Spanish dynasts, Ferdinand and Isabella, so the premature death in 1502

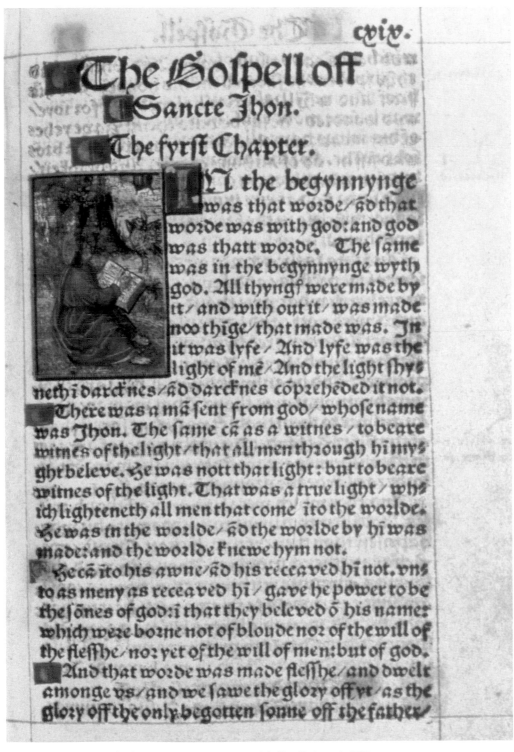

cxix.

The Gospell off Sancte Jhon.

The fyrst Chapter.

IN the begynnynge was that worde/ and that worde was with god: and god was thatt worde. The same was in the begynnynge wyth god. All thyngf were made by itt/ and with out it/ was made noo thige/ that made was. In it was lyfe/ And lyfe was the light of mē/ And the light shyneth i darcknes/ and darcknes coprehēded it not.

There was a mā sent from god/ whose name was Jhon. The same cā as a witnes/ to beare witnes of the light/ that all men through hi myght beleve. He was nott that light: but to beare witnes of the light. That was a true light/ whych lighteneth all men that come ito the worlde. He was in the worlde/ and the worlde by hi was made: and the worlde knewe hym not.

He cā ito his awne/ and his receaved hi not. vnto as meny as receaved hi/ gave he power to be the sōnes of god: i that they beleved ō his name: which were borne not of bloude nor of the will of the flesshe/ nor yet of the will of men: but of god. And that worde was made flesshe/ and dwelt amonge vs/ and we sawe the glory off yt/ as the glory off the only begotten sonne off the father/

Above: The beginning of the Gospel of St John, from Tyndale's New Testament, 1526.
Left: Henry VIII, by an unknown artist, 1520.

of the teenage Arthur, who had indeed been the flower of chivalry his name evoked, was a diplomatic as well as a family disaster. In his late forties and a widower, Henry VII for a while seriously thought about marrying Catherine himself, but in the end it was decided that she should be betrothed instead to Henry, the new Prince of Wales, then just eleven years old. They were supposed to be married four years later when the groom would have been fifteen and the bride nineteen, but the dowry failed to materialize, no small matter for Henry VII for whom money talked. So the prince was kept away from his Spanish princess right up to the time that his father died in 1509, when he was finally able to seize the keys to the kingdom and his long-promised wife.

Henry was now almost eighteen, and he lost no time in making it clear he would be his own master. To ensure that he would not inherit the unpopularity of his father's councillors, Edmund Dudley and Richard Empson (detested for their vigorous tax administration), he had them summarily impeached and executed. He then began to spend the money they had laboriously amassed, not least on a spectacular wedding for himself and Catherine. We tend to think of Catherine of Aragon as the embittered and victimized matron she did indeed become, but portraits confirm contemporary reports that in the early years of her marriage she was not at all unattractive, but dark and voluptuous. From the visible signs of affection between husband and wife the future of the dynasty must have seemed auspicious. Henry VII, after all, had had seven children even if only three of them had survived.

As for Henry himself, you could practically smell the testosterone. Any way and anywhere he could flash his burly energy, he flashed it: in the saddle, on the dance floor or on the tennis court, where a besotted courtier wrote excitedly of the king's skin glowing through his finely woven shirt. Six feet tall (had there *ever* been a short king of England since John?), Henry not only shone, he glittered, literally, his fingers a mass of rings and a diamond as big as a walnut hanging from a neck that was described by another admirer as long, thick and beautiful enough to belong to a woman. Henry dispensed his famous, breezy charm rather like the English weather, in sunny intervals alternating with long, cloudy spells and sudden bursts of heavy thunder. The charm was of the rib-poking, back-slapping, arm-around-the-shoulder, punch-in-the-belly kind, which, depending on the mood of the week, could betoken either rapid promotion or imminent arrest. Henry wallowed in the praise droolingly lavished on him by his courtiers and foreign ambassadors: Henry the gallant, Henry the clever, Henry the nimble, Henry the superstar. He was the only king with his personal band, hired to go touring with him and featuring the eighteen-year-old as lead singer-songwriter.

Early in his reign Henry had a Latin biography of Henry V translated into English, an unsubtle allusion to his belief that he was not so much the Agincourt warrior's descendant as his reincarnation, and that made the first order of the day a nice little war with France. This happened to suit Henry's in-laws, Ferdinand and Isabella, who were eager to help themselves to the border province of Navarre. In 1512 a joint attack was launched, but it petered out ignominiously when the English fleet waited in vain for a Spanish army to materialize. The following year a campaign was planned for Normandy. This was a huge success: farms were indiscriminately ransacked and burned, towns put to the sword. Henry thoroughly enjoyed the whole thing, especially the skirmish dignified as the Battle of the Spurs, in which the French cavalry, finding themselves ambushed, turned and fled, leaving nobles behind as lucrative prisoners. There were even better things to come. Henry's brother-in-law, James IV of Scotland (who was married to his elder sister, Margaret), had gallantly decided to live up to his end of the 'auld alliance' by invading northern Britain, a campaign that ended catastrophically at Flodden in 1513, where a smaller English force led by Thomas Howard, Earl of Surrey (soon to be Henry's Earl Marshal Norfolk), annihilated the Scots, leaving 10,000 dead, including most of the great earls of Scotland and James IV himself.

All this had been managed, somehow, without breaking the bank, the reason being that an extraordinary bank-manager was in charge: Thomas Wolsey, the butcher's son (as all his many enemies reminded him) and omnicompetent minder of the realm. The art of Wolsey's management was his mastery of both matters and men. He had inherited an increasingly sophisticated administration from the Yorkist kings and Henry VII, but he added to it a shrewd understanding of the machinery of power. He could stroke parliament when it was necessary, and he could bang heads (even aristocratic heads) together when that was called for. He was an awesome manipulator of patronage, honours, bribes and threats. In other words, he was a political psychologist in a cardinal's hat.

Wolsey knew just what made people tick – their vanities and their fears – and he also understood the critical relationship between display and authority. He used it to stunning (and ultimately self-destructive) effect at Hampton Court, where he built himself a palace, realizing in bricks and mortar his status as a 'prince of the Church'. And he also used it for Henry VIII, creating carefully measured pools of distance between the person of the king and his routine business. That business was taken care of by Wolsey and the council. Henry's person, on the other hand, was closed off in Privy Chamber, literally a private space patrolled by a select inner corps of sixteen gentlemen-courtiers, the chief of whom was the Groom of the Stole. This was the

Top: Thomas Wolsey, by an unknown artist, *c.* 1570–99.
Above: Catherine of Aragon, by Michiel Sittow, 1503–4.
Left: *The Field of the Cloth of Gold* (detail), by an
unknown artist, *c.* 1520.

job all gentlemen of any ambition killed for: the honour of attending on the king every waking hour, including the times when he was grunting on the close-stool.

The *pièce de résistance* of Wolsey's orchestration of royal ceremony took place in 1520 with the astounding jamboree known as the Field of the Cloth of Gold. It had its political point, meaning to demonstrate to the new Holy Roman Emperor, Charles V, whose vast territories dominated Europe, that if need be the two old cross-Channel foes could stand together against Habsburg intimidation. So instead of the usual war, there was a wondrous demonstration of amity between Henry and the young Valois king, Francis I. It came to war anyway, not with swords and lances but something much more deadly: style.

For weeks on end Francis and Henry competed in displays of outrageous ostentation. In the greatest transportation exercise seen since the campaigns of Edward III, Wolsey shipped over the entire ruling class of England, about 5000 of them, earls, bishops and knights of the shire, including in a display of unconvincing humility himself, riding on a mule, dressed in crimson velvet (with, lest he be thought self-effacing, another 200 identically clad behind him). Francis, alas, won the decor and design prize by having his 3000 horses and 5000 men issue from a 60-foot-high pavilion made from strips of blue velvet and cloth of gold sewn with the fleur-de-lis. At the English end was a half-millennium affair of a fake wood and canvas castle, heavily crenellated and decorated with the ubiquitous Tudor rose. Music – especially music composed by Henry – played; wine flowed from red and white fountains; much heron was consumed; and the two kings spent hours trying on out-fits to stun the opposition. They wrestled not only with knotty problems of state but each other, the fox and the bear, half-naked and all tangled up, the more supple Francis throwing Henry on his back.

No doubt he laughed. No doubt he hated it. No wonder that two years after this orgy of good fellowship and a solemn promise to build a chapel to Our Lady of Peace on the site, Francis and Henry were at war again.

And somewhere in the middle of this over-dressed mêlée was the young woman who would bring down Wolsey's entire house of cards and with it, quite inconceivably, the Roman Church in England. So much has been written about the tragic soap opera of Anne Boleyn's life that 'serious history' seems duty-bound to turn away from it to the weightier and less personal issues that we instinctively think ought to be behind so profound a change as the break with Rome. But if the traditional Church was *not* on its last legs, if Protestantism was in its infancy in England, and if, before his infatuation, Henry VIII showed no sign whatsoever of interest in the Reformation, then it's not only reasonable but essential to come back to Anne Boleyn as both the occasion and cause of the extraordinary change in direction.

She may have been first introduced to the king at the Field of the Cloth of Gold where she was present, not in the English but the French camp as a lady-in-waiting to Queen Claude, the wife of Francis I. But there might not have been much about the girl – long dark hair, a prominent nose – to catch the king's eye, and his attention was, in any case, engaged elsewhere and it wasn't in Catherine of Aragon's bed. Whatever heat had been generated between the king and queen had gone through a prolonged cooling-off after their son Henry had died in 1511, when he was just two months old, notwithstanding all the king's tributes to the Lady of Walsingham. Catherine had become pregnant again, but the child, born in 1516, was a girl, Mary. Although he paid his queen all due respect in public, the king made little effort to hide his disappointment that the Spanish princess, whose fruitfulness had been so heavily advertised, had proved incapable of providing a male heir. When a son was born to his mistress Elizabeth Blount, the king, almost as if to make a point, called the boy Henry fitzRoy and subsequently made him Earl of Richmond, the title his own father had carried to the battlefield at Bosworth! The point of mistresses for someone like Henry VIII (as for all the princes of Europe) was their disposability. And at some point in 1525 he began sleeping with Anne's sister Mary (whose marriage to William Carey seemed only a minor inconvenience). The son born to Mary Boleyn early in 1526 was also called Henry, and there were predictable mutterings about his paternity.

Despite the myth of the Boleyns as obscure country gentry, they were, in fact, at the very top of the Kentish county elite, ambitious and well connected, just the kind of family on which the government depended to see their will done smoothly and efficiently. In return, people like Thomas Boleyn won favours, places at court and, if they stayed on the king's right side, entry into the Privy Council. Thomas's wife was Elizabeth Howard, a member of the greatest aristocratic family in the land and the daughter of the Earl of Surrey, the victor of Flodden. So, from the beginning, Thomas Boleyn was one of the courtiers personally close enough to the young king to take him on as an opponent in the tilts and close enough to be an annoyance to Thomas Wolsey. But Boleyn, who spoke good French and was a well-travelled cosmopolitan, was exactly the kind of person who was useful during the years when Henry was trying to establish himself as a major power in Europe.

Boleyn's diplomatic career brought both his daughters when they were still children into the court life of the great European dynasts. Anne's first experience of this kind would have been at Mechelen in Flanders, at the court of the affable

Habsburg regent of the Netherlands, Margaret of Austria. But when England's foreign allegiance switched from the Habsburgs to France, Anne was transferred along with it, this time to the Valois court of Claude, the wife of the then dauphin, Francis. In the palaces of the Loire, the chief pastime, after hunting, was courtly love, that theatrical form of aristocratic flirtation around which a whole culture had grown up: desire endlessly deferred; sexual passion transfigured into pure, selfless love; troubadours, masks; silk handkerchiefs, a lot of sighing. There were moments, though, when the elaborate pretence was swept aside and basic instincts took command. Anne Boleyn and her sister, Mary, witnessed at close quarters one such moment – the most extraordinary sexual drama of the age.

As part of the strategy developed by Wolsey to counterbalance the increasingly irksome attachment to the Habsburgs, Henry had decided to marry his younger sister, Mary, to Louis XII of France. He was fifty-two; she was barely in her teens, but bright, extremely pretty and able to play her brother like a lute. Her price for being a sacrifice to diplomacy was that she should have a say in the next match. Perhaps Mary knew something her brother did not, for Louis was dead in eleven weeks. His marriage alliance policy foiled, Henry now threw the whole plan into reverse, hoping to tie the Habsburgs more closely to him by exporting his sister to the Archduke Charles, shortly to be emperor. Whatever he had promised Mary was of trifling consequences beside the critical interests of state. He was sure she would see it that way, but she did not. Mary had heard of the famous lantern jaw and exophthalmic eyes, and she informed the king that she would rather die than become Charles's wife. Pending the resolution of his sister's future, Henry sent one of his closest companions and sparring partner in the lists, Charles Brandon, to bring the young widow back from France along with as much of her dowry as he could decently retrieve. Brandon was notorious as a reckless flirt, but when he saw the sweet, tearful face of Mary Tudor, he became putty in her hands. The new king of France, Francis I, was delighted to play dishonest marriage broker and break up an Anglo–Habsburg marriage. But the couple didn't need a Pandarus. Mary threw herself at Brandon and virtually demanded that he marry her. When he heard of the secret wedding between Brandon and Mary, Henry was predictably apoplectic, seeing himself as the dupe of a double betrayal, by his friend and by his sister. Their elopement was virtually, if not technically, an act of treason, since the blood-line of the dynasty was certainly at stake, but after weeks of royal rage and tear-soaked expressions of sorrow by the guilty parties, he relented somewhat and Brandon and Mary were packed off to become the Duke and Duchess of Suffolk.

They had escaped disaster, but only just. The historian who wants to reconstruct

Anne Boleyn (detail), by an unknown artist, 1570–99.

the strength of feeling that made both Mary and Brandon risk their necks for each other, but who is always told that romantic love was an eighteenth-century invention, is at something of a loss. Marriages were hard-headed business arrangements, the product of social, political or economic calculation, not passion. Except sometimes – as in this classic case, right at the heart of the Tudor court – they weren't. So if love isn't the subject matter of, say, the sonnets by Petrarch or Wyatt or Shakespeare, or of *Romeo and Juliet*, whatever we want to call it was certainly up and running with phenomenal urgency by the early sixteenth century. And it would make a difference to English history.

Anne Boleyn and her sister Mary were ladies-in-waiting at the court of Queen Claude of France while the drama of Mary Tudor and Charles Brandon was being played out. (Anne's embarrassing closeness to the event may have been the reason for Mary Tudor's subsequent coldness towards her.) It would have given Anne a precocious education in the politics of passion, a department of human behaviour in which she was to prove a major talent. Around nineteen years old, she returned from France and entered the dangerous, glittering world of the Tudor court as a maid of honour to the woman she would replace, Queen Catherine. Physically Anne was nothing special, despite the long black hair and big dark eyes. Her bosom, reported the Venetian ambassador, who evidently noticed these things, was 'not much risen'. But she exploited her natural vivaciousness to play the games of love for all she was worth. Either instinctively or by education, she knew exactly when to beckon and when to push away; when to flatter men into believing everything they liked about themselves was actually true; and when to disabuse them, so they rolled around in misery like sharply rebuked puppies. Anne gave off articulate self-confidence, the teasing intelligence that made her intensely desirable. To her delight, men fell panting at her feet.

First, there was Henry Percy, the heir to the huge fortune and power of the earls of Northumberland. Independence in the choice of marriage partner was evidently in the air in aristocratic society because Percy and Anne actually contracted a betrothal without asking the earl's permission. Outraged, the Earl of Northumberland got Wolsey to lean heavily on the young man, who was duly crushed into submission. He ended up in an unhappy marriage with the much wealthier Margaret Talbot and died young and childless. The scandal was enough to send Anne back to the French court for another few years, not the best place, perhaps, to encourage her in demure obedience.

When Anne returned, around 1525, she attracted the attention of another admirer who was equally (but for different reasons) unsuitable: the poet-courtier Thomas Wyatt. His family had been neighbours of the Boleyns in Kent, and the two are very likely to have known each other as children. Thomas's father, Henry, had (like Thomas Boleyn) risen far and fast enough from his Yorkshire obscurity to be able to buy Allington Castle, which he restored in the grandiose post-War of the Roses manner to look feudally dangerous on the outside and luxuriously comfortable on the inside. The same was pretty much true for his son, Thomas, a very paragon of the Renaissance courtier, drop-dead handsome (if Holbein is to be believed), famously accomplished in the lists (and therefore smiled on by the king) and so clever and well travelled that he could bring Italian love poetry back to England and make something of it in the mother tongue. Wyatt's poems were, as usual, heavy with sighs at the unattainable object of desire – and at least one of them was meant for Anne Boleyn. By the time he met up with Anne again Wyatt was separated from his own wife, allegedly because of her adultery. But separation was not divorce, and the best he could offer Anne was the role of a mistress: not good enough for an ambitious girl on the make. Wyatt's poem, in which he vainly pursues his 'hind', is heavy with the knowledge of failure:

> Whoso list to hount, I know where there is an hynde
> But as for me, helas, I may no more.
> The vayne travail hath wearied me so sore,
> I am of theme that farthest commeth behinde.
> Yet may I by no means my weried mynde
> Drawe from the Diere, but as she fleeth afore
> Faynting I folowe…

Towards the end of the poem, the forlorn and exhausted hunter cautions anyone rash enough to imagine they might do better:

> …I put him owte of dowbte
> As well as I may spend his time in vain.
> And graven with Diamonds in letters plain
> There is written her fair neck rounde abowte:
> '*Noli me tangere* for Caesar's I ame,
> And wilde to hold though I seem tame.'

'Do not touch' – for Caesar, otherwise known as Henry VIII, had indeed thrown himself into the chase, and the king, as we know, was an inexhaustible huntsman. Wyatt knew when he was beaten. But before he retired from the contest (according

Tho: Wiatt Knight.

Sir Thomas Wyatt, by Hans Holbein, 1538–40.

to his grandson George, who heard it from one of Anne's maids, Anne Gainsford), Wyatt allowed himself at least one little triumph. Henry and the poet were reportedly playing bowls. Smiling at his reported rival, Henry pointed to a throw, using a finger with Anne's ring prominently on it, remarking offhand, 'Mine I believe'. Wyatt responded by taking out from inside his shirt Anne's jewel, suspended from a necklace, and replied: 'If it like Your Majesty give me leave to measure. I hope it will be mine.' Henry was evidently not amused. 'It may be so but then I am deceived.' Game over.

By the summer of 1526 Henry's pursuit of Anne had turned serious. When he danced with her in front of the queen, the contrast between the two women was glaring. Anne was everything Catherine of Aragon was not. Ten years younger, merry rather than pious, spirited, even teasing in the French manner rather than gravely deferential in the Spanish fashion. She opened the way to sexual bliss, domestic happiness and, most important of all, the possibility of a son and heir. Henry now believed that a divine curse had been laid on his marriage for taking his dead brother's wife as his own and that for seventeen years he had been living in an incestuous relationship. Leviticus 20:21 was quite clear about this: 'If a man shall take his brother's wife, it is an unclean thing: he hath uncovered his brother's nakedness; they shall be childless.' It would be wrong to assume that Henry was merely exploiting the scripture as a disingenuous pretext to discard Catherine and satisfy his craving for Anne. He was, certainly, besotted, but he was also a serious and literal Bible reader and the texts in Leviticus would have explained why his marriage had become a barren misery (even though the existence of his daughter Mary hardly corresponded to the curse of childlessness). In 1525 he stopped sleeping with Catherine, and his conviction that he must escape an unholy union grew swiftly into an obsession.

Anne's point-blank refusal to entertain the idea of becoming Henry's mistress only intensified his urgency. During 1526 and 1527 their relationship developed from a courtly flirtation (presents of roebucks and jewellery) to something much more serious. Henry, who normally found writing letters torture, wrote seventeen to Anne, parsing each of her replies with the excruciating obsessiveness of the insecure lover:

Debating with myself the contents of your letter I have put myself in great distress not knowing how to interpret them, whether to my disadvantage as in some places shown or to advantage as in others I understand them; praying you with all my heart that you will expressly certify me of your whole mind concerning the love between us two. For of necessity I must ensure me of this answer, having been now one whole year struck with the dart of love, not being assured either of failure or finding place in your heart and grounded affection. Which last point has kept me for some little time from calling you my mistress since if you love me in none other sort save that of common affection, that name in no wise belongs to you, for it denotes a singular love, far removed from the common.

Anne was quite different from her sister, Mary, who was notorious as an easy conquest. This was, for the first time in his life, hard work. Even his trump card, the promise to make Anne his sole mistress, a formal royal concubine, backfired disastrously when she recoiled in aversion from the suggestion, punishing Henry by disappearing from court altogether. Beside himself with contrition, Henry begged forgiveness, and Anne eventually put him out of his misery, sending the king a little ship with a solitary maiden aboard. It worked like a dream. Henry went into a paroxysm of rapture and responded by proposing something quite different from concubinage:

> Praying you also that if ever before I have in any way done you offence, that you will give me the same absolution that you ask [no doubt for appearing cold], ensuring you that henceforth my heart shall be dedicate to you alone, greatly desirous that my body could be as well, as God can bring to pass if it pleaseth Him whom I entreat once each day for the accomplishment thereof, trusting that at length my prayer will be heard, wishing the time brief and thinking it will be but long until we see each other again.

And at the end Henry signed:

> Written with the hand of that Secretary who in heart, body and will is Your loyal and most ensured servant,
> H autre (AB) ne cherse R [Henry who looks no further than his AB].

All that remained was to secure the divorce, and Henry must have been confident that Wolsey would bring his managerial magic to whatever small obstacles might be set in his way.

But in 1527 something happened, a long way from England, to make those obstacles mountainous. Catherine of Aragon's nephew, the Emperor Charles V, sacked Rome and took Pope Clement VII prisoner. Whatever his own judgement might have been on the matter, it was now out of the question for the pope to oblige Henry on his 'Great Matter' without mortally offending the emperor. Ever the mischief-maker, Francis I suggested that Henry should unilaterally declare himself unmarried.

But even if he took Francis's advice, there was nothing to stop Catherine from appealing to Rome, possibly provoking an excommunication, and certainly ruling out what Henry wanted most: the recognition of his and Anne's children as legitimate heirs.

For the first time Wolsey must have felt uncomfortable in his cardinal's hat. Whichever way he turned, he was in trouble. If he failed to get the king his divorce, he was ruined; if he provoked the pope and the emperor, he lost his diplomatic cachet and his power as a prince of the Church. In the autumn of 1528 he staked everything on a planned mission by the papal legate, Cardinal Campeggio, to hear the case for an annulment. The cardinal was supposed to consider the Crown's argument that, at the time of Arthur's death, the pope had had no authority to grant dispensation from the Leviticus prohibition. In that case, Henry's marriage to Catherine had been, from the beginning, unlawful. But during the long delay before the court actually sat (in June 1529), opinion out of doors and inside was shifting massively in Catherine's favour. To the charges of incest, the queen was insisting that her marriage to Arthur had never been consummated and thus had been no marriage at all. Increasingly seen as a victim, Catherine had never been more popular, and the 'goggle-eyed whore' epithet that would cling to Anne Boleyn for the rest of her life could already be heard in the taverns and streets. Henry had to send her away to her parents at Hever Castle, where she fell dangerously ill with the sweating sickness (evidently a kind of viral influenza). Rattled by the firmness of the queen, Henry made a grotesquely disingenuous speech in which he claimed that he should like nothing better than for his marriage to Catherine to be proved lawful: 'She is a woman of most humility and buxomness, yea and of all good qualities pertaining to nobility.' No one was fooled. All kinds of partisans for the queen suddenly found their voice, including John Fisher, Bishop of Rochester, and even Martin Luther.

At Blackfriars the court turned into a stage for Catherine's genuinely heartrending despair. Henry sat stone-faced while the queen knelt at his feet in floods of tears, sobbing as she made the secrets of their marriage bed the heart of the matter. Only desperation could have forced so naturally modest a woman to speak thus:

> Sire, I beseech you for all the love that hath been between us and for the love of God let me have justice and right. Take of me some pity and compassion for I am a poor woman and a stranger born out of your dominion. I have no assured friend here…When ye had me at the first, I take God to be my judge, I was a true maid without touch of man. And whether this be true or no, I put it to your conscience.

This was too much. The cardinal-legate broke up the court on the pretext of a summer adjournment. The king was livid. Wolsey was finished. He was dismissed, ostensibly for fraud and corruption, by a coalition of anti-Wolseyites that included Anne's own family: her father and her brother, George, Viscount Rochford; her Howard uncle, the Duke of Norfolk; and Charles Brandon, Duke of Suffolk (who may have felt he owed the king a love match). Within a year Wolsey was dead, charges of high treason still hanging over his head.

Getting rid of Wolsey, though, did not solve the problem. His successor as chancellor was Thomas More, who would not touch the poisoned chalice of the divorce. Fisher, annoyingly, kept referring to a passage in Deuteronomy that actually *urged* the taking of a dead brother's wife as an act of compassion! Henry's own confidence in a satisfactory solution failed him enough to renew his suggestion to Anne that perhaps she would reconsider the possibility of becoming his mistress, a suggestion she treated as so offensive that it must have been made 'in mirth' to test her. At some point in 1530 it was Anne herself who decided that she must take matters in hand and steer the whole business in a radically new direction. She put into Henry's hands a copy of William Tyndale's work *On the Obedience of a Christian Man and How Christian Rulers Ought to Govern*, published at the end of 1528 and, in the eyes of the Church, very much a banned book. Although Tyndale, like Luther, was against the divorce, his little book was dynamite, for it flatly rejected any notion of an authority divided between Church and state, insisting instead that 'one king, one law is God's ordinance in every realm'. A true Christian prince, in other words, was governor of *both* Church and state and need not defer to the illegitimately usurped power of the 'Bishop of Rome'. A non-papal solution to Henry's divorce suddenly presented itself. Henry would, in effect, act as his own pope, the governor of the English Church, and award himself the divorce – with, of course, the blessing of the bishops and the parliament of England. The matter had been personal and dynastic. Now it would be national and political.

An air of peculiar unreality hung over the business of Church and state in the spring of 1530. Thomas More was busy burning heretics and their infamous literature, but it was the Roman Church in England that was about to go up in smoke. With a characteristic combination of conviction and self-interest, Anne Boleyn and her family had recruited a think-tank of well-disposed theologians, including the Cambridge scholar Thomas Cranmer, to come up with historical evidence for the royal supremacy. They duly beavered away in the archives and produced a collection of writings, the *Collectanea satis copiosa* (Sufficiently Copious Collection), which asserted that in the earliest days of the Church each 'province' (England, for example)

Henry VIII (detail), by Hans Holbein, c. 1536.

had had its own jurisdiction that was quite apart from and free of Rome, and that God had always intended kings to be rulers of those Churches, accountable only to the Almighty. Beneath the deceptive antiquarianism, the implications of the 'Collection' were as radical as Tyndale's book.

Henry had still not finally resolved to break with Rome. Teams of his lawyers and theologians were sweeping through the universities of Europe with instructions to produce opinions that might still sway the pope. But there were times when the decidedly finite reserves of royal patience were exhausted and Henry began to act and sound like both chief prince and priest. To a startled Church assembly, summoned so that Henry could denounce heresy, he also added that he might personally have to take in hand a translation of the Bible, which would then be given to the laity when he judged it fit and proper. To the imperial ambassador he let it be known that some of the things that Luther said seemed to him to have merit. In fact, the more Henry learned about the royal supremacy the better he liked it. It may have begun as a tactic to intimidate the pope and the English bishops into seeing the divorce his way, but after a while Henry began to internalize the idea as a self-evident truth. One can almost hear him clapping a hand to the bullish brow and exclaiming, 'How can I have been so dull as to have missed *this*?'

The royal ego, never a small part of his personality, ballooned to imperial proportions and it got the palaces to house it – fifty of them before the reign was done. Some of the greatest and grandest had been Wolsey's and were now transferred to the king: York Place in London was renamed Whitehall and personally inspected by Anne to see if its accommodations were suitable, and Hampton Court became the stage for the swaggering theatre of Henrician court life. Nothing measures the imperial scale of that court better than the size of the space needed to feed it. Some 230 people were employed to service the thousand who were, every day, entitled to eat at the king's expense. There were three vast larders for meat alone; a specially designed wet larder to hold fish, supplied by water drawn from the fountains outside; spiceries, fruiteries; six immense fireplaces; three gargantuan cellars capable of holding the 300 casks of wine and 600,000 gallons of ale downed each year. And at the centre of it all, carefully protected by the Privy Chamber from undue exhibition, was England's new Caesar, the forty-year-old king, colossal and autocratic, bestriding the realm, his pose deliberately meant to recall the power of the Roman emperors.

Not surprisingly, then, in the summer of 1530, the word 'imperial' begins to show up with some calculated regularity in Henry's remarks. Emperors, of course, acknowledged no superior on earth. To the papal nuncio Anne's brother, George Boleyn, and Charles Brandon, Duke of Suffolk, said: 'England cares nothing for popes, not even if St Peter should come to life again, for the king is absolute emperor and pope in his kingdom.' The formula would be repeated in 1533 in the preamble to the statute designed to suppress appeals to Rome where the declaration was made that: 'The realm of England is an empire.' With every month that passed without a decision from Rome, Henry became more aggressive. He would not take orders from a pope, he told his envoys, who was himself a well-known bastard. By November 1530 he was insisting out loud that he was 'chief' of the 'spiritual men'.

It may be that the spiritual men supposed that this would all go away – their predecessors had been there before with Henry II and with John, after all – but they were in for a very nasty shock. At the end of 1530 writs of Praemunire, the 'lesser treason' of infringing the king's laws (but for which the penalties were imprisonment and confiscation of property) were issued. William Warham, the Archbishop of Canterbury, was the first named, then a broader group of bishops and, finally, through its insistence on Church courts, the *entire* Church was held to be complicit in this 'lesser treason'. At first, they bought off Henry with a grant of £100,000, but with the scent of their fear in his nostrils, Henry pounced on the quarry, demanding recognition of the title of Supreme Head. By encouraging parliament to issue a long and bitter attack on familiar grievances the Church courts, tithes, the alleged worldliness of the clergy – Henry also made it clear that he was prepared to leave no propaganda tactic unexploited. In the spring of 1532 he moved in for the kill. The oath the clergy took to the pope and the money they paid him each year revealed, he said, just where *their* true loyalty lay. 'Well beloved subjects,' he thundered to a specially summoned delegation, 'we thought that the clergy of the realm had been our subjects wholly but now we have well perceived that they be but half our subjects, yea and scarce our subjects.'

Faced with these very big sticks, the Church cracked wide open. There were still some brave souls, like John Fisher, who remained an impassioned defender of Queen Catherine and who believed that any erosion of papal authority was tantamount to the destruction of the unity of Christendom. But there were some other clerics who were beginning to think the unthinkable: that a king not a pope could be Supreme Head and they themselves might be part of something called the 'Church of England'. In May 1532 the heat melted the resistance. Thomas More resigned as chancellor and Bishop Fisher continued to lecture the king, but the majority of his colleagues delivered their grovelling Submission of the Clergy which caved in to all Henry's demands: future Church convocations would be summoned by royal writ; no new canon law could be passed without the king's consent; and existing law would be reviewed by a committee appointed by the Crown. It was a momentous surrender.

Hand-coloured title page of the Great Bible of 1539, said to
have belonged to Thomas Cromwell.

It was now unarguable that the Church in England had but one master, and he certainly did not reside in St Peter's.

It was a reformation but not the Protestant Reformation. No core doctrines had been touched. The real presence of Christ in the mass was preserved. Priests were still required to be celibate. The monasteries were still standing, and prayers and the Bible were still read in Latin. And now that Henry had found a way to get his divorce, and now that Anne, heavily pregnant, had been crowned in Westminster Abbey by the new Archbishop of Canterbury, Thomas Cranmer, the interference with the traditional Church might have stopped there.

That it did not was due to one of the most remarkable working partnerships in all British history: Thomas Cranmer and Thomas Cromwell. Take either one of them away and the English Reformation would not have happened, or at least not in the way it did. Their agenda was always more daring than the king's, and they both had strong personal as well as religious motives for adopting the cause of reform. In Cromwell's case it would bring him such power and authority that the son of a Putney cloth-worker would die (though not in his bed) the Earl of Essex. And although his convictions were deep, Cranmer was playing an even more dangerous game since just before he was appointed Archbishop of Canterbury he had secretly married a German woman, Margarethe, thereby committing himself to one of Luther's most shocking innovations. Cranmer was also wedded to the old Lollard idea of an English Bible for the laity, although he certainly did not believe that this gave licence to anyone to produce their own version for public consumption. That way lay religious anarchy. Cranmer, like Cromwell, was wedded to the Renaissance idea of a strong prince in a strong Christian state. The people were to be given their officially authorized Bible from on high; no other edition would be tolerated.

The picture of an orderly, even authoritarian, Church of England is exactly what can be seen on the frontispiece of the Great Bible, commissioned by Cromwell and published in 1539. At the top the king-emperor, prince and high priest receives the *Verbum Dei* (Word of God) directly from the Father on High, just like a Solomon, and then passes this to his two trusty lieutenants, Cranmer, on the left, the lord of the spiritual realm, and Cromwell, on the right, the lord of the temporal realm, each of whom in their turn passes it along to grateful throngs of clergy and laity.

Thomas Cromwell may have been the least sentimental Englishman ever to run the country, but he was certainly not the inventor of Tudor coercion. He had been a diligent student of Wolsey's own way with force, and it had, after all, been the king himself who had thought it a splendid idea to celebrate the first year of his independent reign by staging the show trial and execution of his father's ministers.

Cromwell made sure that he reminded Thomas More during his interrogation that More had not exactly been averse to using force to ensure obedience to Rome. But in the last resort Cromwell knew it fell to him to be Henry's hard man: to collude in the lie that, when brutal things needed to be done, the king could be shielded from their ugliness. Above all, Cromwell understood, with a clarity that Henry could never manage, that it would never be enough for the break with Rome to be proclaimed and then expect everyone to fall over themselves in expressions of loyal celebration. He was anticipating a fight, and he was prepared to fight dirty.

Cromwell knew very well that, sooner or later, the pope would wheel his big gun, excommunication, into the battle, and if the king were to win (where John had lost) he had better be prepared to fight back with something more or less novel in the language of politics, namely patriotism. The country had to be aroused to a new sense of its own sovereignty and potency. Rome had to be demonized as 'the foreigner' and 'the enemy', and so it had to be parliament, the voice of the nation, that enacted the laws instituting the royal supremacy, that would drown out any apprehension with a crude kind of bludgeoning, patriotic euphoria, the rejoicing of the demolition squad and the cheer-leading of the 'England, England' brigade. Propagandists like Thomas Starkey and Richard Morison were hired to present this unnerving alteration as a kind of national self-awakening. The pope would now be called the 'Bishop of Rome' and his obstinate adherents would be called 'papists' – a word as yet unknown. The word 'Papa' was to be excised from church services, and sermons were to be preached in the name of the Supreme Head.

To this engine of xenophobic publicity Cromwell added the heavy machinery of state terror. An oath had to be sworn recognizing the royal supremacy, the legitimacy of the heirs of Henry and Anne and the bastardization of the Lady (no longer Princess) Mary. Insulting the new queen was treason; calling the king a schismatic or a heretic was treason. It was treason to write these things or to plot these things, and, for the very first time in English law, it was a crime to say these things.

Cromwell managed to turn England into a frightened, snivelling, jumpy place, where denunciation was a sanctimonious duty and countless petty little scores got settled by people who protested they were just doing the right thing. There were plenty of incautious victims. Mrs Amadas, the self-appointed prophetess, said out loud that the king was 'cursed with God's own mouth' and prophesied that he would be banished and the kingdom conquered by the Scots. There was the Welsh priest, William ap Lli, who wanted to get the king up on Snowdon where 'he would souse the king about the ears till he had his head soft enough'. And there was the Oxfordshire midwife who said she would be happy to attend on Queen Catherine, but as for Anne, she was far too good for the likes of her, she being 'a whore and a harlot for her living'.

These were all loudmouths. But Thomas More was keeping his mouth shut. He had let it be known that parliament was entitled to determine the succession. As for the supremacy itself and the destruction of the pope's jurisdiction in England, More refused to say a word or to take the oath. When Cromwell sent him to the Tower, along with the much more outspoken Fisher and the king's ex-confessor, it was in the hope of extracting concessions from them. The confessor did, in fact, relent and got off free. But Fisher wouldn't shut up and More wouldn't open up. When the pope made Fisher a cardinal, Henry's rage boiled over. More and Fisher were to be made examples as ingrates and traitors. Originally sentenced to be hanged, drawn and quartered, they were spared the torment by the royal mercy of the executioner's axe. But although both died heroically and for the sake of *their* consciences, they certainly did not die for the liberty of anyone else's. After he had been sentenced, More let it be known that all along he had rejected the supremacy as an abomination to God and if he had remained chancellor he would certainly have enforced his version of the truth every bit as fiercely as Cromwell now prosecuted his.

Nowhere in Cromwell's strong-arm regime did his myrmidons enjoy their work more than in the 'visitations' to the monasteries, carried out with lightning speed during 1535 and early 1536. The uprooting of nearly 15,000 monks and nuns and the destruction of an entire, ancient way of life had little to do with reforming zeal. It was, in the first instance, driven by money. The monasteries and abbeys were to be plundered to establish a war chest for the conflict with Catholic Europe that now seemed inevitable. Officially, Cromwell presented the project, not as the weakening but as the strengthening of the monasteries, with the decaying non-viable establishments liquidated, their property and land passing to the Crown for resale, and some of the brothers and sisters consolidated into the bigger, better-run institutions. But Cromwell's flying squads – Leigh and Layton, ap Rees and Tregonwell, who descended on convents, demanding accommodation while they reduced abbots to trembling jellies of misery - do not seem much like men who thought of themselves as renovators. For a start, they enjoyed their work a little too much. 'I laid unto him the concealment of treason,' wrote one of Cromwell's hit-men to his chief about a prior he had at his mercy. 'Called him heinous traitor in the worst names I could devise, he all the time kneeling and making intercession unto me not to utter to you the premises for his undoing.' Such were the pleasures of reform.

Cromwell's 'Visitors' covered an enormous amount of territory very fast – 121 houses and 1000 miles in one dramatic swing through the north. When they arrived they knew exactly what they wanted: a self-incriminating catalogue of sex, fraud, conspiracy and superstition. Sex was at the top of their list of helpful confessions, the juicier the better. The word 'sodomy' (sometimes meaning homosexual practices, sometimes just masturbation) recurs over and again in the reports. 'Incontinence' – another favourite – meant fornication between the sexes. Reports of children born to nuns, abbots in bed with prioresses. Slanders against the king and queen, obstinate deference to Rome or just a suspicious silence was enough to prove 'conspiracy'. 'Superstition' proved extremely fruitful for the Visitors, who carried off cartloads of purported relics – jars of doubtful goop said to be the Virgin's milk, bits of rusting iron venerated as the 'chains of St Peter', which pregnant women bound around them at the time of their delivery, were all merrily itemized for Cromwell's entertainment. In Bury St Edmunds the nuns of the convent remained silent, even though the Visitors used 'much diligence in the examination', but at the abbey the Visitors hit the jackpot. The abbot was a gambling addict, 'much delighted in playing cards and dice'; the abbey gate was a turnstile for tarts; and the closets disgorged a Portobello Road of sacred junk: 'as the coals of St Lawrence was toasted withal; the parings of St Edmund's nails; St Thomas Canterbury's pen knife and boots and divers skulls for the headache'.

For the tens of thousands of men and women cast out into the world, what happened in 1536 and the years that followed was no joke. The property redistribution was on a scale that no other English revolution ever approached. Priories, like Lacock in Wiltshire, were offered at bargain prices, and loyalty to the new order was secured with bricks and mortar. The former residents were soon forgotten or reduced to family legends of headless nuns and spectral monks. And by filling the Crown's coffers with the proceeds, the dissolution gave Henry the wherewithal to stand up to the worst that the Catholic powers could throw at him. It was an achievement of *realpolitik* that Wolsey in his wildest dreams could hardly have imagined.

But Cromwell had been close enough to Wolsey to treat the cardinal's fate as a cautionary lesson. Beware, lest you think yourself invulnerable. Watch out for back-biting aristocrats who, however patronizing their smiles, actually despise you as a jumped-up, power-mad, inky-fingered lout. The king is your saving grace. Do what he wants before he knows he wants it and they can't lay a finger on you. And Cromwell was only too painfully aware that what Henry wanted, desperately, achingly, miserably, was a son. Anne had, so far, failed to give him the promised prize. A baby daughter, Elizabeth, was born in September 1533. Henry laid his hand on the baby's head, acknowledging her as his legitimate daughter and hoped for better luck next time. Eighteen months later Anne was pregnant again. In January 1536 there was

Top: Thomas Cromwell, by Hans Holbein, c. 1530.
Above: Anne of Cleves, miniature by Hans Holbein, 1539.

more good news. Catherine of Aragon had died. 'God be praised,' said Henry. 'We are free from all suspicion of war.' It may have been at this point that Cromwell's machinery of anticipation began to buzz and whir. With the emperor's aunt, Catherine, dead, why not bring about a reconciliation between Charles and Henry. But the price of peace would be the re-legitimizing of Lady Mary, and to that Anne would never agree. The logical conclusion was that she must go.

Everything turned on the result of Anne's pregnancy. On 19 January she miscarried. The child would have been a boy. The disaster re-awakened Henry's pessimism and rage. 'I see now that God will never give me a male heir,' he told Anne, before curtly informing her that he would see her when she left her bed. Black melancholia began to fester into something much more grotesque as he thrashed around looking for someone to blame. The curse was still on him. It was not God but the devil who had brought him this marriage, and he had been seduced into it by witchcraft. Witches were known to induce impotence, and the virile king was having a little problem. The marriage was unclean, doomed to sterility. It needed a quick exorcism.

Cromwell knew that few would grieve for the Boleyns. Catherine's death had stimulated another outpouring of sympathy for the Lady Mary, and Anne's family were detested by the dukes of Norfolk and Suffolk as greedy and presumptuous parvenus. Personally, Cromwell didn't give a fig one way or the other. The Boleyns were in the way of state business; that was all. But he respected Anne too much to do anything by half. If she was going to be removed, she and everyone around her had better be destroyed, flattened, with no chance of getting off the mat.

What he then cooked up was a thing of pure devilry; a finely measured brew, one part pornography, one part paranoia. Moments of dalliance, nothing really untoward in the Renaissance court – a handkerchief that did not belong to the king dropped at a May Day tilt; a dance taken with a young man, also not the king; a blown kiss, a giggle – were twisted by Cromwell into a carnival of unholy, traitorous sex. As a witness under oath at Anne's trial put it, 'the Queen, following her daily frail and carnal lust did procure divers of the King's daily and familiar servants to be her adulterers'. Anne, it seems, had done it with everyone. She'd had sex with her court musician; she'd had sex with the Groom of the Stole; she'd screwed the king's tennis partner Francis Weston and the courtier William Brereton; she had even slept with her own brother. Anne had presided like some possessed Messalina over a diabolical orgy of treason, perhaps planning to pass off the poisoned fruit of all this hectic copulation as a royal heir.

It was the confession of the carpenter's son and court musician, Mark Smeaton, extracted under torture, that provided a fig leaf of legality for Cromwell's judicial murders. On 27 April Smeaton's confession was given to Henry, and he bought every word of it. Three days later, holding her baby Elizabeth in her arms and with cannon booming in the Tower as the first of her friends was brought to prison, Anne made a desperate attempt to plead with the king to make him see reason. It was in vain. Terrified by the monster that Cromwell had let loose, the great and the good ran for cover just as fast as they could. The glamorous Duke of Norfolk, Anne's own uncle, presided over the kangaroo court. Cranmer, who without Anne would still have been toasting his own muffins in a Cambridge college, fussed and fretted, having believed the queen the noblest and most virtuous woman that ever lived but now seeing that he had been most wickedly deceived. Most obscenely, her father Thomas Boleyn decided to pretend that the adulteries were true in order to save his own neck while his children lost theirs. Others from Anne's past came very close to destruction. Thomas Wyatt, her old flame, was arrested on suspicion of (what else?) adultery and sent to the Tower, where through a grating in his cell in the Bell Tower he watched the execution of Anne's brother and friends.

> The Bell Tower showed me such a sight
> That in my head sticks day and night
> There I did learn out of a grate
> For all favour, glory, or might
> That yet *circa Regna tonat* [around the throne the thunder roars].

Two days later, on 19 May, four months to the day after her miscarriage, it was Anne's turn. As a special boon, an expert swordsman had been imported from France. 'I hear the executioner is very good,' Anne is said to have told the constable of the Tower, 'and I have a little neck.' And then she put her hands around her throat and burst out laughing. On the scaffold, dressed in black damask trimmed with ermine, she declared: 'I am come neither to accuse no man nor to speak anything of that whereof I am accused and brought here to die but I pray God save the king and send him long to reign over you for a gentler nor a more merciful prince was there never.' Among those watching the first execution of a queen of England were her own uncle, the Duke of Norfolk, Thomas Cromwell, the Earl of Suffolk and the Lord Mayor of London. Wyatt's sister, Margaret, was probably one of the ladies waiting on the queen to the last. He himself watched the final act through his little grating.

> These bloody days hath broken my heart.
> And lust, my youth did them depart...

Still, Wyatt not only survived Anne's ruin but actually became close to Cromwell and was duly rewarded by being made sheriff of Kent.

The beheading was a tonic for Henry VIII. The day before Anne's execution he had his marriage annulled by Cranmer on the grounds of her adultery, making Elizabeth as well as Mary a bastard, a fact that seemed to cheer up the older sister enormously. The day after the execution the king announced his betrothal to Jane Seymour. Eighteen months later he was a father, this time to the long-awaited boy, and less than two weeks later he was, again, a widower. Well, no matter, a queen had at last done her job.

When the news of Anne Boleyn's death reached Dover, it was said that church tapers spontaneously re-lit. For the vast majority of the country, which despite the break with Rome still regarded itself as Catholic, her death seemed a long-overdue judgement on those they called heretics and twopenny bookmen. With the king now so thoroughly undeceived, they assumed he would put matters back the way they had been. And when this failed to happen right away, they took it on themselves to rescue him from the evil councillors who were obviously obstructing his true will. Marching under the banner of the Five Wounds of Christ, an army of 10,000 in the north and east demanded a restoration of the old ways. Or rather petitioned, for their leader, Robert Aske (as so many insurgents before and after him), adopted a posture of loyal supplication. His anthem-chanting host was, he believed, not a rebellion but a pilgrimage, the Pilgrimage of Grace, and it asked the king to do only what they truly believed he wished to do, once free of the wicked Cromwell and Cranmer: restore the monasteries, legitimize Mary, prosecute heretics with the ardour shown by Wolsey and More, and preserve the old ceremonies.

The crusade, as it imagined itself, caught fire. By December 1536 there may have been as many as 40,000 mustered beneath the banner of the Five Wounds. By now, not only country gentlemen like Aske but also leading northern aristocrats, like the Percys, were involved. It was, in effect, the first act of the English wars of religion that mapped itself – as it would for centuries – as a Catholic north and west against a more reform-minded, or at least more heavily governed, southeast. For the moment, however, since it could not yet mobilize a force strong enough to confront and defeat the rebels, the government had no alternative but to pretend that it would at least listen to their demand for a general amnesty and a Catholic restoration. The Duke of Norfolk, who was known to be hostile to the evangelicals and had just sent his niece, Anne, to the execution block, was sent to do the dirty work at Doncaster and did so with aplomb, agreeing on the king's behalf to most of the demands, the restoration of the monasteries excepted. Robert Aske pulled off his badge of the Five Wounds, proclaiming, 'we will wear no badge but the badge of our sovereign lord,' and the pilgrims went home ecstatic, believing the king, in his goodness, had granted their wishes.

But it was, of course, a replay of the tactics of 1381, when the king had temporized by appeasing the Peasants Revolt. Once the immediate threat had vanished, Henry outdid Richard II at his most autocratic, swearing retribution on the rebels. 'Our pleasure,' the king wrote to the Duke of Norfolk, '[is] that you shall cause such dreadful execution to be done upon a good number of every town village and hamlet that have offended as they may be a fearful spectacle to all others hereafter that would practise any like matter.' And we can be sure that he complied.

Different lessons were drawn from the Pilgrimage of Grace by different factions. The more traditionally minded, like Norfolk, believed that the rising had shown the need to rein in some of the more intrusive innovations, to avoid provoking future outbreaks. But Cranmer and Cromwell drew precisely the opposite conclusion: that the unwitting association of Catholicism and treason had given them an opportunity to push their theological offensive faster and further than they had previously dared. In 1538 Cromwell sent out a new batch of 'Injunctions' to the clergy, designed to lean heavily on 'superstition'. His targets were all those traditional practices that brought together large numbers of people, for he understood very well that crowds, especially crowds that believed they had Christ and the saints on their side, might get up the courage to do things that individuals might shrink from. So pilgrimages, saints' days and the display of relics were banned, and the most egregious objects of veneration were smashed and burned in public, the better to cow the credulous. In one economical act of terror, the miracle-working statue of St Derfel was burned alongside a Franciscan friar who refused to accept the new order.

The two most famous pilgrimage shrines in England were the object of special displeasure. At Canterbury the travelling evangelical playwright, John 'Bilious' Bale, was hired to rewrite the Becket story as a play, *The Treason of Becket*, in which the traitorous archbishop dies as the result of an accidental scuffle. It was performed at Canterbury while Cromwell's iconoclastic goons comprehensively demolished the shrine. No more old ladies stumbling to the tomb for a cure; no more processions of the barefoot on the roads of Kent. And at Walsingham, where Henry had given thanks for the birth of a son twenty-seven years before, the statue of the Virgin was burned. The account book for 1538 records, for the first time: 'Payment for the King's great candle; salary for the abbot: nil.'

Cranmer and Cromwell were gambling that, since they could present their iconoclastic offensive as an attack on the enemies of the king's royal state, they could take him with them. But their confidence was misplaced. For as Henry grew older the distinction between the royal supremacy (good) and a Protestant reformation (bad) became more, not less, absolute in his own mind. Matters like chantries and the excessive veneration of obscure saints had, after all, been the objects of criticism in the time of his father and grandmother as part of the programme of Catholic reform. But in all the issues of doctrine that most offended Protestantism – the real presence of Christ in the mass, the celibacy of priests and the relevance of good works to salvation – Henry was not just a conservative, he was a perfectly orthodox Catholic. So when Cranmer and his protégés produced a 'Bishop's Book' publicizing a heavily Protestant version of the new Church, Henry not only refused to authorize it but filled page after page with his own corrections. In the preface to the second edition of the Great Bible, Cranmer expressly said that it was 'for all manner of persons, men, women, young, old, rich, poor priests, laymen, lords, ladies, officers, tenants and mean men, virgins, wives, widows, lawyers, merchants, all manner of persons of whatever estate and condition'. But Henry had no intention of tolerating this commonwealth of believers, and in 1546 he expressly forbade women and the lower classes (that is, the vast majority of his subjects) from reading the English Bible lest they be led astray. For many this was a grievous deprivation. On the fly leaf of a small religious tract is an inscription by an Oxfordshire shepherd: 'I bought this book when the testament was abrogated that shepherds might not read it. I pray God amend that blindness. Writ by Robert Williams, keeping sheep upon Saintbury Hill.'

Cromwell was really pushing his luck, then, when he attempted to align Henry with the league of Lutheran princes by contracting a marriage alliance with a German princess. The union with poor Anne of Cleves collapsed as soon as Henry discovered that she was a lot less appealing than Holbein's adorable miniature had advertised. Cromwell, just elevated to the earldom of Essex, was swept away in a court coup, organized by Norfolk and Suffolk, that was every bit as ruthless as those he himself had managed. Parliament passed the Six Articles, which outlawed marriage for priests on pain of death and upheld the real presence of Christ in the mass. Somehow, Cranmer, whose own marriage was, of course, still kept a deathly secret from the king and who, after briefly defending Cromwell, prudently repudiated him just as he had repudiated Anne, was spared. Although he supposed him misguided, the king was somehow emotionally attached to the archbishop who had steered him through so many storms. Increasingly, though, real theological power lay with much more conservative bishops, like Stephen Gardiner.

In the last years of his reign the king was becoming more rigid, both physically and theologically. He was now in his fifties, and the body that had once caused swooning fits of admiration on the tennis court had become a vast, bloated, arthritic hulk. A little cart was built to wheel him from room to room in Hampton Court. But for a dizzy moment he deluded himself that Norfolk's nubile niece, Catherine Howard, was actually as besotted with him as he was with her and he embarrassingly played the part of the lusty husband, until, that is, he discovered that queen number five (unlike queen number two) had been to bed with her cousin Thomas Culpeper. His last wife, Catherine Parr, was exactly what Henry needed in his fading years: nurse, auntie and matron. She would humour his rages and indulge his fantasy that he was still the great warlord, provoking him to a last disastrous campaign against the French. But when his prize warship, the *Mary Rose*, sank in Portsmouth harbour it was as if the whole, top-heavy Henrician fantasy empire had gone to the bottom of the sea with it.

Chief among the fantasies with which Henry consoled himself was the notion that by slamming on the brakes he had healed the bitter divisions in the country. In the massive portrait from the studio of Holbein, which was done for the College of Barber Surgeons, Henry appears not just as an unearthly English Caesar, but also as 'Great Physician', which is exactly how the king liked to see himself: the Tudor medicine man, who had laid out the body of England on the operating table and had cut out the cankers of papist superstition. The patient was now recovered; the nation was grateful, the operation a complete success.

Except, of course, it wasn't. Henry would be followed by his three children, each of whom had utterly different ideas about what was best for the spiritual and political health of the country. Between Edward, the heir apparent, and his half-sisters, Mary and Elizabeth, England would move right through the spectrum of belief from intense Protestant evangelicalism to equally militant Catholicism. And the direction taken by the English Church would, more than ever, depend not on any confessional programme, as on the lottery of royal births, marriages and deaths.

Henry's funeral, as vast and imposing as he had been, offered no guidance for what was about to happen. Dirges and masses were sung for the repose of his soul, and his mighty entrails were ceremonially interred at Whitehall. The most conservative bishops – Stephen Gardiner at Winchester and Edmund Bonner in London – were still in their sees, but in the very last year of Henry VIII's reign the Catholic party had been fatally compromised by over-confidence. The Earl of Surrey had gone to the block, and his father, the Duke of Norfolk, was a prisoner in the Tower. So Cranmer, Edward's godfather and one of the executors of the late king's will, was in a position to become the dominant figure in the Edwardian cultural revolution. Quite soon, wearing the beard that made him look like an Old Testament prophet, Cranmer sounded a new note when in a sermon he spoke of the nine-year-old boy as 'Josiah'. Josiah was the boy-king of Israel whose mission had been the smashing of idolatry, and solemn little Edward was to take this very much to heart. Although St Edward's spurs had to be taken off him at his coronation in Westminster Abbey lest he trip over them, he was still God's little crusader, and during his reign a transformation would take place so sweeping as to make everything that happened in his father's time seem just a stiff breeze before the whirlwind.

Cranmer was the moving spirit; Edward Seymour, Duke of Somerset and the Lord Protector, provided the power. Together they unleashed a true reformation. In the first year of the reign, in July 1547, a special 'injunction' from the royal council banned almost all the traditional customs and ceremonies. There would be no more blessings of the candles at Candlemas, no more 'creeping to the cross' on Good Friday. Doves would no longer be released from the roof of St Paul's on Whit Sunday. In the second year the religious guilds and fraternities went. In their place, poor boxes were posted in the churches. Any cults of saints and processions that had survived Cromwell's onslaught were now done away with. In due course, Edward himself took care to expunge any mention of St George from the Order of the Garter. Carts and wagons were filled with the smashed-up debris of the old church: roods, stained glass, vestments and vessels. Bells were taken down from the belfries. At Durham a commissioner jumped up and down on a large Corpus Christi monstrance to make sure it was battered to destruction. Pots of limewash were brought into the churches of England to obliterate the wall paintings; this was probably the moment when the saints of Binham Priory were whitened out. Sounds as well as sights were banished from the liturgy. 'Alas, gossip,' bewailed one woman. 'What shall we do at church since all the godly sights we were wont to have are gone and we cannot hear the piping, singing, chanting and playing upon the organ that we could before?'

In the third year, 1549, disreputable literature was done away with and in its place came translated Bibles, no fewer than sixty of them during Edward's reign and available now to all those dangerous people whom Henry had wanted to keep away from the *evangelion*. Books of homilies explained to the laity how their salvation was a free gift of God's grace, made possible by the sacrifice of his son. And a new Book of Common Prayer, required in all parishes for the first time, made English the dominant language of the church service. There would be no exorcism of the salt at baptism, no blessing of the ring at marriages.

To take the measure of the Edwardian revolution, one need only go to Hailes church in Gloucestershire. Years before, Anne Boleyn had sent her own commissioners to the abbey to inspect the cross, which was said to liquefy with the blood of

Top: Anti-papal Allegory of the Succession, 1549. Henry VIII on his deathbed gestures to his successor. On Edward VI's left stands Somerset, while the royal council sits around the table. Above: Thomas Cranmer, by Gerlach Flicke, 1546.

Christ. They had exposed the fraud as a mixture of wax and duck's blood. But in 1550 something much more radical took place at the church. Instead of the stone altar, set in the place of honour at the east end of the church where bread and wine had become the flesh and blood of Christ, a plain wooden table was placed in the middle of the chancel, and the priest, dressed in a simple surplice like a parish clerk, broke bread and gave it to the congregation, who were sitting alongside him. The redesign of the church was expressly meant to abolish the distance between the priest (as he was still called) and the flock. The screen, which had acted as a barrier protecting the mystery of the mass, was now just a way in to the communion, a gathering of the faithful along with their priest. No room was left for any kind of miraculous transformation, just a symbolic remembrance of Christ's sacrifice. As if this were not shocking enough, at some point in 1550 the priest would have invited the congregation to partake of communion using those English words never before heard in church, 'Dearly beloved'. The familiarity of the address must have bewildered many and made others feel uncomfortable, rather like being exhorted to call the vicar 'Bob'. Worse, men and women were supposed to line up for communion on opposite sides of the table, which must have reminded everyone of the opening of a country dance.

But momentous things were happening to the relations between the sexes as a result of the Edwardian reforms. Priests could, and did, now live openly with their wives. Thomas Cranmer, the first married Archbishop of Canterbury, composed a wedding service with English texts that, for the first time, treated marriage not as a sacrament but as a moral human relationship, 'for mutual help, society and comfort…that the one ought to have of the other both in prosperity and adversity'. And if marriage were no longer a sacrament, then it could be broken by divorce. Another first during Edward's reign were the women who took advantage of this freedom to obtain divorces as a result of the adultery of their husbands, and this might include the 'spiritual adultery' of his obstinate attachment to papism!

England was now a divided country. It was, in the first instance, divided by generation. In the cities and towns of the southeast, where the Reformation was strongest, Edward's own generation could have had no memory of the old pre-1530 Church. Teenagers, especially male teenagers, watched as all sorts of old stuff – relics, statues, glass – were breezily trashed by the commissioners. Now they were free to have some fun at the expense of the back-number Church, too. Priests were pelted with stones or subjected to joke masses or just bad-mouthed by smart-alecks standing around on street corners. Miles Huggarde, an indignant Catholic, complained bitterly that the young had 'no regard at all to repair to the church upon the holy days but flock in clusters upon stalls either scorning the passers-by or with their testaments utter some wise stuff of their own device'. But in places like Norwich or London there was a different kind of church to attract the young. For the first time going to hear itinerant preachers, sometimes outdoors, became a pastime. In fact, you could go to the *same* place – like the Privy Garden – and see bear-baiting one day and a hot gospeller the next. Star turns delivered thundering sermons on the iniquities of mankind that got the blood racing and the heart pounding: thrill time for the sinful. This was their religion – of the word, the psalms turned into English rhymes – and they felt the surge of excited loyalty that came from membership of the troops of the righteous.

It wouldn't do to sell the exhilarating appeal of Protestantism short by representing it as some sort of frivolously adopted counter-culture. The very simplicity of its call to sweep away all the encrusted custom and unquestioned authority of the centuries was viscerally thrilling. If there was destruction of the false gods and idols, it was only so that the purity of the gospel truth could be brilliantly revealed. Being told that each and every believer might find for themselves that gospel truth in scripture alone was a genuine liberation. For the first time in the history of Christianity individualism was sanctified. To those who experienced this rush of freedom and self-sufficiency, it was like being reborn: like drinking clear water, breathing the purest oxygen.

The Roman Church had always been described as a mother. Well, now it was time to grow up. Leaving home, though, was not for everyone. In Lancashire or Cornwall in the 1540s the young were just as attached to the old ways as their elders, perhaps more so. In the west and north priests kept the Latin mass alive surreptitiously, nervously aware that Bonner and Gardiner, the bishops who had protested at Cranmer's new regime, were now in prison and their sees given to reformers. But there were some who were determined to resist, whatever the cost. At Helston on 6 April 1547 Wolsey's illegitimate son, William Body, who was overseeing the destruction of images in Cornwall, was beaten to death in front of the church. Two years later the forcible introduction of the Book of Common Prayer triggered a massive rebellion in the southwest, culminating in a thirty-five-day siege of Exeter and a pitched battle at Sampford Courtenay in which 4000 Devonians and Cornishmen were killed.

As if this wasn't bad enough, rebellions against the Book of Common Prayer broke out in Oxfordshire and Buckinghamshire, and a much more serious revolt, driven by social and economic grievances in hard times of high prices and land enclosures, occurred in East Anglia, with 3000 artisans, urban craftsmen and yeomen camped at Mousehold Heath outside Norwich. They were led by the tanner Robert

Kett, who 'hath conceived a wonderful hate against all gentlemen and taketh them all as their enemies'. Specifically, the Mousehold rebels demanded a prohibition on lords using common land or keeping sheep at the expense of the tillage of the common people. Before this revolt was also suppressed with more thousands dead, Somerset's authority was in ruins. For a while there was talk of making Princess Mary regent, but with the support of the new leading magnate, John Dudley, Earl of Warwick, Cranmer held stubbornly to the principles of his reformation, if anything sharpening them, confiscating the redundant vessels of the mass and inviting famous (or, depending on your point of view, notorious) Protestants to live in England and take up posts in Oxford and Cambridge.

None of this could have happened without the active endorsement of the king himself. And as he grew from child to teenager, it became apparent that Edward VI was very much his father's son and not at all the pasty-faced weakling of popular myth. Edward had the same insatiable appetite for riding, hawking and hunting as Henry; the same volatile temper (especially when failing to get what he thought a proper allowance); and the same conviction that he was perfectly qualified to be Supreme Head of the Church. But unlike his father, Edward had no reservations about the old religion. Along with friends and relatives – his half-sister Elizabeth, and the grandchildren of Charles Brandon and Mary Tudor – he had been educated by enthusiastic and learned Protestants, including John Cheke, his tutor. From the beginning he was primed, loaded and ready to blast away at the idolatry of benighted papists. Even when he had been just ten years old he had let it be known that the pope was 'the true son of the Devil, an anti-Christ and an abominable tyrant'. In 1550 he learned that, despite the Act of Uniformity of 1549, which outlawed the mass, his half-sister Mary not only persisted in her Catholic forms of worship but made no attempt to hide them. Edward himself reported on the ill-fated meeting that took place to try to resolve the issue. 'The Lady Mary, my sister, came to me at Westminster where after salutations she was called of my Council into a chamber where it was declared how long I had suffered her Mass. She answered that her soul was God's and her face she would not change nor would she dissemble with contrary doings.' But although Mary was emotionally devoted to her brother, she was much more devoted to the old Church and actually increased her attendance at the mass to two and even three times a day. 'When they send me orders forbidding me the Mass, I shall expect to suffer as I suffered once during my father's lifetime,' she said. 'I am like a little ignorant girl and I care neither for my goods nor for the World but only for God's service and my conscience.'

Mary's colossal martyr-complex was, of course, the result of her mother's ordeal

and her own humiliation in the years that followed, when she was demoted from
Princess Mary to the illegitimate 'Lady Mary'. But by the time of her brother's reign
she was not as helpless as she made out. In 1543 Catherine Parr had persuaded Henry
VIII to reinstate both Mary and Elizabeth in the line of succession and had brought
the girls to her own household. A portrait painted around 1544 on a precious azurite
blue ground shows Mary not as the dowdy, nun-like creature of myth, but as a
Renaissance princess, covered in jewels and brilliantly coloured French velvets.
Thanks to her father's guilty generosity, which showered her with palaces and castles
in East Anglia, Mary had become a power in her own right. And she had a powerful
ally in her cousin, the Emperor Charles V, who threatened war if she were denied her
masses and to whose hospitality Mary attempted to flee from the evangelical regime
of Cranmer.

So when Edward's lingering feverish cold degenerated into a respiratory infection in the spring and summer of 1552, it was obvious to the guardians of the *evangelion* that, unless something drastic were done, Mary would take England back to its
pre-Reformation past. The ailing, fifteen-year-old king conspired with John Dudley,
now Earl of Northumberland, to pre-empt this disaster. Acting with dire haste,
Northumberland married his son, Guildford Dudley, to Lady Jane Grey, the dependably Protestant granddaughter of the famous elopers, Charles Brandon and Mary
Tudor. With Edward's pulmonary infection (which was *not* tuberculosis) steadily
deteriorating, producing ulcers on his lungs and subjecting him to long coughing fits,
Jane Grey and Guildford Dudley were ordered to get on with producing an heir as
quickly as possible. It was not quickly enough, for Edward died on 13 April 1553.
Northumberland summoned Jane to tell her that she was now queen and had a royal
canopy placed over her head. As the architect of the pre-emptive strike, however,
he had made one very serious mistake: failing to make sure that he first had Mary
under lock and key.

Northumberland had fatally misjudged both the national mood and Mary herself. Far from being intimidated by his coup, now that her moment of redemption
had arrived she was determined to fight like a crusader. Moving quickly north
from her house at Hunsdon in Hertfordshire, she travelled through Cambridgeshire
and raised her standard at Framlingham Castle in Suffolk on the ancestral estate of
the Duke of Norfolk, who had been in prison since 1547. Thousands upon thousands
immediately rallied to her, for the truth was that Mary had long been popular
among the largely Catholic county gentry and knights of the shires. There were those
who remembered how shabbily her mother had been treated; there were those who
thought she would rescue them from the alien ways of the Reformation; and there

were those – perhaps the majority – who, even though they may have been estranged
from the Roman Church, still believed that Mary ought to succeed to the throne
because the will of her father had clearly said she should. All of these were good
reasons to take up her cause. Sailors in Queen Jane's navy at Ipswich mutinied;
soldiers from Northumberland's own army deserted and flocked to her banner. In
Cambridge Northumberland pathetically attempted to save his neck by throwing his
cap in the air and crying 'God save Queen Mary'. Mary herself reviewed 15,000
troops on a white horse with tears in her eyes. She spoke of this as God's miracle –
and who can blame her?

In September 1553 Mary entered London in a triumphal chariot. The streets
were deep in flowers. For a moment it seemed as if she would turn back the clock
to the last, conservative years of Henry VIII's reign. She received her sister Elizabeth,
who arrived to pay her respects (prudently attended by a small army of 2000 horsemen); released bishops Bonner and Gardiner from captivity; and had parliament
quickly repeal the entire religious legislation of Edward's reign. But Mary's mission
was, in fact, more radically reactionary. She wanted to restore the Church not as it
had been in 1546 but as it had been in 1526: obedient to Rome. And once she had
made it clear that the land sold during the dissolution of the monasteries would not
be restored, there was little resistance to her campaign. The papal legate, Cardinal
Pole, returned from exile, and in 1554 both houses of parliament knelt in tearful
atonement for all the sins they had committed since the 1530s. Cranmer, the man the
queen blamed most for the schism, was arrested and sent to the Tower along with
other offending evangelical bishops. Orders went out for the repainting of churches,
the carving of roods, the restoration of stone altars and the Latin mass. On
30 November 1554 Mary officially proclaimed the return of England to Rome and
ordered that that day (St Andrew's Day, as it happened) should be celebrated henceforth as the greatest of all national holidays.

Only one anxiety cast a shadow over Mary's exultation: the ticking of her biological clock. She was thirty-eight, by sixteenth-century standards an advanced age for
conception. Nonetheless, it was her sacred duty to produce the heir who would keep
England in faithful obedience to Rome. She had always looked to the Emperor
Charles for guidance, and so a logical choice for husband was his son, Philip of Spain.
Parliament was appalled by the choice, imploring her to choose someone from within
the realm instead. Even the ultra-conservative Bishop Gardiner attempted to dissuade
her. Adamant, the queen threw a little tantrum, protesting that if she was forced to
marry someone she disliked it would be the death of her within weeks and the end
of any possibility of an heir. The best was done to protect England. Philip was to

be made king in title only and was to be sworn to protect and preserve English institutions. If the queen died before him, he was still to be excluded from the line of succession. Philip himself was not, in fact, interested in importing *autos-da-fé* to the streets of London. But despite all these cautions, there is no doubt that the Spanish marriage caused irreversible damage to the queen's popularity. 'The queen is a Spaniard at heart,' it was said, 'and loves another realm better than this.'

The forebodings of the pessimists seemed vindicated when Thomas Wyatt, the son of Anne Boleyn's old poet-admirer, led an army of about 3000 gentlemen and commoners all the way from Kent to the gates of London. Words that had become popular and significant in the reign of Edward – *commonwealth* and *liberty* – featured prominently in Wyatt's propaganda, in which he cast himself as the defender of the nation's freedom, pledged to the 'avoidance of Strangers'. In the minds of some at least, Protestantism and patriotism were beginning to become linked.

But Mary rose to the occasion, going to the Guildhall in her crown and state robes and declaring (a little disingenuously) that she was marrying because her council had implored her to. If there was discontent, the matter would be discussed in parliament, but for the moment the people must stand with her against rebellion. And so they did. More than 20,000 Londoners volunteered to defend the city. Wyatt's army failed to penetrate Ludgate, then rapidly crumbled away. His cause and his life were forfeit. Mary naturally assumed that this, too, had been God's work: a sign that he approved her marriage. The marriage duly took place at Winchester Cathedral in July 1554. Philip was gallantly affable to his older bride, unlike the Venetian ambassador, who described Mary at this time as having 'no eyebrows. She is a saint. She dresses badly.' The Spanish entourage found the English 'white, pink and quarrelsome', and when they left the cathedral they stepped into the classic summertime weather of a steady downpour. Nothing, however, could dampen Mary's ecstasy. For the first time in her lonely life she believed she had someone she could depend on. She even believed that Philip was a paragon of princely chastity. (It was just as well she never knew that within months of the wedding he was off with two mistresses in the Netherlands.) Now, with the help of God and Philip, she could set about cleansing the realm of the pollution of heresy.

The burnings began in 1555. In three years 220 men and 60 women died on Mary's bonfires. At first, they alarmed, then they horrified people, and not just Protestants or moderate Catholics. Before he died in November 1555, old Bishop Gardiner, Cranmer's arch-enemy, spoke strongly against them. Philip and some of his closest advisers were dismayed by Mary's increasingly fanatical ardour and predicted it would alienate the Crown from the people. They were right.

Early on there was an emphasis on show trials, payback for the Edwardian years (in which, however, not a single Catholic had gone to the stake). One of the first to be burned was John Hooper, Bishop of Gloucester, who died a lingering death when the gunpowder thrown on the faggots refused to explode. He was followed by Nicholas Ridley, Bishop of London, and Hugh Latimer, Bishop of Worcester, who were brought to Oxford for a farcical examination of their opinions, in which their views were decreed to have been formally confounded. On 14 February 1556, they went to the stake in Broad Street, but not before Latimer had told his fellow-martyr: 'Be of good comfort, Master Ridley, and play the man. We shall this day light such a candle by God's grace in England, as I trust shall never be put out.' At Thomas Cranmer's trial, also in Oxford, where he was made to stand up high in Christ Church Cathedral rood loft (the kind of place he had been eager to destroy), Cranmer listened to a litany of the evils it was said he had brought on England. For a while he resisted, then when the writ for his burning was issued, he crumbled, signing a recantation. If he had hoped to save his life, he was wrong. Instead, the queen demanded that he make a formal statement of contrition in St Mary's, the university church, and then be burned anyway. But instead of the expected words of atonement and remorse, Cranmer defiantly reiterated his Protestant beliefs. Uproar broke out. Shouting 'As for the pope I refuse him as anti-Christ,' Cranmer was dragged from the pulpit and to the stake. With the fire set, he thrust the hand that had signed the false recantation into the flames, punishing it for its insincerity.

Most of the Marian martyrs were much simpler people – cloth-workers, chandlers, cutlers – and many of them were young, members of the generation who had felt the excitement of finding truth through their own reading of the English Bible. Some were even illiterate, like Rawlings White, a fisherman who paid for his son to go to school and learn to read so that the boy might read the Bible to him each night after supper, or Joan Waist of Derby, a poor blind woman who saved up for a New Testament and paid people to read it to her. The vivid details of the simple, powerful faith of White, Waist and others are recorded in the book that, more than any other, would come to define Protestant England or rather rewrite history so that England's destiny was always somehow meant by God to be separate from Rome. This was John Foxe's *Acts and Monuments*, more usually known as his 'Book of Martyrs'. First published in 1563, in the reign of Elizabeth, and using a powerful mix of texts and woodcut images, the book turned the Marian burnings into a national epic of sacrifice and redemption. Just as Christ had sacrificed himself to redeem humanity, so the Marian martyrs had died so that England might be saved from *foreign* tyranny and the rule of the anti-Christ.

Top: Mary I, by Master John, 1544.
Above: The burning of Thomas Haukes in Essex,
June 1555; woodcut from Foxe's 'Book of Martyrs'.

Foxe's book had most impact in the abridged form created by Timothy Bright, a physician turned ordained clergyman, who published it in a convenient quarto format in 1589, just a year after England's narrow escape from the Spanish Armada. By that time, there was no question but that the nation's destiny and history had been linked to Protestantism, and Foxe's treatment of the ordeal of the martyrs seemed yet more evidence that they had, somehow, been patriotic, as well as spiritual victims. But propaganda though it undoubtedly was, Foxe's book still contained an essential kernel of moral truth. Unspeakable cruelties *were* committed in Mary's reign, and neither the fact that her father had burned heretics, nor the fact they were being burned in even greater numbers elsewhere, nor the quiescence of the majority of the population, nor historical impatience with stereotypes about 'Bloody Mary', in any way dilutes the enormity of the crime.

To an increasing number of people there was, in fact, something wrong with both Mary and her government. Twice she was pronounced pregnant and twice nothing came of it. Twice Philip departed, deeply uncomfortable with his role both as husband and consort. The queen was suffering not only from delusions but from ovarian or cervical cancer. In 1557 the humiliating loss of Calais, the last remnant of the Plantagenet empire – which coincided with galloping inflation and severe unemployment in the towns – seemed just another of the plagues that had been laid on suffering England. Said one ardent Elizabethan, Thomas Smith: 'I never saw England weaker in money, men and riches…nothing but fining, hanging, quartering and burning, levying and beggaring and losing our strongholds abroad. A few priests ruled all who, with setting up of six foot roods, thought to make all cocksure.' On 17 November 1558, the day Mary died in great pain and mortification that her theologically unsound sister Elizabeth would succeed her, she managed to issue a warrant for two more burnings.

From the very beginning, Elizabeth made it clear that she would undo the excesses of Mary's Counter-Reformation. When priests in the royal chapel lit a candle, they were told to put it out 'for we see very clearly'. But it was much less clear whether Elizabeth would restore the reformed Church of her conservative father or her evangelical brother. In 1559 the Act of Uniformity attempted to find a middle way that would allow both Catholics and Protestants to practise their religion. The mass was abolished and the Book of Common Prayer re-imposed, but priests were encouraged to remain celibate and saints' days remained in the calendar. Much latitude was left to the parishes.

Styling herself 'Supreme Governor', rather than 'Supreme Head' like her father, Elizabeth wanted, above all, to end the religious war that had opened up such a deep wound in the body politic of the country. But during the reigns of her half-brother and half-sister the country had become more, not less, polarized between camps whose versions of truth, faith and obedience were mutually exclusive. For Catholics in the 1560s there was still some possibility of remaining faithful to both their Church and queen, but only if they grasped what Elizabeth had offered them and attempted to work within the Church of England. For most of them, unhappily, this was not enough. For Rome it was nothing at all, for in the 1560s the Counter-Reformation took on the character of an implacable war, centrally directed and militantly disciplined. The faithful, marooned in pariah England, were ordered to stay away from heretical churches. If they were forced to conform outwardly to spare themselves persecution, they had to find secret churches to continue the old obedience. And their duty now was to look beyond England for help – from Spain, from the Catholic queen of Scotland, from the pope. In 1570 the pope promised the blessings of a martyr's reception in heaven to anyone who would assassinate Elizabeth I.

To be cut off from the priesthood was, of course, a lingering death sentence for a Church whose liturgy depended on priests. To be deprived of public ceremonies was to destroy the entire sense of shared community on which the old Church had thrived. What was left? An underground existence, a portable Church existing in things that could be easily smuggled and concealed: tracts, miniature images, jewels and rosaries. Faith and nation parted company in these years. English Catholic priests trained in foreign seminaries would be smuggled into the country and end up dead or in hiding with Catholic families rich and powerful enough to protect them. So *this* is what happened to Catholic England: it ended up down a priest-hole, the ceremonious grandeur of a Long Melford reduced to a faith on the run.

7

Godfrey Goodman fell for Elizabeth I when he was five years old and she was fifty-three. Much later, when he was Bishop of Gloucester in the reign of Charles I, he could still remember the evening in the tense Armada year of 1588 when he was living 'at the upper end of the Strand near St Clements Church, when suddenly there came a report unto us (it was December much about five o' clock at night and very dark), that the Queen was come to Council and if you will see the Queen you must come quickly'. Godfrey and his friends scampered as fast as their little legs could take them through the streets of London to Whitehall Palace, where the gates of the court-yard stood wide open. The space was packed with people and lit by a blaze of torches. After an hour Elizabeth emerged 'in great state. Then we cried "God Save Your Majesty". Then the Queen turned to us and said "God bless you all my good people." Then we cried again "God Save Your Majesty". Then the Queen said "You may well have a greater prince but you shall never have a more loving prince"…This wrought such an impression…on us that all the day long we did nothing but talk what an admirable queen she was and how we'd adventure our lives to do her service.'

She had that effect on all kinds of people, especially men, even when they got older and should have known better. John Selwyn of Walton-on-Thames was so determined to impress Elizabeth with his virile devotion that during a hunt in the royal park at Oatlands he leapt from his horse on to the back of a stag and rode it towards the queen before killing it with a sword thrust to the animal's throat. She was, after all, supposed to be Diana (not to mention Belphoebe, Cynthia, Astraea and Sirinx). But although the poets and balladeers sang her praises as if she were a goddess, Elizabeth I was only too obviously made of flesh and blood. She was vain, arrogant, spiteful, bloody-minded, frequently unjust and even more frequently maddeningly indecisive: an authentic Tudor, in other words. But she was also brave, intelligent, startlingly articulate, an eyeful to behold and, on occasions, genuinely wise. She had charisma in bucketfuls, and she understood people, high and low, with

THE BODY OF
THE QUEEN

The 'Armada Portrait' of Elizabeth I (detail), by George Gower, *c.* 1588.

uncommon shrewdness. She was, in fact, the first true woman politician in British history. Although she seldom flinched from intimidation, she also knew that, in the end, allegiance was strongest when it sprang from devotion. In the end it doesn't matter that much of this devotion was cranked up through the manipulation of her public image. Which political regime in our history has not attempted to do the same? Elizabeth succeeded in making the English happy to be who they were (no small achievement) and to feel that she cared for nothing so much as them. The Faerie had warts all right, but she was, nonetheless, the case for the monarchy. The only problem – and it was a big one – was that she made herself, literally, unreproducible.

In February 1603, shadowed by melancholy, Elizabeth was also in severe pain. Throat ulcers made it difficult to spoon anything but a little pottage down her gullet. Her hands had long been racked by rheumatism, and now the fingers that courtiers had stooped to kiss were so badly swollen that a decision was made to file away the queen's coronation ring, which had become deeply embedded in her skin and flesh. No matter whether she had actually made a show of displaying the ring at her coronation as the wedding band that united her with her people, everyone had for years believed that she had. A ballad writer had her sing to her suitor, Merrie England:

> Here is my hand
> My dear lover England,
> I am with thee both with mind and heart
> For ever to endure
> Thou mayst be sure
> Until death we two do part.

That parting seemed imminent now.

She was supposed to be immortal, of course, *semper eadem* (always the same), as the motto, taken from her unlucky mother, proclaimed. The older she got, the younger her portraitists made her appear, gillyflowers and pansies perpetually blooming on her stomacher. In 1602, a year before her death, the poet John Davies was gallantly insisting:

> Time's young hours attend her still
> And her eyes and cheeks do fill
> With fresh youth and beauty.

And the odd thing was that, despite the garish wig and the blackened teeth and the withered breasts (uncovered to the end, as befitted a virgin), foreigners like the

Venetian ambassador Scarinelli, who saw her with pearls like pears roped about her brow, did indeed think that Elizabeth's beauty 'though past' had not entirely faded. And the German Thomas Platter swore he had seen behind the mask a young woman, 'no more than twenty years of age'. When she died on the eve of the Annunciation of the Virgin and 'so easily' it was said 'like a ripe apple [falling] from a tree' and her undergarments were taken from her body, it was seen that they still fitted the contours of a maid: wasp-waisted, slim-hipped, long-limbed.

This was all the more remarkable since, according to the physicians, women's bodies that had not fulfilled the purposes for which God had fashioned them ran the danger of infected discoloration, specifically the 'swart, weasel' hue that was the sign of the virgin's disease, chlorosis, or 'the greensickness'. The condition was the result of unexpended female sperm (which contemporary medicine supposed were stored in the uterus) becoming corrupt and contaminating the upper parts of the body. In 1554 John Lange, who was the first to publish a diagnosis of greensickness, recommended the expulsion of dangerously retained seed through salutary copulation. And there had been a time when the councillors of Elizabeth I had desperately hoped that the queen would avail herself of it, for the sake of the health of her realm as well as herself, for they were one and the same. Elizabeth was meant to have joined herself to a husband and produced an heir to keep the peace and piety of the country secure for posterity. She had not done this. Still, when they laid her body in its tomb few people believed that Elizabeth had failed England. She had been peculiar, certainly, an island unto herself, but she had given everyone due warning. At the very beginning of her reign she had told her people that she had two bodies, one 'naturally considered', that of a woman, but the other, by God's permission, 'a body politic, to govern'. And she had proceeded to subject her body natural to her body politic, inventing something quite new in the history of the monarchy: the androgynous virgin prince.

She would never escape the politics of sex. Biology had made her mother queen and biology had killed her. In 1542, six years after Anne Boleyn's death, when Elizabeth was eight years old and certainly beginning to be aware of the revolving door of her father's court or at least of royal stepmothers who came and went, her Howard cousin, Catherine, was condemned and executed for having sex with another cousin, Thomas Culpeper, while Henry VIII was away hunting. So if women were generally thought to be governed by their lust, rather than their reason, the Howard women seemed to have a particular problem in this area. But Catherine Howard's sins and crimes had done nothing to mitigate those of Anne Boleyn. She stood forever damned as an incestuous, adulterous witch. It probably didn't help that Culpeper's access to Catherine Howard had been abetted by Elizabeth's aunt, Lady Rochford, her mother's sister-in-law. Since it was a truism that children inherited characteristics with their mother's milk, who knew how Elizabeth's Tudor blood might not be polluted by nursing at the dugs of a sorceress?

So the girl with the red-gold hair was a suspect who badly needed a guardian and one, moreover, who would think the best, not the worst, of her. In her last step-mother, Catherine Parr, Elizabeth finally found just such a protectress. It was Henry VIII's sixth queen who persuaded him to rewrite his will reinstating both his daughters in the line of succession, and in 1544 an act of parliament made it official. Catherine brought Elizabeth into her household at Chelsea and for a brief time she was able to relax in the warmth of approval and even affection. Her bad-tempered, pachydermal father bestowed favours and smiles on her as he rested his ulcerated leg on Queen Catherine's lap. She was now the picture of virtue, not a reminder of vice. In 1545 the twelve-year-old presented her father with her own translation, in French, Italian and Latin, of the queen's exemplary *Prayers and Meditations*, bound in crimson cloth and embroidered with Henry and Catherine's intertwined monograms, sewn in silver and gold. Restored to favour, Elizabeth also became close to her brother Edward, who was, after all, just three years her junior. When Henry died in January 1547 the news was given to brother and sister together, and Edward, beside himself, sobbed in his half-sister's arms. They also shared the same tutors, including the dauntingly learned Cambridge humanist, John Cheke, whose instruction made no concessions to the stereotypes of female light-headedness. Roger Ascham, who taught her in 1548, wrote to a scholarly friend, marvelling that:

> her mind has no womanly weakness and her perseverance is equal to that of a man and her memory long keeps what it quickly picks up. She talks French and Italian as well as she does English and has often talked to me readily and well in Latin, moderately in Greek. When she writes in Greek and Latin nothing is more beautiful than her handwriting. She delights as much in music as she is skilful in it. In adornment she is elegant rather than showy.

Ascham happened to be much more important than a humble don, flattered by a post at court. He was a master calligrapher, surely responsible for Elizabeth's exquisite hand, and the advocate of a stern 'double-translation' method, which had students take Latin texts that had been rendered into English and translate them back again, unseen of course, into Latin. Ascham was also Public Orator at Cambridge University and it was in this role that he put Cicero's *De Oratore* in front of Elizabeth. The outlandish idea was to instruct the teenage girl in a discipline that most thought

Princess Elizabeth aged thirteen, by an unknown artist.

profoundly unfit for a woman at all: the art of public speech. And although her sister Mary intermittently showed some skill and courage, rhetoric was from the outset the strongest in Elizabeth's arsenal of political weapons. Her speeches were always by herself and worked painstakingly through several drafts. Although at the beginning of her reign the speeches were read by male speakers, after a while Elizabeth delivered them herself, evidently to extraordinary effect. Her ringing, finely thought-out oratory could strong-arm or seduce, tease or threaten. Whenever she took it out for an airing, her adversaries and critics flinched, for they knew they were in for a very, very hard time.

The portrait of the teenage princess, painted at Edward's express request, is of a Renaissance paragon: pious and learned. The king called her 'Sweet Sister Temperance', and her person is already festooned with the virgin's pearls that would be her visual autograph. Watchful intelligence describes the face, with its strong set of jaw and the long, rather bony nose, while the index finger of her left hand marks the page of her book as if impatient to continue a grudgingly interrupted reading. Elizabeth already knew her strengths, even when she was being disingenuously modest about her other qualities. 'For the face I *might* well blush to offer,' she wrote to her little brother-king, 'but for the mind I shall never be ashamed to present.'

She was not yet free of suspicion, though. Until she became queen on 17 November 1558 Elizabeth's life was finely balanced between vindication and disgrace. Out of the dark Boleyn eyes she watched herself being watched. But she was an adolescent, playful like her mother, and inevitably there were times when her guard was down. One of those times nearly ruined her.

It came when it was least expected. Until they were interrupted by scandal, the first years of Edward VI's reign were the best times of Elizabeth's young life. The hitherto unimpeachably Christian queen dowager, Catherine Parr, had raised eyebrows by marrying the man with whom she had been amorously involved before Henry VIII came along, interrupting their own marital plans. He was the Lord High Admiral, Thomas Seymour, Edward VI's uncle, and the brother of the power in the land, Edward Seymour, Duke of Somerset and Lord Protector. Thomas was thirty-eight, charismatically good-looking and consumed with ambition. Very soon, much too soon for some people, Catherine was pregnant. And that, according to the testimony given against Seymour in 1549, was when the trouble started.

Before he married Catherine Parr, Thomas Seymour had decided that he might himself be a match for Elizabeth, then just fourteen but by the aristocratic standards of the time certainly nubile. His brother, the Lord Protector, had been appalled at the temerity and had forbidden it out of hand. But in the Seymour ménage at Sudeley

Castle, Gloucestershire, where Elizabeth spent some months, the admiral turned horseplay into something dangerously like flirting. According to Elizabeth's governess, Kat Ashley, he would come into her bedchamber early in the morning 'before she were ready' dressed 'only in his nightgown...bare-legged'.

> If she were up he would bid her good morrow and ask her how she did, and strike her upon the back or the buttocks familiarly...And if she were in her bed he would put open the curtains...and make as though he would come at her. And she would go further into the bed so that he could not come at her. And one morning he strave [*sic*] to have kissed her in bed and this examinate [Kat] was there and bade him go away for shame.

But was Kat Ashley laughing or frowning when she said this? Was the bottom-slapping just innocent merriment in keeping with the improbable English reputation for physical displays of affection? Or was the wicked uncle groping the heir to the throne? For a while, Catherine herself joined in the fun, if that's what it was, restraining Elizabeth while the admiral slashed a black dress she was wearing to ribbons. Soon Catherine stopped smiling and started scowling. Pregnant and 'suspecting the often access of the Admiral to the Lady Elizabeth's Grace [Catherine] came suddenly upon them, where they were all alone (he having her in his arms) wherefore she fell out both with the Lord Admiral and her Grace also'. The demure Elizabeth, who at twelve had given Catherine a translation of Marguerite of Navarre's *Meditations of a Sinful Soul,* with its warnings against fornication with false lovers, had been unmasked as a shocking little tease, or at the very least, a victim of Seymour's criminal impulsiveness. For everyone's sake she was sent packing.

The serious business, however, had only just begun. Catherine Parr died in childbirth just a few weeks after Elizabeth's departure from her house. Undaunted, Thomas Seymour busied himself with a conspiracy to substitute the power of his brother with his own. Edward VI was to be kidnapped and married to Lady Jane Grey. He would be the new Protector. Slightly drunk, he got as far as the king's bedroom door before Edward's loyal spaniel did his duty and barked the plot into fiasco. Seymour was arrested, taken to the Tower and charged with thirty-three separate offences. One of them was the design to marry Elizabeth without the consent of council, itself an indisputable act of treason.

Kat Ashley was interrogated along with Elizabeth's cofferer who had witnessed the goings-on at Sudeley, and although she supplied all the details of the romps in the princess's bedroom at Sudeley, much to the exasperation of her interrogator Sir

Robert Tyrwhit, Kat refused to incriminate the princess in any kind of conspiracy against the king, the council or the state. When Elizabeth was herself interrogated, unsettling memories must have come rushing back – of the stories told about her mother and of cousin Catherine – but, as so often when she was in deep trouble, Elizabeth drew on deep reserves of fortitude. She told the truth plainly, with no attempt to fudge or extenuate, admitting she knew about Seymour's ambition to marry her but denying that she ever gave him the least encouragement. To the Lord Protector Somerset she protested her innocence of Seymour's designs on her:

> My Lord. Master Tyrwhit and others have told me that there goeth rumours abroad which be greatly against my honour and honesty (which above all I esteem) which be these: that I am in the Tower; and with child by my lord admiral. My lord these are shameful slanders for the which besides the great desire I have to see the King's Majesty I most heartily desire your lordship that I may come to the court after your first determination that I may show myself there as I am.
>
> Written in haste from Atfelde [Hatfield] this 28 January
> Your assured friend to *my* little power
> Elizabeth

She was, remember, just fifteen. But it took great art to seem this artless. Scared though she must have been, Elizabeth was sufficiently in command of herself to ask, indeed almost to demand, that the Lord Protector publish a proclamation 'into the countries' (counties) ordering people to 'refrain their tongues declaring how the tales be but lies'. Even though she could have no memory of her mother's fate, Elizabeth was fighting as Anne could not, to protect her crucial asset: the good name that would preserve her claim to the throne and her claim to a powerful marriage. No one was going to want an unchaste princess for a bride.

In March 1549 the hapless Thomas Seymour was executed. On his last night on earth he used the metal ferrules on the laces that tied his stockings to his doublet to write letters of explanation and sheepish regret to both Elizabeth and Mary. In his idiotic way he was obviously deeply fond of them both. The letters, of course, never reached their destination.

It was a brutally early education in the perils of sexual politics. Elizabeth's sense of disquiet that any day she might be a victim of innuendo could not have been helped when her half-sister, Mary, had the first parliament of her reign declare lawful the marriage of her own mother Catherine of Aragon with Henry VIII. This made

Elizabeth, once more, a bastard. Although no one dared, formally, to annul her place in the succession, she was humiliated by having the daughters of Henry VIII's sisters given precedence over her at court and by being spied on as a potential focus for Protestant resistance. When Wyatt made his futile attempt to prevent Mary from marrying Philip of Spain, Elizabeth was bound to be in very serious trouble. On the scaffold Wyatt insisted she had had no prior knowledge of the plot, and Elizabeth herself denied ever receiving the letter it was claimed he had sent her. But she was, nonetheless, held in close confinement at St James's Palace. Then came the ominous order from the queen and council to have her moved to the Tower. Her cousin, Jane Grey, the two-week queen, was still in the Tower, certain to face death on the block. Just beyond the walls, the disembowelled remains of the Wyatt rebels were still hanging from gibbets.

As she was being taken by barge to the prison, Elizabeth suddenly remembered a remark made by Somerset before he, too, had been executed: that if he had allowed his brother, Thomas, a last-minute interview, he probably would not have condemned him to the block. Not unreasonably, Elizabeth now became convinced that only an audience with Mary would save her. So she wrote a letter insisting on her innocence, quoting Somerset's remorse and imploring the queen to see her. Her state of mind makes its way into her beautiful hand only as the tight, elegant calligraphy of its opening lines gives way to larger swooping letters towards the end as her thoughts and words become more agitated. At the bottom, to forestall any ill-disposed parties adding anything compromising to her own words, Elizabeth drew freehand diagonal lines, flowing down the page like wavelets on the Thames. And as she wrote and wrote, the tidal water of the river rose − so that by the time she was done there was no room beneath London Bridge to take her to the Tower. Who says that good handwriting can't save your life?

The following day she was rowed again to the Tower, entering not, as legend says, by the Traitor's Gate but by the tradesmen's entrance at the side. But this was not a hospitable place to be. Tradition has it that, sitting on the damp stone, her voice barely rising above the tears, Elizabeth said to her little company of servants: 'I pray you all good friends and fellows bear me witness that I come in no traitor but as a true woman to the Queen's majesty as any now living.' Elizabeth spent two months in the Tower. There were quarrels about her food, Queen Mary insisting that she eat from the lieutenant's table like any other prisoner rather than from her own provisions. She could walk on the leads between Beauchamp and Bell Tower, under close watch. In April 1554 she was released and taken to Richmond Palace, so nervous that she assumed that this was to be the place of her execution. But after a year of house arrest at Woodstock, she finally got her audience with Mary, who was displeased that Elizabeth 'stiffly persevere[d] in the truth'.

This time, biology was her friend. Concerned that Mary's pregnancies might herald not life but death, her husband King Philip took prudent steps to become reconciled with Elizabeth, dissuading Mary from any thought of excluding her from the succession and, in fact, persuading the queen to set her at liberty. A Protestant England, Philip hoped, might better be pre-empted by marrying Elizabeth off to a suitable Catholic prince, but grateful though she was for her freedom, Elizabeth was not about to surrender it. Writing to Mary she protested:

> I so well like this estate [spinsterhood] as I persuade myself there is not any kind of life comparable unto it…What I shall do hereafter I know not but I assure you upon my truth and fidelity and as God be merciful unto me I am not at this present time otherwise minded than I have declared unto you, no though I were offered to the greatest prince of all Europe. And yet percase the Queen's Majesty may perceive this my answer rather to proceed of a maidenly shame-fastedness than upon any certain determination.

By the autumn of 1558 it was obvious to everyone except Mary that her swollen abdomen was a tumour not a baby. The heretics were still going up in smoke, but the roads to Hatfield House in Hertfordshire, where Elizabeth now lived, were jammed with traffic as the loyal English nobility overtook each other to trade allegiance. The Spanish ambassador, Count Feria, who went to see her amid the throng, was disconcerted by the difference between the two Tudor half-sisters. 'She is a very vain and clever woman. She must have been thoroughly schooled in the manner in which her father conducted his affairs and I am very much afraid that she will not be well-disposed in matters of religion…There is not a heretic or traitor in all the kingdom who has not joyfully raised himself from the grave to come to her side. She is determined to be governed by no one.'

On 17 November 1558 a messenger arrived from London with the long-awaited news. A cherished tradition has it that Elizabeth was standing or seated beside an ancient oak when she heard of her sister's death, taking the ring that had been removed from Mary's finger and slipping it on her own. Kneeling beneath the tree she then spoke in Latin a verse from Psalm 118: '*A domino factum est mirabile in oculis nostris*' (This is the Lord's doing and it is marvellous in our eyes).

It is one of the most familiar and cherished tableaux in all English history: the golden girl beneath the oak, about to inaugurate the nation's great age. But the supporting role taken by the tree is crucial to the mythical effect. So much of English history is oaken. Ancient Britons were thought to have worshipped them; righteous outlaws are sheltered by them; kings on the run hide in them; hearts of oak go to sea and win empires. It would only be in the next century – in, for example, John Evelyn's *Sylva* (1664) – that ancient trees would be explicitly seen as symbols of national durability. But the Hatfield oak – knotty and gnarled, storm-struck but standing – is Elizabeth's first loyal supporter. It was, in effect, England bringing the strength and weight of its tradition to the proclamation of a momentous rebirth.

But did the English really feel like this? There's no doubt that many, rich and poor alike, looked to the new monarch for desperately needed relief. The last years of Mary's reign had brought brutal winters, pitiful, sodden harvests and soaring food prices; there were armies (so it was said) of vagabonds on the road; the plague had returned; and Calais had been humiliatingly lost (the direct result of fighting a war for King Philip). When Elizabeth made her formal entry into London before the coronation (the date, 15 January 1559, decided by her astrologer John Dee as the most auspicious), there was snow on the freshly gravelled roads but, according to one contemporary, 'nothing but gladness, nothing but prayer and nothing but comfort'. Of course, the celebrations and pageants were elaborately staged propaganda events, paid for by the corporations of merchants who were eager to see an end to Mary's wars and the recovery of prosperity. And they were carefully designed to inaugurate a scripture of the young queen as the personification of wisdom, piety and justice: the new Deborah. Although it was customary for all monarchs to stay in the Tower of London before their coronation, Elizabeth's second journey there by water, of course, took on personal meaning, both for herself and for the people, erasing painful memories of her captivity and replacing them with festive anticipation. In the very first speech of her reign she compared her own history to that of the prophet Daniel, brought safely out of the lion's den (and there *were* lions in the Tower) by God's miraculous deliverance. Each stage of the planned route was carefully designed to distinguish her reign from that of her sister. In another obviously rehearsed move, Elizabeth graciously received an English Bible from the allegorical personification of Truth and, according to the official eulogistic book of *The Queen Majesty's Passage*, 'reverently did she with both her hands take it, kiss it and lay it upon her breast to the great comfort of the lookers on'.

For the most ardent Protestants, however, this charade of piety was not enough to compensate for the misfortune of having another woman on the throne, at best a hazardous state of affairs and at worst a wholly unnatural reversal of the divinely sanctioned relation between the sexes. The stock description of women as 'the weaker vessel' had first appeared in Tyndale's 1526 English Bible, and Protestant manuals on the proper household regimen routinely repeated it together with the necessary sub-servience of women to men. And what was the kingdom, after all, but a household writ large? To John Knox, the Scottish Calvinist preacher, Marian exile and author of *The First Blast of the Trumpet against the Monstrous Regiment of Women* (1558), the reign of so many women – Mary Tudor, Mary of Guise in Scotland, Catherine de' Medici in France – was a 'monstriferous abomination', a species of plague. It was, in fact, the obvious explanation why the times were so manifestly out of joint. Women, Knox wrote, echoing the commonplaces of the day, 'ought to be constant, stable, prudent and doing everything with discretion and reason, virtues which women cannot have in equality with men…Nature I say doth paint [women] further to be weak, frail, impatient, feeble and foolish and experience hath declared them to be inconstant, variable and cruel and lacking the spirit of counsel and regiment…in the nature of all women lurketh such vices as in good governors are not tolerable.'

Learning of Elizabeth's accession, Knox was concerned enough not to damage the chances for a Protestant government in England to write to William Cecil, the queen's new secretary of state, and explain (though not retract) his diatribe. Like many other critics of female rule, Knox was prepared to concede that Elizabeth might be considered a special case, sent by God to fulfil his purposes of restoring the gospel. But his insistence that she must nevertheless acknowledge that womanly rule was 'repugnant' to the Almighty's proper order was not calculated to endear him to the young queen. There was, however, plenty of support for Knox's views within England itself. *The Homily of the State of Matrimony*, read from the pulpit in Protestant churches, reiterated the litany of failings lodged in female flesh, 'all weak affections'. John Aylmer, later to be Bishop of London, whose *An Harborowe for Faithfull and Trewe Subjects* (1559) was supposed to be a refutation of Knox's tract, nonetheless felt obliged to write that God's otherwise bewildering selection of another woman, 'weak in nature, feeble in body, soft in courage, unskilful in practice, not terrible to the enemy', to be ruler could only be explained as a test of his ability to work miracles.

Everyone in the ruling class (and beyond) knew the remedy for this misfortune: matrimony. To the objection (perhaps felt by Elizabeth herself) that she could not in good conscience subject herself to a husband without compromising her magisterial authority, Aylmer neatly invoked the convenient doctrine of the prince's two bodies. As a natural woman, he observed, Elizabeth might, indeed, be subordinate to her hus-band, but as ruler she would be subject to no one but God. With the husbandly authority problem taken care of, parliament was petitioning the queen to marry as early as February 1559. And Elizabeth may not have been as marriage-averse as most

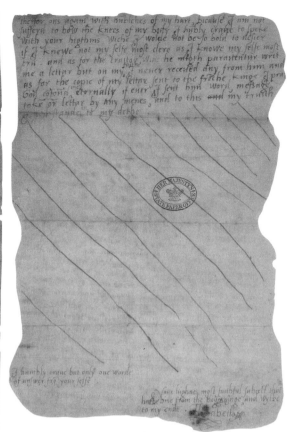

Top: The 'Tide Letter', written by Elizabeth as she travelled to the Tower by barge on the Thames in 1554.
Above: Elizabeth in her coronation robes, by an unknown artist.

biographers have assumed. When Prince Erik of Sweden had offered himself during Edward's reign, it is true that she had asked her half-brother if she might not 'remain in that estate I was which of all others best liked and pleased me', her maidenhood. And she had said something of the sort again in Mary's time. But now the security of the realm and the fate of the Protestant settlement depended on her capacity to give the country an heir. And Elizabeth, who always had a steely grip on political reality, knew just what was required of her. The famous response to parliament's petition, always invoked as evidence of her reluctance to be married, was, in fact, put into her mouth by William Camden many decades later. Its great peroration, that 'in the end this shall be for me sufficient, that a marble stone shall declare that a Queen having reigned such a time lived and died a virgin', sounds more like a prospective epitaph than a declaration of intent. It was surely part of the propaganda of the later part of her reign, when the queen's perpetual virginity was turned from a liability into a patriotic cult. But it was not what Elizabeth said at the time. Instead, she concentrated not on *whether* she should marry (which was all but taken for granted), but on the credentials of the likely candidates. In particular, she promised that: 'Whensoever it may please God to incline my heart to another kind of life, ye may well assure yourselves my meaning is not to do or determine anything wherewith the realm may or shall have just cause to be discontented. And whomsoever my chance shall light upon I trust he shall be as careful for the realm and you.'

In other words, Elizabeth would not make Mary's mistake of marrying a prince whose ambition and religion would damage, rather than sustain, the interests of England. Better take some time to find the right man than to hurry along to the altar and to disaster. Others, though, felt the queen did not have the luxury of leisurely selection. For Secretary Cecil nothing could be more urgent. He and his Edwardian Protestant colleagues on the council, like his brother-in-law Nicholas Bacon, and Francis Knollys, had all personally suffered through the years of Mary's counter-Reformation, either as exiles or banished to the political wilderness. They knew perfectly well that the majority of the country was still Catholic, either actively or passively. The compromise religious settlement of 1559, with its conciliatory demotion of the sovereign from 'Supreme Head' to 'Supreme Governor' of the Church, had barely passed through parliament and then only over the opposition of *all* the bishops and seven lay peers. For that matter, there must have been times, even early in the reign, when Cecil wondered just how much of a good Protestant the queen actually was. For although she had stormed out of the Chapel Royal when a priest attempted to celebrate mass at Christmas, she later made it known that she would like a crucifix there. Elizabeth was also prepared to allow wafers (though unornamented) in communion, had communion tables moved up to the chancel where stone altars had been positioned and positively insisted on traditional vestments for the clergy. For Cecil, this may all have been a distasteful holding operation, needed to keep English Catholics loyal while very gradually evangelizing the country, but was uneasily aware that no one was really satisfied by the compromises, except possibly Elizabeth herself.

The dilemma faced Cecil every day at council. Even though he had drastically reduced the size of the council, the better to monitor its loyalty, he still had to sit across the table from a number of Mary's councillors, like Sir William Petre and the Marquis of Winchester, whom the queen had hoped to neutralize by co-option. Many of the great magnates of the country – the Percys and Dacres, as well as Pembroke and Arundel – were still very much Catholics, and all this only heightened Cecil's sense of insecurity. He and his colleagues knew just how little it took for everything to be undone. Elizabeth might fall victim to the plague, the sweating sickness or smallpox, the last of which did, indeed, bring her close to death in October 1562, or she might be assassinated, like so many other princes of high estate who vainly imagined themselves impregnable to the knife or bullet.

So although the queen kept telling parliament and the Privy Council that in good time she would see to the matter of her marriage but that it was her, not their, business, Cecil and the others could hardly forbear from reminding her of England's desperate need for an heir. As a New Year's gift in 1560 Sir Thomas Chaloner gave the queen a book singing the praises of her father, adding in the dedication the hope that she would 'bestow the bonds of your modesty on a husband…For then a little Henry will play in the palace for us.' She may well have bridled a little at the implication that her own reign was nothing more than an unfortunate interruption in the proper continuity of kings and that her principal duty was to make good the deficiency by supplying another one.

The emphasis that she was more than a 'mere' woman began early. But *if* a candidate came along who fitted all the proper criteria – high station, pragmatic in confession, impeccable lineage, massive wealth – the young Elizabeth was certainly prepared to give him a look. Between 1559 and 1566 there was no shortage of suitors. The most powerful, Philip II, had virtually begun his courtship before his wife's death, but since Elizabeth had gone to such lengths to dissociate herself from her half-sister's reign and insisted so often that she would never compromise the country for the interests of a foreign prince, his candidacy was never a real possibility. Philip's crime, in the sight of English opinion, had not, in fact, been the burning of heretics so much as the loss of Calais in a war believed to have been fought for

Spanish interests. Other possibilities, such as the Archduke Charles of Austria, were also handicapped by their ardent Catholicism. Elizabeth and even some of the Protestant members of council could see their way to having a Catholic consort, provided that he could be expected, in due course, to convert, provided that he observed his rituals in private and provided that he agreed to children being brought up in the Reformed Church. But these were precisely the concessions that none of the serious Catholic candidates, either Habsburg or French, was prepared to make.

There were some Protestant suitors in the long line for her attention. But like Sir William Pickering, whose name was being bandied about early in the 1560s, they were generally thought (not least by Elizabeth herself) to be embarrassingly beneath her station and dignity. And there was one more painful headache for Cecil. If he pushed the queen too hard, too soon, she might just plump for the man everyone assumed she really loved. He was Protestant and he was English. Unfortunately for Cecil, he was also Robert Dudley.

Dudley was everything Cecil was not. His line did not, in fact, go back very far, but he gave himself the airs of ancient aristocratic pedigree. He was flashily gallant rather than sober and temperate; impetuous rather than judicious. He was exuberant, impassioned and, not least, incredibly good-looking, especially on a horse. To a queen who more than once dismissed from her presence those (of either sex) she thought physically unpleasing, this mattered a lot. They would make, undeniably, a handsome couple. What was more, she and Robert Dudley shared a lot of past. His father, John Dudley, Earl of Northumberland, had ousted Protector Somerset from power and sent him to the block before he, in turn, had been executed for attempting to put Lady Jane Grey on the throne. So Robert and Elizabeth were, in some sense, both orphans of the scaffold. He had been educated with her half-brother Edward, and had shared the formidable Ascham with Elizabeth. In the grim years of Mary's reign, he had sympathized with her troubles and, more importantly, he had done something about it, selling some of the Dudley lands to make Elizabeth's life a little easier at a time he could ill afford it. Things like that she never forgot. Whatever else they were, there was a sense in which they thought of each other as soulmates, almost brother and sister. Her nickname for him was 'Eyes', and he signed his letters to her 'OO'. No one at court watching them dance the volta thought they had eyes for anyone else.

How much of a couple were they? It's not just Hollywood movie-makers who have thought that Elizabeth and Dudley were lovers. The demonstrative physical affection they showed startled contemporaries and had gossips all over Europe, including the Spanish ambassador in England, convinced they must have been sleeping together. Rumours abounded that the queen was pregnant by Dudley, and long into her reign stories circulated in popular culture of their bastards, sometimes two, sometimes four, spirited away by ships or even killed in infancy. An English spy caught in Madrid in 1587 told King Philip's English secretary that he was really one 'Arthur Dudley', the illegitimate son of Robert and Elizabeth. At least one country priest was reported to have called Elizabeth a whore because she was a dancer and as far as he was concerned one was the same as the other. Their intimacy was all the more shocking given that it seemed to pay no account to Dudley's marriage to Amy Robsart. Elizabeth, of course, was well aware of Amy, but she also knew that Dudley's wife was very ill, probably of breast cancer, and unlikely to survive for much longer. Sleeping with your intended was not unusual in Tudor England. Close to one in five brides were pregnant on their wedding day, and given low rates of conception this suggests that a lot more than 20 per cent of engaged couples were having premarital sex. And of course it was not only common but expected for male sovereigns to keep themselves healthy by the regular expulsion of sperm, courtesy of a mistress.

But what passed as matter of fact among the people, or among male princes, would still have been seen as outrageous for a queen who had displayed the unshorn tresses of the virgin at her coronation. Given the history of her mother and the Seymour scandal (however innocent Elizabeth's part in it), she would hardly need reminding that as far as many of her subjects were concerned, her body natural and her body politic were one and the same, and she was not free to do with either what her heart desired. When pressed about the innuendos, however, she reacted with defensive vexation, informing the busybodies that while the rumours were a disgraceful slander, should she ever choose to lead the 'dishonourable life' there was no one she knew of who had the authority to stop her.

Cecil, of course, was beside himself. Impotently watching Elizabeth shower honours, money and gifts on Dudley in September 1560, he told the Spanish ambassador that he was staring at 'the ruin of the realm' through Dudley's 'intimacy with the queen who surrendered all affairs to him and meant to marry him'. For Cecil this was tantamount to handing over England to what he believed was a self-serving dynastic faction. (Robert's brother Ambrose was also a member of council, but so was Cecil's brother-in-law, Sir Nicholas Bacon.) Secretary Cecil stopped at nothing to thwart the love match, spreading malicious stories that Dudley was actually poisoning his wife. And two days after he had poured out his chagrin to the Spanish ambassador his worst nightmare seemed to have come true. Amy Dudley had been found at the bottom of a staircase in the house of friends, dead of a broken neck. Suicide seems a distinct possibility, for she must have been in dreadful pain and had insisted that her hosts leave the house some hours before her life ended. The coroners called it accidental death. It was said that the advanced breast cancer from which she had been suffering had made her bones so brittle that a fatal fall was likely. But to those who had a dim view of the Dudley–Elizabeth romance, an accident of that kind seemed much too convenient to be credible. This was the golden age of gossip, and gossip did not believe Amy Dudley had fallen. Gossip believed she had been pushed.

Without wasting any time, the queen ordered the court into mourning and sent Dudley away to Kew until he was cleared of any sinister suspicion, which officially he was. But although Elizabeth loyally insisted that he had been completely vindicated from anything untoward, she well knew that what had happened had made their marriage impossible. She very badly wanted, even in 1560, to be a sovereign loved by her people. And a marriage with a suspected accomplice in marital murder guaranteed (as the history of Mary of Scotland would demonstrate) a public relations disaster.

Even so, neither the queen nor, especially, Dudley himself was quite ready to give up. In 1561, the Spanish ambassador was asked on to a barge from which Dudley and Elizabeth were happily watching a water pageant, and he reported that: 'She, Robert and I being alone on the galley, they began joking which she likes to do much more than talking about business. They went so far with their jokes that Lord Robert told her that if she liked I could be minister to perform the act of marriage and she, nothing loath to hear it, said she was not sure whether I knew enough English.' But this may have been a lot less comical than the ambassador thought. For Dudley was so desperate to see the marriage come about that he planned something unthinkable. He held out the promise that he and Elizabeth would return England to Rome if Philip II would lend his support to the marriage and help deal with the guaranteed disaffection. The plan went so far that soundings were actually made of the pope.

It would have been the most shocking irony of all: the English Church as the plaything of the Tudors' marriage bed. The mother's desire had brought about the break with Rome. Now the daughter's passion would repair it.

But Cecil was not about to let this happen. He made sure to leak the story, and the storm of outrage he had been counting on broke immediately, both among the older nobility, who did not much care for Dudley, and the people in the cities. Anti-Catholic riots seemed close. The partners hastily backed off, denying that there had ever been any plans to restore the old Church or to do any kind of deal with Spain.

Even though the danger was past, William Cecil never quite relaxed on the subject of the Master of the Horse. Pushing his own favourite nominee, the Archduke

Charles of Austria, he made a list of 'pros and cons' in which Dudley (created Earl of Leicester in 1564) came off worse in every category of comparison.

	Charles	Dudley
In degree	Archduke *born*	Earl MADE
In wealth	By report 3000 a year	All of ye Queen and in debt
In knowledge	All qualities belonging to a prince	Meet for a courtier
In reputation	Honoured of all, named to ye empire	Hated of many, his wife's death

Perhaps Cecil need not have worked quite so hard, because the truth is that Elizabeth herself was not quite sure that Dudley was grand enough for her. In 1565 she told the French ambassador that: 'As for the Earl of Leicester, I have always loved his virtues but the aspiration to greatness and honour which is in me could not suffer him as companion and husband.'

Perhaps, though, he might still father an heir to the throne – but not by her. For by 1563 Elizabeth was seriously prepared to offer him up in marriage to Mary Stuart, the queen of the Scots.

Scotland had always mattered desperately to the Welsh Tudors. Something about the kingdom to the north provoked their characteristic combination of arrogance and insecurity. That something was, of course, the 'auld alliance', in which the English imagined themselves attacked simultaneously on two fronts, by the French and the Scots. But the relationship between cause and effect depended, of course, on which side of the Tweed you stood. From the Scottish side it was the (largely correct) suspicion that the Tudors clung to the old Plantagenet fantasy of imposing their 'overlordship' on Scotland that left them no alternative but to seek help from France. The Stone of Destiny, after all, was still in Westminster Abbey So the two paranoias bounced off each other, generation after generation, with invariably tragic results.

The Tudors had two Scottish strategies, neither of them enormously subtle: whackings and weddings. Henry VII's preference had been for weddings, and he married his elder daughter, Margaret, to the Stewart king James IV. But this did not stop Henry VIII from going to war with Scotland twice, at the beginning and end of his reign, both times with equally devastating results for Scotland. Among the indirect casualties of the battle of Solway Moss in 1542 was Henry VIII's nephew, James V, who survived the slaughter of his own nobles and soldiers, but died shortly after in a state of traumatized misery. James left behind two Marys: his French widow, Mary of Guise, as regent and their infant daughter, Mary, already the baby queen of the Scots.

Two possible courses of action were open to Mary of Guise and her councillors. She could cut her losses by a reconciliation with England, based on the marriage Henry VIII was offering between his infant son, Edward, and the little Mary, or she could plump for her enemy's enemy, her own countrymen, the French, and continue the war for as long as it took. The difficulty with the pro-English solution was that the regent was sister to both Henry II, the king of France, and the Cardinal of Lorraine, both of them the most implacable enemies of the Protestant Reformation. However conservative and quasi-Catholic Henry VIII might have appeared at the end of his reign, he was still a heretic who had usurped the authority of the Holy Father in his realm. To send her little Marie south to be brought up as a bride for a Protestant prince was, in the end, too much to stomach. And there was the additional suspicion that the enticing vision of a peaceful union of the realms promised by Henry Tudor would, somehow, not turn out to be an equal partnership. So the infant princess was shipped back to France to grow up at the French court, with the understanding that one day she would be queen to a good Catholic Valois.

Henry took the rejection personally and began his 'rough wooing' by burning down most of the Scottish lowlands. But not all the Scottish nobility were, in fact, affronted by the strong-arm tactics. There was an important party led by Princess Mary's illegitimate half-brother, James Stewart, Earl of Moray, who saw the English as saviours not bullies. And the reason was that many of them had converted to Protestantism. An English alliance was a way to get the French troops imported by Mary of Guise out of Scotland and bring the country to the true Kirk. Fired up with the Calvinist righteousness provided by John Knox and his fellow preachers, in 1557 the Scottish Protestants made a covenant among themselves, binding themselves as the 'Lords of the Congregation'. Their aim was the overthrow of Mary of Guise and the irreversible establishment of a reformed Scotland. Two years later, the Lords of the Congregation made an alliance with the English government (heavily promoted by Cecil) in which English intervention was promised to 'restore the ancient liberties and freedom of Scotland'. This sort of thing, of course, sets off alarm bells in nationalist history as a tactic of transparently disingenuous imperialism, but at the time neither side saw the alliance as a Trojan horse for English annexation. Cecil's aim was just to secure a friendly, Protestant neighbour to the north. At a time when England was virtually encircled by Catholic armies – in France, in the Netherlands and in Spain – it would simply be one headache less.

So there was yet another campaign in the spring of 1560. But Elizabeth (as so often was the case when it came to military matters) was chronically indecisive, kept fretting about whether she should put the whole thing into reverse and was ruinously

Top: Elizabeth I: the 'Clopton Portrait', by an unknown artist, *c*. 1560–5.
Above: Queen Elizabeth dancing the volta with Robert Dudley, by an unknown artist, *c*. 1581.

conservative when it came to providing adequate supplies of men and money to do the job. For their part, her commanders, like the Duke of Norfolk, felt they had to do something swiftly before she could pull out. So they botched a siege of Leith in which, to add insult to injury (and there were *many* injuries), a company of Scottish whores, unhappy about the imminent expulsion of their steady French clientele, threw burning coals down on the attacking English troops. An embarrassing fiasco was forestalled only when Mary of Guise died unexpectedly, leaving her many enemies to sign the Treaty of Edinburgh. To sweeten the peace, Cecil added something momentous even if as yet unofficial: that it might be possible to recognize Mary Stuart as the presumptive heir to the throne of England should the queen herself remain unmarried and childless. Britain was in the offing.

But there were two crucial conditions. First, the claim (made by Henry II of France on Mary Tudor's death) that Mary of Scotland was the rightful sovereign of England and that Elizabeth was still illegitimate had to be formally renounced right away. Second, now that Mary's husband, the next French king, Francis II, had died (of the worst ear infection in European history) and she was free to remarry, Elizabeth should have the right to ensure that any future husband would not be a threat.

There was, of course, one handy solution to both these problems, which began as a joke made by Mary herself, and then developed into a rich fantasy by Elizabeth's ambassador to Scotland, Nicholas Throckmorton. 'Methinketh it were to be wishes of all wise men and Her Majesty's Good Subjects that one of these two queens of the Isle of Britain were transformed into the shape of a man to make so happy a marriage as thereby there might be a unity of the whole.'

No one even bothered to ask, of course, which of the two would play the man. (Robert Cecil would later remark that Elizabeth was 'more than a man and, in truth, less than a woman'.) Lurking beneath the fantasy was the sense, instinctively felt by many in both countries, that the queens were, in fact, the two halves of a single personality. It wasn't just that Tudor blood ran in both their veins – they shared the same great-grandfather, Henry VII, and the same long nose – it seemed, somehow, that their histories were, for better or worse, already fatefully connected.

They had grown up quite differently. For the most part Elizabeth had lived in aristocratic, but relatively modest, provincial houses; sternly educated, her routine had been punctuated by elation when things went well, and terror when they went wrong. By the time of her accession she already had the skills of a survivor and was suspicious of fair-weather friends. Mary, on the other hand, had been treated as the darling of the most glittering court of Europe precisely at the moment when at Fontainebleau, Amboise and Chenonceau it was creating the greatest masterpieces of

Renaissance palace architecture. The fact that her mother was off in Scotland governing as regent only made her uncle, Henry II, cosset her more lavishly: the fair-faced little Scottish doll cultivated as a northern flower amid the heavily perfumed lilies of the Valois court. So *la belle des belles*, as Mary was called, grew up in a culture of gallant desire. With her heart-shaped face, creamy complexion, auburn hair and almond-shaped, heavy-lidded eyes, she evidently had the stuff to make men, especially poets, pant with dreams of possession.

She was, however, not just a pretty face. When she arrived in Scotland in 1560 it was Mary, not Elizabeth, who might well have seemed the more serious and responsible of the two queens. She, after all, was not deep in a reckless flirtation. Elizabeth had behaved badly, almost irrationally, towards her cousin, denying her safe-conduct through England and forcing Mary to sail the long route offshore to Scotland. Elizabeth's point (as it would be for years to come) was that Mary had not yet signed the treaty removing the offensive claim to the English throne. But Mary responded to Elizabeth's harshness with the brand of theatrical self-pity that would colour the relationship between the two women. Before her departure she told Elizabeth's envoy in France: 'I trust the wind will be so favourable as I shall not need to come on the coast of England and if I do, Monsieur l'Ambassadeur, the Queen your mistress shall have me in her hands to do her will of me and if she be so hard-hearted as to desire my end, she may then do her pleasure and make sacrifice of me, peradventure that casualty might be better for me than to live.' It did not, of course, come to this. There was a passing of royal galleys on the high seas with nothing more serious exchanged between them than a salute. Once in Scotland, Mary wrote many times in an attempt to meet Elizabeth, hoping that the tantalizing matter of the succession could be settled face to face. But although this was never far from Elizabeth's mind, the more she thought about it, the less she liked the idea of a public statement making Mary her heir. Already feeling insecure and threatened, such an announcement would, she thought, be an invitation for her removal. In Elizabeth's own words it would be to 'require me in my own life to set a winding sheet before my own eyes. Think, you, that I could love my own winding sheet?'

The ill-will would evaporate, though, into cousinly warmth once Mary made a choice of husband that Elizabeth deemed politically friendly: hence her willingness to serve up Robert Dudley. But if Elizabeth thought Dudley too much her social inferior to marry him, why should Mary feel differently? And in any case, since the death of his wife he was damaged goods. To accept the queen of England's compromised cast-off was not exactly what *la belle des belles* had in mind. On the other hand, Lord Henry Darnley, the poster-boy of the Scottish nobility, seemed quite a different prospect. Unlike Dudley, his pedigree was impeccable, being a cousin of both queens, yet another grandchild of the adventurous sister of Henry VIII, Mary Tudor, who after Brandon's death had married Darnley's father, the Earl of Lennox. Even by Renaissance standards, Darnley was, as long as he kept his mouth shut, a walking work of art. One look at those finely chiselled cheekbones and the smoothly modelled calves and Mary was hopelessly smitten. It was only after the nuptials in 1565 that she discovered that, in addition to the blood royal flowing through his veins, there was a great deal of strong liquor. When he was not smashed, Darnley, who was now supposed to be a working king of Scotland, was usually absent without leave, hunting, hawking or whoring and certainly not available for the tedious drudgery of state business.

Left to her own devices, Mary increasingly depended on her own court circle and, in particular, on one of her private secretaries, the Italian David Riccio, who, much to the displeasure of the Scottish magnates, jealously guarded access to the queen. Worse still, the leader of the Protestant nobility, her half-brother, the Earl of Moray, suggested to the English government that Mary was considering a full counter-Reformation in Scotland. In fact, although much of the country, especially in the north and west, was still overwhelmingly Catholic, Mary was not that rash. Since returning to Scotland she had followed her mother's careful distinction between private observance and public policy. She made no secret of her Catholic faith but equally professed she would never foist it on the country by force. This, of course, did nothing to satisfy the likes of Knox, who treated her to regular lectures on the abominations of papist idolatry. Barely a year before, the Protestant Scots had been dismayed by Mary's serious consideration of marriage with Prince Carlos, Philip II's son. And then she had insisted on marrying Darnley according to the Catholic rite. When they looked at France and saw the all-out war being waged by her Guise family on the Huguenots, it took very little to convince them that Mary was, indeed, planning a counter-Reformation.

Darnley managed to whine about never being given enough dignity or responsibility and then whine even more when he got it. His increasing estrangement from his wife and his undisguised wish to be treated as a real, rather than as a titular, king gave the disaffected Protestant nobles an opening they eagerly took. A group of them – the Earl of Morton and Sir William Maitland in particular – approached Darnley and proposed a violent *coup d'état*. Get rid of the detestable Riccio, whom they said out loud was Mary's lover, notwithstanding the fact that he was a hunchback and a half-size bigger than a dwarf. Everyone knew about the wicked lechery of hunchbacks. The revelation must have suddenly lit a candle in the dimness of Darnley's pretty head. It would explain the queen's hostility and surliness. She needed to be shown in no uncertain terms who was master and before the child she was carrying was born, or else there would be someone else to push him aside. So began a sequence of events as bloodcurdling as anything in the more gruesome pages of Elizabethan melodrama. On 7 March 1566 Darnley, who seldom showed up for dinner, burst into the chamber at Holyrood Palace where Mary was dining and began to harangue her drunkenly about Riccio. He was swiftly followed by a group of the conspirators, led by Lord Ruthven (whom most people had thought was on his own deathbed), ominously got up in full armour and shouting for 'Davy' to be brought forth. Riccio was dragged from his hiding place, screaming with terror. Brushing aside Mary's infuriated demand that Ruthven leave or be arrested, Riccio's clinging hands were torn from Mary's skirts and he was stabbed to death in front of her. Between fifty and sixty wounds were found on his body after it was discovered, thrown down the privy staircase.

But if the plotters assumed that the violence would reduce Mary to a weepy, cringing wreck, pathetically dependent on the hard men, they were about to be disabused. Instead of throwing herself on Darnley's mercy, she kept cool, correctly confident that all the suspicions of her among the Scots would disappear once the story of the murder got out, including the detail of a pistol being pointed at her heavily pregnant belly. Faced with her resolution, it was Darnley whose fire turned to water, his brief exultation replaced by quaking guilt. Deploying a nicely calculated combination of intimidation and wifely sympathy, Mary persuaded Darnley to abandon the conspirators, if only to save his own neck. Beyond the palace walls, trading on her pregnancy and the assault on it by the plotters, Mary rapidly assumed the status of a persecuted heroine and mother of Scotland's future: quite her favourite part. Nine days after Riccio's murder she re-entered Edinburgh at the head of 8000 soldiers.

The plot was not yet played out. Mary, who had once been so besotted with Darnley, now became consumed by an equally violent hatred. She wanted to be rid of him. It is possible that all she meant by this was that she wished to be rid of him as a husband and consort. Once her child was born, perhaps Darnley could be persuaded into a divorce and his many transgressions could be used to bring the Church round to an annulment. But there were those among her devotees, including the Earl of Bothwell, who took her sighs and words to mean something altogether more decisive.

Bothwell was not some sort of primitive desperado. He came from the great magnate clan of the Hepburns, whose territorial base lay in southeast Scotland. He was rich and sophisticated, he spoke good French, and he could turn on the gallantry copiously enough to make Mary turn to him in her distress as a protector. Comforted by his solicitude, she returned Bothwell's loyalty, even riding 20 miles to see him after he had suffered a riding accident. On 19 June 1566 she gave birth to the child who would be King James VI of Scotland and James I of England. On hearing the news Elizabeth cried out operatically as if she had been struck with a dagger: 'Alack the queen of the Scots is lighter of a bonny son and I am but of barren stock.'

With a healthy baby boy in the cot, Darnley was expendable, and Mary turned ingeniously Machiavellian. Instead of aggressively hunting down the principal culprits in Riccio's death, she let them sweat out their guilt and then implied, through intermediaries, that they could beat one murder charge by committing another. Homicide, after all, seemed to be their thing. So although the grandest of the grandees, like Morton and Maitland, had some misgivings about signing on for another murder having barely escaped punishment, human or divine, for the first, and even greater misgivings about Bothwell, whom they feared and hated, a contract was duly drawn up with Darnley as the target.

On the evening of 9 February 1567 Darnley was lying in bed at the house of Kirk o' Fields on the outskirts of Edinburgh, a nice little place, thoughtfully suggested by the queen (although he wanted to be at Holyrood) as somewhere he might convalesce from a grave fever, probably a side-effect of his galloping syphilis. She did not want to take any chances, she said, with the health of the infant prince. The atmosphere between husband and wife seemed to have warmed a little, and he was grateful to her for her concern for his illness and looked forward to returning to the court once he was well. The queen had dressed for a masque to be held in honour of the marriage of one of her most trusted servants. Darnley was unhappy about her going, an interruption to what had become a surprisingly cosy routine of bedside readings and games of cards, but she went anyway. At a pre-arranged moment, Bothwell left the masque, removed his silver and black costume and, somewhere in the vicinity of Kirk o' Fields, supervised the lighting of a fuse.

At two o'clock in the morning an immense explosion was heard throughout the city, as loud as thirty cannon firing all at once. When they eventually found Darnley's body, dressed only in a nightshirt, amid the rubble of what had been Kirk o' Fields, there were no signs of scorch. It turned out that just minutes before the detonation he had heard some disturbance in the garden and had had himself lowered from a window to the ground on a chair hanging by a rope. Running through the garden in his nightshirt, he had collided with a group of the plotters completing their preparations. They had strangled him to death as the sound and fury rocked Edinburgh.

If Riccio's murder had energized Mary, Darnley's end seemed to have the opposite effect. Whether she had truly wanted it or not, it was a death too many. She had carried her baby through the carnage and managed to see him safely into the world. Now, though, Mary was well beyond the limit of her equanimity and was losing control of that much fought-over body. She would retch uncontrollably for long periods, black and bloody mucus issuing from the pale face, and her temper swung between exhaustion and hysterics. She needed help, and James Bothwell was there to give it.

For if Mary's sense of direction faltered, Bothwell knew exactly where he was going: straight to the top and into her bedroom. A farcical trial, the verdict influenced by the presence of thousands of Bothwell's armed followers, delivered an acquittal. The queen's dependence on him deepened. He summoned a meeting of Scottish nobles at Ainslie and, striking the unlikely pose of statesman, declared that for the proper government of the country, it was essential that the queen take a husband. Very decently he offered himself for the job. The little criminals, compromised by their association with at least one if not two murders, meekly signed on. All that remained were what, for someone like Bothwell, were technicalities: overnight divorce from his inconvenient wife and the 'persuasion' of Mary herself. While *en route* to Edinburgh the queen's train was ambushed by Bothwell and his men, and they led Mary still in her weird trance-like state of passive fatalism to his grim pile of a castle at Dunbar. There, the formalities over, Bothwell planted his flag as prospective king of Scotland by planting himself inside her body.

This was Bothwell's version of a marriage proposal. He assumed that she would have no choice but to marry her rapist, and the assumption was correct. A few weeks later the pair were united at Holyrood, this time according to Protestant rites. There were some brave souls who said out loud just what they thought. John Craig, one of John Knox's colleagues in the Kirk, for example, refused to publish the banns until Mary affirmed that she had not been raped or held against her will. Even then, Craig publicly supplied a list of objections to the match: 'the law of adultery, the ordinance of the Kirk, the law of ravishing, the suspicion of collusion between him and his wife, the sudden divorcement and proclaiming within the space of four days and at last, the suspicion of the king's death which her marriage would confirm.'

Her predicament was, in a peculiar way, the mirror image of Elizabeth's trouble with Dudley, but the response of the two women could not have been more different. Amy Dudley's death, whether or not Robert had anything at all to do with it, translated into Elizabeth's temporary repugnance for, and anger at, him. Instead of it bringing her pastoral dream closer to realization, it ruled it out. Darnley's murder, on

Top: Henry Stewart, Lord Darnley (detail), by an unknown artist, late 1550s.
Above: Miniature of the Earl of Bothwell, by an unknown artist.
Opposite: Mary Queen of Scots, by François Clouet, 1558.

the other hand, actually made Bothwell not desirable but, in some monstrous way, necessary for Mary's own survival. It not only made her violently sick; it made her slightly crazy. Given every possible option, she now invariably took the worst. If she had had no foreknowledge of the murder plot, it was still possible for her to restore her legitimacy by tracking down the assassins and bringing them to justice. Instead, she married their ringleader.

The result was the same rebellion that Elizabeth would have faced had she followed her heart and married Dudley. On 15 June 1567, at Carberry Hill, near Musselburgh, Mary and Bothwell's army faced their opponents. The rebels' banner was itself a brilliant propaganda device: white for murdered innocence and featuring a green tree beneath which lay the body of the murdered king. Beside the body was the baby James and the legend 'judge and avenge my cause O Lord'. Bothwell affected not to notice this and issued a personal challenge to the opposition leaders to settle the issue in personal combat, an invitation that (since the numbers were on their side) they declined. While all the shouting was going on, Bothwell's own troops were disappearing into the woods. With his army disintegrating, Bothwell turned his own horse around and galloped away for reinforcements from Dunbar, leaving Mary the defenceless prisoner of the rebels. It was the last she saw of him. Years later he died in a Danish prison, tied to a stone pillar, befouled with his own excrement.

Mary's humiliation began immediately. By the time she got back to Edinburgh, she was filthy and weepy. The city crowds turned on her, shouting, 'Burn the whore, she is not worthy to live. Drown her.' Handbills featuring Mary as a mermaid (the euphemism for a whore) appeared on walls and doors. The next day she appeared at a window, pleading with the hissing crowds for help. *La plus belle des belles* now resembled an alehouse slattern: her chemise torn open to the waist, her breasts exposed, her hair hanging in dirty hanks, her face streaked with tears and grime. A forced abdication swiftly followed, as Mary renounced the throne in favour of her infant son and established her Protestant half-brother, the Earl of Moray, as the regent during James's minority. She was twenty-five years old. Her history seemed done.

It was not, of course. Banished to the castle of Lochleven in the midst of a cold, deep lake, Mary used her last weapon: her air of tragically damaged beauty. Her jailer, one of the usually hard-bitten Douglas clan, melted in a puddle of adoration. Ten months after being locked up, in May 1568, Mary made a dramatic getaway across the loch and set about raising an army against the regent. This she managed with an ease that would be surprising were it not for the fact that Moray was almost as disliked as the ex-queen. In any case, having got herself an army, she carelessly threw it away in an inglorious defeat at Langside, near Glasgow.

Now there was only one way back, and it was a route she must have had deep anxieties about: a return to Scotland via England. Mary undoubtedly knew that Elizabeth's disgust with the murder of Darnley was exceeded only by her profound horror at rebellion and abdications under duress. She extrapolated from that the notion that Elizabeth would be prepared to help her, militarily if necessary, recover her throne. So when she planned a flight across the border Mary thought of it as merely a temporary refuge, pending the triumphal return. She must have supposed that her stay in England would last perhaps months, a year at most?

Had she known the real answer, nineteen years, she would surely have avoided the passage across the Solway Firth. But there she was, a bedraggled, dead-tired figure, the famous auburn tresses cropped for disguise, sitting in an open boat, hunched up against the raw northern wind, her eyes fixed on the disappearing shoreline of Scotland. At her back was the little Cumbrian fishing port of Workington and her cousin Elizabeth's kingdom. Halfway across she was said to have had a sudden premonition that something was wrong; that she should have fled to France, not England; that she might never see Scotland again.

Mary's abrupt appearance in England threw Elizabeth's government into turmoil. It was one thing to have made routinely cousinly noises, sympathizing with her plight and condemning rebellion; it was quite another to know what to do about it, especially since the regent of Scotland was, of course, a committed Protestant. Cecil himself went into a spasm of indecisiveness, relieved only by one of his famous pro- and con memoranda: 'come of her own accord', 'deposed against her will' etc., etc. Perhaps he hoped that no matter how awkward Mary's presence, it would at least have the effect of at last concentrating his procrastinating queen's mind on the matter of her future, which was also the country's. Elizabeth was, after all, not getting any younger – she was thirty-five in 1568. The royal laundresses were still sending monthly evidence of her capacity to produce children, but her will seemed more stubborn than ever. If she would not discuss marriage, surely she had a duty to provide for the succession. If she did not grasp this nettle herself, others would, and since Mary was well known to have the greatest claim, these others might create an alternative court somewhere up there near the border.

But it took a brave man to make Elizabeth face facts. When she thought Dudley was still badgering her, she turned on him, exclaiming: 'If you think to rule here, I will take a course to see you forthcoming. I will have but one mistress and no master.' In the same year, 1566, when parliament had tried to do just that by threatening to deny her money unless she dealt with the matter, she threw a major royal tantrum, insisting that these things were her own personal affair or, at most, an item for discussion in council, not in parliament. And if they wanted discussion about personal matters, well everyone knew that the Duke of Norfolk was, more or less, a traitor and as for the Marquis of Northampton, he had fouled his marriage nest so badly he needed a statute to sort it out. There was a lot more in this vein. Aghast, Cecil attempted to prorogue the session: 'It seemeth very uncomfortable to the Queen's Majesty to hear of at this time.'

She knew not 'seemeth'. On 5 November 1566, her poise somewhat restored, Elizabeth addressed a specially summoned parliamentary delegation. After criticizing the Commons for not observing correct procedure but instead attempting blackmail, she went on to deliver one of the great perorations in the history of British oratory. It was also one of the slyest, using the classic tactic of refuting a charge that no one had, in fact, laid at her door: that she was recklessly indifferent to the fate of her subjects. Do you, she asked in effect, take me for some *stranger*?

> Was I not born in the Realm? Were my parents born in any foreign country? Is not my kingdom here?…Whom have I oppressed? Whom have I enriched to another's harm? What turmoil have I made in this Commonwealth that I should be suspected to have no regard to the same? How have I governed since my reign? I will be tried by envy itself. I need not use many words, for my deeds will try me…I will never break the word of a prince spoken in a public space for my honour's sake. And therefore I will say again that I will marry as soon as I can conveniently…And I hope to have children, otherwise I would not marry.

It got even better. Laying on the guilt, Elizabeth reminded her audience of what she had suffered under Mary because of her proximity to the succession and said she would never inflict that on anyone else.

> As for my own part, I care not for death for all men are mortal. And though I be a woman, yet I have as good courage answerable to my place as ever my father had. I am your anointed Queen. I will never be by violence constrained to do anything. I thank God I am indeed endowed with such qualities that if I were turned out of the Realm in my petticoat I were able to live in any place in Christendom.

When *she* judged it safe and proper she would inform *them* about the succession, not be dictated to about it, 'for it is monstrous that the feet should direct the head'.

This was vintage Elizabethan rhetoric, so dazzling that no one noticed the usual *non sequiturs*: I am a petticoated woman who wants to marry and have children, but then again I'm not just a woman, so no one will give me orders as to when and to whom I might wed; in fact, I am both king and queen, so just pipe down and go away and I'll let you know all about it when I'm good and ready.

It solved nothing. Eighteen months later, Mary's unlooked-for appearance brought home the real costs of not having these critical matters properly settled. Now, certain questions were unavoidable. Was Mary Stuart her heir or wasn't she? If not her, then who? How was she to be treated? As the next-in-line or as a temporary guest and ally? Not exactly. Mary's first request from her cousin was for some clothes and ornaments befitting her rank to replace the rags she had arrived with. What she got, after much complaining, was a chest of linen. It may have been just as well that Mary did not know Elizabeth was already wearing the ropes of pearls that had been stolen by Moray and sent as a sweetener to the English queen!

Elizabeth was, in fact, deeply torn about what to do. Her strong sense of princely obligation disposed her to help Mary, but she still suspected Mary's complicity in the murder of her other cousin, Darnley. Her grip on *realpolitik* told her that she had no interest at all in replacing a friendly, grateful Protestant regime in Scotland with a Catholic queen, who would probably open up the country to the French once again. As usual, when conflicting matters of state arose, Elizabeth did nothing and hoped it would all go away.

When her personal appeals for a meeting with Elizabeth went unheeded, Mary was puzzled, assuming that perhaps her letters had been intercepted. But when Elizabeth's chosen messenger, Sir Francis Knollys, explained that Mary would not be received at court until her case had been thoroughly examined and her conduct exonerated, Mary began to understand that she was a captive not a guest and, not surprisingly, went into a state of high dudgeon. In vain. The more she raved, the deafer Elizabeth became to her entreaties. By October 1568, when the commission of inquiry opened at York, most of Elizabeth's council were hoping that Moray would present such a damning case against Mary that her cause would be doomed. He did just that, bringing an incriminating casket of letters, perhaps forged, perhaps not, written by Mary to Bothwell before Darnley's death, urging him to kill her husband.

As she would for the rest of her life, Mary disdained to answer to any charge of wrongdoing or even to accept the jurisdiction of an English court to try the conduct of a queen of Scotland. She had a point. But after the commission she could be under no illusion that she was anything except a prisoner. She was shuttled from house to house under the guard of George Talbot, Earl of Shrewsbury, who had the unenviable job of being her jailer. Some houses, like Tutbury in Staffordshire, were little more than rain-soaked ruins. Others, like South Wingfield in Derbyshire, were more tolerable, and she was allowed to ride to hunt and to make tapestries for Shrewsbury's wife, the formidable Bess. But Mary was always watched, for she had become, as both Cecil and Francis Walsingham (now Elizabeth's Secretary of State), insisted to the queen, her most dangerous security problem.

As an ardent Protestant, Walsingham would hardly be expected to be sympathetic to Mary's plight. In his view, as long as she was alive, wherever she was, she was trouble. Exiled to France, she was trouble. Sent back over the Tweed to Scotland, she was *big* trouble. Under lock and key in England – the holding strategy – she was *still* trouble, for, as Elizabeth's presumptive heir, she would attract the disaffected like flies to a honeypot. Walsingham may have been the classic secret policeman – cold-blooded, devious, single-minded – but he was not paranoid, for overnight Mary did indeed become a magnet for conspiracy. The most dangerous was a plan to spring her from prison and marry her to the premier peer of the realm, Thomas Howard, 4th Duke of Norfolk, who, three times a widower, was now freshly available. Nor was this a plot hatched by some marginal gang of Catholic fanatics and dreamers. It came from men close to the very heart of government, including Arundel, who had once set his cap at Elizabeth herself. They were men of broad acres and massive patronage who had had enough of Cecil's growing dominance of the queen, and their number included Dudley himself, despite the fact that he and Norfolk had had a bitterly prolonged feud ever since a tennis match in which Dudley had taken a kerchief from the watching queen and wiped his brow with it, an action deemed so presumptuous and unseemly by the duke that he threatened to hit Leicester with his racket.

In hindsight, the scheme might look crackpot, but at the time it had something going for it. Norfolk, like all the Howards, may have been Catholic at heart, but officially he was Protestant, conforming to the Elizabethan Church. Leicester, Sussex, Arundel and the rest of them might even have imagined that the marriage of Mary and Norfolk was a way to bind up the wounds of religious schism that were far from healed in England. At a stroke, all the old divisions – between the English and the Scots; the Protestants and the Catholics; the north and the south – would disappear. A new and better Britain would be the result, and Cecil would drop off its map.

Not surprisingly, Elizabeth did not see it this way. Mischievously, she asked Norfolk whether the rumours of his marriage to the queen of the Scots were true? 'I prefer to sleep on a safe pillow,' was his reply. Elizabeth was not fooled, however. Norfolk's father had been executed as a traitor by her father, and she sensed an annoying characteristic about the Howards: their undeserved conviction that they were somehow the betters of the Tudors. The queen gave Norfolk every opportunity to tell the truth about the plan, but in the end it was a panicky Leicester who came clean – and got royal thanks rather than punishment. It was Norfolk who went to the Tower in October 1569.

The liberation of Mary, though, was not just the business of court politicians like Arundel and Leicester. Or, rather, those same court politicians and councillors were, in another guise, great regional magnates, masters of money, acres and men. And the blueprint for a different England, a British England, meant most to the people furthest away from London and the choruses of adoration that attended the progresses of the queen. In the north and west, where Catholicism had not only not been uprooted but where it was flourishing on the resentments of the great Marcher dynasties, the Dacres and the Percys, the temptation to exchange Mary for Elizabeth was especially strong. They had been there in Northumberland and Westmorland, they told themselves, when the Tudors were still in the brewing trade in Wales, and they were by now heartily sick of being told by some jumped-up quill-pusher from the south what they could or couldn't do, either in the government of their shires or their religion. For these people Mary Stuart was not just a successor. She was a replacement.

When the southern branch of the revolt caved in, there was a pause for thought. But then the women took charge, especially the Duchess of Westmorland, who just happened to be Norfolk's tougher sister. 'What a simple man, the duke [her brother] is,' she wrote witheringly, 'to begin a matter and not go through with it.' When the northern earls received a summons to go to London and explain themselves to council, the duchess persuaded the northern nobles that their choice was now either outright resistance or a craven walk to the block.

So they fought, the Earls of Westmorland and Northumberland leading the rebellion in November 1569. And for a while it even looked as if they might win, at least in the north. For although Tudor power looked very impressive as a show of spectacle, much of it was a precarious façade, and the further north you went in England, the shakier that façade became. Against the rebels, the government could produce at first only some hundreds of mounted knights and a thousand or so of men-at-arms. The army of the north, marching beneath the old banner of the Five Wounds of Christ that had last been seen during the Pilgrimage of Grace in 1536–7, swept through its homeland, in Lancashire, Yorkshire and Northumberland. In November 1569 Durham Cathedral was reconsecrated for Rome. English Bibles were rounded up and destroyed. The stone altar was restored, and the Latin mass sounded again through the chevron-striped columns of the vast Norman basilica.

Red-chalk drawing of Elizabeth I, by Federico Zuccaro, 1574.

Top: Red-chalk drawing of the Earl of Leicester, by Federico Zuccaro.
Above: Elizabeth's procession arriving at Nonsuch Palace, Surrey, in 1568;
pen and watercolour drawing by Joris Hoefnagel.

It must have seemed that the Church of the English saints had been reborn. And the rebels believed that if they could sit tight through the winter, Spanish help would be on its way in the spring.

But Elizabeth's government now understood the gravity of the situation and that another act of the English wars of religion was being played out. Mary was moved, in the nick of time, from Tutbury, where a flying squad of the northerners was coming to get her, and taken instead to the massively defended Coventry. After some initial chaos, a formidable, overwhelmingly southern army of 12,000 men was mobilized, adding more to its numbers once it reached the north. The rebellion was brutally crushed, the earls fleeing over the border to Scotland. With those who were caught, Elizabeth was disinclined to be lenient. Norfolk, who luckily for him was in the Tower when the rising peaked, was spared, but the queen's directives for reprisal and punishment were so savage that local justices of the peace decided on their own account, and to avoid generations of bitter recrimination, not to carry them out to the maximum letter of retribution. Even so, 450 were executed, three times the number Henry VIII had condemned after the much bigger Pilgrimage of Grace. Men of low rank were hanged, cut down while still alive and disembowelled.

The terror worked. The rising of the northern earls was the last serious insurrection to disturb Tudor England. Looking at the massive dispossession of rebel estates and the transfer of property to loyalist southerners, the discontented were made to see that there was too much at stake to hazard another attempt to change the regime. For the most passionately Catholic, however, 1570 brought a terrible dilemma. In that year, with poor timing, the pope, Pius V, published a bull excommunicating Elizabeth and calling on the faithful to rise up and depose their heretic queen, if necessary lethally. The Catholics of England now had a choice of betrayals: their Church or their monarch?

Some, inevitably, chose the latter. In 1571 a plot organized by the Florentine banker Roberto Ridolfi was discovered. Its aim had been to liberate Mary through the combined force of an uprising in England and a Spanish army of invasion, sent from the Netherlands. Elizabeth was to be killed and Mary enthroned in her place. Astoundingly, the Duke of Norfolk, who had been released from the Tower on good behaviour, had allowed himself to be drawn into the plot. Did the man never learn *anything*? Even with utterly damning evidence against him, Elizabeth flinched from her own subconscious taboo against cousin-killing and procrastinated over Norfolk's trial. Despite parliament demonizing the queen of the Scots as 'the monstrous and huge dragon and mass of the earth', Elizabeth was even less ready to have Mary attainted or even, at that stage, removed from the line of succession. But a sacrifice was necessary lest the queen appear to her subjects to be her own and their worst enemy. Norfolk was finally tried by a jury of his peers, unanimously condemned and beheaded at the Tower like his father before him, joining the gang of the headless beneath the flagstones at St Peter ad Vincula.

At the end of the northern rising Cecil wrote: 'The Queen's Majesty hath had a notable trial of her whole realm.' He and she both knew that for all the fanfares and flowers, the line between glory and disaster was never more than razor-thin.

For a time in the mid-1570s it must have seemed that trouble was somewhere else. Across the North Sea in the Netherlands, the Dutch and the Spanish were at each other's throats. Cities were being starved into submission or burned to the ground. In Paris Protestants (including, it was reported, women and babes in arms) had been slaughtered in the St Bartholomew's Day Massacre of 1572 and the bodies thrown into the Seine. 'The greatest crime since the Crucifixion,' was Cecil's comment.

But that was Abroad. At home the Bishop of Salisbury declared that never was England 'better in worldly peace, in health and body, in abundance of victuals'. The word 'abundance' came easily to the celebrants of Elizabeth's England, as if the country had only one season: golden high summer. The queen herself might not have borne fruit (though she wore cherries as earrings), but her reign had. Flanders' disasters had been England's gift, with the influx of capital and skilled labour. And Elizabeth, in imitation of Antwerp's bourse, opened the country's first stock exchange. The economy underwent spectacular, if erratic, industrial expansion. All kinds of manufactured goods, from tin and iron, linen and lace, glass, soap and salt, were now made in England rather than imported. It became common to install glazed windows in even fairly modest houses, and pewter replaced wood for tableware and utensils. It was a country in the throes of a profound transformation. Of course, the horn of plenty did not drop its bounty into everyone's lap, for there was also an abundance of people: 5 million of them by the century's end (against about half a million Scots). The period saw the greatest population explosion since the years before the Black Death. There were more bodies to feed, but there was less work to go round, less bargaining power and lower wages for those who could get it. In the countryside the enclosure of common land, usually for profitable flocks of sheep, closed off the possibility of self-sufficient subsistence for countless numbers of villagers, who were either depressed to landless wage-labourers or took to the roads to join the legions of the transient poor. In response, the Elizabethan parliaments passed poor laws providing alms for the disabled, residential poor but savage penalties for 'vagabondage': whipping and boring through the ear for first offenders, hanging for recidivist vagrants.

In Warwick in 1575 the human eyesores were made to disappear, one way or another, when the queen's progress was imminent. Instead, she could persuade herself of the clemency and charity of her government by looking at the special home for aged military veterans established by Dudley, Earl of Leicester. But for the burgesses of Warwick, who were faced with the immense cost of a royal visit, it might have been hard to decide which lot of travellers, the beggars or the courtiers, were more trouble. As cartloads of the unwashed were moved out, 200 cartloads of the court baggage moved in. Each wagon was pulled by a team of six horses. That meant a great deal of stable room and a great deal of hay. A week before the great day men from the Office of Purveyors would have descended on Warwick, buying up everything in sight at prices they decided were about right. No wonder some houses and towns had decidedly mixed feelings when they heard that they had been selected for a visit, for there was much that could go wrong. The ladies and gentlemen of the court, so many visions in satin and pearls, might be displeased by the entertainment and make their displeasure known. And then there was Queen Bess herself, a gem-encrusted apparition, a goddess on earth, but like most of those immortals as frightening as she was majestic. One might suppose that the town official selected to deliver a public speech might have been shaking in his shoes, but his long disquisition on the history of the town – 'We read in old writings and authentical chronicles the fame to have been a city or walled towne in the time of the Britons, then called Carwar...' – suggests he was well up to his job. The most scared man appeared to be the recorder, who was required to say something to the queen but who, at the crucial moment, was evidently stricken by tongue-tied panic, giving Elizabeth, with her perfect timing, a chance to touch his life with a drop of magic. 'Come hither little Recorder,' she is reported to have said. 'It was told me that you would be afraid to look upon me or to speak boldly, but you were not so afraid of me as I was of you and I now thank you for putting me in mind of my duty.' 'And so thereupon,' continues the Black Book of Warwick, 'showing a most gracious and favourable countenance to all the burgesses and company said again, "I most heartily thank you all my good people".'

Things could still go amiss. A great firework display had been planned by the Earl of Warwick, complete with guns and squibs he had brought from the Tower of London, where he was warden. But flames from the dragon's mouth set fire to four houses at the end of the town and 'suburbs were on fire at once whereof one had a ball come through on both sides and made a hole as big as man's head'. The next morning, with the town smelling a little of saltpetre, Elizabeth had the old couple whose house had caught fire while they were still in bed brought to her, and she gave them money to make up their losses. It was, of course, money got from her courtiers.

Elizabeth I: the 'Pelican Portrait', by Nicholas Hilliard, c. 1574.

The queen was generosity itself with other people's money. But dunning her courtiers only made the good burgers of Warwick love her even more.

They were not the only ones. The 1570s was the decade in which the religion of Elizabeth was being inaugurated. Her accession day, 17 November, became the greatest of all national holidays, more sacred than all the events on the heathen papist calendar. On that holy day there were bonfires and bells, and two days later there were the great tilts, where Sir Henry Lee, the Queen's Champion, jousted for her honour and crowds admitted to the spectacle for a shilling could voice their acclaim. Made by exiled Flemish artists, like Marcus Gheeraerts, and massively reproduced in prints, miniatures and medals, her image was everywhere. In defiant response to the papal excommunication, her nobles and gentlemen wore the miniature as a badge on their costumes. And as hopes of her marriage waned, the cult of her virginity (making the best of a bad thing) took off. Many of her subsequent symbolic personifications – the phoenix, the ermine, the crescent moon, the rose and the pearl – had been emblems of the Madonna and were now transposed to the Virgin Queen. She also appeared as the chaste Diana and Tuccia, the Vestal Virgin (who proved her chastity by carrying a sieve of water without spilling a drop), or with a snowy white ermine or the pelican which, according to sacred iconography, sacrificially fed its young from the blood of its own breast. Or again Elizabeth might be the sun, whose radiance gave the beams of the rainbow their colours. She was everything, and as the eyes and ears on the 'Rainbow' portrait make clear, she heard and saw everything. For those who were unable to see the paintings at court or in the great country houses – the 'prodigy houses' – built to receive her, she would appear in illustrations to histories, like Edward Hall's chronicle of the miraculous rise of God's own Protestant Commonwealth and its consummation in the reign of the chaste queen.

Even those in the know, who could, if they wanted, plainly see the elaborate scaffolding from which the image of Gloriana was projected and who knew that the pale moonglow of the queen's face was just so much pulverized borax, alum and mill-water, were still hopelessly captive to the cult. Christopher Hatton, for example, a Northamptonshire gentleman and obscure member of parliament who had caught Elizabeth's eye at a masque when Leicester was out of favour, became so drastically infatuated that he seemed close to losing his mind when separated from her presence. When Hatton fell sick and Elizabeth sent him to a spa for his own good, he wrote back like a teenager in delirious torment: 'Would God I were with you one hour… My wits are overwrought…I love you. I cannot lack you…Bear with me most dear sweet lady. Passion overcometh me. I can write no more. Love me for I love you… Ten thousand farewells…'

Hatton was just another casualty of Bessiemania. But then there was something slightly unhinged about the razzle-dazzle of the 'prodigy' years: houses like Hardwick 'more windows than walls'; ballrooms the size of football fields (for there *was* Elizabethan football); libraries with acres of unread classics; even a bathing pool, on Lord Bacon's property, where the walls and floor were studded with jewels that would sparkle through the water. In contrast to the relative sobriety of the first half of the century, Elizabethan glamour called for jewellery; some of it from exotic sources like topazes and emeralds from Brazil, or peridots and chrysoberyls from the East. The extraordinary 'Cheapside hoard', representing the stock of a London jeweller towards the end of the sixteenth century and early in the seventeenth, makes it clear how the jewellery habit had spread out from the court into the wealthier sections of the mer-cantile classes. Leicester's New Year's gifts to the queen invariably featured colossal gems, as big and gaudy as his own personality.

By rights, Leicester's involvement in the Norfolk–Mary marriage plot ought to have finished him, but Elizabeth's soft spot for her old paramour was large and deep. In 1575 she let him stage an enormous entertainment for her benefit at Kenilworth Castle, which she had given to him. By this time, he and the queen were playing an elaborate game. He would pretend to be, still, her ardent lover, and she would pretend to tolerate his excessive adulation. The fact that Leicester had a son, Douglas Sheffield, by his mistress was neither here nor there. That was a different kind of game, so the entertainment at Kenilworth in 1575 was, in effect, their last great date, with a cast of thousands looking on. Leicester had added an entire wing to the castle in which the queen could reside on the few occasions when she came to stay. There was scarlet leather on the walls, blue Turkey rugs and thousands of candles glittering at night; there were crystal chessboards, an aviary stocked with dazzling exotic birds and white marble fountains, filled with marble, naked, kissing nymphs in imitation of the Venetian nymphaea; and a banquet of 300 dishes. A field in front of the castle was flooded to make a huge artificial lake, on which floated an island with boys dressed as girls piping a greeting as the queen arrived. Hairy wild men emerged from arcadian woods, and fireworks exploded so exuberantly that as Kenilworth's gatekeeper wrote: 'the waters surged, the castle shook and made me, hardy as I am, very vengeably afeared.'

Leicester, now a little stout for a Master of the Horse, presided over all this with rosy-faced satisfaction. It was just because he could no longer be taken seriously as a suitor that he became an object of public affection, naughty Uncle Robin. It was quite different, though, with the Duke of Alençon, who was the youngest brother of Henry III, the king of France. Elizabeth took Alençon's suit seriously enough to invite him to England. She was in her forties. Even when she was forty-five a physician pronounced her capable of bearing children. Historians have mostly thought that her calculations, first in 1572–3 and then again in 1579–81, were essentially political and diplomatic – a way to press France to intervene against the Spanish in the Netherlands, thereby relieving England of the trouble and expense. This was certainly Cecil's calculation. But in the teeth of much opposition in the council and among the public, the queen made public displays of affection towards Alençon in 1579 – notwithstanding the fact he was very short and hideously pock-marked – and called him 'her frog' (an ominous sign when someone received a coveted nickname). Leicester had just married again, to one of Elizabeth's court ladies, Lettice Knollys, so it is not beyond all possibility that she was, in fact, seriously fond of Alençon and thought him possibly her last chance.

For the first time, England became jealous. Hatton sent a ring to the queen, guaranteed to expel 'infectious airs' provided she wore it 'betwixt the sweet dugs – the chaste nest of pure constancy'. Leicester and Hatton, both experts in wounded sensibility, proceeded to orchestrate a tremendous campaign of patriotic opposition, featuring songs like 'The Most Strange Marriage of the Frog and the Mouse', and broadsides and sermons were printed. In August 1579 John Stubbs published *A Discoverie of a Gaping Gulf wherein England is like to be Swallowed*, warning that the entire Valois dynasty was infected with disease as God's punishment and that the queen had no business contaminating herself and by extension the body politic. His reward was trial for libel and a sentence (along with his printer and distributor) to have his right hand cut off. The printer was spared, but when Stubbs's hand was amputated with a cleaver, driven home with a mallet, he managed, with his good hand, to raise his hat in the air and cry 'God Save the Queen' before passing out. William Camden, who witnessed the gruesome spectacle, wrote: 'The multitude standing about was altogether silent; either out of horror of this new and unwonted punishment, or else out of pity toward the man, being of honest and unblameable report, or else out of hatred of the marriage which most presaged would be the overthrow of religion.'

Not surprisingly, the queen's reputation suffered badly as she toyed both with Alençon, the council and the public. On Accession Day 1581 she finally exchanged rings and announced a betrothal, but only to rescue the duke's honour and get him out of England. By the end of the year there was no more talk of a French marriage. Now, whether she wanted it or not, she was certain to stay the Virgin Queen.

Around twilight on 6 April 1580 there was an earthquake in England. Its epicentre was the east coast of Kent, but at the Tower of London the shock was strong enough to set the lions in the royal zoo roaring. In theatres like The Curtain playgoers

TANDEM SI

Sir Christopher Hatton, by an unknown artist, 1589.

were frightened enough to jump from the gallery. The previous October a comet had appeared, followed in the winter by massive snowfalls, the likes of which no one could remember. The queen put a brave face on these omens. To the horror of her courtiers she opened her window to see the sallow flare of the comet more clearly. Everyone else knew God had sent these things as a warning of dark times to come.

But, for better or worse, England had its own dark angel to see it through the worst: Francis Walsingham, swarthy and melancholy enough for Elizabeth to call him her 'Moor'. 'Intelligence is never too dear,' was Walsingham's motto, and his entire career was an applied demonstration of the modern truism that knowledge is power. In his person, the notion that 'intelligence' could mean both understanding and espionage was made real. Walsingham, who was related to the queen through his step-father, had been made one of the two secretaries of state in 1572 when Cecil had been promoted to lord treasurer. Thereafter, the two of them were the bookends of Elizabeth's Privy Council: able to work together but always leaning against each other in judgement and temper.

The differences between Cecil and Walsingham were not just personal. They reflected different views of the world and England's place in it. Cecil was a Socratic pragmatist, who always managed to see two sides of any issue and then struggled, optimistically, to reconcile them. This is how he saw the greatest division of his day: the war of faiths. Cecil thought that the Church settlement of 1559, with its require-ment that people attend Anglican churches and occasionally take communion, but without being forced to swallow the whole of Protestant doctrine, was gentle enough to bring the majority of the country, slowly but surely, round to the new order.

Walsingham, on the other hand, was not interested in reconciliation. He was interested in winning. The ways of power, he thought, might be complicated but the world was really very simple, divided cleanly between the good and the bad, Protestants and Catholics. He had been in Paris in 1572 during the St Bartholomew's Day Massacre, and he was under no illusions. Treaties and alliances were all very nice but they were tactics. The strategic reality was a war to the death. To see both sides of the question, to compromise with anti-Christ, was to guarantee you would lose. And if Walsingham had anything to do with it, England was not about to lose.

The simple test of how seriously anyone thought about England's survival in the years of an apparent Catholic crusade was how they felt about the war in the Netherlands, which had begun in 1568 and showed no signs of ending. Was it some far-off incomprehensible civil war that was none of England's business, or was it *the* struggle on which the island's fate would ultimately depend? Walsingham knew that Cecil and the queen wanted no part of it and thought it a battle between two parties of equally deplorable fanatics. Many in the council saw no compelling need to rush to the aid of the Dutch when they had been attacking English ships peacefully trading with Spain. But Walsingham was adamant that if Spain succeeded in crushing the Dutch revolt, England would be next. Cecil's response was a grudging acceptance of the need to do something, but to have that something done by proxy, by the French; hence his hope that a French marriage would somehow work out.

But neither the marital nor the military strategy succeeded. Within a few years all the barriers between England and its moment of truth had fallen away. The French proxy campaign in the Netherlands collapsed. In 1584 the great hero of Dutch resistance, William the Silent, was assassinated on the staircase of his residence at Delft. The armies of the Duke of Parma moved rapidly through Flanders to the sea. By 1585 they controlled Antwerp and faced the coast of England.

Both inside the government and throughout the country, the crisis produced a soul-searching debate; it was the first time that England was confronted with a question that would return many times in its history: Is Europe our business? Are the blood-lettings of continentals our concern or our interest? Cecil and Walsingham had opposite answers. With Dutch resistance apparently crumbling and the North Sea and Channel threatened, Cecil conceded that it was only a matter of time before England and Spain confronted each other directly. But all his instincts were deeply insular. Why fritter away men and money 'over there' when both were needed to build Fortress England? Stand or fall, it had to be done on their own. For Walsingham this was, literally, self-defeating. Stand aside from the fray in Europe, doom the Dutch to go down and you merely postpone the evil day and make the enemy a hundred times stronger. Hit him now, and hit him with everything you've got and everywhere you can: on the high seas, in the Netherlands, in America and in the English shires where Catholic gentry hid Jesuits. Make him scatter and run and you have a fighting chance.

Leicester, whose Protestantism grew stronger as the years passed, agreed with Walsingham, and as the situation across the North Sea grew grimmer and intelligence reports confirmed that Spain was planning an invasion launched from the Netherlands, finally, with many misgivings, so did the queen. A total of 8000 troops were to be sent to Antwerp, with Leicester himself as their commander. But the queen, as usual, was not about to issue any kind of blank cheque. She had barely made the decision before she was making contingencies for countermanding it. From the outset Leicester was hamstrung by his orders to fight a strictly defensive war, and since the queen had turned down the offer of sovereignty of the United Provinces after the death of William the Silent, Leicester was ordered emphatically not to accede to any kind of request to become their governor.

Needless to say, within months he had done just that and had been solemnly invested as governor-general at The Hague. His justification for countermanding his commission was that some sort of commanding authority was needed in the notoriously disunited Netherlands if they were to fight an effective war. But when Elizabeth heard the news she became apoplectic with rage. 'We could never have imagined, had we not seen it fall out in experience, that a man raised up by ourself, and extraordinarily favoured by us above any other subject of this land, would have in so contemptible a sort broken our commandment, in a course that so greatly toucheth us in honour…' It was all Walsingham could do to prevent the queen from shutting down the campaign then and there. When he heard of the queen's fury, Leicester quailed with contrition. All he could hope for now, he said, was to find a job in her stables 'to run the horses' heels'.

But Elizabeth could still be brought round to see things the hawks' way by being reminded of what might happen if Spain won the battle of the North Sea: invasion, Catholic rebellion, Mary Stuart liberated and enthroned at Westminster. Walsingham was now fighting his war at home as well as abroad, and he had taken the gloves off. He knew that the pope, Pius V, had not only excommunicated 'that guilty woman of England', but promised 'whosoever sends her out of the world…not only does not sin but gains merit in the eyes of God'. Against this invitation to regicide, Walsingham created Bonds of Association: vigilante organizations of gentlemen sworn to destroy anyone threatening harm to the queen. The second step was to expel Jesuit missionaries, now redefined as accomplices to murder. If they stayed they were to be automatically treated as traitors. Any person found sheltering a Catholic priest or receiving mass would be guilty of a felony. Thousands upon thousands of Catholics were now forced to a terrible choice: disobey the Church or disobey the law. From now on, the idea of a loyal Catholic (though there were many who protested they were just that) was treated as a dangerous absurdity.

Elizabethan England became Walsingham's national security state. Infiltrators and double-agents were kept busy, and the rack and the thumbscrew were in full operation. One over-zealous sadist called Topcliffe (himself imprisoned for exceeding his commission) kept a rack inside his own house where he regularly tortured suspects, including a priest named Portmort, who took revenge by denouncing Topcliffe for having boasted of feeling the queen's breasts and belly. The Privy Council even discussed the government of the country were the queen to be killed and came up with an interesting solution. Parliament would be sovereign and the government run by a 'grand council'. But if Walsingham was ferocious he was not paranoid. Underground plots *were* being organized in France, Rome and Spain, and they were all working to one end: the death of Elizabeth and her replacement by Mary Stuart.

For years, under the watchful eye of the Earl of Shrewsbury and his terrifying wife, Bess Talbot, Mary had been leading the life of a country gentlewoman, permitted to hunt and hawk and to keep a decent, if not extensive, household. Physically, she had deteriorated, the slender beauty thickening. But she had never become reconciled to her captivity, nor had she ever forgiven the cousin whom she had imagined to be her friend and ally. Horrified when her son James made a treaty with England that repudiated his own mother, Mary signed her own rights of succession over to the king of Spain. This only confirmed Walsingham in his pessimistic view that with a native-born heir to the throne no longer a possibility, the mere existence of Mary Stuart was a dagger pointed at the heart of Elizabeth.

So he designed an elaborate entrapment to take care of the matter. In December 1585, without telling Cecil, Walsingham made an important change in the conditions of Mary's captivity. She and her household were suddenly packed up and sent to Chartley House near Sheffield and provided with a new and much harsher jailer, the puritanical Amyas Paulet, who made no attempt to hide his intense distaste for his prisoner. At Chartley the conditions of her confinement could be minutely monitored and if necessary engineered to bring about her destruction. Imagine Mary's happiness when she discovered that a new and ingenious method had been devised by parties working on her behalf to smuggle letters to and from her agent in Paris and to her latest sworn avenger and champion, the wealthy London merchant Anthony Babington. The coded letters were put in a watertight pouch and slipped through the bung hole of beer casks delivered and removed from Chartley. What Mary did not know was that it was Walsingham who had thought this up and whose cipher clerks were busy decoding her messages hours after they had been sent off. The entire Chartley regime had been rigged as a set up designed to nail Mary once and for all.

Nail her it did. Babington obligingly supplied Mary with details of his plot: the six gentlemen who would murder Elizabeth; how she would be freed; the expected invasion and rising. On 19 July 1586 Mary replied, encouraging the plotters but as usual putting her own liberation at the top of their priorities. If anything should go wrong, she gratuitously warned Babington, just imagine *my* fate. Hours after they left her hand they were being copied and decoded by Walsingham's cipher clerks before being sent on their way to Babington.

In Westminster Elizabeth suddenly became inexplicably distraught about her security, imagining the assassin's knife behind every shadow and curtain. She knew what had happened to William the Silent. They had got to him. Whatever Walsingham said, they could get to her. She fell deathly ill.

At Chartley Mary felt the skies lighten; her liberty and vindication were close after twenty years of unjust imprisonment. On 11 August 1586 Paulet actually suggested she go for a ride. Good for the old lungs don't you know. From a distance Mary saw a small group of riders approach. This was it, she must have imagined: deliverance.

It was, in fact, the warrant for her arrest. Babington and his fellow-plotters had been arrested and under torture had confessed. Mary was taken away, while her rooms at Chartley were searched, turning up hundreds of incriminating documents and the keys to sixty different codes. In London Elizabeth wrote an ecstatic letter to Paulet: 'Amyas, my most faithful and careful servant. God reward thee treblefold for the most troublesome charge so well discharged.' She spoke of Mary as a 'wicked murderess'. Hanging and live disembowelment, she told Cecil, was not good enough for traitors as evil as the Babington plotters.

There was just one more stop, one more castle in the tragic career of the wandering Mary, Queen of Scots: Fotheringhay, the great Yorkist pile in Northampton-shire where Richard III had been born. If anyone expected her to pen a tear-stained confession, though, they evidently had something to learn about her. Faced with the endgame, Mary drew on some inner resource that made her disconcertingly lofty, as if raised above the squalid charades of power. Asked to own up to her crimes, Mary stood on her sovereignty. To Paulet's hectoring demand that she confess, she replied: 'As a sinner I am truly conscious of having often offended my Creator. I beg him to forgive me. But as Queen and sovereign I am aware of no fault or offence for which I have to render account to anyone here below.'

Her second tactic was to lie her head off, denying all knowledge of the Babington plot until, that is, she was shown the letters to him bearing her signature. But Walsingham had overreached himself by adding forged statements to the genuine article, and this allowed Mary to accuse him of having set the entire conspiracy up in order to be rid of her. This was, after all, not far from the truth, and she was even closer to the mark when she reminded her interrogators on the Privy Council that she had come to England freely and in response to a promise of aid against her enemies in Scotland. 'I was at once imprisoned,' she added bluntly.

Elizabeth didn't exactly see it that way. She wrote to Mary as if the queen of the Scots had been an ungrateful house-guest who, instead of writing thank-you notes for the hospitality, had made off with the towels. Mary 'had planned in divers ways and manners to take my life and ruin my kingdom by the shedding of blood. I never proceeded so hastily against you. On the contrary I have maintained you and pre-served your life with the same care which I use for myself.'

On 15 October 1586 the formal trial began in the great hall of Fotheringhay. In a typical gesture, half plea, half threat, Mary had warned her prosecutors to look to their consciences and 'remember that the theatre of the world is wider than the realm of England'. It was to that audience – worldwide and across the ages – that she now played out her part, centre stage.

She hobbled into the room, shockingly, painfully infirm, dressed head to foot like a glamorous mother superior, swathed in black velvet, capped by a white head-dress and veil. Seeing a grandiose chair standing on a dais Mary naturally assumed that this was her place, only to be crushingly informed it represented the presence of the queen of England. She was ushered to a small crimson chair of the accused. She began bravely. Deprived of access to the evidence marshalled against her; deprived of a defence counsel, a secretary or even pen and ink, Mary turned to Cecil and Walsingham and said that in such circumstances 'there is not one, I think, among you, let him be the cleverest man in the world but would be incapable of resisting or defending himself, if he were in my place'. Defend herself she did, however, insisting that she never meant to take the throne of England while Elizabeth was alive but had merely asserted her irrefutable claim to succeed as the nearest in line. Far from confessing, Mary then turned the tables on her prosecutors, putting them in the dock, accusing Walsingham of forging the entirety of the Babington letter and forcing him into an unaccustomed but careful defence of his conduct: 'As God is my witness…as a private person I have done nothing unworthy of an honest man, and as Secretary of State nothing unbefitted of my duty.' The cat and mouse game continued with the mouse on the offensive when it was Cecil's turn to examine her. Questioned about her transfer of the rights to the throne to Philip II, Mary replied loftily that it was not for men such as *him* to concern himself with the affairs of princes. When he pressed her to say how she would have acted in the event of a Spanish invasion, Mary said she wanted nothing but liberty from unlawful detention.

In the end it did not matter what she said. Since she proved such an adroit defendant, the trial was adjourned and resumed in London without her. Ten days later the commission passed swiftly to her conviction. When the sentence was made public there was rejoicing in the streets of London, and parliament petitioned the queen for a speedy execution. But this was precisely what Elizabeth was incapable of providing. For months she had ranted at the infamy of the 'murderess', but when it came to killing her off, the old, deep horror of the axe at the neck of those she felt and knew were kin – Norfolk and Mary – made her balk. And there was something about Mary's veiled threat that revenge would be taken for her sacrifice which also may have made Elizabeth afraid. 'We princes are set as it were upon stages in the sight of the world,' Mary had said and Elizabeth knew it was true.

For three months Elizabeth agonized over the fate of her cousin – a record even by her standards of procrastination – but on 1 February 1587 she finally signed the death warrant and asked her private secretary, William Davison, to attach the Great Seal of England and take it to Walsingham. The execution, she insisted, had to be done away from the public gaze, at Fotheringhay itself. In fact, what Elizabeth really wanted, she let it be known, was for the whole ugly business to be taken out of her hands by some loyal person who would just get rid of Mary in the time-honoured way reserved for redundant monarchs. But Paulet, normally so obliging, was horrified by the suggestion: 'God forbid that I should make so foul a shipwreck of my conscience or so leave so great blot on my poor posterity as to shed blood without a warrant.'

If Elizabeth dreaded the publicity, Mary revelled in her coming martyrdom. All the chaos, squalor, reckless adventuring and rash conspiracy; all the delusions, histrionics, skin-of-her-teeth escapes and battlefield fiascos; the apparently arbitrary madness of her life suddenly assumed direction and meaning. God had led her through all her tribulations so that she might arrive at this one transfiguring moment: a sacrifice for the truth and endurance of the eternal Church. So when Mary was informed by a weeping Scottish courtier that she would be executed the following morning, 8 February 1587, she told him to be joyful: 'for the end of Mary Stuart's troubles is now done…Carry this message from me and tell my friends that I died like a true Scottish woman and a true French woman.'

The incredible performance was played for all it was worth, right to the end. Harangued by Richard Fletcher, the Dean of Peterborough, she turned her back on him, rejecting his invitation to join his prayers. 'Mr Dean I am settled in the ancient Roman Catholic religion and mind to spend my blood in defence of it.' Undeterred, Fletcher walked round to the other side of the scaffold and continued to berate Mary. The two voices, English and Latin, rose in unseemly competition. Attempts were made to prevent her from kissing her crucifix. When, finally, she undressed for the executioner, the demure black gown fell away to reveal a petticoat of blood-red crimson: the stain of the martyr. Her eyes were tied with a white silk cloth, embroidered in gold, and she lay with such complete stillness that it gave the executioner a bad case of sweaty palms. His first blow cut deep into the back of her head. She was heard to cry softly 'sweet Jesus' before the second blow severed all but a hanging tendon so that the executioner was now forced to use his axe like a hacksaw.

And Mary, of course, was not going to allow a little matter like death to get in

Top: Woodcut of the trial of Mary Queen of Scots.
Above: The execution of Mary Queen of Scots;
watercolour by an unknown Dutch artist, *c.* 1608.

the way of her total domination of the proceedings. With the large audience of invited spectators in shock, the lips on her severed head, so witnesses reported, continued for some minutes to move as if in silent prayer. And when the executioner, by now probably wanting to die himself, went to perform his obligatory duty of holding up the head and calling out 'God Save the Queen', he made the mistake of grasping it by the mass of auburn curls. It was, of course, a wig. To general horror, Mary's skull, covered only with a mat of grey stubble, fell from the hair and rolled across the floor like a bowling ball. The next task was to remove the clothes from the headless trunk to prepare the body for embalming – and to deprive the relic trade of valuable inventory. But as the blood-soaked petticoat was being pulled away, something moved from within its folds and began to howl. The something was Mary's lapdog, a Skye terrier, which gripped the gory fabric with his teeth. When it was finally detached from the wreckage of his mistress, the dog was scrubbed down. But it was no good. The clots clung to his coat. Clean or dirty it made no difference. The dog refused food, languished and died, just another sad little victim of Mary's tragic touch. The dog was Mary's first mourner. But he certainly wouldn't be her last.

While bells rang and Londoners sang 'An excellent ditty made as a general rejoicing for the cutting off of the Scottish queen's head', Elizabeth I plunged into an abyss of remorse. If the messenger who brought her news of Mary's death was expecting a show of gratitude, he was in for a surprise. Fearing yet another change of mind, Cecil and Walsingham had decided not to tell Elizabeth of the appointed time until it was all over. No matter how many times they flattered the queen by telling her – or by tolerating others to tell her – how much more than a 'mere' woman she was, there were times when they thought and acted as if she was just that: the chronically irresolute and inconstant female, ruled by the ebb and flow of her emotions, just as surely as her under-utilized matrix was ruled by the cycles of the moon and stars. Usually, they got away with the *faits accomplis*, but not this time. When Elizabeth got the news of Mary's death, according to William Camden: 'her countenance changed, her words faltered and with excessive sorrow she was in a manner astonished insomuch as she gave herself over to grief putting herself into mourning weeds and shedding abundance of tears'. And instead of congratulating her servants on doing her bidding, Elizabeth turned on them, banishing Cecil from her presence for an unprecedented six months and attempting to have secretary Davison, who had taken the warrant to Walsingham, arrested and hanged for insubordination. This was not a disingenuous show and the tears were not crocodile tears; rather, a massive case of denial. Elizabeth really did seem to think that she had expressly told Davison to delay the execution, not hasten it, and that he had violated her orders. But it was inconceivable that he would have taken this risk, knowing full well lives, including his own, depended on it. Everyone took their portion of the unmerited blame, knowing that the queen had to be allowed to wail and rave and delude herself that Mary's death had happened in spite of, not because of, her.

Elizabeth's inability to face the truth may have been prompted by a bad conscience but also by a well-grounded anxiety about the consequences that Mary's execution would have on European politics. She might now be branded a killer of princes as well as a notorious heretic, and instead of stopping conspiracy in its tracks, the execution at Fotheringhay might actually reinforce the determination of those who thought they might please the pope by getting rid of the queen of England. Instead of isolated plotters, she might now have to face a full-scale war of sovereigns.

She was right. Even before Mary's trial, Philip II had accelerated plans for an 'Enterprise of England', an invasion to restore the Catholic Church. But although he invoked the papal bull that had called Elizabeth 'an incestuous bastard begotten and born in sin of an infamous courtesan', for Philip the Armada was always a matter of imperial self-defence rather than religious retribution. For years, even while the English government was ostensibly discussing peace, the committed Protestants on the council, such as Leicester and Walsingham, had been encouraging pirates like Francis Drake and John Hawkins to attack Spanish shipping. The jackpot would have been the great treasure fleet, which every spring and autumn carried huge quantities of silver from the mines of Peru back to Seville and which alone sustained the immense war effort in the Netherlands. Drake and Hawkins never quite made the big hit, but throughout the late 1570s and 1580s they managed nonetheless to haul home considerable amounts of booty, much to the delight of their investors, including, of course, the risk-free sleeping partner, Elizabeth I. To the queen it all made sense as part of a two-prong effort to get the Spanish out of the Netherlands. Instead of using an immense and costly army over there, they should cut the supply lines. By all means try peace negotiations, but use the pirates to give Spain an incentive to come to terms. To Philip, however, this was bare-faced hypocrisy. The raids on Spanish America were just state-sponsored acts of terrorism, and if Elizabeth would not stop them, he would have to go to the root of the problem in England itself.

Not only did the raids not stop, but in the spring of 1587 the maritime attacks reached a new peak of audacity. While Elizabeth was sending envoys to talk peace, Drake pulled off his cheekiest raid yet, attacking the Spanish fleet in Cadiz harbour itself, destroying ships and sailing with impunity through its roadsteads: a sixteenth-century Pearl Harbor. In Madrid the news was greeted with fury and panic. Was the king of Spain's authority to be of no account in his own waters?

But although Philip had virtually no alternative now but to launch the Armada, from the beginning many of his councillors foresaw the inevitability of its disaster. When the great Spanish admiral Santa Cruz estimated that, to have any chance of success, between 50,000 and 90,000 troops and 200 ships would be needed, he must have assumed that this kind of scale would be prohibitive. But Philip merely stripped the size of the effort down, just to the point where he virtually guaranteed its failure.

What followed, in the summer of 1588, was one of the great epics of insular patriotism. Whenever, in subsequent generations, England seemed to be facing impossible odds, the 'Fires over England' (the coastal beacons lit to warn of the approaching invaders) were re-lit, in print and celluloid. In 1798 Henry Dundas, William Pitt's colleague, alarmed by news of a planned French invasion, consulted the speeches of Elizabeth I and was comforted to find her anticipating his own provisions. But despite the undoubtedly terrifying spectacle of the 130-odd ships sailing past the Lizard in July, the odds actually favoured the defenders not the attackers. Drake was right to keep cool and finish his apocryphal game of bowls. As they sailed towards their moment of truth, the Spanish commanders knew this too. From bitter experience they were well aware that the English ships had a huge edge in speed and manoeuvrability and especially in the rapid-fire technology of their guns, which could discharge a full fusillade once an hour rather than, as in the Spanish case, once a day! They also knew that the English fleets were not about to sit and wait for them to join with the Duke of Parma's barge-borne invasion army before taking them on. All this made the Spanish deeply uneasy, and more than once the admirals attempted, in vain, to persuade Philip to call the whole thing off before it was too late.

At every stage it was geography and the weather that decided the outcome. The Armada survived Drake's initial attacks on it in the Solent with hardly enough casualties to be noticed and sailed on imposingly towards Calais and its rendezvous with Parma and his forces in the Netherlands. But there, the wind did indeed turn Protestant, halting the progress of the barge flotilla that carried the troops and making it impossible for them to reach their deepwater junction. At the same time, the Armada, hit by English fire-ships, couldn't get close enough into the shallows to take the soldiers aboard. It was those few miles of deadly Channel seabed that made the difference between disaster and triumph.

The battle of Gravelines, fought over 28–29 July, was now a struggle, not for the survival of England but for the survival of the Armada. When its commander, the Duke of Medina-Sidonia, finally pulled away from the battle, eleven ships short, and set a course northeast to begin a long, ruinous odyssey home, his fleet was still substantial enough to deter pursuing attacks. It was when the Armada rounded the northwest tip of Scotland and ran into merciless Hebridean gales and tempests that it was destroyed. Ironically, then, it was in the waters between Scotland and Ireland that the Enterprise of England truly came to grief: the sailors and soldiers were drowned, starved, ravaged by typhus or picked off by the Irish.

It wouldn't do to write off the narrow escape of 1588 as purely patriotic mythology. If, with hindsight, we can see that the chances of a successful Spanish invasion were always slight, that is certainly not the way it was seen at the time. Philip II went into mourning for the 15,000 dead and his annihilated fleet, but the defeat was not so overwhelming that he could not try again in the 1590s. In England the response to the crisis was perhaps even more important than the military logistics, for it produced a moment of intense national self-definition. If you asked yourself what was a queen *for*, the answer was for 1588, to give a sense to the people, indoors and on the streets, in great houses and in taverns, that the nation was somehow more than the sum of its parts, and that its prince, somehow both king and queen in one frame, was its authentic and imperishable embodiment. It was Elizabeth's genius (as it was Churchill's in 1940) to understand how to project this to her fearful, agitated people, and Leicester, grievously ill, probably with stomach cancer, but rehabilitated as Her Majesty's Lieutenant against Foreign Invasion, was ready to campaign one last time as the impresario of her public image. He may have been a hopeless commander of armies and an even worse foreign diplomat and politician, but when it came to patriotic shows there was no one to touch him.

Like the rest of the council he had been dismayed by Elizabeth's apparent determination to lead her armies in person, should it come to fighting a Spanish invasion force in England itself – 'Your person being the most dainty and sacred thing we have in this world to care for, a man must tremble when he thinks of it' – and in early August the danger was by no means past. Instead, Leicester organized the extraordinary occasion at Tilbury camp (where he had complained of alarming disorder) on 9 August when the queen reviewed and addressed the defence levies. Paradoxically, the very abundance of reports and images of what happened at Tilbury makes it difficult to know for certain exactly what Elizabeth wore or what she said, but she certainly arrived on 8 August in a great gilded coach and was escorted by 2000 ecstatic troops to her lodgings at Arden House. The next day she probably did walk on foot through lines of men before mounting a grey gelding with Leicester holding the bridle, accompanied by pikemen, drums and pipers. She may not, in fact, have actually worn the breastplate said in some versions to have been produced by Leicester, but she certainly made an impression on the troops as a commander as much as the virgin-mother of the country. An eyewitness, James Aske, described her as 'king-like' and a 'sacred general'.

The speech, which was repeated the next day by the military chaplain, Leonel Sharp, has deservedly passed down to posterity as one of the greatest orations of British history, all the more extraordinary for being delivered at a moment of such trepidation.

My loving people, We have been persuaded by some that are careful of our safety to take heed how we commit ourselves to armed multitudes for fear of treachery, but I assure you I do not desire to live to distrust my faithful and loving people. Let Tyrants fear; I have always so behaved myself under God, I have placed my chiefest strength and safeguard in the loyal hearts and good-will of my subjects. And therefore I am come amongst you, as you see, at this time not for my recreation and disport, but being resolved in the midst and heat of the battle to live and die amongst you all. To lay down for God, my kingdom and for my people, my honour and my blood even in the dust. I know I have the body of a weak and feeble woman, but I have the heart and stomach of a King and a King of England too and think it foul scorn that Parma or Spain or any Prince of Europe should dare to invade the borders of my realm; to which, rather than any dishonour shall grow by me, I myself will take up arms, I myself will be your General, Judge and Rewarder of every one of your virtues in the field. I know already for your forwardness you have deserved rewards and crowns; and we do assure you, on the word of a Prince, they shall be duly paid you.

There are other versions of the speech, less Shakespearean, but preserving the essence of Elizabeth's performance: a sovereign imagined not as a remote and a forbidding presence but as one of the people in their hour of crisis. And though she was a woman, the love her subjects bore her made her an Amazon, a Penthesilea, a fighter: in the words of the 1612 version 'the enemy perhaps may challenge my sex for that I am a woman, so may I likewise charge their mould for that they are but men'. And there is no doubt whatever that at Tilbury Elizabeth assumed the status of a national icon. Shortly after, Leicester wrote to the Earl of Shrewsbury that 'Our Gracious Majesty hath been here with me to see her camp and her people, which so inflamed the hearts of her good subjects as I think the weakest person amongst them is able to match the proudest Spaniard that dare land in England.' An extraordinary panel in the church of St Faith at King's Lynn shows the haloed Virgin Queen enthroned, as if in heaven, above the spectacle of the Armada in flames, while her Tilbury persona on the dappled grey rides before the troops.

The image of the androgynous warrior-empress was manufactured time and again in the difficult years that closed the Tudor century, most spectacularly, of course, in the several versions of George Gower's 'Armada Portrait' (see page 331). The men who had brought her to this apotheosis did not themselves long survive it. Leicester died in October 1588. The queen was said to have grieved so bitterly that her locked door needed to be broken down before she could be persuaded to emerge and face the rest of her life. Walsingham died in 1590, and Christopher Hatton in 1591, not before the queen had spoon-fed him cordial in his last days. Cecil (created Lord Burghley in 1571), old and arthritic, died in 1598, having passed on the heaviest burden of state business to his second son, Robert, the hunchbacked 'pigmy', as shrewd as his father. For the last decade and a half of the reign, Robert Cecil was locked in battle with his arch-rival, Robert Devereux, Earl of Essex, Leicester's step-son, with a third commanding figure, Walter Ralegh, more often than not supporting Cecil against Essex. In fact, the 1590s seemed strangely like an echo-chamber of the past, with Cecil playing his father's part of studious pragmatist and Essex taking Leicester's role of impetuous belligerent and regal toyboy, constantly in and out of hot water for squandering men and money on mismanaged military campaigns (especially in Ireland), disobeying the queen's instructions and failing to clock in for the required hours of craven adoration.

The Elizabethan court had never exactly been a church of sobriety. But in the 1590s the disjunction between social reality and allegorical reverie bordered on the grotesque. Personal feuds were stoked by fashion wars and soap-opera slights. Ralegh and Essex nearly fought a duel when their men showed up for the tilts wearing identical orange livery. Essex began the estrangement that would end in his abortive *coup d'état* and execution in 1601 when, after a fierce dressing down from the queen, he turned his back on her and she in turn slapped him, very hard, on the face. This last insult may well have pushed Essex over the edge. For some time he had resented the queen's refusal to distribute what he believed was adequate patronage to his followers. Genuinely very popular with the people, Essex took this ale-house appre-ciation for a mandate. When he abruptly returned from Ireland to force himself on parliament and the council, he began his campaign by marching into the queen's private chamber while her royal face was still in process of being elaborately con-structed. Seeing her wigless and toothless, Essex might as well have seen her naked, for he had penetrated the mask, an unforgivable act of *lèse-majesté*. The punishment for looking on the naked Diana was, of course, death.

Inevitably, the distance between the mythology of Elizabeth's ageless body politic and the shrivelled reality of her body natural became more glaring.

Surrounded by sycophantic courtiers and image-makers, who pretended she was still a slip of a thing and who turned out panegyrics to the second Golden Age, Elizabeth obliged the fantasists by dressing herself ever more extravagantly in the diaphanous tops that still proclaimed her virginity, and even, on one occasion, going completely topless, and when hot, unbuttoning herself all the way to the royal navel. Fantasists like the astrologer Simon Forman were provoked into feverish dreams of the queen, envisioned as a little old woman but somehow still desirable, trailing her white petti-coat in the dirt and rescued from red-haired bravos (like Essex) by the dreamer who announced that he would attend, not under but *upon* her to make her belly bigger for England.

It is hard not to feel that there was something a little too strenuously gorgeous about the over-dressed masquerades of the late-Elizabethan world. Was it entirely a coincidence that the unprecedented burst of literary invention for which we most remember this period was devoted to many kinds of make-believe exactly at the time when life in the country and town was becoming most difficult? When the barren regime itself looked shaky and impatient and men like Essex were already looking beyond it for their own fortunes, history was being rewritten to flatter the Tudor view that the dynasty was the consummation of God's plan for the Protestant nation and that they alone had created union from the warring clans of the late Middle Ages. At a time when social hierarchies had never been more rigid and niceties of rank more likely to provoke violent disputes, the dream-makers conjured up arcadian fairylands in which the sexes traded places, men and immortals mingled, servants talked back to their masters and the mighty got their come-uppance. In 1592 Marcus Gheeraerts the Younger painted the most memorable of all the Elizabethan portraits for the recently retired Queen's Champion, Sir Henry Lee, on the occasion of his last entertainment for his goddess (see Frontispiece). Her face silvery with moonglow, her dress deco-rated with the white roses and pearls of chastity, Elizabeth stands with her slippers at the fountainhead of the Thames, close to Lee's Oxfordshire estate at Ditchley. Queen and country have become literally united, the one an extension of the other. Mapped from a godly altitude, England too looks imperishable: well-watered, little clumps of forest dotting the landscape, neat towns and hamlets studding the space between – a vision indeed of demi-paradise.

The reality was more prosaic. All the evils that the official histories claimed had been banished by the Tudors were glaringly evident in the 1590s: punitive taxation to pay for endless wars; high unemployment; a succession of disastrous harvests from 1594–7; sky-rocketing food prices. In 1596 there were riots, and magistrates, con-fronted with a crime wave, sent felons to the gallows in record numbers. Fairyland

Elizabeth I at Tilbury; panel painting in St Faith's Church, King's Lynn, Norfolk.

was strewn with gibbets. In 1598 a Kentish labourer let it be known that he 'hoped to see such war in this realm to afflict the rich men of this country, to requite their hardness of heart towards the poor'.

For the first time in many decades, a chorus of complaint about being ruled by a woman – an *old* woman, it was said, despite the pretence of perpetual youth – became audible, especially in the courts where men were being pilloried or mutilated for abusing the queen. John Feltwell, a labourer of Great Wenden in Essex, was said to have wanted to 'pray for a king'. When asked why, he replied: 'the Queene is nothing but a woman and ruled by noblemen...so that poor men could get nothing... We shall never have a merry world while the queen liveth.' In 1599 a 'common wanderer' called Thomas Vaughan claimed that the youth who had died in 1553 had not been Edward VI at all but someone put in his place and that the real Edward, king of Denmark, had come to Ireland and Wales to save the poor from starvation.

What England needed, these dangerously outspoken men and women let it be known, was a king who would give them work and ale and bread. What they were getting instead were imperial adventures and castles in the air. For although Gower's 'Armada Portrait' shows the queen with her hand confidently on the Indies, the ocean bed of Gloriana's empire was littered with the wrecks of crazy projects, many of them dreamed up by makers of literature. The young John Donne went on Essex's futile voyage to the Azores that was supposed to bring the Spanish empire to its knees. Ralegh's settlement at Roanoke, Virginia, the original pipe dream, lasted barely two years before being killed off by disease and starvation. Spenser's extravagant fantasy of a similar 'Plantation' in Ireland, where the natives would be rescued from their unfortunate barbarism by the blessings of Anglo-Scottish Protestant virtue, ended in a hideously bloody and prolonged war, which only confirmed to both Gaelic and Old English Ireland how little they had in common with a country that treated them as so many bog-dwelling Calibans.

The dreams had a nasty way of ruining the dreamers, especially when they got translated into stone and mortar. The most extravagant of the 'prodigy houses', with their eruptions of chimneys, pinnacles and gables, were built to receive the queen exactly at the moment when she was restricting her progresses to short journeys. The most prodigious of them all was Wollaton Hall, near Nottingham, which was created for Sir Robert Willoughby by the specialist in exuberant masonry and brickwork, Robert Smythson. Willoughby must have desperately hoped that the splendour of Wollaton would complete his elevation from provincial industrial baron into aristocratic magnate. But all that he and his heirs were left with were massive debts. For the queen never came.

Of all the stories of thwarted homage and castles in the air, none is more poignant than that of the Northamptonshire master-builder Sir Thomas Tresham. The family had risen quickly, starting as lawyers, one of them making it all the way to attorney-general under Henry V. Sir Thomas's grandfather, like so many other county gentlemen, had loyally served both Henry VIII and Edward VI, while still remaining a Catholic. For a while Thomas himself had managed to abide by the Church settlement of 1559, just as Cecil and Elizabeth herself had hoped. He had been knighted in 1575, and had married well, fathering ten children. But when Walsingham's terror and the Jesuit missions had forced a decision on those who wanted to be loyal Catholics, Tresham had decided for faith, throwing off the compromise ceremonies of the Elizabethan regime and undergoing a complete reconversion back to the old Roman Church. He became a recusant, refusing to attend Anglican services, and paying steep fines for his absenteeism. Even so, when called on by the Walsingham regime to declare his allegiance, Tresham never ceased to profess passionate loyalty to Elizabeth.

Out of that touching confidence in an England that could be European and Catholic as well as Protestant and insular, came Tresham's resolve to build himself a house that would express what was, in every sense, his good faith. And from that resolution came the most beautiful ruin in Britain.

Like so many of the grand projects of the Elizabethan twilight, Lyveden New Bield is a pious fantasy. It was the product of a doomed optimism that you could be, at the same time, a Catholic and a loyal country gentleman. Prevented from saying his creed out loud, Tresham decided to have his architecture speak for him: to make the sign of the cross in the ground-plan and the windowframes, and to venerate the Passion in the stone frieze travelling round the exterior walls. The end result looks nothing like any other architecture we habitually think of as 'English' or 'British' — more an alien classical transplant from France or Italy — but Tresham meant it to be as natural as the Northamptonshire landscape in which it is set. And if there ever was to be a native Anglo-Catholic style, Lyveden New Bield is it.

It was an astoundingly ambitious project, conceived by a true visionary. In his library Tresham had the great textbooks of classical architecture, Vitruvius, Serlio and Palladio, and had seen those designs come to life in Venice when he visited Italy. At Lyveden, too, there would be rooms of mathematically perfect proportions, gracefully fluted pilasters and a great pantheon-like cupola to crown the house. Since this was meant as a private hermitage for Tresham's retirement, there would be an oratory for his devotions and a wealth of sacred, emblematic inscriptions and devices carved into the walls.

Top: Wollaton Hall (front façade), Nottinghamshire.
Above: Lyveden New Bield, Northamptonshire.

Alone on his holy isle, Tresham was unable to work miracles. After Elizabeth died, reality caught up with him and instead of spending his last days in his luminous ante-chamber to paradise, he spent them in the darkness of a prison, locked away for his faith. One son became a Gunpowder Plotter, saving his life only by turning king's evidence. The family fortunes crumbled, making the completion of Lyveden, much less the beautiful dome that was supposed to crown it, prohibitively impracticable. It was never finished. All that was left of Tresham's glorious vision were just sad ghosts and the secrets of the stones.

But perhaps even if Tresham had managed to complete the house, it would still have stuck out like a sore thumb. Because as he was doing his best to reconcile, in his own person, faith and taste, England and classical Europe, history was pushing them apart. In the writings of chroniclers, geographers and playwrights, churchmen and parliamentary antiquarians, what was *truly* English was being newly and narrowly redefined. What was authentically English was a liturgy in the native tongue; a literature that threw off foreign idioms and mannerisms. And if, as now seems possible, Shakespeare was himself a clandestine Catholic, he could get away with it only by writing the ultimate anthem to the insular separateness of England and putting it in the mouth of the dying John of Gaunt.

For the first time, too, as anxious panegyrists looked north beyond the Tweed towards the queen's successor, James VI, the God-blessed island began to be imagined as something more than England, as *Britannia*, the title of William Camden's extraordinary compilation of history and geography dedicated to the queen. By the time that Elizabeth died in March 1603 the idea of 'Britain' would still have been largely alien and incomprehensible to most of the country. But the old queen herself might well have been one of the few for whom it had some real meaning. For as she lay dying and her 'wedding ring' was filed away, she might well have thought that perhaps God did indeed have some sort of plan when he destined her to remain a virgin. For by remaining unmarried she had, in the end, brought about a momentous union: that of Scotland and England, not yet in one kingdom, but in one person; the child of her cousin, enemy and victim, Mary Stuart. She had not been barren then, after all. There had been no greensickness. She had brought forth fruit, the fruit of her body politic. And its name, already, was *Magna Britannia*: Great Britain.

SELECT BIBLIOGRAPHY

Abbreviations BM Press – British Museum Press; CUP – Cambridge University Press; OUP – Oxford University Press; UCL – University College, London; UP – University Press

PRINTED PRIMARY SOURCES

Adomnan of Iona, *Life of St Columba*, trans. R. Sharpe (Penguin 1995)

Alfred the Great: Asser's Life of King Alfred and Other Contemporary Sources, trans. S. Keynes and M. Lapidge (Penguin 1983)

Aneirin, *Y Gododdin,* trans. and ed. A.O.H. Jarman (Gomer Press 1988)

Anglo-Saxon Chronicle, trans. and ed. Michael Swanton (Dent 1996)

Arthurian Chronicles by Wace and Layamon, trans. Eugene Mason (Dent 1962; University of Toronto Press 1996)

Barbour, John, *The Bruce*, ed. A.A.M. Duncan (Cannongate 1997)

Bede, *Ecclesiastical History of the English People*, ed. D.H. Farmer, trans. L. Sherley-Price (Penguin 1990)

Beowulf, trans. Seamus Heaney (Faber 1999)

Blind Harry's Wallace, introduction by Elspeth King (Luath Press 1999)

Bower, Walter, *Scotichronicon*, ed. D.E.R. Watt, 9 vols. (Aberdeen UP/Mercat 1987–98)

Caesar, Julius, *Gallic Wars*, trans. H.J. Edwards (Loeb Library, Harvard UP 1986)

Camden, William, *The Annals of Elizabeth* (1615)

Camden, William, *Britannia*, trans. Philemon Holland (1637)

Chronicle of Richard of Devizes of the Time of King Richard the First, ed. J.T. Appleby (Thomas Nelson 1963)

Chronicle of Walter of Guisborough, Previously Edited as the Chronicle of Walter of Hemingford, ed. Harry Rothwell (Royal Historical Society 1957)

Chronicles of Matthew Paris: Monastic Life in the Thirteenth Century, trans. and ed. Richard Vaughan (Sutton 1984)

Early Irish Myths and Sagas, trans. Jeffrey Gantz (Penguin 1981)

English Historical Documents, Vols. I–VI:
  Vol. I *c.* 500–1042, ed. D. Whitelock (Routledge 1995)
  Vol. II 1042–1189, ed. David C. Douglas and G.W. Greenaway (OUP 1996)
  Vol. III 1189–1327, ed. Harry Rothwell (OUP 1996)
  Vol. IV 1327–1485, ed. A.R. Myers (OUP 1969)
  Vol. V 1485–1558, ed. C.H. Williams (OUP 1997)
  Vol. VI 1558–1603, ed. D. Price (Methuen 1988)

Flores Historiarum, ed. H.R. Ward, Vol. III (1890)

Froissart, Jean, *Chronicles*, trans. and ed. Geoffrey Brerton (Penguin 1968)

Geoffrey of Monmouth, *The History of the Kings of Britain*, trans. Lewis Thorpe (Penguin 1976)

Gerald of Wales, *The History and Topography of Ireland*, trans. J.J. O'Meara (Penguin 1951)

Gerald of Wales, *The Journey Through Wales*, trans. Lewis Thorpe (Penguin 1978)

Gildas, *The Ruin of Britain*, trans. and ed. Michael Winterbottom (Phillimore 1978)

Harrison, William, *The Description of England*, ed. Georges Edelen (Dover Reprints, Constable 1994)

John of Fordun, *Chronicle of the Scottish Nation*, trans. Felix J.H. Skene and ed. William F. Skene (Llanerch 1993)

Leland, John, *John Leland's Itinerary: Travels in Tudor England*, ed. John Chandler (Sutton 1993)

The Mabinogion, trans. Gwyn and Thomas Jones (Dent 1993)

Nennius, *British History and Welsh Annals*, ed. J. Morris (Phillimore 1980)

Orderic Vitalis, *The Ecclesiastical History of England and Normandy*, trans. T. Forester, Vols. I and II (Bohn 1905)

Paris, Matthew, *Illustrated Chronicles of Matthew Paris*, ed. Richard Vaughan (Sutton 1984)

Paston Letters and Papers of the Fifteenth Century, ed. Norman Davis (Clarendon Press 1971–6)

St Patrick, *His Writing*, ed. A.B.E. Hood (Phillimore 1978)

Smith, Thomas, *De Republica Anglorum* (Leiden 1630)

Stones, E. L. G. (ed.), *Anglo-Scottish Relations 1174–1328: Some Selected Documents* (Clarendon Press 1963)

Stow, John, *A Survey of London written in the Year 1598*, ed. Henry Morley, introduction by Antonia Fraser (Sutton 1994)

Tacitus, *Agricola*, trans. M. Hutton, rev. ed. R.M. Ogilvie (Loeb Library, Harvard UP 1980)

Vita Edwardi Secundi – The Life of Edward II by the so-called Monk of Malmesbury, trans. by N. Denholm-Young (Thomas Nelson 1957)

OVERVIEW AND GENERAL SOURCES

Bartlett, Robert, *The Making of Europe: Conquest, Colonisation and Cultural Change, 950–1350* (Penguin 1993; Princeton UP 1993)

Black, Jeremy, *A History of the British Isles* (Macmillan 1996; St Martin's Press 1996)

Broun, Dauvit *et al.* (eds.), *Image and Identity: The Making and Re-making of Scotland through the Ages* (John Donald 1998)

Cannon, John (ed.), *The Oxford Companion to British History* (OUP 1997)

Connolly, S.J. (ed.), *The Oxford Companion to Irish History* (OUP 1998)

Davies, John A., *History of Wales* (Penguin 1994; Viking Penguin 1994)

Davies, Norman, *The Isles: A History* (Macmillan 1999; OUP 1999)

Davies, R.R., *Age of Conquest: Wales 1063 to 1415* (OUP 1992)

Davies, Wendy, *Wales in the Early Middle Ages* (Leicester UP 1982)

Foster, R.F. (ed.), *The Oxford History of Ireland* (OUP 1989)

Frame, Robin, *The Political Development of the British Isles 1100–1400* (OUP 1990)

Given-Wilson, Chris, *The English Nobility in the Late Middle Ages* (Routledge 1987)

Grant, Alexander and Stringer, Keith J. (eds.), *Uniting the Kingdom: The Making of British History* (Routledge 1995)

Hallam, Elizabeth (ed.), *The Plantagenet Chronicles* (Tiger Books and Random House 1995)

Hanawalt, Barbara, *The Middle Ages – An Illustrated History* (OUP 1998)

Harbison, Peter, *Guide to National and Historic Monuments of Ireland*, 3rd ed. (Gill & Macmillan 1992)

Kearney, Hugh, *The British Isles – A History of Four Nations* (CUP 1989)

Lynch, Michael, *Scotland: A New History* (Pimlico 1991)

Morgan, Kenneth O. (ed.), *The Oxford History of Britain* (OUP 1999)

Platt, Colin, *The Architecture of Medieval Britain: A Social History* (Yale UP 1990)

Pounds, Norman John Greville, *The Medieval Castle in England and Wales: A Social and Political History* (CUP 1990)

Prestwich, Michael, *Armies and Warfare in the Middle Ages* (Yale UP 1996)

Samuel, Raphael, *Theatres of Memory*:
    Vol. 1 Past and Present in Contemporary Culture (Verso 1994, 1996)
    Vol. 2 Island Stories. Unravelling Britain, ed. A. Light with S. Alexander and G. Stedman Jones (Verso 1997, 1999)

Somerset-Fry, Plantaganet, *Castles of Britain and Ireland* (David & Charles 1996; Abbeville Press 1997)

Williams, Gwyn A., *When Was Wales?* (Black Raven Press 1985)

Wright, Patrick, *On Living in an Old Country. The National Past in Contemporary Britain* (Verso 1985)

SECONDARY SOURCES
CHAPTER ONE

Abels, Richard P., *Alfred the Great. War, Kingship and Culture in Anglo-Saxon England* (Longman 1998; Addison-Wesley 1998)

Barber, Richard, *King Arthur: Hero and Legend* (Boydell & Brewer 1994)

Birley, R.E., *Vindolanda. A Roman Frontier Fort on Hadrian's Wall* (Thames and Hudson 1977)

Bland, Roger and Johns, Catherine, *The Hoxne Treasure* (BM Press 1994)

Bowman, Alan K., *Life and Letters of the Roman Frontier: Vindolanda and its people* (BM Press 1998; Routledge 1998)

Breeze, David, *The Northern Frontiers of Roman Britain* (Batsford 1993)

Breeze, David and Dobson, Brian, *Hadrian's Wall*, 3rd rev. ed. (Penguin 1991)

Brown, Peter, *The Rise of Western Christendom: Triumph and Diversity AD 200–1000* (Blackwell 1997)

Campbell, James *et al.* (eds.), *The Anglo-Saxons* (Penguin 1991)

Carver, Martin, *Sutton Hoo: Burial Ground of Kings?* (BM Press 1998; University of Pennsylvania Press 1998)

Crummy, Phillip, *City of Victory: The Story of Colchester* (Colchester Archaeological Trust 1997)

Cunliffe, Barry, *Ancient Celts* (Penguin 2000)

Cunliffe, Barry, *Iron Age Communities in Britain*, 3rd ed. (Routledge 1991)

Cunliffe, Barry, *Roman Bath* (Batsford/English Heritage 1995)

Dodwell, C.R., *Anglo-Saxon Art: A New Perspective* (Manchester UP 1982)

Dumville, D., 'Sub-Roman Britain: History and Legend', *History*, Vol. 62, 1977

Esmonde-Cleary, A.S., *The Ending of Roman Britain* (Batsford 1989 and Routledge 2000)

Fletcher, Richard, *The Barbarian Conversion: From Paganism to Christianity* (University of California Press 1999)

Hanson, R.C.P., *St Patrick: His Origins and Career* (Clarendon Press 1968)

Higham, N.J., *The English Conquest: Gildas and Britain in the Fifth Century* (Manchester UP 1994)

Higham, N.J., *An English Empire: Bede and the Early Saxon Kingdoms* (Manchester UP 1995)

Higham, N.J., *Rome, Britain and the Anglo-Saxons* (Sealoy 1992)

Hines, John (ed.), *Anglo-Saxons From the Migration Period to the Eighth Century: An Ethnographic Perspective* (Boydell & Brewer 1997)

Hodges, Richard, *The Anglo-Saxon Achievement: Archaeology and the Beginnings of English Society* (Cornell UP 1994)

James, Simon, *Atlantic Celts: Ancient People or Modern Invention* (BM Press 1999)

James, Simon, *Britain and the Celtic Iron Age* (BM Press 1997)

Johnson, S., *Hadrian's Wall* (Batsford/English Heritage 1989)

Morris, John (ed.), *Arthurian Period Sources*, Vol. IV: *Places and Peoples and Saxon Archaeology* (Phillimore 1995)

O'Kelly, M.J., *Early Ireland* (CUP 1989)

Ottaway, Patrick, *Archaeology in British Towns: From the Emperor Claudius to the Black Death* (Routledge 1992)

Potter, T.W., *Roman Britain* (BM Press 1983; University of California Press 1993)

Renfrew, Colin, *The Prehistory of Orkney BC 4000–1000 AD* (Edinburgh UP 1985)

Ritchie, Anna, *Prehistoric Orkney* (Batsford 1995)

Salway, Peter, *Oxford Illustrated History of Roman Britain* (OUP 1993)

Salway, Peter, *Roman Britain* (OUP 1981, 1984)

Sawyer, Peter (ed.), *The Oxford Illustrated History of the Vikings* (OUP 1997, 2000)

Smyth, Alfred P., *King Alfred the Great* (OUP 1996)

Stenton, Frank M., *Anglo-Saxon England*, 3rd ed. (OUP 1971, 1989; Gordon Press 1977)

Thomas, Charles, *Celtic Britain* (Thames & Hudson 1997)

Todd, Malcolm, *Roman Britain* (Blackwell 1999)

Waddell, John *et al.* (eds.), *Book of Aran: The Aran Islands, County Galway* (Tir Eolas 1994)

Wood, Michael, *In Search of the Dark Ages* (BBC Books 1987)

CHAPTER TWO

Barlow, Frank, *Edward the Confessor* (Yale UP 1997)

Bates, David, *William the Conqueror* (George Philip 1989)

Bates, David and Curry, Anne (eds.), *England and Normandy in the Middle Ages* (Hambledon Press 1994)

Chibnall, Marjorie, *Anglo-Norman England 1066–1166* (Blackwell 1986)

Chibnall, Marjorie, *The World of Orderic Vitalis: Norman Monks and Norman Knights* (Boydell & Brewer 1996)

Clarke, Peter A., *The English Nobility under Edward the Confessor* (OUP 1994)

Davis, R.H.C., *The Normans and their Myth* (Thames and Hudson 1976)

Douglas, David, *William the Conqueror* (Yale UP 1999)

Fleming, R., *Kings and Lords in Conquest England* (CUP 1994)

Gameson, Richard (ed.), *The Study of the Bayeux Tapestry* (Boydell & Brewer 1997)

Golding, Brian, *Conquest and Colonisation: Normans in Britain 1066–1100* (Macmillan Press 1994)

Grape, Wolfgang, *The Bayeux Tapestry* (Prestel Verlag 1994)

Hallam, Elizabeth (ed.), *Domesday Book* (Random House 1995)

Higham, N.J., *The Death of Anglo-Saxon England* (Sutton 1998)

Hinde, Thomas (ed.), *Domesday Book: England's Heritage Then and Now* (Bramley Books 1996)

Holt, J.C., *Colonial England 1066–1215* (Hambledon Press 1996)

Holt, J.C. (ed.), *Domesday Studies* (Boydell & Brewer 1990, 1995)

Lemmon, C.H. *et al.*, *The Norman Conquest* (Eyre & Spottiswoode 1966)

McLynn, P.F., *1066: The Year of the Three Battles* (Pimlico 1999)

Rowley, Trevor, *English Heritage Book of Norman England* (Batsford 1997)

Stafford, Pauline, *Unification and Conquest: A Political and Social History of England in the 10th and 11th Centuries* (Edward Arnold 1995)

Stenton, Frank *et al.*, *The Bayeux Tapestry. A Comprehensive Survey* (Phaidon 1957)

Strickland, M.J., *Anglo-Norman Warfare: Studies in Late Anglo-Saxon and Anglo-Norman Military Organization and Warfare* (Boydell & Brewer 1994)

Walker, Ian W., *Harold: The Last Anglo-Saxon King* (Sutton 1997)

Williams, Ann, *The English and the Norman Conquest* (Boydell & Brewer, 1997)

Wright, Peter P., *Hastings* (Windrush Press and Interlink Publishing 1997)

CHAPTER THREE

Barlow, Frank, *Thomas Becket* (Phoenix Press 1986, 1997)

Barlow, Frank, *William Rufus* (Yale UP 2000)

Bartlett, Robert, *England Under the Norman and Angevin Kings, 1075–1225* (OUP 2000)

Bartlett, Robert, *Gerald of Wales 1145–1223* (Clarendon Press 1982)

Bradbury, Jim, *Philip Augustus: King of France, 1180–1283* (Longman 1998; Addison-Wesley Longman 1997)

Bradbury, Jim, *Stephen and Matilda: The Civil War of 1139–1153* (Sutton 1998)

Brand, Paul, *The Making of the Common Law* (Hambledon Press 1992)

Butler, John, *The Quest for Becket's Bones: The Mystery of the Relics of St. Thomas Beckett of Canterbury* (Yale UP 1996)

Chibnall, Marjorie, *The Empress Matilda: Queen Consort, Queen Mother and Lady of the English* (Blackwell 1993)

Crouch, David, *William Marshal: Court, Career and Chivalry in the Angevin Empire, 1147–1219* (Longman 1994)

Duby, Georges, *William Marshal: The Flower of Chivalry* (Pantheon 1985)

Duby, Georges, *The Three Orders: Feudal Society Imagined* (University of Chicago Press 1982)

Duby, Georges and Birrell, Jean, *Women of the Twelfth Century, Vol. 1* (Polity Press 1997; University of Chicago Press 1997)

Duby, Georges and Birrell, Jean, *Women of the Twelfth Century, Vol.2* (Polity Press 1998; University of Chicago Press 1998)

Flanagan, Marie Therese, *Irish Society, Anglo-Norman Settlers and Angevin Kingship* (Clarendon Press 1989)

Gies, Frances, *The Knight in History* (HarperColllins 1987)

Gillingham, John, *The Angevin Empire* (Holmes & Meier 1984)

Gillingham, John, *Richard I*, 2nd ed. (Yale UP 1999)

Holt, James C., *The Magna Carta*, 2nd ed. (CUP 1992)

Holt, James C., *Robin Hood* (Thames and Hudson 1982, 1989)

Hudson, John, *The Formation of English Common Law* (Longman 1996)

Jolliffe, John E., *Angevin Kingship* (A. & C. Black 1963)

Kelly, A., *Eleanor of Aquitaine and the Four Kings* (Harvard UP 1950)

Leyser, Henrietta, *Medieval Women: A Social History of Women in England 450–1500* (St Martin's Press 1998)

Mortimer, Richard, *Angevin England 1154–1258* (Blackwell, 1996)

Owen, D.D.R., *Eleanor of Aquitaine: Queen and Legend* (Blackwell 1993)

Seward, Desmond, *Eleanor of Aquitaine* (Barnes & Noble 1998)

Turner, Ralph V., *King John* (Longman 1994)

Warren, W.L., *Henry II* (Yale UP 1973)

Warren, W.L., *King John* (Yale UP 1998; Eyre Methuen 1998)

Weir, Alison, *Eleanor of Aquitaine* (Cape 1999)

CHAPTER FOUR

Alexander, John and Binski, Paul (eds.), *Age of Chivalry: Art in Plantagenet England, 1200–1400* (Royal Academy in association with Weidenfeld & Nicolson 1987)

Barrow, G.W.S., *Kingship and Unity, Scotland 1000–1306* (Edinburgh UP 1981)

Barrow, G.W.S., *Robert the Bruce and the Community of the Realm of Scotland*, 3rd ed. (Edinburgh UP 1988)

Binski, Paul, *Westminster Abbey and the Plantagenets: Kingship and the Representation of Power, 1200–1400* (Yale UP 1995)

Carpenter, D.A., *The Reign of Henry III* (Hambledon Press 1996)

Cosgrove, Art (ed.), *A New History of Ireland, Vol. II: Medieval Ireland, 1169–1534*, 2nd. ed. (OUP 1993)

Coss, P. R., *The Knight in Medieval England, 1000–1400* (Sutton 1993)

Davies, R.G. and Denton, J.H. (eds.), *The English Parliament in the Middle Ages* (Manchester UP 1981)

Davies, R.R., *The Age of Conquest: Wales 1063–1415* (OUP 1987)

Davies, R.R., *Dominion and Conquest: Ireland, Scotland and Wales, 1100–1300* (CUP 1990)

Duffy, Sean, *Ireland in the Middle Ages* (St Martin's Press 1997)

Duncan, A.A.M., *Scotland: The Making of the Kingdom* (Edinburgh UP 1992)

Dyer, Christopher, *Standards of Living in the Later Middle Ages c.1200–1520* (CUP 1989)

Fawcett, Richard, *Stirling Castle* (Batsford 1996)

Fawcett, Richard, *Scottish Abbeys and Priories* (Batsford 1994)

Fisher, Andrew, *William Wallace* (John Donald 1986)

Harding, Alan, *England in the Thirteenth Century* (CUP 1993)

Hicks, Michael, *Bastard Feudalism* (Longman 1995)

Keen, Maurice, *Chivalry* (Yale UP 1984)

Mackay, James, *William Wallace: Brave Heart* (Mainstream 1996)

McNamee, Colm, *The Wars of the Bruces: Scotland, England and Ireland* (Tuckwell Press 1996)

Maddicott, J.R., *Simon de Montfort* (CUP 1996)

Mundill, Robin R., *England's Jewish Solution: Experiment and Expulsion* (CUP 1998)

Prestwich, Michael, *Edward I* (Yale UP 1997)

Prestwich, Michael, *The Three Edwards: War and State in England, 1272–1377* (Routledge 1997)

Prestwich, Michael, *War, Politics and Finance under Edward I* (Gregg Revivals 1992)

Watson, Fiona, *Under the Hammer: Edward I and Scotland, 1286–1307* (Tuckwell Press 1998)

Webster, Bruce, *Medieval Scotland: The Making of an Identity* (Macmillan 1997)

Young, Alan, *Robert the Bruce's Rivals: The Comyns, 1212–1314* (Tuckwell Press 1997)

CHAPTER FIVE

Allmand, Christopher, *Henry V* (Yale UP 1993)

Binski, Paul, *Medieval Death: Ritual and Representation* (BM Press 1996; Cornell UP 1996)

Brewer, Derek S., *Chaucer and his World* (D. S. Brewer 1992, 1996)

Burrow, J.A., *Medieval Writers and Their Work* (OUP 1982)

Cam, Helen, *England Before Elizabeth* (Harper Row 1960)

Carpenter, Christine, *Wars of the Roses: Politics and the Constitution in England, 1437–1509* (CUP 1997)

Cohen, Kathleen, *Metamorphosis of a Death Symbol. The Transi Tomb in the Late Middle Ages and Renaissance* (University of California Press 1973)

Dobson, R.B. (ed.), *The Peasant's Revolt 1381*, 2nd ed. (Macmillan 1983)

Gies, Frances and Joseph, *Life in a Medieval Village* (HarperCollins 1990)

Gillespie, J.L., *The Age of Richard II* (Sutton 1997; St Martin's Press 1997)

Gillingham, John (ed.), *Richard III: A Medieval Kingship* (St Martin's Press 1993)

Gottfried, R.S., *The Black Death. Natural and Human Disaster in Medieval Europe* (The Free Press 1983)

Griffiths, R.A., *The Reign of Henry VI* (Sutton 1998)

Hanawalt, Barbara, *Growing Up in Medieval London: The Experience of Childhood in History* (OUP 1993, 1995)

Hanawalt, Barbara, *The Ties That Bound: Peasant Families in Medieval England* (OUP 1986)

Hatcher, John, *Plague, Population and the English Economy, 1348–1530* (Macmillan 1977, 1986)

Herlihy, David, *Black Death and the Transformation of the West* (Harvard UP 1997)

Horrox, Rosemary (trans.), *Black Death* (Manchester UP 1994)

Horrox, Rosemary (ed.), *Fifteenth-Century Attitudes: Perceptions of Society in Late Medieval England* (CUP 1994, 1997)

Horrox, Rosemary, *Richard III: A Study of Service* (CUP 1991)

Horrox, Rosemary (trans.), *Black Death* (Manchester UP 1994)

Hughes, Jonathan, *The Religious Life of Richard III: Piety and Prayer in the North of England* (Sutton 1997)

Keen, Maurice H., *English Society in the Later Middle Ages, 1348–1500* (Penguin 1991)

Lander, J.R., *Government and Community: England, 1450–1509* (Arnold 1980; Harvard UP 1980)

McFarlane, K.B., *The Nobility of Later Medieval England* (OUP 1973)

McNeill, William H., *Plagues and Peoples* (Doubleday 1977; Peter Smith 1992)

Nicholas, David, *The Later Medieval City, 1300–1500* (Longman 1977)

Ormrod, Mark and Lindley, Phillip (eds.), *The Black Death in England, 1348–1500* (P. Watkins 1996)

Ormrod, W.M., *The Reign of Edward III* (Tempus Publishing 1999)

Platt, Colin, *King Death: The Black Death and its Aftermath in Late Medieval England* (UCL Press 1996; University of Toronto Press 1996)

Richmond, Colin, *The Paston Family in the Fifteenth Century: Fastolf's Will* (CUP 1996)

Ross, Charles, *The Wars of the Roses* (Thames and Hudson 1986)

Ross, Charles, *Richard III* (Methuen 1981; University of Chicago Press 1983)

Saul, Nigel (ed.), *The Oxford History of Medieval England* (OUP 1997)

Saul, Nigel, *Richard II* (Yale UP 1997, 1999)

Sumption, Jonathan, *The Hundred Years War, Vol. 1: Trial by Battle* (Faber 1999; University of Pennsylvania Press, 1999)

Sumption, Jonathan, *The Hundred Years War, Vol. 2: Trial by Fire* (Faber 1999; University of Pennsylvania Press 1999)

Tuck, Anthony, *Crown and Nobility: England 1272–1461: Political Conflict in Late Medieval England*, 2nd ed. (Blackwell 1999)

Tuck, J.A., *Richard II and the English Nobility* (Arnold 1973)

Virgne, R. (ed.), *The Illustrated Letters of the Paston Family* (Macmillan 1989)

Waugh, Scott L., *England in the Reign of Edward III* (CUP 1991)

Webster, Bruce, *The Wars of the Roses* (University of California Press 1997)

Ziegler, Philip, *The Black Death* (Sutton 1998)

CHAPTER SIX

Ackroyd, Peter, *The Life of Thomas More* (Chatto & Windus 1999)

Anglo, Sydney, *Images of Tudor Kingship* (Seaby 1992)

Aston, Margaret, *England's Iconoclasts – Laws Against Images* (Clarendon Press 1988)

Aston, Margaret, *The King's Bedpost: Reformation and Iconography in a Tudor Group Portrait* (CUP 1995)

Bossy, J., *The English Catholic Community, 1570–1850* (Darton, Longman & Todd 1975)

Brigden, S., *London and the Reformation* (OUP 1989)

Chadwick, Owen, *The Reformation* (Penguin 1964)

Collinson, Patrick, *The Birthpangs of Protestant England: Religious and Cultural Change in the 16th and 17th Centuries* (Macmillan 1988, 1991)

Collinson, Patrick, *The Religion of Protestants: The Church in English Society, 1559–1625* (OUP 1984)

Cressy, David, *Bonfires and Bells – National Memory and the Protestant Calendar in Elizabethan and Stuart England* (Weidenfeld & Nicolson 1989)

Cressy, David, *Birth, Marriage and Death: Ritual and Religion in Tudor and Stuart England* (OUP 1997, 1999)

Daniell, David, *William Tyndale: A Biography* (Yale UP 1994)

Dickens, A.G., *The English Reformation,* 2nd rev. ed. (Batsford 1991; Pennsylvania State UP 1991)

Donaldson, Gordon, *The Scottish Reformation* (CUP 1960)

Doran, Susan and Durston, Christopher, *Princes, Pastors and People* (Routledge 1991)

Duffy, Eamon, *The Stripping of the Altars: Traditional Religion in England, 1400–1580* (Yale UP 1994)

Dymond, David and Paine, Clive, *The Spoil of Melford Church* (Suffolk Books 1992)

Ellis, Steven G., *Tudor Ireland, 1470–1603* (Longman 1985)

Elton, G.R., *Policy and Police: The Enforcement of the Reformation in the Age of Thomas Cromwell* (CUP 1972)

Elton, G.R., *Reform and Reformation: England 1509–1558* (Arnold 1977)

Erickson, Carroly, *Bloody Mary: Life of Mary Tudor* (Robson Books 1995, 1997)

Fletcher, Anthony and MacCulloch, Diarmaid, *Tudor Rebellions Seminar,* 4th ed. (Longman 1997)

Guy, John, *Tudor England* (OUP 1988)

Guy, John, *The Tudor Monarchy* (Arnold 1997)

Haigh, Christopher, *English Reformations: Religion, Politics and Society under the Tudors* (OUP 1993)

Haigh, Christopher (ed.), *The English Reformation Revised* (CUP 1987)

Haigh, Christopher, *Reformation and Resistance in Tudor Lancashire* (CUP 1975)

Hearn, Karen (ed.), *Dynasties: Painting in Tudor and Jacobean England 1530–1630* (Tate Publishing, 1995)

Hoak, Dale E. (ed.), *Tudor Political Culture* (CUP 1995)

Hutton, Ronald, *The Rise and Fall of Merrie England: The Ritual Year 1400–1700* (OUP 1996)

Ives, E., *Anne Boleyn* (Blackwell 1986)

Kamen, Henry, *Philip of Spain* (Yale UP 1997, 1999)

King, John N., *Tudor Royal Iconography: Literature and Art in an Age of Religious Crisis* (Princeton UP 1989)

Lacey, Robert, *The Life and Times of Henry VIII* (Abbeville Press 1992)

Lloyd, Christopher and Thurley, Simon, *Henry VIII: Images of a Tudor King* (Phaidon Press 1996)

Loach, Jennifer, *Edward VI* (Yale UP 1999)

Loades, David, *Power in Tudor England* (Macmillan 1996; St Martin's Press 1996)

Loades, David, *Tudor Government: Structures of Authority in the Sixteenth Century* (Blackwell 1997)

MacCulloch, Diarmaid, *The Later Reformation, 1547–1603* (Macmillan 1990)

MacCulloch, Diarmaid, *The Reign of Henry VIII: Politics, Policy and Piety* (Macmillan Press 1995)

MacCulloch, Diarmaid, *Thomas Cranmer: A Life* (Yale UP 1996)

MacCulloch, Diarmaid, *Tudor Church Militant: Edward VI and the Protestant Reformation* (Allen Lane 2000)

Marshall, Peter, *The Catholic Priesthood and the English Reformation* (OUP 1994, 1997)

Marshall, Peter, *The Impact of the English Reformation 1500–1640* (Arnold 1997; OUP 1997)

Platt, Colin, *The Great Rebuildings of Tudor and Stuart England* (UCL Press 1994)

Rex, Richard, *Henry VIII and the English Reformation* (Macmillan 1993; St Martin's Press 1993)

Rosman, D., *From Catholic to Protestant: Religion and the People in Tudor England* (UCL Press 1993 and 1996)

Rowse, A.L., *Tudor Cornwall* (Cape 1941)

Scarisbrick, J. J., *Henry VIII* (Yale UP 1968)

Scarisbrick, J. J., *The Reformation and the English People* (Blackwell 1995)

Thomas, Keith, *Religion and the Decline of Magic: Studies in Popular Beliefs in Sixteenth and Seventeenth Century England*, new ed. (Weidenfeld & Nicolson 1997; OUP 1997)

Thurley, Simon, *The Royal Palaces in Tudor England: Architecture and Court Life, 1460–1547* (Yale UP 1993)

Todd, M., *Reformation to Revolution* (Routledge 1995)

Warnicke, Retha M., *The Marrying of Anne of Cleves: Royal Protocol in Tudor England* (CUP 2000)

Warnicke, Retha M., *The Rise and Fall of Anne Boleyn* (CUP 1991)

Watt, Tessa, *Cheap Print and Popular Piety 1550–1640* (CUP 1993)

Whiting, Robert, *The Blind Devotion of the People: Popular Religion and the English Reformation* (CUP 1989)

Wormald, Jenny, *Court, Kirk and Community: Scotland, 1470–1625* (Edinburgh UP 1991)

CHAPTER SEVEN

Collinson, P., *The Religion of Protestants: The Church in English Society 1559–1625* (OUP 1982)

Ellis, Steven, *Tudor Frontiers and Noble Power: The Making of the British State* (OUP 1995)

Falls, Cyril, *Elizabeth's Irish Wars* (Constable 1996, 1997; Syracuse UP 1997)

Fletcher, Anthony, *Gender, Sex and Subordination in England 1500–1800* (Yale UP 1996)

Fletcher, Anthony and Stevenson, John (eds.), *Order and Disorder in Early Modern England* (CUP 1985)

Fraser, Antonia, *Mary, Queen of Scots* (Weidenfeld & Nicolson 1990; Dell 1993)

Frye, Susan, *Elizabeth I: The Competition for Representation* (OUP 1996)

Graves, Michael A., *Elizabethan Parliaments*, 2nd ed. (Longman 1996; Addison-Wesley Longman 1996)

Guy, John (ed.), *The Reign of Elizabeth I: Court and Culture in the Last Decade* (CUP 1995)

Hackett, Helen, *Virgin Mother, Maiden Queen: Elizabeth I and the Cult of the Virgin Mary* (Macmillan 1995; St Martin's Press 1995)

Helgerson, Richard, *Forms of Nationhood: The Elizabethan Writing of England* (University of Chicago Press 1992, 1994)

Levin, Carole, *The Heart and Stomach of a King: Elizabeth I and the Politics of Sex and Power* (University of Pennsylvania Press 1994)

MacCaffrey, Wallace T., *Elizabeth I and Religion* (Routledge 1993)

MacCaffrey, Wallace T., *Elizabeth I: War and Politics, 1588–1603* (Princeton UP 1994)

Martin, Colin and Parker, Geoffrey, *The Spanish Armada*, 2nd ed. (Mandolin and Manchester UP 1999; W.W. Norton 1992)

Mattingley, Garrett, *The Defeat of the Spanish Armada* (Pimlico 2000)

Neale, J.S., *Elizabeth I and Her Parliaments* (Cape 1957)

Patterson, Annabel, *Reading Holinshed's Chronicles* (University of Chicago Press 1994)

Quinn, D.B., *The Elizabethans and the Irish* (Cornell UP 1966)

Rowse, A.L., *The Elizabethan Age: The England of Elizabeth*, 2 vols. (Macmillan 1955)

Russell, Conrad, *The Crisis of Parliaments 1529–1660* (OUP 1971)

Salgado, Gamini, *The Elizabethan Underworld* (Sutton 1992, 1997)

Somerset, Anne, *Elizabeth I* (Phoenix Press 1997)

Strong, Roy, *The Cult of Elizabeth: Elizabethan Portraiture and Pageantry* (Pimlico 1999)

Walker, Julia M., *Dissing Elizabeth: Negative Representations of Gloriana* (Duke UP 1998)

Williams, Pendry, *The Later Tudors, England 1547–1603* (OUP 1995)

Williams, Pendry, *Tudor Regime* (Clarendon Press 1979)

Wilson, Charles, *Queen Elizabeth I and the Netherlands* (Macmillan 1970)

Woodfield, D. B., *Surreptitious Printing in England 1550–1640* (Bibliography Society of America 1973)

Yates, Frances A., *Astraea* (Routledge 1999)

INDEX

Page numbers in italics refer to illustrations

PICTURE CREDITS

Frontispiece NPG, London; p.18-19 Michael Jenner; pp.22, 23, 27l Ian Bremner; p.27r British Museum; p.35 English Heritage/Skyscan Balloon Photography; p.37 Vindolanda Trust; p.39t Ian Bremner, b Michael Jenner; p.42 Martin Davidson; p.50 Michael Holford; p.55 AKG London; p.63 Ashmolean Museum; p.67 Michael Holford; p.70t Museum of London, b AKG; p.75 British Library; p.79 John Parker; pp.87, 90t Michael Holford; p.90bl, br British Museum; p.99t Collections/ Michael George; pp.99b, 102 Michael Holford; p.111t The Art Archive, b Mike Ibeji; pp.115, 119 British Library; p.122 Musées du Mans; p.131 Sonia Halliday and Laura Lushington; p.135t British Library, b Bridgeman Art Library; pp.146, 147, 151 British Library; pp.155, 158t AKG London; p.158b John Parker; p.163t Ian Bremner, b AAAC; p.167 Martin Davidson; p.170t Society of Antiquaries of London, b British Library; p.171 Ian Bremner; p.183 Collections/Malcolm Crowthers; p.187t British Library, b Public Record Office; p.195 Collections/Roy Stedall-Humphreys; p.199t & b British Library; p.202l Collections/Jeffery W. Whitelaw, r Michael Holford; p.206t Collections/Gary Smith, b National Library of Scotland; p.211 Ian Bremner; p.219 British Library; p.223 AKG London; p.227t Bridgeman Art Library, b British Library; p.231 Ian Bremner; p.234t & b Bridgeman Art Library; p.239 British Library; p.242 John Parker; p.243t Mike Ibeji; pp.243b, 250, 251 British Library; p.259t & b National Gallery, London; p.263t Ian Bremner, b Dean & Chapter of Westminster; p.266 NPG, London; p.270 Michael Holford; p.271 John Parker, b Mike Ibeji; p.275 Tim Kirby; p.278l Michael Holford, r John Parker; p.279 Bridgeman Art Library; p.283 John Parker; p.286 NPG; p.287 British Library; pp.290-1 Royal Collection; p.291tr NPG, br Bridgeman Art Library; p.295 NPG; p.298 Royal Collection; p.303 Museo Thyssen-Bornemisza; p.306 St John's College, Cambridge; p.311t Bridgeman Art Library, b Bridgeman Art Library/Victoria & Albert Museum; pp.319t & b, 327t NPG; p.327b Bridgeman Art Library; p.331 Woburn Abbey; p.334 British Museum; p.335 Royal Collection; p.343tl & tr Public Record Office, b NPG; p.351t Bridgeman Art Library, b Viscount de L'Isle; p.358t & b Scottish National Portrait Gallery; p.259 Royal Collection; pp.366, 367t British Museum; pp.367b, 370 Bridgeman Art Library; p.375 NPG; p.383t AKG London, b Scottish National Portrait Gallery; p.391 Bridgeman Art Library; p.394t & b John Parker.

Abbreviation NPG = National Portrait Gallery

OTHER CREDITS

The quotation from Vladimir Nabokov's *Speak, Memory* on page 7 is reproduced by permission of Vintage Books, a division of Random House, Inc.. Excerpt from "End of a Year" from *History* by Robert Lowell. Copyright © 1973 by Robert Lowell. Reprinted by permission of Farrar, Straus and Giroux, LLC.